The New Public Personnel Administration

Third Edition

The New Public Personnel Administration

Third Edition

FELIX A. NIGRO
University of Georgia

LLOYD G. NIGRO
Georgia State University

F.E. PEACOCK PUBLISHERS, INC.
ITASCA, ILLINOIS 60143

TO E.H.N., C.L.N., and K.F.N.

Contents

Preface

In the mid-1980s, issues of public personnel policy continue to be debated pro and con, and we discuss new developments since publication of the second edition of this book in 1981. We have added new chapters, substantially rewritten others, included new appendices, and updated all material.

One of the new chapters, Chapter 11, Performance Appraisal and Merit Pay, analyzes the experience with new systems in the federal, state, and local governments. In Chapter 15, Constitutional Rights and the Public Employee, a new section is added on the liability of public employees and of public jurisdictions for infringements of the constitutional rights of members of the public, and the most important court rulings to date are presented. The intensely-debated issue of comparable worth is analyzed in Chapter 9, Job Evaluation and Pay: Pressures and Conflicts. In Chapter 10, Selection, there is a mini-case study of the "politics of test validity," with the discontinued main federal government entrance examination, PACE, the example. The failure in Britain to implement the principal recommendations of the Fulton Committee is explained in Chapter 4, The Career Concept, as part of the comparative analysis of the efforts in the United States, Britain, and France to establish true career systems. The final chapter, Chapter 16, The Future of Public Personnel Administration, is entirely rewritten and reflects our judgments after years of study and observation of the state of public personnel policies and practices in the United States.

As to new appendix material, there are excerpts from the Public Employe Relations Act of the State of Pennsylvania and the full text of an arbitration decision.

Our theoretical framework for conceptualizing public personnel administration remains the same as in the two previous editions, and we include some new material on employee motivation in Chapter 3, Personnel and Organizational Performance.

The appendix material, Affirmative Action Plan Components, is reprinted by permission of the publisher, the Labor-Management Relations Service of the U.S. Conference of Mayors. The author is Karen Ann Olsen. The appendix material, Arbitration Decision, is reprinted by permission from *Labor Arbitration Reports*, copyright 1982 by the Bureau of National Affairs, Inc., Washington, D.C. (The three appendices in this book appear after Chapter 16, just prior to the Index.)

For this third edition, we are particularly indebted to Jim Hellings of the Office of Personnel Management for information on federal government developments. We, of course, accept full responsibility for the accuracy and soundness of the materials and interpretations in this book.

Edna H. Nigro made her usual excellent contribution with criticism, editing, typing of the manuscript, and proofreading.

Felix A. Nigro
Lloyd G. Nigro

Athens, Georgia
February 1985

1 Value Inputs and Conflicts

In this book, we view personnel administration as a key element in the efforts of organizations of all kinds to achieve their goals. In Chapters 2 and 3, we discuss in detail a systems resources model for understanding the contributions the personnel function can make to organizational effectiveness. The present period is one of increasing public dissatisfaction with the effectiveness of government programs. Criticisms of government personnel policies and practices antedate by many years the current widespread disillusionment with government in general. More than any other time in the nation's history, questions of personnel policy have emerged as prominent items on the public agenda of important issues to resolve. Personnel administration has in the past been regarded as a largely technical function; in this book we attempt to explain its real significance as a set of interrelated societal and organizational problems.

At the outset, let us clarify terms we will be using. We employ "civil service" and "merit system" interchangeably although we are aware some writers make a distinction between them because civil service often has not fulfilled merit objectives. Since so few civil service agencies can truly be said to have achieved complete application of the merit principle, we will be using civil service to refer to any public personnel system established by law to make appointments and promotions on a competitive basis and to make other personnel decisions for merit rather than partisan or other reasons not related to ability. When we use the term "personnel administration," it will mean any program or system that deals with personnel matters. In government, even in the absence of a civil service or merit system law, many formally organized personnel programs exist. The term "central personnel agency," sometimes abbreviated to "personnel agency," will mean the commission, board, or other agency that is responsible for the personnel function on a jurisdiction-wide basis. Finally, "personnel office" will refer to personnel offices located within the line agencies of government such as public health, agriculture, police and fire protection, and so forth.

Values of individuals and groups and of society as a whole influence—or seek to influence—public personnel systems, just as in the case of other activities of government. Yet, because personnel administration has so widely been perceived as "technical," somehow "value-neutral," the impact of values on personnel policies and practices has not received sufficient emphasis. In this first chapter, "Value Inputs and Conflicts," our purpose is to demonstrate how various conceptions of the personnel function have influenced actual policy and practice throughout United States history.

■ CONCEPTS OF THE PERSONNEL FUNCTION

Four principal views of the role of public personnel administration have manifested themselves on the American scene, as they have in many other countries.

1. The *merit* concept, namely, that appointments, promotions, and other personnel actions should be made on the basis of relative ability. For appointments and promotions, this has usually meant the administration of competitive examinations, scores on which have been believed to distinguish between the candidates according to capacity to perform satisfactorily on the job. For other personnel actions such as salary increases, reduction-in-force, and dismissals the assumption has also been that the employee's "merit" could be determined and that he or she should be treated accordingly.

    The word "merit" is placed in quotation marks because there are many versions of what it means and how to measure it. For example, as we elaborate in later chapters of this book, in recent years the interpretation of merit has been broadened to mean much more than ranking candidates according to measures of their ability. Merit is now defined by many persons and groups and by law to include guaranteeing equal employment opportunity to minority groups and women. This necessitates affirmative action programs, requiring intensive searches for candidates that previously were not characteristic of many personnel agencies. To unions and employees, merit now also means pay that compares favorably with that in the private sector for comparable jobs, and it means due process and other rights now recognized by the courts.

2. The *political reward* concept—namely, that government jobs should be awarded to those who have campaigned for or otherwise rendered valuable service to the party in power. This is often referred to as the "spoils" or patronage view of public employment.

   Politicians and others who support patronage in the form of government jobs often say that public employees could not be made "responsive" if there were no patronage. Many elective officials also maintain that since they are discriminating in deciding which political supporters to reward with jobs they are applying merit standards. While the latter contention may seem farfetched, in fact many of these officials do evaluate the job qualifications of their supporters—but they eliminate from consideration persons who support opposing political parties or candidates.

3. The *need* concept—providing government jobs for those who are unemployed or underemployed. True, the private economy in the United States has generally been so strong that it has not been necessary to practice the welfare view of public employment common in many developing nations. Notwithstanding, there has been substantial unemployment and the federal government has on occasion provided funds for public service employment of many unemployed and underemployed, a recent example being jobs in state and local governments under the Comprehensive Employment and Training Act of 1974 (CETA), a program that has been terminated.

4. The *preference* concept—giving special advantage in public employment to groups in society deemed to deserve such treatment. Historically, the best example is veterans' preference, which in the United States has its antecedents in colonial times and by World War I had become solidly established at all levels of government. In recent years, proposals, adopted to some extent, have been made to give preferential treatment to members of disadvantaged groups that previously were discriminated against in public employ-

ment. Preference for such persons is justified in terms of social justice, and it is maintained that a true merit system does not exist unless it embodies considerations of social justice.

Clearly, these four views of public employment overlap, particularly since arguments can be found to justify the political reward, the need, and the preference concepts in terms of redefinition of merit. Furthermore, one concept may be applied in filling one kind of job; another in filling a different kind. There may be a conscious effort to limit application of one of the concepts to certain kinds of positions, for example, restricting patronage jobs to those not requiring specialized qualifications. Of course, the number of jobs that can be filled on a political basis is often limited by law.

The extent of use of each of the four approaches has varied during particular periods of United States history. For example, patronage jobs, once the general rule in the federal service, now are a small percentage of positions in the national executive branch. This brings us to our last observation about the four concepts, namely, that there is much variation in their use by level of government and among individual agencies at each level.

The Four Approaches in United States History

A brief historical review will show the evolution of these four approaches to public employment in the United States and indicate their impact at particular times.

Policies of the first presidents (1789 to 1829)

In general, the policy of the first six Presidents was to make appointments on the basis of fitness for office—a merit concept. Fitness for office meant not only good character and competence but also conformity with the political views of the President. George Washington and John Adams required their appointees to be supporters of the Constitution and the Federalist cause, and similarly Jefferson, Madison, and Monroe required adherence to their political views. All six Presidents made some removals on this political partisan basis, but in general they chose persons they believed to be capable of carrying out the tasks of the particular job.[1]

---

[1]Paul Van Riper, *History of the United States Civil Service* (New York: Harper & Row, 1958), pp. 11–27.

The selection of candidates was, however, very much limited from the standpoint of social class. American society at that time was very stratified, and as Van Riper writes, "The government of our early days was a government led by the well-educated, the well-born, the prosperous, and their adherents."[2] Thus, during this period the federal service was very exclusive, rather than inclusive of all population groups. Taking into account the requirement of political loyalty, it can hardly be said that the first six Presidents followed a merit system in the modern sense, but no clean sweep of federal offices was made, and the federal service had a "good reputation for integrity and capacity."[3] The picture was very different at the state and local government level where from 1800 to 1829 the spoils system of handing out jobs simply on the basis of partisan political support had entrenched itself in states such as New York and Pennsylvania.

The period from 1829 to 1883

Andrew Jackson's views on public personnel policy differed from those of his predecessors in important respects. He believed the service should be democratized and opened to all segments of society and that there was no need for permanence because, as he saw it, the duties of most federal jobs were simple and did not require experience. Accordingly, to him rotation in office was the best policy. These views of Jackson responded to "widespread resentment at the monopolizing of public office by representatives of the upper classes." Some families "had maintained themselves from father to son in the civil service."[4]

According to Mosher, Jackson was only "modestly successful" in democratizing appointments to the top-level positions. In filling these positions, he showed "no less concern about ability and competence" than his predecessors, and, because the "pool of qualified men was still limited," he did not reduce the upper-class background of this part of the service by very much.[5] However, the long-term effect of Jackson's emphasis upon egalitarianism was to open the gates for the spoils politicians at the national level. His

---

[2]Ibid., pp. 17–18.

[3]Ibid., p. 27.

[4]Ibid., p. 33.

[5]Frederick C. Mosher, *Democracy and the Public Service* (New York: Oxford University Press, 1968), p. 62.

successors made many more removals, the objective being principally to strengthen the party machinery—a conception of political reality, rather than an egalitarian ideal. By 1860, the spoils system had progressed so far it "had an adhesive grip upon the political machinery of the United States,"[6] and the same was true in state and local governments.

Some scholars, such as historian Carl Russell Fish, believe that for much of American history the President's patronage club over members of Congress strengthened his leadership in the system of separation of powers.[7] Yet Abraham Lincoln, looking at a crowd of job seekers in his outer office, remarked that "the spoils system might in course of time become far more dangerous to the Republic than the rebellion itself."[8]

The civil service reform movement

The civil service reform movement has been characterized as basically negative in character because it aimed at "keeping out the rascals" rather than recruiting the most competent persons available for public service. But this is a perspective from a later period in American history; certainly the objectives of the civil service reformers were very positive for their times. The scandals of the Grant administration had made abundantly clear to much of the public that the spoils system and graft went hand-in-hand and that this constituted an evil that had to be extirpated from American society.

The writings of the reformers did abound in emotional appeals and rhetoric. Wrote Dorman B. Eaton, "The theory that a party can be kept together only by the hope and reality of spoils is in fact but the mere survivorship, in a milder form, of the once universal theory that an army could only be raised and kept in efficiency by the prospects of pillage."[9] Yet Eaton and other leaders of the reform movement wanted the spoils system eliminated as a first step towards providing more efficient public services. The really negative-minded were those who for many years after the

[6]Van Riper, *History of the United States Civil Service*, p. 42.

[7]See Carl Russell Fish, *The Civil Service and the Patronage* (Cambridge, Mass.: Harvard University Press, 1904).

[8]Van Riper, *History of the United States Civil Service*, p. 44.

[9]See Dorman B. Eaton, *Civil Service in Great Britain* (New York: Harper & Bros., 1880), p. 171.

introduction of civil service systems concentrated on "fighting the spoilsman" in circumstances where the spoilsmen no longer were as great a threat.

Civil service legislation was finally passed by Congress in 1883 after the assassination of President Garfield by a disappointed office seeker, but the immediate reason for approval of the legislation was the Republicans' fear that the next President would be a Democrat who would remove all Republican officeholders. The victory was not an overwhelming one, for coverage of the new competitive system was limited to only about 10.5 percent of the positions in the executive branch.

The administrative machinery established to carry out the Pendleton Act was a civil service commission rather than an executive agency directly under the President. The commission form of organization was chosen to protect the civil service system from partisan political control. However, the President was given an important role because he appointed the three civil service commissioners, subject to Senate confirmation, and his approval was required for promulgation of civil service rules and regulations recommended by the commission. When state and local governments later adopted civil service, they followed the federal example and also created commissions or boards to administer the legislation. The President was also given the power to place additional positions under civil service and to remove positions from such coverage.

Civil service from 1883 to World War II

The first civil service systems were poorly funded and struggled to survive. Besides being limited in coverage, they were narrow gauged; basically, they gave examinations, mostly of an unimaginative character, maintained records, and did little else. They were staffed largely with clerks, and it was clerks who took care of the personnel chores in the departments.

The first state to adopt civil service was New York in 1883, followed by Massachusetts in 1884. That civil service was not a flood of reform is revealed by the fact that no new state civil service laws were approved in the next two decades. Albany, New York—now a stronghold of the old machine politics—was the first municipality to adopt civil service (1884). Cook County, Illinois, another example of boss control, was the first county to do so (1895). Often, when civil service was adopted, it was taken over by machine politicians, and the commissions became "a front for spoils."[10]

Although more civil service systems were established during the first three decades of the 20th century, the activities conducted remained restricted. During this period the scientific management movement had some impact on government and the efficiency concept was of increasing importance in American society, but civil service at all levels of government remained much the same.

Birth of modern personnel administration. In 1938 Franklin D. Roosevelt issued an executive order requiring the principal federal agencies to establish bona fide, professionally staffed personnel offices. Because the personnel function, although much criticized, is generally accepted today, it seems inconceivable that this should have occurred so late in United States history. At that time, however, the necessity for personnel offices had not been established.

Roosevelt's order signaled the arrival of "modern" personnel administration based on the efficiency approach. Modern meant expanded personnel services, improvement of basic techniques such as position classification, and in general the use of the scientific method in selection and other personnel processes. Since this required staffing of the central personnel agency and departmental personnel offices with persons with appropriate training, college graduates soon began to replace the clerks. The concept of personnel administration as a tool or arm of management began to take hold, not only in the federal government but also in some state and local governments. Looking back on this period, the accomplishments and even some of the thinking may not seem impressive compared with improvements since then, but by the end of World War II the old era of civil service as a routine activity with limited technical content and little relation to management needs had largely receded into the past.

Between World War II and the 1960s

The efficiency approach soon revealed weaknesses of its own. Basically, two criticisms of the new personnel offices were made: (1) they frequently hampered rather than helped line officials, and (2)

---

[10]Albert H. Aronson, "Personnel Administration: The State and Local Picture," *Civil Service Journal* 13, no. 3 (January–March 1973): 38.

they concentrated on procedures and paper work and neglected human considerations.

A familiar complaint was that the personnel workers carried a rule book they followed rigidly and were prone to deny line officer requests. It seemed that whereas line officials previously were suspected of wanting to violate the merit principle now they were held in contempt as being unappreciative of the advantages of an efficiently functioning personnel office. This kind of criticism was inevitable; it is often made of persons serving in staff roles since in their sphere of expertise they exercise control over line officials. Yet there was enough justification in the complaints for leaders in the personnel field to appeal to their colleagues to adopt a more flexible attitude. Many speeches were made and articles written in which personnel workers were reminded that their mission was to facilitate the work of the line agencies. Such admonitions are still being made, although more recently the phraseology is to "bring personnel into the mainstream of management," or some such statement.

As to the second criticism, although the objective of personnel programs presumably was the obvious one of serving human needs, personnel workers did not seem at all "people-minded." They spent most of their time on day-to-day personnel tasks, applying technical skills but showing little interest in developing the potential of the employee as a valuable human resource. The human relations approach, stemming from the research of Elton Mayo and associates at the Hawthorne plant of the Western Electric Company, was having some effect in the private sector but hardly any in the mechanistic world of public personnel administration.

This began to change after World War II as an "accent-on-people" emphasis gained adherents. The human relations approach is, of course, broad in its implications, but it became clear that it could be applied to the personnel function in the following specific ways:

1. Stimulating employees to give forth their best efforts. It does not suffice simply to find qualified persons and place them in the right jobs; they must be properly motivated.
2. Developing the people-centered phases of the personnel program, such as in-service training which had been given little attention. Analyzing employees' training needs and helping them develop their potential evidences concern for them as humans and benefits the organization.

3. Recognizing that supervisors constitute the focal element in the personnel program because they have the closest contact with the employees. Accordingly, they should be helped in all their personnel relations.
4. Undertaking personnel research because it is essential to understand the wellsprings of human motivation and effort. Very little such research was being conducted at the time.
5. Expecting personnel workers to have sufficiently broad backgrounds of training and experience to understand human behavior. The mark of their value should not solely be expertise in techniques such as classification or testing; they should also be schooled in human relations theory and its application. The desirability of broader preparation and deeper insights for personnel workers became increasingly recognized.

Summing up for this period, it basically was one in which at the federal level and in a growing number of state and local jurisdictions progress was made in making personnel systems more efficient, better related to management needs, and more concerned with the employee as a person. Just how much progress was made is a matter of opinion; in many state and local jurisdictions civil service remained negative and unimaginative in outlook. For the country as a whole, however, the conception of the personnel function had perceptibly broadened.

■ THE NEW PUBLIC PERSONNEL ADMINISTRATION

Beginning with the 1960s, the changes have been so great that it can be said that a "new public personnel administration" has emerged. Several strong forces have been responsible for very substantial changes in traditional policies and practices: (1) the rapid spread of collective bargaining in the public service; (2) legislative, judicial, and administrative policy requirements for equal employment opportunity and affirmative action programs; and (3) court decisions establishing constitutional and other rights of public employees. In the 1970s and 1980s, a fourth force has developed impetus—that for civil service reform centering on such innovations as special personnel systems for executives, merit pay for supervisors, delegation of personnel authority to the line agencies, and, in general, elimination of rigid practices believed to have contributed to the widely perceived failure of government to "deliver" programs effectively.

The Spread of Collective Bargaining

Before 1960, only one state, Wisconsin in 1959, had passed legislation requiring the public employer to bargain collectively with
public employees. (The 1959 Wisconsin statute applied to municipal governments.) In the federal service, there was no law or executive order providing for collective bargaining or any
governmentwide labor relations policy. The present picture is very
different. By 1985, 40 states and the District of Columbia had statutes or executive orders establishing legal frameworks for collective
bargaining with some or all of their employees.

About half of all state and local government full-time employees
now are members of employee organizations, and the percentage
of organized full-time employees is high in such governmental
functions as education, highways, public welfare, hospitals, police,
fire, and sanitation services.[11] In the federal service, collective bargaining, first provided for by an executive order of President Kennedy issued in January of 1962, is now a statutory requirement.
The Postal Reorganization Act of 1970 provided collective bargaining rights for postal employees, and Title VII of the Civil Service
Reform Act of 1978 grants similar rights to nonpostal employees.
Close to 70 percent of federal postal and nonpostal employees combined are represented by unions serving as bargaining agents.

Under collective bargaining, decisions on employment policies
are reached through negotiations between representatives of management and representatives of unions—a bilateral, rather than
unilateral, process. Historically, civil service systems have been
paternalistic: The public employer, after whatever consultation
with employees it found appropriate, unilaterally determined
terms and conditions of employment. Although the extent of consultation was often criticized by employees as insufficient, most
employee organizations themselves did not demand collective bargaining rights, and they relied on traditional lobbying methods to
protect their interests. After two and a half decades of rapid spread
of collective bargaining in government, this bilateral process—so
repugnant at first to many public officials, as in many places it
continues to be—no longer is a novelty.

In many jurisdictions, both civil service and collective bargaining

---

[11]Bureau of the Census, U.S. Department of Commerce, Labor-Management
Services Administration, U.S. Department of Labor, *Labor-Management Relations
in State and Local Governments* (Washington, D.C.: Government Printing Office,
1976), pp. 1–7.

systems exist. Whereas previously to understand the personnel policies and procedures of a jurisdiction one had only to consult the civil service law and rules, now one must also study the contents of collective agreements entered into by the public employer with a union or unions. Furthermore, the unions are very much involved in the administration of personnel policies and procedures. Through stewards and other representatives, unions monitor management actions and supervisory performance to assure compliance with contract terms. In a real sense, this gives the union a partnership role with management in personnel administration.

There are many conflicts between public employers and the unions, and often the relationships are hostile. The union role can be condemned or lauded, depending on one's point of view and what actions management and the unions have taken in a particular situation. Obviously, neither side is always right. The essential point is that under collective bargaining the *nature* of the relationship between management and employees changes drastically. Management deals with the union on the formulation and implementation of personnel policies, rather than with individual employees. Under collective bargaining, for the most part the employee voice is heard through the union. Many public officials have found it difficult to adjust to this collective, rather than individual, relationship with employees.

Chapters 5 and 6 of this book are devoted in their entirety to the unions; in the other chapters, specific union impact on the aspect of personnel administration treated is described. Chapter 5 discusses the background of collective bargaining in the private sector, its rise in the public sector, the different kinds of public employee organizations, and other general characteristics of unions and collective bargaining in government. Chapter 6 presents in detail the components of a collective bargaining system and analyzes the whole area of potential and actual conflicts between civil service and collective bargaining.

Equal Employment Opportunity

Equal employment opportunity means prohibition of discrimination in employment for reasons of race, sex, color, religion, national origin, or condition of being physically handicapped.

Under traditional civil service, the very low representation of minority groups in the public service and their concentration in the lowest ranking jobs were generally not viewed as a violation of the merit principle. So long as there was no overt discrimination, the failure of blacks and other minorities to qualify for appointment in anywhere near the same numbers as the rest of society was viewed as unfortunate but no fault of the civil service system. Actually, there was overt discrimination, as documented by the findings of the U.S. Commission on Civil Rights in a 1969 report on state and local government personnel systems: "Administrators of merit systems have frequently violated the merit principle and practiced conscious, even institutionalized, discrimination."[12] The commission's basic finding, however, was that "static" civil service procedures were mostly responsible for excluding minority groups; it cited as examples the use of unvalidated written tests, rigid education requirements, and automatic disqualification for an arrest record. The report also stressed that most merit system agencies made no positive efforts to recruit minorities, as by visiting colleges with large enrollments of blacks or sending recruiters into the ghettos.[13]

At the time this report was issued, equal employment opportunity had made some progress in the nation, and some federal lower court decisions, based on the Fourteenth Amendment to the federal Constitution and on the Civil Rights Acts of 1866 and 1871, had made clear that the judiciary would void discriminatory practices and insist on affirmative action programs if public employers did not adopt such programs. (The Civil Rights Act of 1964 as originally enacted applied to the private sector only, but it was amended in 1972 to cover the public sector as well.)

In 1971, the U.S. Supreme Court made its decision in *Griggs* v. *Duke Power Company*. In 1964, the Duke Power Company ended a policy of confining blacks to low-paying laborers' jobs but at the same time established the new requirement that to qualify for better jobs the employee, black or white, had to have a high school diploma and pass an intelligence test as well as a mechanical comprehension test. The black employees bringing the court action charged that in practice this continued the old discriminatory policies because the only jobs exempted from the new requirements

---

[12]U.S. Commission on Civil Rights, *For All the People . . . By All the People: A Report on Equal Opportunity in State and Local Government Employment* (Washington, D.C.: Government Printing Office, 1969), p. 64.

[13]Ibid., pp. 32–37, p. 65.

and therefore the only ones for which they could qualify were menial ones in the company's labor department. The Court found that the new standards were not demonstrably related to successful job performance and that they served to disqualify blacks at a substantially higher rate than whites. As to the company's defense that its intentions had been good, the Court said that "good intent or absence of discriminatory intent does not redeem employment procedures or testing mechanisms that operate as 'built-in head-winds' for minority groups and are unrelated to measuring job capability."[14]

The Court emphasized that nothing in the Civil Rights Act of 1964 precluded the use of testing or measuring procedures and that Congress had not

> . . . commanded that the less qualified be preferred over the better qualified simply because of minority origins. . . . Far from disparaging job qualifications as such, Congress has made such qualifications the controlling factor, so that race, religion, nationality, and sex become irrelevant. What Congress has commanded is that any tests used must measure the person for the job and not the person in the abstract.[15]

Griggs has had profound effect because it established the rule that if employers use a selection requirement that has a disparate effect on the basis of race, sex, religion, or national origin they must prove the requirement is job-related. If they cannot do so, the requirement constitutes illegal discrimination.

Court decisions since Griggs relating to employment of minorities. Since *Griggs*, there have been many lower court decisions enjoining the use of selection methods the court believes have not been proven to be related to satisfactory performance of the duties of the job in question. The judges review the validity evidence submitted in court and decide whether or not it is acceptable— which means that the judiciary is heavily involved in technical selection questions. Judges have ordered personnel agencies to prepare new tests and issued guidelines for validating these new tests; ruled a violation of the Civil Rights Act of 1964 recruitment of firefighters by "word of mouth and encouragement from friends

---

[14]401 U.S. 424 (1971).
[15]Ibid.

already on the force, where 99 percent of the force is white";[16] and required outreach recruitment, pretest tutoring sessions, and other changes in personnel programs to improve the employment possibilities of minorities. They have also imposed remedial numerical hiring ratios to rectify past discrimination, such as hiring one black for each white until the percentage of blacks employed equals the percentage of blacks in the jurisdiction's population. The judges have justified these remedial hiring ratios as necessary on a temporary basis, but there has been much criticism that the ratios are in fact quotas prohibited by the Civil Rights Act.

In *Albemarle Paper Company* v. *Moody* (1975), the U.S. Supreme Court repeated the requirements for test validity set forth in *Griggs*. The Court also decreed that back pay should be awarded whenever necessary to fulfill the purposes of Title VII of the Civil Rights Act of 1964.[17] In *Regents of the University of California* v. *Bakke* (1978),[18] the issue before the U.S. Supreme Court was *not* the use of remedial hiring ratios, but it was widely believed that the Court's decision in this case might have clear implications for such ratios. Allen Bakke, a white, had been denied admission to the Medical School of the University of California at Davis. The school had reserved 16 of its 100 admissions for blacks and Hispanics, some of whom had been rated by the school as less qualified than Bakke. The California Supreme Court had found this admissions plan unconstitutional, ordered Bakke admitted, and enjoined *any* consideration of race in future admissions.

By a five-to-four vote, the U.S. Supreme Court ordered Bakke's admission to the Davis medical school but ruled that college admission programs which take race into account *are* constitutional. The Davis admission plan violated the Civil Rights Act of 1964 because black and Hispanic applicants competed among themselves for the 16 admissions reserved for them, not with the white applicants. The Civil Rights Act of 1964 provides: "No person in the United States shall, on the grounds of race, color, or national origin, be excluded from participation in, be denied the benefits or be subjected to discrimination under any program or activity receiving Federal financial assistance."

---

[16]Bureau of Intergovernmental Personnel Programs, U.S. Civil Service Commission, *Equal Employment Opportunity Court Cases* (Washington, D.C., 1976), p. 19.

[17]422 U.S. 405 (1975).

[18]See United States Commission on Civil Rights, *Toward an Understanding of Bakke* (Washington, D.C.: Government Printing Office, May 1979).

The *Bakke* decision relieved those who were concerned about the future of government programs providing preferential treatment for minorities; the California Supreme Court's ban on giving race any consideration at all had been rejected. Justice Powell referred approvingly to admission plans such as that at Harvard College, where race is taken into account, together with other factors, as a means of achieving diversity in the student population.

The arguments in the *Bakke* case were based both on the Civil Rights Act of 1964 and the equal protection clause of the Fourteenth Amendment to the federal Constitution. In another widely publicized case before the U.S. Supreme Court, *United Steelworkers of America* v. *Weber* (1979),[19] violation of the equal protection clause was not alleged, and the issue was interpretation of the Civil Rights Act of 1964, specifically whether in the private sector, unions and companies can adopt voluntary affirmative action plans calling for preferential treatment for blacks. Weber, a white worker, maintained that a Kaiser Company-Steelworkers' affirmative action plan negotiated as part of a nationwide collective bargaining agreement violated the Civil Rights Act because it reserved half the places in training programs to black workers. Weber had more seniority than two blacks accepted for training in one of the Kaiser plants.

By a five-to-two vote, the Court ruled that the Kaiser-Steelworker affirmative action plan did *not* violate the Civil Rights Act. Writing for the Court majority, Justice Brennan said that the legislative history of the Civil Rights Act indicated clearly that it was not the intention of Congress to "prohibit all race conscious affirmative action plans." In passing the legislation, Congress was concerned over the trend to relegating blacks largely to unskilled jobs—jobs without a future. Wrote Brennan: "It would be ironic indeed if a law triggered by a Nation's concern over centuries of racial injustice and intended to improve the lot of those who had been 'excluded from the American dream for so long' constituted the first legislative prohibition of all voluntary, race-conscious efforts to abolish traditional patterns of racial segregation and hierarchy." Besides, had Congress meant to forbid voluntary affirmative action plans, it would have written a provision to that effect into the legislation.

Since both *Bakke* and *Weber* have no clear bearing on remedial

---

[19]"Excerpts from High Court's Opinions," *New York Times*, June 28, 1979.

numerical hiring ratios in public employment, determination of the constitutionality of such ratios remained for later U.S. Supreme Court decision. When Ronald Reagan assumed office, his administration took the strong position that remedial hiring ratios represented reverse discrimination and violated both the Civil Rights Act and the equal protection clause of the Fourteenth Amendment to the Federal Constitution. In December of 1983 the Justice Department urged the Supreme Court to rule unconstitutional an affirmative action plan entered into voluntarily by the Detroit Police Department providing for the hiring and promotion of blacks and whites in equal numbers, but the Court declined to hear the case. As a *Christian Science Monitor* editorial notes,

> opposition among whites has risen in recent years as a formerly expanding economy contracted, throwing more blacks and whites into job competition. . . . White males realize now that they compete not only with blacks for jobs but also with women and the growing Hispanic and Asian minorities. . . . Part of the controversy is over the conflict between those who see progress as individual and those who believe group progress is most feasible for blacks. The Reagan administration has come down on the side of the individual. Some others, such as the American Civil Liberties Union, hold that the only feasible way for substantial numbers of qualified blacks to gain good jobs is through quotas. That debate will persist.[20]

Sex Discrimination

United States society has been characterized not only by discrimination against ethnic minorities but also against women. Like minority groups, because of discriminatory practices, women have been confined to lower-grade jobs both in the private and public sectors. Traditionally, their employment has been confined to clerical and service jobs—so-called women's jobs according to the employers' stereotype.

Although the courts have interpreted the prohibitions in the Civil Rights Act of 1964 to include sex discrimination, this condition of occupational segregation into lower-paying jobs has continued and has even worsened somewhat.[21] While the U.S.

---

[20]*Christian Science Monitor*, editorial page, December 8, 1983.

[21]See Michael Evan Gold, *A Dialogue on Comparable Worth* (Ithaca, N.Y.: Cornell University, New York State School of Industrial and Labor Relations, 1983), p.6.

Supreme Court has found racial classifications inherently suspect, a majority of its judges has yet to rule similarly for sex classifications. However, the courts have clearly established that, to be upheld, sex classifications must have a rational basis, that is, be justified in terms of a rational relationship between sex and occupational qualification. As a result, women are now being employed in many kinds of positions previously considered too strenuous or otherwise unsuitable for females. Nonetheless, just as in the case of minority groups, women still are very poorly-represented in higher grade professional and executive positions, and some employers have flimsy reasons for not employing women in certain positions.

Discrimination for Reasons of Age or Handicapped Condition

Equal employment opportunity protections also apply to those between the ages of 40 and 70 and to the handicapped.

The Age Discrimination in Employment Act of 1967, as amended in 1978, which applies to both the private and public sectors, prohibits employers from discriminating against persons age 40 to 70 in terms, conditions, and privileges of employment. This legislation is not violated if the employer can prove that age is a legitimate employment qualification; but the courts are requiring reasonable evidence that a certain entrance or retirement age is disqualifying. Employers may not favor younger employees simply for reasons of age unrelated to ability to do the job.

The Rehabilitation Act of 1973, which applies to federal contractors, prohibits discrimination in all employment decisions and requires the contractor to have a written affirmative action program for the handicapped. Reasonable accommodation must be made by the employer to facilitate the employment of handicapped persons.

Constitutional Rights of the Public Employee

Since this subject is dealt with in an entire chapter (Chapter 15), the only point we make here is that the courts have not basically retreated from a series of decisions overruling the ancient privilege doctrine of public employment, that is, that government employees had no constitutional rights in their jobs. Certain recent U.S. Supreme Court decisions have created doubt that the Court is protecting these constitutional rights as carefully as previously, but the courts continue to review personnel actions taken in government where the employee's interest is believed to be substantial enough to warrant constitutional protection.

Civil Service Reform

Collective bargaining, equal employment opportunity, and court decisions establishing constitutional rights of public employees— all these can certainly be considered to have profoundly changed public personnel administration. However, these are not the changes to which the term "civil service reform" now usually refers. It refers instead to efforts to reform the "bureaucracy," to improve personnel practices in government and the quality and performance of public employees as part of a total program to make "government work."

Civil service reform in this context has its source in the dissatisfactions of various elements in society with the performance of administrative agencies and of government in general. The public is concerned that efforts by government to achieve targeted objectives in such problem areas as poverty, unemployment, inflation, and crime have failed. Business, civic, professional, and other groups have long been convinced that civil service machinery and practices are outmoded and hamper rather than facilitate good management. Line officials in government continue to protest that civil service denies them the flexibility they need in order to manage programs effectively, and they say that under civil service it is virtually impossible for them to dismiss incompetent employees. Departmental personnel offices complain that insufficient personnel authority is delegated to them by the central personnel agency. Employees themselves see little relationship between the quality of their performance and promotion, salary increase, and other rewards. To many elective officials, civil service reform means first of all making changes to assure that the "bureaucracy" is responsive to their policy directives. Many legislators are equally concerned that the administrative agencies are not sufficiently responsive to legislative requests and wishes. Employee union leaders usually are suspicious that civil service reform proposals are disguised efforts to politicize the bureaucracy, but as noted in later chapters, some unions have negotiated agreements with public employers to make significant changes in traditional practices (e.g., incentive pay).

Civil service reform proposals vary in their content, nor has civil service reform as yet become a major force throughout the country. Major legislation has been passed at the federal level—the Civil Service Reform Act of 1978 (CSRA)—and certain changes in traditional practices have been made by law and/or administrative policy in a number of state and local governments. Major provisions of the CSRA will be discussed in later chapters of this book, and reference will be made to similar reform efforts at the state and local level.

■ NEW EMPHASES IN PUBLIC PERSONNEL ADMINISTRATION

In concluding this first chapter, we want to discuss certain new emphases in public personnel administration that increasingly are replacing or modifying traditional civil service practices. By traditional is meant the policies, practices, methods, and attitudes of personnel agencies in government administering merit systems. In part, these new emphases reflect values of what we have called the new public personnel administration, so our discussion here will to that extent be an elaboration of points made earlier in this chapter. Since each of these new emphases constitutes a model we distinguish the following: (1) the management flexibility model, (2) the political and public responsiveness model, (3) the social justice and individual rights model, and (4) the collective bargaining model.

Before taking up each of these models, it must be stated that they do overlap to some extent. For example, the first and second overlap in their quest for flexibility, but the second stresses political and public accountability. Similarly, the collective bargaining model rests on considerations of social and individual justice, but equal employment opportunity and court decisions recognizing and expanding the constitutional and legal rights of public employees are not a part of the collective bargaining movement as such and thus warrant separate treatment.

The Management Flexibility Model

This model emphasizes the need of the chief executive, department heads, and program managers to control the personnel function. Supporters of this model maintain that since their inception civil service systems have functioned with far too much independence from chief executives and that they have imposed numerous restrictive controls over line management. The contention is that when civil service began with the passage of the Pendleton Act in 1883, it was based on an assumption that was basically wrong and that for many years now has been outmoded—namely, that for a merit system to survive and function well the personnel operation had to be kept a safe distance from chief executives and line managers.

Thus, a separation between general management and personnel administration was created despite the fact that personnel, like finance, is an integral part of the management function in any organization. Understandably, the civil service reformers had to be concerned about protecting the new merit systems from destruction by the spoils politicians, and understandably it still remains essential to protect against political abuses, but this split between executive management and the personnel function is intolerable. Merit systems can be developed that protect against the spoils system but also serve the needs of chief executives and program officials.

Among the changes recommended by proponents of the management flexibility model are the following:

(1) The traditional independent civil service commission should be abolished and replaced by a personnel director appointed by the chief executive, with or without senate confirmation, and reporting directly to him or her. The entire jurisdiction-wide personnel management function would be under the personnel director and the chief executive, with an independent board or commission established to hear employee appeals and make investigations of personnel practices to prevent political abuses.

The Civil Service Reform Act of 1978 made this change in the federal service by providing for an Office of Personnel Management whose director reports directly to the President, and a Merit Systems Protection Board responsible for the appellate and a merit "watchdog" function. In state and local governments, various prestigious study groups and organizations, such as the Municipal Manpower Commission in 1962[22] and the National Civil Service League in 1970,[23] have recommended similar organizational arrangements,

[22]Municipal Manpower Commission, *Governmental Manpower for Tomorrow's Cities* (New York: McGraw-Hill, 1962), p. 108.

[23]*A Model Public Personnel Administration Law*, National Civil Service League, Chevy Chase, Md., 1970, p. 5.

and while the traditional civil service commission with personnel policymaking, appellate, and administrative responsibilities still remains in many jurisdictions, in a growing number the commission has either been abolished or limited to advisory, appellate, and investigatory roles. As personnel authority W. Donald Heisel stresses, independent civil service commissions have agendas of their own and often fail to follow personnel policies desired by chief executives.[24]

(2) Central personnel agencies and the personnel offices in the line departments should eliminate numerous unnecessary controls they maintain over line officials in personnel matters. An example, but only one, of such restrictive control is the requirement that department heads obtain prior approval of the central personnel agency before they can make even minor personnel decisions, such as extension of a temporary appointment.

The proper role of the central personnel agency is to provide policy, technical, and other guidance to line departments, to delegate the details of the personnel function to these departments, and to evaluate departmental personnel programs and be vigilant to detect any failure to follow merit system requirements. As stated so well in a recent report of the National Academy of Public Administration, the responsibility for personnel administration should be *"placed squarely in the hands of the manager, and not in the personnel organization."*[25] Since it recommends such sweeping delegation, the Academy—a prestigious group of distinguished persons in the public administration field—can be said to advocate an advanced form of the management flexibility model, but the thrust of its recommendation makes clear what the objectives of that model are.

(3) Establishment of special personnel systems for executives that make possible more flexible and effective use of their services and rewarding them with salary and other recognition commensurate with the quality of their performance. Success with government programs depends greatly upon the quality, motivation, and performance of career executives, yet civil service rigidities prevent utilizing their services effectively and providing adequate rewards for outstanding accomplishment.

---

[24]W. Donald Heisel and Warren Bennis, "Reforming the Civil Service," *New York Affairs* 4, no. 2 (Spring 1977).

[25]*Revitalizing Federal Management: Managers and their Overburdened Systems*, National Academy of Public Administration, Washington, D.C., 1978, p. 38.

This is the rationale for senior executive services, such as that established in the federal government by the Civil Service Reform Act of 1978 and now found in several state governments and under active consideration in others. In a senior executive service, rank is in the person, not in the job; this prevents the downgrading always possible under civil service when someone is assigned to another job if the position classifiers rule that the duties are less responsible although the agency management has an urgent need to make the transfer. For various reasons, discussed in Chapter 9, entering salaries and salary increases for executives in government generally are well below those for comparable positions in the private sector.

In the federal Senior Executive Service (SES), department heads have much discretion in setting the entrance salaries of executives and in granting them salary increases and bonuses. The SES members are untenured and may be returned to non-SES ppositions if their performance evaluations are not sufficiently high—a further element of flexibility for management.

(4) Instituting sound systems of performance evaluation and merit pay for all employees, and a removal policy and procedure that make it possible to weed out employees for inadequate performance. Under civil service, for various reasons it usually is difficult to remove unsatisfactory employees.

Other components of the management flexibility model could be mentioned but this is unnecessary because our purpose has been to give enough examples to make clear what flexibility is sought.

The flexibility approach is based on certain assumptions that can be challenged. One such assumption is that private sector practices should be followed, such as organizing the personnel function under the top executive. But the top executive in government necessarily is a political figure, and the political factor permeates the government environment and makes it very different from that in business. The more control the chief executive has over the personnel function and the more discretion department heads have in taking personnel actions, the greater the chance they have to evade and ultimately undermine the merit principle—this is the basic fear about introducing substantial management flexibility.

Certainly there is much evidence, past and present, to demonstrate that these fears are justified. However, the existence of a U.S. Civil Service Commission failed to prevent merit system evasions planned and executed by White House staff during the Nixon presidency, and similar manipulations occurred under other presidencies. Still, this does not convince those who believe that the opportunity for political abuses was widened when the Commission was abolished and the Office of Personnel Management established.

Many federal employees, and particularly union leaders, were very apprehensive about such innovations as the SES, merit pay, and bonus awards because they thought it likely that department heads would reward favorites and find ways of removing those they disliked from the SES. The General Accounting Office reports no systematic, widespread violation of merit principles in the SES to date,[26] but there have been some verified instances of such violations, and in any case many of those who opposed an SES, merit pay, and other greater discretion for management have not changed their minds.

Supporters of flexibility maintain that the advantages clearly outweigh the risks. In truth, this has been an age-old dilemma for public personnel administration: how to achieve urgently-needed change without exposing the merit principle to undue risk. Since there are conflicting values in society about public personnel policies, this dilemma will always remain, a theme emphasized in the final chapter of this book.

The Political and Public Responsiveness Model

This model also emphasizes flexibility but the primary purpose of the discretion sought is to establish and maintain political control over the administrative branch of government.

A long-standing dissatisfaction of Presidents, Governors, and other chief executives is that civil service extends so far upward in the administrative hierarchy that there are too few exempt positions they can fill with persons in whose loyalty to their policies they can trust. The issue here is not political spoils but rather the ability to be in control of the administrative branch, to carry out electoral mandates, and to be able to deal effectively with any bureaucratic sabotage by career officials.

Throughout the first decades of this century, a stated goal of

---

[26]*Report to the Chairwoman, Subcommittee on Civil Service, House Committee on Post Office and Civil Service, Testimony of the Comptroller General on the Impact of the Senior Executive Service*, General Accounting Office, Washington, D.C., December 30, 1983.

merit system supporters was to extend coverage of the competitive system upward, downward, and horizontally so that most of the administrative branch was included. So much success was achieved in this respect that after World War II complaints were increasingly heard that as a result of such extensive civil service coverage the bureaucracy was unresponsive to political leaders and the people. Nor were these complaints limited to elective chief executives: city managers reported they could not manage efficiently because department and assistant department heads not distinguished by great competence were protected by civil service. A countertrend developed in governments like that of the state of Oregon where only a handful of positions had been exempted from civil service and where several years ago substantial numbers of top posts were placed in the exempt category.

Just how many positions and which ones should be excluded from civil service remains a much-disputed question. When they believe they have too few top positions they can fill, chief executives sometimes try to establish control by evading civil service requirements. This occurred for a time during the Eisenhower administration when a White House aide developed a plan for reviewing the "fitness" of holdover c ⁀icials from the previous Democratic administration, including sc ne in civil service grades, but because of pressures from the National Civil Service League and other organizations, as well as opposition within the administration, this plan was terminated. More recently and still fresh in the memories of career officials in the federal service, during the Nixon presidency the White House directed and skillfully implemented a calculated strategy for ridding the bureaucracy of officials not considered loyal to the President and his policies. As Hugh Heclo points out,[27] tactics of this type did not originate with Nixon, and both the Kennedy and Johnson administrations worked around civil service requirements to assure loyalty of career officials to the President's policies.

A senior civil service makes it easier for chief executives and department heads to maintain control because the SES members can be moved from one post to another and, since they are untenured, can be removed from the SES itself. Many career officials and union leaders believe that this is the chief executive's real

---

[27]Hugh Heclo, *A Government of Strangers: Executive Politics in Washington* (Washington, D.C.: Brookings, 1977).

reason for wanting an SES. While transfers and other treatment of SES members may not be made on a partisan political basis, the fear of reprisals can and does inhibit some career officials in the free expression of their opinions (see Chapter 4).

Thus, consideration of the political responsiveness model leads inevitably to a dilemma similar to that in the management flexibility approach: how to assure responsiveness and democratic control of the administrative branch without damaging the essence of the merit principle.

The Social Justice Model

This model rests on the conviction that a true merit system is one which provides equal employment opportunity in the public service for all segments of society. Specifically, this means EEO for minority group members and for women, and affirmative action plans to achieve EEO.

Historically, lofty as its merit ideals were, civil service was not based on considerations of social justice. Civil service administrators did not consider it their role to redress injustices in society by reshaping public personnel policies and practices to promote better opportunities for minorities. The dominant element in their value system was adherence to the merit principle and, if minorities qualified only for relatively few civil service positions except menial ones, that was unfortunate but a problem for "society" to remedy.

With passage of the Civil Rights Act of 1964, "society," imbued with new values, did legislate a remedy—EEO—and affirmative action plans were instituted in government.

Previously, merit system administrators thought any special help for minorities violated the merit principle. Now, as one example, "outreach recruitment" and other programs to increase the number of minority group member applicants for public service jobs are an acknowledged responsibility of the civil service agency.

In society, there remain deep disagreements about which forms of assistance for minorities and women are acceptable from the policy standpoint and which violate the essence of merit selection and advancement. The most important of these disagreements is over remedial hiring ratios, popularly known as "quotas," the pros and cons of which are discussed in Chapter 7.

Just like the collective bargaining model, to be discussed next, the social justice approach has made profound changes in public personnel administration. In both cases, the impact has been to broaden considerably the definition of merit.

The Collective Bargaining Model

Because collective bargaining is a joint decision-making process by management and the unions, where it has been adopted it has radically changed public personnel administration. Before the spread of collective bargaining in government, employee input was very limited. With collective bargaining, that input is greatly increased as is that of the unions. The unions still rely heavily on lobbying with elective and appointive officials, but when wages, benefits, and many personnel policies and procedures must be negotiated with their representatives, they have a much more important role in government.

Before the 1960s, most merit system administrators thought of collective bargaining as something peculiar to the private sector that had no place in government. In truth, they had little familiarity with collective bargaining and knowledge of its institutional significance as a system of internal governance in private establishments. When collective bargaining began to spread in government, they considered it a real menace to preservation of the merit principle and thought the goal of most public employee union leaders was to wipe out civil service laws and regulations and replace them with collective agreements. As subsequent chapters of this book explain (see particularly Chapter 6), this has not happened although there are frequent conflicts between merit system administrators and the unions.

It is one thing for legislatures and civil service commissions to develop personnel policies and oversee their enforcement. It is another for public management to have to develop these policies jointly with the unions through the bargaining process which often is prolonged and basically is an adversary relationship, no matter what "partnership" agreements are reached. The unions believe that it is only through collective bargaining that policies that are fair to the employees and respect their dignity as persons can be reached.

Union leaders further maintain that collective bargaining is the best method available for achieving good, stable labor relations because it provides for recognition of a majority union that advances and defends the interests of all employees in the bargaining unit whether or not union members. Many merit system administrators have adjusted to collective bargaining, and some believe it is advantageous for management to deal with the employees through a responsible union. Yet many are unhappy with the big expenditures of staff time and other expense that must be devoted to the negotiation of agreements and afterwards to consultations with union officials over contract administration. As elaborated in Chapter 6, the impact of collective bargaining has been to improve public personnel administration in important respects but also to harm it in others. Whether the benefits outweigh the negative ffects is a matter of opinion. The overall record indicates to us t at they clearly do, that collective bargaining in government obviously is here to stay and the constructive energies are those that seek to maximize the benefits and avoid the dangers.

In the chapters of this book that follow, additional information is given about each of these alternative models to traditional civil service. This preliminary discussion is intended to provide a framework for understanding the new directions in public personnel administration.

BIBLIOGRAPHY

Gold, Michael Evans. *A Dialogue on Comparable Worth*. Ithaca, N.Y.: Cornell University, New York State School of Industrial and Labor Relations, 1983.

Heclo, Hugh. *A Government of Strangers: Executive Politics in Washington*. Washington, D.C.: Brookings, 1977.

House Committee on Post Office and Civil Service. *History of Civil Service Merit Systems of the United States and Selected Foreign Countries*. 94th Congress, 2d Session. Washington, D.C.: Government Printing Office, 1976.

Macy, John W., Jr. *Public Service: The Human Side of Government*. New York: Harper & Row, 1971.

Mosher, Frederick C. *Democracy and the Public Service*. New York: Oxford University Press, 1968.

National Academy of Public Administration. *Revitalizing Federal Management: Managers and Their Overburdened Systems*. Chapter 5: New Concepts for Personnel Management. Washington, D.C., November 1983.

Nigro, Felix A. "Public Personnel Administration: From Theodore

Roosevelt to Ronald Reagan." *International Journal of Public Administration* 6, no. 1 (March 1984).

———. "The Politics of Civil Service Reform." *Southern Review of Public Administration* 3, no. 2 (September 1979).

Personnel Literature. Washington, D.C.: Office of Personnel Management. Monthly bibliography.

Rabin, Jack; Vocino, Thomas; Hildreth, W. Bartley; and Miller, Gerald J., eds. *Handbook on Public Personnel Administration and Labor Relations*. New York: Marcel Dekker, 1983.

Schiesl, Martin J. *The Politics of Efficiency*. Berkeley, Calif.: University of California Press, 1977.

Tolchin, Martin, and Tolchin, Susan. *To the Victor . . . Political Patronage from the Clubhouse to the White House*. New York: Vintage Books, 1972.

Van Riper, Paul. *History of the United States Civil Service*. New York: Harper & Row, 1958.

2 Organizations and the Personnel Function

In a pluralistic society such as ours, personnel policies and practices must serve diverse and sometimes conflicting interests. The organization itself is one such interest. In this chapter and the next one, we will present an overview of the ways in which personnel systems can contribute to the performance capabilities of public organizations. Detailed discussions of many of the topics raised will be found in the chapters that follow. Our frame of reference is the public agency as a social and technical system, and our focus is on the part personnel management plays in promoting or undermining the capabilities of these organizations to survive and to accomplish their goals.

■ THE SYSTEMS RESOURCES MODEL

In the final analysis, the effectiveness of organizations should be judged in terms of the degree to which they accomplish their formal and informal objectives. But what makes one organization more or less successful than another one? In this connection, it would be very helpful if we could identify types of challenges that all organizations must deal with successfully if they are to be effective. In an effort to provide a set of criteria against which *all* formal organizations can be evaluated, Seashore and Yuchtman set forth what they call a *systems resources model*.[1] In this model,

[1]Stanley E. Seashore and Ephraim Yuchtman, "A System Resource Approach to Organizational Effectiveness," *American Sociological Review* 32, no. 6 (December 1967): 891–903. See also Paul S. Goodman, Johannes M. Pennings, and Associates, *New Perspectives on Organizational Effectiveness* (San Francisco: Jossey-Bass, 1977).

effectiveness is the "ability of the organization, in either relative or absolute terms, to exploit its environment in the acquisition of scarce and valued resources."[2] Effectiveness is best understood in terms of the universal needs of organizations to *extract* essential human and material resources from their environments. Goal accomplishment, therefore, is dependent upon effective resources extraction.

The systems resources model is based on the observation that all human organizations are *open systems* which continuously interact with their environments. In order to function and to survive, they must be able to respond appropriately to the opportunities and constraints presented by their environments. At least initially, human and material resources needed to carry out organizational activities must be acquired from the external environment. For many reasons, some organizations and their administrators are more successful than others in influencing outside agents to provide political support, skilled personnel, and finances. The relative ability of agencies to capture resources from their environments is their *external extraction capability*.[3] Effective (powerful) organizations perform well in this respect and are more likely to be able to mobilize the skills and technologies needed to attain their objectives.[4]

We now turn to a discussion of the strategies used by public administrators as they try to build the external extraction capabilities of their agencies. Specifically, we will concentrate on those aspects of external extraction strategy that directly involve the personnel function.

■ ORGANIZATIONAL TASK ENVIRONMENTS AND THEIR COMPONENTS

The external environments of public agencies often are complex and dynamic, and they are always political. If they are to be effective, public administrators must recognize that:

---

[2]Seashore and Yuchtman, "A System Resource Approach to Organizational Effectiveness," 898.

[3]Daniel Katz and Robert L. Kahn, *The Social Psychology of Organizations*, 2d ed. (New York: Wiley, 1978).

[4]Eugene Lewis, *Public Entrepreneurship: Toward a Theory of Bureaucratic Power* (Bloomington, Ind.: Indiana University Press, 1980); and Francis E. Rourke, "Variations in Agency Power," in F. E. Rourke (ed.), *Bureaucratic Power in National Politics*, 3d ed. (Boston: Little, Brown, 1978).

A public organization is part of a policy subsystem, an arena of individuals, groups, and organizations, of "relevant others" affected
by and interested in a given policy. The relevant others have a role
to play or an interest in influencing an area of policy for which a
particular public organization has prime concern. These relevant
others represent a variety of actors in and out of government: interest groups, competing public organizations, superior organizations, individuals, appropriation subcommittees, subject matter
committees, and staff agencies. They may be competitive, cooperative, hostile, overseeing, reviewing, controlling, but regardless of
their role they shape the mandate and the conditions of existence
for a public organization.[5]

Those relevant others that have a significant impact on the goals
and goal-attainment capabilities of an organization make up what
James D. Thompson calls the *task environment*.[6] In administrative
terms, the task environment is the most important aspect of an
organization's external setting because its elements control needed
resources. Consequently, external resources extraction strategies
are directed at key actors in the task environment. Task environments are composed of *suppliers, competitors, clients,* and *regulators*.[7] These are ways of behaving, and the same organizations,
groups, or individuals may play two or more of these roles.

Suppliers

Suppliers produce and distribute the many kinds of political, material, and human resources needed by public agencies. Organized
interest groups, legislators, and executive policymakers often act
as suppliers. As such, they must be convinced that an agency's
programs, performance, and potential justify support through, for
example, a larger budget or an expanded mandate. Universities,
vocational schools, and labor unions are examples of suppliers of
trained personnel. Clearly, public administrators must meet the
challenge of building and maintaining productive relationships with

[5]Gary L. Wamsley and Mayer N. Zald, *The Political Economy of Public Organizations* (Lexington, Mass.: Heath, 1973), p. 26.
[6]James D. Thompson, *Organizations in Action* (New York: McGraw-Hill, 1967),
pp. 25–38.
[7]Koya Azumi, "Environmental Needs, Resources, and Agents," in Koya Azumi
and Jerald Hage (eds.), *Organizational Systems* (Lexington, Mass.: Heath, 1972),
pp. 91–100.

a wide variety of suppliers, including those who control—either directly or indirectly—access to human resources.

Competitors

Valuable resources are by definition limited, but there are never enough of them available, at an acceptable price, to satisfy the needs of all concerned. Public employers often face strong competition from the private sector as well as other governmental agencies. Because money, skills, and political support are scarce commodities, administrators may be expected to favor personnel practices that protect and enhance their competitive positions.[8]

Clients

Clients are those actors in the task environment who buy or use an organization's services or products, or somehow benefit from its activities. In the United States, clients often form organized interest groups which can become powerful actors in the public policymaking process. Big, disciplined, well-run interest groups are valuable allies in the competition for budgetary and other resources. Administering programs benefiting large numbers of voters is a distinct advantage, because legislators and elected executives, for obvious reasons, are not inclined to reduce or abolish such programs. Consequently, on all levels of government public administrators devote considerable attention to satisfying the needs of powerful and politically active constituencies.[9]

Regulators

Regulators mediate or control certain aspects of the relationships among an organization and its suppliers, competitors, and clients. Broadly speaking, regulators make, interpret, and administer laws or rules dealing with task environment interactions that affect the public interest. For example, labor-management relations, the investment of pension funds, and employment practices are all under some form of regulation in most, if not all, public jurisdictions.

---

[8]Thompson, *Organizations in Action*, pp. 28–50.
[9]Francis E. Rourke, *Bureaucracy, Politics, and Public Policy*, 3d ed. (Boston: Little, Brown, 1978); also Eugene Lewis, *American Politics in A Bureaucratic Age: Citizens, Constituents, Clients, and Victims* (Cambridge, Mass.: Winthrop, 1977).

Examples of regulators are the courts, commissions and boards such as the Interstate Commerce Commission, the National Labor Relations Board, and the Merit Systems Protection Board, state public utility commissions, and agencies like the Environmental Protection Agency and the Food and Drug Administration.[10]

Legislative bodies, civil service commissions, state and federal courts, equal employment opportunity commissions, and executive agencies such as the Office of Management and Budget (OMB) and Federal Labor Relations Authority (FLRA) routinely act as regulators in matters directly concerning the personnel and labor relations activities of public agencies. Regulators play a central role in creating the conditions under which administrators must work as they try to extract human and material resources from the task environment. The key positions and powers of regulators in public personnel administration should not be underestimated, and their capacity to hinder as well as to promote effective external extraction must be recognized.[11]

■ THE TASK ENVIRONMENT AS A SYSTEM

Each public agency is at the center of a complex system of interdependencies and interactions; some of these relationships involve direct transactions with one or more elements of the task environment. However, many relationships are indirect because, for example, dealings with a supplier may be through a regulator or a clientele group. To add further to the complexity of the situation, interactions among elements of the task environment, in which the organization does not participate directly, may nonetheless be of major importance. For example, the decision to eliminate the federal government's Professional, Administrative, Career Examination (PACE) made it necessary for individual federal agencies to develop other selection methods for positions that previously had been filled using the PACE register.[12] Figure 2.1 shows some of the possible lines of interaction in an organization's task environment.

[10]Louis M. Kohlmeier, Jr., *The Regulators* (New York: Harper & Row, 1969); also James Q. Wilson (ed.), *The Politics of Regulation* (New York: Basic Books, 1980).

[11]See Phillip J. Cooper, *Public Law and Public Administration* (Palo Alto, Calif.: Mayfield, 1983).

[12]See "Pace Exam Abolished for Federal Employment," *Public Administration Times*, June 1, 1982.

FIGURE 2.1.

Possible Lines of Interaction in an Organization's Task Environment

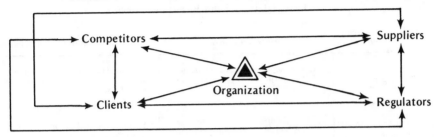

Strategies for Extracting Human Resources

In their efforts to obtain human resources for their agencies, effective administrators must use a variety of situationally-tailored strategies. In general, these strategies are designed to: (1) reduce agency dependence on any single element of the task environment, and (2) improve control over the behavior of key actors in the task environment. In both cases, the objective is to increase or to protect the organization's power or capacity to influence the behavior of its task environment. Figure 2.2 shows the linkages likely to develop.

In James D. Thompson's words, "an organization has power, relative to an element of its task environment, to the extent that the organization has capacity to satisfy needs of that element and to the extent that the organization monopolizes that capacity."[13] Thus, to recall a dramatic event, the Federal Aviation Administration used supervisory personnel and borrowed military controllers in order to escape the dependency upon which the Professional Air Traffic Controller Organization (PATCO) had counted for success in its ill-fated strike in 1981. Ultimately, PATCO was decertified and most of the striking controllers lost their jobs permanently. Fortunately, the vast majority of interactions among *interdependent organizations* are not of the "win-lose" variety. Given the opportunity, administrators may try to establish positions of overwhelming power in relationships with other organizations, but under most conditions outright domination of the task environment is not possible.[14] Therefore, a continuous effort

---

[13]Thompson, *Organizations in Action*, pp. 30–31.

[14]See Kenneth McNeil, "Understanding Organizational Power: Building on the Weberian Legacy," *Administrative Science Quarterly* 23 (March 1978): 65–90; Jeffrey Pfeffer and Gerald R. Salancik, *The External Control of Organizations: A Resource Dependence Perspective* (New York: Harper & Row, 1978); and Robert A. Caro, *The Power Broker: Robert Moses and the Fall of New York* (New York: Vintage Books, 1975).

FIGURE 2.2.

Linkages in the Task Environment—Areas of Control and Dependence-
Uncertainty and the Resulting Exchanges

Task Environment Element	Areas of Control	Areas of Dependency-Uncertainty
Public Agency	Expertise; Existing Authorizations; Program Implementation; Respon-① siveness	Funding; Human Resources; Legislative-Executive Priorities; Rules and Procedures
Supplier of Human Resources	Trained Personnel; Technology and Skills Needed to Produce Human ② Resources; Political Support	Funding Needed to Operate and Staff Organization
Clientele-Interest Group	Political-Ideological Support, Contributions, Campaign ③ Workers	Legislative-Executive and Agency Program Priorities and Funding, Level of Implementation
Legislative-Executive Actors	Authorizations; Program Priorities; Funding, Enabling Laws ④	Political Support; Policy Implementation; Agency Responsiveness
Regulatory Units	Facilitating and Constraining Rules and Procedures ⑤	Political-Ideological Support; Legislative Mandate; Funding

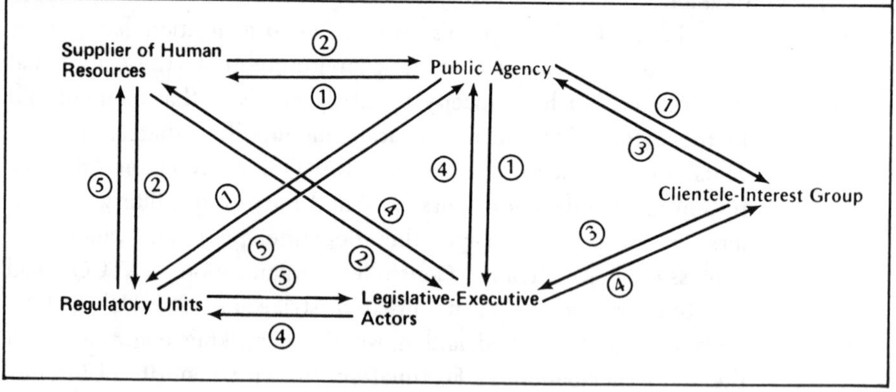

to establish and to maintain favorable relationships with key actors
in the task environment is required.[15]

Two kinds of strategies for managing relationships with task environments have been described by students of formal organizations—*competition* and *cooperation*.[16] If these strategies do not
work, a third option is to escape dependence on an element of the

[15]Wamsley and Zald, *The Political Economy of Public Organizations,* pp. 25–56.
[16]Thompson, *Organizations in Action,* pp. 32–38.

task environment by *incorporating* it, that is, by developing an internal capacity that eliminates or reduces the need to compete or to cooperate. In combination, competition, cooperation, and incorporation are used to build what administrators hope will be predictable access to human resources.

The competitive strategy

The heart of the competitive strategy is a sustained effort to control the costs of human resources to the organization. "Costs" are in two different but interrelated forms: (1) dependence on suppliers, and (2) actual expenditures of funds and other resources associated with the recruitment, hiring, and compensation of personnel. Dependence on a single supplier is to be avoided because this gives that supplier the power to impose terms and conditions and to command very high prices for its products or services. From a competitive standpoint, if alternative (competing) suppliers do not exist, they must be created. The presence of a labor market not dominated by a few suppliers or consumers allows employers to pay wages and to offer benefits that are economically "efficient."[17] If these conditions do exist within the task environment, it should be possible to gear at least some aspects of the external extraction process to a competitive model.

Competitive approaches stress achieving success through superior organizational performance in several key areas. First, the organization must be able to offer "competitive" material and social-psychological inducements to prospective as well as current employees. Second, a capacity to manipulate job designs and work procedures is a great advantage in efforts to exploit the *available* labor pool. Third, personnel management procedures and administrative structures can be designed to encourage adaptive responses to conditions in the task environment. Finally, considerable advantage may be gained if the public employer is able to stimulate and sustain competition among rival suppliers in the task environment.

Competitive inducements. Pay, benefits, working conditions, and career opportunities are basic elements of an agency's competitive position. For the most part, public employers rely on legislative

---

[17]See Milton and Rose Friedman, *Free to Choose* (New York: Harcourt Brace Jovanovich, 1980), pp. 9–37.

and executive support for the funds needed to compete successfully with the private sector and other governmental agencies. Historically, legislatively-fixed pay schedules and benefits have tended to adjust slowly and often inadequately to changes in the task environment; for some categories of scientists, professionals, and technicians the result has been to make the public sector an unattractive place to work. In other parts of the labor market, public employers have actually offered superior inducements and been able to compete quite effectively. More recently, the public sector has been severely affected by the "taxpayers revolt" and a spreading hostility toward "big government" and "bureaucrats." Increasing demands are now being placed on static, if not declining, resources. By the mid-1980s, a decade of "fiscal stress" and "cutback" had seriously eroded government's competitive capacities, and no relief from the downward spiral was in sight.[18] Robert Behn describes the current situation in the following terms:

> The task of attracting, keeping, and motivating high quality personnel is facilitated by (1) resources with which to reward talented individuals, (2) a critical mass of personnel and support facilities to provide collegial interaction and necessary assistance, and (3) the creation of new positions into which valuable people can be promoted. Thus, in an era of retrenchment, when these are not available, it is particularly difficult to maintain a work force that is productive. The most mobile and thus, by definition, the most talented employees are the first to leave, further decreasing morale, motivation, and work.[19]

As Behn points out, government's ability to attract and retain qualified personnel has been impaired by declining tax bases and budgets; however, an equally important factor may be the status or prestige of public employment. Public attitudes about government work and beliefs about career opportunities are significant variables. In contrast to many nations where the public sector is the high status job area and important administrative, professional, and technical positions are virtually monopolized by government,

---

[18]See Charles H. Levine, "Organizational Decline and Cutback Management," *Public Administration Review* 38 (July–August 1978): 316–325; John J. DeMarco and Stephen H. Holley, "The Use of Productivity Criteria in Local Government Cutback Decision Making," in Lloyd G. Nigro (ed.), *Decision Making in the Public Sector* (New York: Dekker, 1984); and E. S. Savas, *Privatizing the Public Sector* (Chatham, N.J.: Chatham House, 1982).

[19]Robert D. Behn, "Leadership in an Era of Retrenchment," *Public Administration Review* 40 (November–December 1980): 603.

the United States is a business- or market-oriented society.[20] From a competitive standpoint, the tendency—especially among career-oriented professionals—is to see government as a refuge for second-raters and those seeking security. These perceptions, in combination with a more recent public inclination to be openly contemptuous of public employees, can be a serious disability. In one observer's words:

> Inevitably, negative rhetoric about our public servants becomes a self-fulfilling prophesy, making it difficult to recruit and maintain high quality people in government. The cumulative impact of the negative aspects of the lives of government officials at all levels— negative attitudes about government, demanding interest groups, unrelenting news media, time consuming and rigid decision making procedures, and financial sacrifice—is making government service unnecessarily frustrating and unattractive to many.[21]

The problems created by less than sympathetic attitudes toward the public service are not limited to the impact on those considering where to work since relations with some or all of the elements of the task environment may be affected. Thus, legislators, elective officials, corporate leaders, members of clientele groups, and others may be hostile or at best noncommittal about the talent, commitment, and responsiveness of civil servants. Resources and support are withheld, and the competitiveness of the public employer further reduced. In the long run, the quality of the public service declines, attitudes about it become more negative, and levels of support drop even more.[22]

Obviously, changing the public's image of how public personnel systems operate is an important factor in any effort to break this vicious circle. Merit staffing, equal employment opportunity, political neutrality, responsiveness to executive leadership, and pay-for-performance all tap values widely shared in American society. If the American public *believes* that the public service actually practices these values, it may be more inclined to be supportive

---

[20]See Max Lerner, *America as a Civilization* (New York: Simon and Schuster, 1957), and Robert A. Goldwin and William A. Schambra (eds.), *How Capitalistic Is the Constitution?* (Washington, D.C.: American Enterprise Institute, 1982).

[21]Bruce Adams, "The Frustrations of Government Service," *Public Administration Review* 44 (January–February 1984): 5.

[22]See Jerome M. Rosow, "Public Sector Pay and Benefits," *Public Administration Review* 36 (September–October 1976): 538–543, and Charles T. Goodsell, "The Grace Commission: Seeking Efficiency for the Whole People?" *Public Administration Review* 44 (May–June 1984): 196–204.

in material as well as other ways.[23] Along these lines, Alan K. Campbell, the first director of the U.S. Office of Personnel Management, stated that one of the purposes of the Civil Service Reform Act (CSRA) was to improve the reputation of the federal civil service.[24]

Adapting to conditions in the labor market. Adaptiveness is often a key to competitive success. Conditions in the organization's task environment must be responded to in an effective and timely manner. Often, this challenge can be met only if the organization is capable of making needed adjustments in its jobs, technologies, and administrative arrangements. For example, public employers may find that they are competing for skills or experience that are in short supply relative to demand because the labor market has a limited capability to produce them. Even with competitive pay and benefits, an agency will have difficulty locating and attracting enough candidates for these kinds of positions. These so-called *inelastic* supply conditions are caused by a number of factors, including limited capabilities of suppliers such as universities and technical schools, long training or apprenticeship periods, policies of regulatory or licensing bodies, and social biases against certain kinds of work.

Eventually, the market will probably respond, but matching supply with demand may take several years or more and, as school teachers, aerospace engineers, and others working in fields requiring extensive education and experience can testify, achieving such a balance is extremely difficult. Usually, the segment of the labor market that is most quickly responsive to changes in demand is unskilled or semiskilled labor because workers are not required to have a great deal of education or experience and they need only brief on-the-job training. A competitive strategy that fails to monitor and to anticipate labor market conditions with a view to adjusting the organization's needs leaves the employer open to an unanticipated and perhaps very disruptive situation: a chronic in-

[23]Thompson, *Organizations in Action*, pp. 33–34; Charles Perrow, "Organizational Prestige: Some Functions and Dysfunctions," *American Journal of Sociology* 66 (January 1961): 335–341; Herbert Kaufman, "Fear of Bureaucracy: A Raging Pandemic," *Public Administration Review* 41 (January–February 1981): 1–9; and Laurence J. O'Toole, Jr., "American Public Administration and the Idea of Reform," *Administration and Society* 16 (August 1984): 141–166.

[24]Alan K. Campbell, "The Institution and Its Problems," in Eugene B. McGregor, Jr. (ed.), "Symposium: The Public Service as Institution," *Public Administration Review* 42 (July–August 1982): 305–308.

ability to fill certain key positions and an oversupply of candidates for other jobs.[25]

One way to improve the match between agency needs and market supply is to make adjustments in internal task structures and technologies. It is often possible to redesign jobs, to restructure relationships among jobs, and to alter supervisory patterns in ways which meaningfully improve the organization's capacity to make good use of those human resources available to it. Some jobs can be simplified or broken down into several less complex tasks while others can be enlarged or enriched. Paraprofessionals may be employed to reduce the numbers of highly trained, expensive, and scarce professionals such as doctors, registered nurses, lawyers, and engineers that an organization needs. With paraprofessional support positions, professional personnel may be used differently and more effectively. Mechanized or automated systems can be installed to replace or to supplement human resources in ways that reduce labor costs, lower or redistribute skill requirements, and increase overall efficiency. Minimum job requirements and job progression may be altered to accommodate postentry upgrading and retraining; similarly, on-the-job training or educational opportunities can be provided in order to make it possible to fill positions through promotions and transfers.[26]

Public personnel systems have long had the reputation of being unimaginative human resources planners, of legalistic rigidity in their approaches to job design and classification, and of an inclination to assume that the labor market will respond readily to their staffing requirements. To the extent that this reputation is deserved, it signals a serious competitive disability, a weakness that is particularly apparent when resources are limited and the public employer is facing a "sellers' market." There is no reason why public agencies should be internally inflexible or passive in the

---

[25]See Charles T. Kerchner, "Shortgages and Gluts of Public School Teachers: There Must Be a Policy Problem Here Somewhere," *Public Administration Review* 44 (July–August 1984): 292–298; and Albert C. Hyde and Torrey Whitman, "Workforce Planning—The State of the Art," in Jay M. Shafritz (ed.), *The Public Personnel World: Readings in the Professional Practice* (Chicago: International Personnel Management Association, 1978).

[26]Alyce M. Kwiecinski (ed.), "Mini-Symposium on Manpower Planning," *Public Administration Review* 44 (March–April 1984): 162–176; Robert D. Lee and William Lucianovic, "Personnel Management Information Systems for State and Local Government," in Shafritz (ed.), *Public Personnel World*; also, Robert Blakeney, Michael Matteson, and James Huff, "The Personnel Function: A Systemic View," *Public Personnel Management* 3 (January–February 1974): 83–86.

face of stiff competition and an other-than-perfect balance between supply and demand in the labor market.

Using administrative designs that improve competitiveness. Traditionally, public personnel systems have used administrative structures that emphasize control and standardization. Centralization of policy and rulemaking authority is typical of merit systems with their roots in the original civil service reform movement. While these administrative arrangements may be effective in keeping "the rascals" out and seeing to it that merit principles are protected by limiting managerial discretion, they are notoriously slow to recognize and to respond to changes in the social environment. Theory and research on organization-environment relationships suggest that effective organizations employ administrative structures that are well-adapted to their environment.[27] Typically, organizations facing dynamic, highly competitive task environments rely heavily on decentralized decision-making and stress managerial flexibility and discretion. From a competitive standpoint, the administrative arrangements used to "deliver" a personnel program must promote adaptive and timely responses to environmental conditions.[28]

Highly centralized, bureaucratic models for personnel administration seem to work relatively well when human resources are readily accessible through routinized recruitment and selection procedures. Likewise, generalized rules that standardize recruitment, testing, selection, compensation, and other personnel functions are effective when the range of likely situations is known and tested ways of dealing with them are available. Under these conditions, it is not inappropriate to centralize authority and to house responsibility for personnel administration in specialized units separated from line management. However, when time and material resources are limited, competition is intense, and environmental conditions are rapidly changing, a structural capacity to "read" or monitor the environment and to "tailor-make" responses is often

---

[27]Thompson, *Organizations in Action,* and Barry Bozeman, "Organization Structure and the Effectiveness of Public Agencies," *International Journal of Public Administration* 4, no. 3 (1982): 235–296.

[28]Paul Lawrence and Jay Lorsch, *Organization and Environment* (Homewood, Ill.: Irwin, 1969); Michael C. White, Michael Crino, and Ben Kedia, "Environmental Turbulence: A Reappraisal of Emery and Trist," *Administration and Society* 16 (May 1984): 97–116; and Robert P. McGowan and John M. Stevens, "Local Government Management: Reactive or Adaptive?" *Public Administration Review* 43 (May–June 1983): 260–267.

needed. In practice, this means that the authority and expertise necessary for diagnosing situations, making decisions, and implementing personnel strategies should be located as close as possible to the existing problems. One way of accomplishing this objective is to deploy personnel "generalists" as consultants to and resources for line administrators who have the authority to act within a framework of very general rules and regulations. Another option is to retain the central personnel office or department model, but to create paralleling staffs on the agency headquarters and field levels, each having considerable discretion to develop policies and methods best suited to its clients' situations.[29]

Creating resources and stimulating competition. In the United States, the federal and state governments have long histories of efforts to promote economic development and to stimulate the creation of the human resources required to support that development. While the bulk of this activity has been aimed at the private sector, some of it has been directly concerned with human resources for the public sector, and a great deal of it has indirectly affected the public employer by either expanding or limiting the available resources. To be effective or rational from an organizational standpoint, a competitive strategy should be employed in environments that offer alternative suppliers capable of satisfying an agency's or government's needs. Public education and federal and state support of private education represent major investments in the human resources base of society. These and a broad range of other human resources development programs have increased the numbers of suppliers and improved their capacity to educate, train, or otherwise prepare people well- qualified for jobs in the public and private sectors. In competitive terms, these programs have in many instances allowed public employers to escape dependency on a small number of suppliers (e.g., schools of law, engineering, and social work). Of course, the existence of many competing suppliers increases the probability that, in addition to being available, personnel will not be extremely "expensive."[30]

---

[29]James E. Stafford and Don Domm, "The Generalist Approach to Personnel Administration," *Public Personnel Review* 31 (October 1970): 254–260; and Steven W. Hays and T. Zane Reeves, *Personnel Management in the Public Sector* (Boston: Allyn and Bacon, 1984), pp. 91–95.

[30]See Michael Reagan and John Sansone, *The New Federalism*, 2d ed. (New York: Oxford University Press, 1981); and John J. Kirlin, "Policy Formulation," in G. Ronald Gilbert (ed.), *Making and Managing Policy* (New York: Dekker, 1984), pp. 13–24.

Contracting out as a competitive strategy. As a method of holding down the costs of services and reducing dependency on single sources of supply, contracting recently has received a great deal of attention. The contracting out of services traditionally provided by the public sector is attractive to administrators because it uses competition in one or more of the following ways. First, competitive bidding for government contracts keeps costs, including those for contractor personnel, within boundaries set by the supply and demand functions of the marketplace. Second, under certain conditions, contracting out may keep the costs of publicly provided services down while upgrading their quality by putting them into competition with private "for-profit" or "not-for-profit" providers. At a minimum, such public-private competition allows public administrators to evaluate the costs of "in-house" service delivery, and, therefore, to make more informed decisions about staffing patterns and other human resources issues confronting their agencies. A third, and highly controversial, use to which contracting may be put is to undercut the power of employee unions. A willingness and capacity to contract out services gives management an alternative to the union as a supplier of human resources; reduced dependency on the union means that management is in a stronger negotiating position. Since, from the union point of view, the public employer is a supplier of jobs, the contracting out possibility places the union in the position of having to "compete" with potential contractors for these jobs.[31]

Public employers have resisted the idea that they should embrace competition as a framework for personnel policy and the design of personnel systems. Although reforms in some civil service systems have increased agency flexibility in activities such as position classification and selection and strengthened line management's hand in pay administration, for the most part public personnel systems are still highly formalized and rules-oriented. In practice, standardization and adherence to merit procedures are given greater weight than competitiveness.[32] Clearly, there are as-

---

[31]See E. S. Savas, "An Empirical Study of Competition in Municipal Service Delivery," *Public Administration Review* 37 (November–December 1977): 717–724; and E. S. Savas, "Intracity Competition Between Public and Private Service Delivery," *Public Administration Review* 41 (January–February 1981): 46–52.

[32]Charles Perrow, *Complex Organizations: A Critical Essay* (Glenview, Ill.: Scott, Foresman, 1972), p. 31; Wallace Sayre, "The Triumph of Technique Over Purpose," *Public Administration Review* 8 (Spring 1948): 134–137; and E. S. Savas and Sigmund Ginsburg, "The Civil Service: A Meritless System?" *The Public Interest* 32 (Summer 1973): 70–85.

pects of public personnel administration where a competitive posture would be inappropriate because the task environment
conditions or needed organizational capabilities do not exist and
cannot be created. There may also be important political, legal, or
ethical reasons that limit or prevent competitive behavior.

Equal employment opportunity laws and affirmative action programs, for example, require hiring procedures that may legiti-
mately limit an agency's ability to act quickly in response to
changes in the labor market. Classification standards, negotiated
contracts, and wage and salary schedules may severely constrain
management's discretion with regard to pay and other inducements. Politically, competition with the private sector has often
been discouraged, especially if workers under contract might be
able to provide the goods or services at lower cost.[33] Nonetheless,
there is growing pressure on those in the personnel function to
develop more effective and lower-cost alternatives to largely passive and inward-looking approaches to the acquisition of human
resources. In some cases, a competitive strategy may be indicated
if necessary task environment conditions exist, the organization has
the needed capacities, and suppliers and regulators are supportive.
However, if competition is not a promising or possible option, cooperation is an alternative strategy.

The cooperative strategy

Like competition, cooperation is a strategy designed to reduce the
chances that essential human resources will be cut off or become
more expensive than they should be. Basically, cooperation means
entering into more-or-less formal commitments with elements of
the task environment. These commitments are *bilateral* or *multi-
lateral*, and are intended to lower the levels of uncertainty or risk
faced by those involved.[34] We will concentrate on three major
forms of cooperation that have direct relevance for public personnel administration: intergovernmental joint ventures and contracts;
contracting out to private producers of goods and services; and
negotiated agreements with public employee organizations.

[33]See Raymond G. Hunt, "Cross-Purposes in the Federal Contract Procurement
System: Military R&D and Beyond," *Public Administration Review* 44 (May–June
1984): 247–256.

[34]Thompson, *Organizations in Action*, pp. 34–36; and Jeffrey Pfeffer and Gerald
Salancik, *The External Control of Organizations*, pp. 142–187.

Joint ventures. Agencies may be able to solve common problems by pooling or sharing their resources. In addition to increasing effectiveness, these arrangements may also improve efficiency by lowering overall costs. For example, in some cases, competition among levels of government and public agencies for personnel has been supplemented by cooperative recruitment, testing, and placement services. Since 1970, the federal government has been authorized to join with states and localities in joint recruiting and testing programs. Costs are shared by the participating employers.[35] Where such cooperative arrangements have been tried, the results have been encouraging.[36] It is also possible for states to sponsor joint ventures among their local jurisdictions, and such cooperation is likely to become increasingly important as federal aid to cities and states continues its sharp decline.[37] Whereas the federal government was previously a leader in fostering intergovernmental joint ventures through such legislative initiatives as the 1968 Intergovernmental Cooperation Act (ICA) and the 1970 Intergovernmental Personnel Act (IPA), more recently the Reagan administration has moved to greatly reduce the federal role in state and local personnel administration.[38]

Other examples of intergovernmental cooperation include joint ventures to provide training programs and agreements whereby governments and agencies use one another's personnel under specified conditions. In the training field, it has been possible for some state and local employees to attend federal training programs that deal with problems or policy issues that require intergovernmental attention and cooperation, such as those offered by the Federal Bureau of Investigation, the Internal Revenue Service, and the Federal Executive Institute (FEI). User-funded state-wide or mul-

[35]See *The Intergovernmental Personnel Act of 1970* (Public Law 91-648, 84 Stat. 1909, January 5, 1971); and J. David Palmer, "Recruitment and Staffing," in Winston W. Crouch (ed.), *Local Government Personnel Administration* (Washington, D.C.: International City Management Association, 1976), p. 105.

[36]See Robert Agranoff and Valerie A. Lindsay, "Intergovernmental Management: Perspectives From Human Services Problem Solving at the Local Level," *Public Administration Review* 43 (May–June 1983): 227–237; and Carl W. Stenberg, "Beyond the Days of Wine and Roses: Intergovernmental Management in a Cutback Environment," *Public Administration Review* 41 (January–February 1981): 10–20; and John W. Macy, Jr., "The Future of the Institution," in Eugene B. McGregor, Jr. (ed.), "Symposium: The Public Service as Institution," 308–310.

[37]U.S. Office of Personnel Management, "OPM Marks Tenth Anniversary of IPA," *OPM Notes* (January–February 1981), pp. 4–5.

[38]See President's Commission on Law Enforcement and Administration of Justice, *Task Force on the Police* (Washington, D.C.: Government Printing Office, 1967), pp. 76–77.

tistate regional training centers for police and fire fighters provide levels of training well beyond the individual capacities of the governments that send their personnel to these centers for basic or advanced training. Direct sharing of personnel is possible under agreements negotiated between jurisdictions. Cities may agree to share police and fire personnel under emergency or other special conditions. Costs are shared and the participating jurisdictions usually retain "recall" rights, but emphasis is placed on recognizing interdependency and dealing with it through mutual support as opposed to very expensive, perhaps futile, efforts to become "independent."[39] Within jurisdictions, interagency joint ventures are also possible, an interesting example being the "cross-training" of workers in two or more organizations (e.g., police and fire departments) so that they are able to back each other up and, if need be, move from one job to another in response to shifting work loads.[40]

Governments also contract with each other for services in functional areas such as law enforcement, fire protection, sanitation, and street repairs. Under these intergovernmental contracts, one government undertakes to provide services to another for a fee. For example, Los Angeles County "sells" law enforcement services to many of the incorporated municipalities within the county. Other services commonly contracted for are water supply, sewage treatment, tax collections, and libraries.[41] Intergovernmental contracting is used by small jurisdictions because it is cheaper or is thought to be less expensive than building an in-house capacity to deliver the services concerned. It gives the user access to the established personnel systems, equipment, and skills of the supplier. It appears that intergovernmental contracting can reduce costs to smaller communities, mainly because of the economies of scale enjoyed by large contractors. From the provider's side, the contract allows it to sell unused or underutilized capacity and, there-

---

[39]Anne C. Cowden, "California Local Government Contracting After Proposition 13," *International Journal of Public Administration* 4, no. 4 (1982): 405.

[40]See Sidney Sonenblum, John J. Kirlin, and John C. Ries, *How Cities Provide Services: An Evaluation of Alternative Delivery Structures* (Cambridge, Mass.: Ballinger Publishing Co., 1977); and Joseph F. Zimmerman, "Intergovernmental Service Agreements and Transfer of Functions," in Advisory Commission on Intergovernmental Relations, *Substate Regionalism and the Federal System*, vol. 3, *Challenge of Local Government Reorganization* (Washington, D.C.: Government Printing Office, 1974).

[41]Cowden, "California Local Government Contracting"; Savas, *Privatizing the Public Sector*; and Bruce Smith (ed.), *The New Political Economy: The Public Use of the Private Sector* (New York: Wiley, 1975).

fore, to build its resources base with a resulting "profit." Each side enhances its productivity through cooperation as opposed to competition.

A potentially important drawback to intergovernmental contracting is that the services involved are often available from only one source. Thus, from the standpoint of the buyer, there is a risk that the supplier will exploit its monopoly position through excessive fees or by imposing undesirable terms and conditions. Cost cannot be controlled through competitive bidding, and the supplier may not be sufficiently responsive to local needs and community values. In comparison to in-house personnel and organizations, the user of contracted-for services loses administrative and political control over many aspects of program staffing and execution. There is also the possibility that the contractor will not be able to uphold its side of the bargain because of changes such as budgetary cutbacks or court decisions. One way to at least partially avoid such risks is to do whatever is feasible to expand the number of potential suppliers in the task environment, including private contractors.[42]

Contracting out with private suppliers. While contracting with private suppliers for many goods and services has been a traditional and, given the nature of the U.S. economy, necessary practice on all levels of government, as we have noted earlier fiscal stress and changing philosophies of government have generated considerable interest in and support for the contracting out of services ordinarily provided by government workers. Thus, parks and recreation, building inspection, sanitation, fire prevention, prisons, and even general administration are a few of the many functions now considered possibilities for contracting out.[43] While competition among available contractors may bring costs down, contracting out establishes a basically cooperative relationship between supplier and consumer. In James D. Thompson's words:

> Using cooperation to gain power with respect to some element of the task environment, the organization must demonstrate its *capacity to reduce uncertainty* for that element, and *must make a commitment* to exchange that capacity. . . . Thus an agreement between A and B specifying that A will supply and B will purchase,

---

[42]See Patricia S. Florestano and Stephen B. Gordon, "Private Provision of Public Services: Contracting by Large Local Governments," *International Journal of Public Administration* 1, no. 3 (1979): 309–310; Cowden, "California Local Government Contracting," 402–407; and Macy, "Future of the Institution," 309.
[43]Ibid.

> reduces uncertainty for both. A knows more about its output targets
> and B knows more about its inputs. . . . Under cooperative strat-
> egies, the effective achievement of power rests on the exchange of
> commitments, the reduction of uncertainty for both parties.[44]

Contracting out, therefore, involves the negotiation of "an agreement for the exchange of performances in the future."[45] However,
contracting out should not be seen as a device for eliminating administrative responsibilities; contracts must be negotiated and administered, and contractor performance has to be evaluated in
political as well as technical and economic terms. In personnel
administration, the current "popularity" of contracting out has several sources. First, under certain conditions, it reduces the cost of
public services. In a study of local government responses to Proposition 13 in California, Cowden observes that "Contracting out is
considerably cheaper when wage rates are lower in the private
sector, when fringe benefits are less, or when private parties have
internal labor and organizational arrangements which permit increased economies."[46]

Second, contracting out increases administrative flexibility in the
external extraction process. Rather than build expensive in-house
capabilities which involve long-term commitments, when they
have missions or mandates requiring skills and technologies not
usually controlled by public agencies administrators can often satisfy these needs through contracts with private suppliers. Programs
can be terminated or changed without the need to go through the
demoralizing, costly, and protracted reduction-in-force procedures
that are typical of merit systems. Also, in situations where private
employers can offer superior pay and benefits to highly skilled people, public employers may be able to use contracting to tap these
resources because it allows them to avoid many of the constraints
and uncertainties imposed by personnel ceilings, wage and salary
scales, and staffing processes. Finally, by shifting responsibility for
day-to-day management to the contractor, government may be able
to reduce or at least slow the growth of administrative "overhead"
costs associated with ongoing programs; similarly, it may be possible to escape having to add supervisory personnel when new
programs are acquired or existing ones are expanded.

A third reason why contracting out can be advantageous is that

---

[44]Thompson, *Organizations in Action*, pp. 34–35.
[45]Ibid., p. 35
[46]Cowden, "California Local Government Contracting," 402–403.

it builds interdependencies with suppliers and clients in the task environment that are the ingredients of supportive political coalitions. Corporations and labor unions often come to rely heavily on the resources (money and jobs) they get through government contracts; they develop a vested interest in the "health" of their public suppliers. From an agency point of view, the support of concerned (self-interested) contractors and other clientele groups is vitally important when budgets have to be defended against cuts and, of course, when efforts are being made to grow in one way or another.[47] A related value of contracting is to "buffer" public agencies from criticism that they are overgrown and encroaching on the proper domain of private enterprise. Since public attention is easily drawn to the size of the public workforce, significant expansion is more than likely to draw attacks from those fearing increased taxes, "creeping socialism," or "big government." While, as the Department of Defense budget amply demonstrates, contracting out does not necessarily mean smaller budgets or even high levels of efficiency, it is a strategy for acquiring facilities and human resources without endangering an agency's ideological or political support.

Negotiated agreements with employee organizations. Although public attention is drawn to the conflictual aspects of labor-management relations in the public as well as private sector, collective bargaining actually is a process intended to promote *interorganizational* cooperation and to reduce uncertainty. A contract or collective agreement is a document detailing the terms under which management and the union will jointly administer certain key elements of the personnel system. It also specifies how each side will supply the other with some of the "inputs" it needs to function effectively.

For example, management typically agrees to pay clearly stipulated wages and salaries, to provide fringe benefits such as a pension plan and health insurance, and to maintain safe and comfortable working conditions. Under negotiated contracts, workers know that they can appeal certain actions by supervisors. Management may further reduce uncertainty for the union by agreeing to various forms of so-called union security (e.g., dues checkoff and an agency or union shop). The union, on the other hand,

[47]See Aaron Wildavsky, *The Politics of the Budgetary Process*, 3d ed. (Boston: Little, Brown, 1979).

agrees to "deliver" human resources and to participate in the good faith administration and enforcement of the rules established in the contract. Finally, most agreements set up systems for resolving disputes between management and the union over interpretations of the contract that do not threaten either party's status or access to human and material resources.

Viewed in these terms, collective bargaining is a way of identifying and formulating cooperative solutions to problems presented by the interdependence of management and labor. Walton and McKersie describe labor negotiations as a type of *social negotiation,* or "the deliberate interaction of two or more social units which are attempting to define or redefine the terms of their independence."[48] Where employee organizations or unions are an important part of the task environment, the public employer must be equipped to deal with them effectively. Disruptive or uncertain labor relations constitute a failure to build and to maintain cooperative relationships with employee organizations. So-called "win-lose" confrontations resulting in job actions, strikes, court sanctions, firings, and the like are almost inevitably very costly to all concerned. Therefore, considerable attention is now paid to the development of effective labor relations programs in government. Personnel and labor relations officers on all levels of government are now expected to have the expertise necessary to organize and carry out negotiations and to assist management in the administration of the resulting contracts.

The incorporation strategy

Competition and cooperation are external extraction strategies that will work if the task environment contains suppliers having the needed capacities. However, if an agency faces an external environment that is unpredictable or is chronically incapable of providing it with necessary resources, creating *internal* suppliers may be the most appropriate strategy. Thus, uncertainty may be reduced by expanding or restructuring the organization to "place [its] boundaries around those activities which if left to the task environment would be crucial contingencies."[49] In practical terms, this means that the source of uncertainty (e.g., a supplier or regulator)

---

[48]Richard E. Walton and Robert B. McKersie, *A Behavioral Theory of Labor Negotiations* (New York: McGraw-Hill, 1965), p. 3.

[49]Thompson, *Organizations in Action,* p. 38.

is made a part of the organization or is brought under its direct administrative control.

For ideological reasons, or because their private economies are inadequate, socialist and most developing countries rely heavily on direct governmental provision of a wide variety of goods and services. In the United States, where many but not all of these goods and services are available from private sources, the prevailing attitude is to resist placing public agencies in competition with these sources. Indeed, some groups now argue strongly that governments in the United States should be divesting themselves of internal capabilities and functions by moving to extensive contracting out and through "privatization."[50] On the other hand, real uncertainty regarding access, price, or market is a powerful incentive to incorporate a capacity or activity.[51] This reality is often illustrated by mergers and expansions in the corporate world; similarly, use of public agencies and civil servants to provide a common core of essential services (national defense, police and fire, education, and a variety of welfare programs) is another manifestation of this organizational drive to reduce and contain uncertainty.

Ideological reasons aside, variations in the degree to which governments and their organizations rely on external as opposed to internal suppliers are tied to variations in the capacities of their task environments. Since there is little or no capacity to train military officers in the U.S. private sector, the military academies (incorporation) and ROTC (cooperation) have been used to carry out this function. On the other hand, in some communities, the private sector has been able to marshal the resources necessary to build and run mass transit systems; in others, it has been necessary to create public authorities such as Atlanta's Metropolitan Area Rapid Transit Authority (MARTA) and New York's Port Authority.

On the federal level, good examples of the incorporation strategy may be found in the field of training and development. The Federal Executive Institute, an OPM facility, provides broad-gauged administrative training for high-ranking executives. Established in 1968, the FEI was designed to fill what was seen to be a serious gap in the federal system for developing senior career executives. It caps an extensive technical and managerial training and career

---

[50]E. S. Savas, *Privatizing the Public Sector*.
[51]Thompson, *Organizations in Action*, pp. 39–50.

development system that gives the federal government a valuable internal complement to external suppliers. Because the system is financed, staffed, and administered internally by OPM and the federal agencies, the content and methods of training can be closely controlled and designed to meet specific needs. These internal training and development resources reduce uncertainty and risk because they greatly increase the probability that federal agencies will have access to qualified personnel when they need them. Dependency on external suppliers is reduced, and the probability that quantitative as well as qualitative gaps in the capacities of the task environment can be overcome is increased.

Incorporation is a strategy designed to reduce uncertainty and dependence on the task environment. Over the past 50 years, government on all levels in the United States has grown in response to public pressures for new and expanded services. Where governmental effectiveness is crucial and a capacity to perform services such as police, fire, air traffic control, national defense, and public health is essential, a long-term investment in the necessary human resources and the support systems they require is certainly justified. Equally justified is an effort to avoid building expensive internal capabilities that are readily and predictably available from external suppliers at lower cost to the taxpayer. While the issue of *what* services governments will or should deliver is always on the political agenda of a democracy, as an *organizational* function public personnel administration is more directly concerned with *how* effectively and efficiently to mobilize the human resources needed to provide public services. Our purpose here is to point out that incorporation is one of several approaches potentially available to public policy makers.

■ EXTERNAL EXTRACTION AND THE ROLE OF THE PERSONNEL ADMINISTRATOR

Today's public employers face very severe human resources extraction problems. Funds are limited and the public sector is for many an unattractive career choice. Increased pressures for efficiency and public expectations that agencies be able to show, among other things, direct relationships between budgets and service levels, and between pay and performance present professional public personnel administrators with a major challenge. This challenge is to develop the expertise required for playing an important positive role in helping their agencies anticipate and meet critical human resources needs. In order to meet this challenge, personnel specialists must understand the structures and dynamics of the task environments their organizations face; they must be willing to look beyond the boundaries of their agencies or units and to work actively at solving the problems associated with managing relationships with the external environment. From an administrative standpoint, a personnel program that stops at the organization's boundary with the task environment is simply not an acceptable response to very difficult problems.

Professional personnel administrators should be prepared to play a major role in the development and implementation of external extraction strategies intended to meet agency and governmental needs. These strategies must bridge the internal and external environments of organizations and function to bring them into productive alignment. If they are able to operate at this level of responsibility, personnel specialists should be able to make important contributions to organizational effectiveness.[52]

BIBLIOGRAPHY

Campbell, Alan K. "Running Out of Esteem?" *Civil Service Journal* (January–March 1978).

Glueck, William. *Personnel: A Diagnostic Approach*. Dallas: Business Publications, 1978.

Kimberly, John R., and Nielsen, Warren R. "Organization Development and Change in Organizational Performance." *Administrative Science Quarterly* 20 (June 1975).

Klingner, Donald E., and Nalbandian, John. "Personnel Administration by Whose Objectives?" *Public Administration Review* 38 (July–August 1978).

Levine, Charles H., and Nigro, Lloyd G. "The Public Personnel System: Can Juridical Administration and Manpower Management Coexist?" *Public Administration Review* 35 (January–February 1975).

————, and Wolohojian, George. "Retrenchment and Human Re-

---

[52]See T. F. Cawsey, "Why Line Managers Don't Listen to Their Personnel Departments," *Personnel* (January–February 1980): 11–20; and Chester A. Newland, "Public Personnel Administration: Legalistic Reforms Vs. Effectiveness, Efficiency, and Economy," *Public Administration Review* 36 (September–October 1976): 529–537.

sources Management." In *Public Personnel Administration,* edited by Steven Hays and Richard Kearney. Englewood Cliffs, N.J.: Prentice-Hall, 1983.

Schiesl, Martin J. *The Politics of Efficiency.* Berkeley: University of California Press, 1977.

Shapek, Raymond A. "Federal Influences in State and Local Personnel Management: The System in Transition." *Public Personnel Management* (January–February 1976).

Simon, Herbert A. *Administrative Behavior,* 2d ed. New York: Free Press, 1956.

Thompson, Frank J., ed. *Classics of Public Personnel Policy.* Oak Park, Ill.: Moore Publishing Co., 1979.

Walker, David B. *Toward a Functioning Federalism.* Cambridge, Mass.: Winthrop, 1981.

3 Personnel and Organizational Performance

In this chapter, we discuss personnel management's potential contribution to the process of internal extraction. From an organizational standpoint, internal extraction is a problem in the design and management of social, psychological, and technical systems that enhance the contributions employees make to the accomplishment of *organizational ends*. Since personnel policies and procedures are central elements of the internal extraction strategies of public agencies, the modern personnel manager's role demands considerable expertise in the meshing of the behavioral and technical requirements of organizations with the needs, abilities, and expectations of the workers.

Functionally, public personnel management has increasingly concentrated on the development and use of incentives that promote effective internal extraction. To the degree possible, the methods used should serve a variety of purposes, some of which are at least potentially in conflict. Effective policy implementation, bureaucratic responsiveness, managerial control, and economic efficiency or productivity are certainly major purposes.[1] In the United States, public administrators are asked to pursue these ends while also promoting values affirming the intrinsic worth and dignity of individuals. Thus, as Buchanan and Millstone observe:

> . . . we find in *any* agency numerous structural embodiments of democratic morality. There are Civil Service grievance procedures and liaison officers whose purpose is to protect the rights of em-

---

[1]See Victor Thompson, *Without Sympathy or Enthusiasm: The Problem of Administrative Compassion* (Alabama: University of Alabama Press, 1975).

ployees who feel unjustly used by superiors or agency procedures. There are Affirmative Action offices and officers, intent on securing compliance with Civil Service dictums on the hiring of disadvantaged minorities, thereby promoting equal opportunity and representative democracy. . . . Each of these structural instruments for the protection of individual rights is capable of disrupting or slowing program operations, in the interest of securing *priority* attention for the "equal protection" or "procedural due process" rights of individual citizens. This fosters a *de facto* co-equality between program structures [administrative rationality] and structures aimed at promoting democratic morality.[2]

Cultural norms, laws, and merit principles limit the methods public managers may use as they try to improve the internal extraction capabilities of their organizations. Several decades of social science research on motivation and performance in organizations also indicate that "punishment-centered" extraction systems are less effective than positive or "reward-" oriented techniques.[3]

■ BEHAVIORAL REQUIREMENTS OF ORGANIZATIONS

To be effective, internal extraction must elicit certain behaviors of the members of an organization. These behaviors are crucially important to organizational effectiveness and efficiency. Specifically, sought-after behaviors include:

1. Regular attendance and participation in organizational activities (low absenteeism);
2. A desire to stay with the organization (low turnover);
3. Consistently good performance in the technical and behavioral requirements of assigned roles, including meeting or exceeding quantitative and qualitative standards; and
4. A willingness to carry out more than formalized role requirements by actively cooperating with others, helping to protect the organization, developing innovative ways to solve problems, endeavoring to keep skills current and to acquire new abilities, and contributing to improving the external extraction capabilities of the organization.[4]

---

[2]Bruce Buchanan and Jeff Millstone, "Public Organizations: A Value-Conflict View," *International Journal of Public Administration* 1, no. 3 (1979): 273–274.

[3]See Daniel Katz and Robert L. Kahn, *The Social Psychology of Organizations*, 2d ed. (New York: Wiley, 1978), pp. 405–425.

[4]Derived from Katz and Kahn, *The Social Psychology of Organizations*, p. 403.

Clearly, these behavioral goals are often difficult to achieve, and organizations devote enormous amounts of human and material resources to the effort. The basic assumption underlying these investments is that the organization must be able to *transact* profitably with its membership.

■ THE INDUCEMENTS-CONTRIBUTIONS EQUATION

As we use the term "behavioral resources," it means the contributions that members make available to the organization. Management, representing the organization and its purposes, tries to offer inducements that will influence members to make the needed contributions. The terms "inducement" and "incentive" are often used interchangeably in this context. In William G. Scott's words:

> An *incentive* is a *stimulus* which incites action. In its broad usage "incentive" is applicable to any inducement, material or nonmaterial, which impels, encourages, or forces a person to perform a task to accomplish a goal.[5]

From a managerial perspective, the problem is to be able to identify and to supply inducements which make it "rewarding" for members to behave in ways that expand the pool of behavioral resources available to the organization. As Scott's definition of incentives implies, the reward involved may be escape from or avoidance of punishments in the form of deprivations or direct attacks on the individual's physical or psychological being.[6] However, the inducements-contributions equation concept is keyed largely to an exchange of values that produces a material or psychological *profit* for *both* sides. As George C. Homans has written, "The open secret of human exchange is to give the other man behavior that is more valuable to him than it is costly to you and to get from him behavior that is more valuable to you than it is costly to him."[7] If this frequently difficult objective is accomplished, both parties emerge from the interaction feeling that they have profited. Furthermore, they will be inclined to maintain the relationship because they anticipate future benefits.

---

[5]William G. Scott, *Organization Theory: A Behavioral Analysis for Management* (Homewood, Ill.: Richard D. Irwin, 1967), pp. 284–285. (Italics in original).

[6]See B. F. Skinner, *Beyond Freedom and Dignity* (New York: Vintage Books, 1971), pp. 56–95.

[7]George C. Homans, *Social Behavior: Its Elementary Forms* (New York: Harcourt Brace & World, 1961), p. 62.

Using the Inducements-Contributions Concept

Although the logic of the inducements-contributions equation is appealing in the abstract, successful implementation by management has been a chronic problem. There appear to be two sources of difficulties. First, existing knowledge about human motivation and its successful use in directing human behavior in public as well as private organizations is far from complete. Second, what has been established is not easily converted into internal extraction strategies that are manageable in traditional terms or, perhaps, even "rational" from a bureaucratic standpoint.

Management must understand the needs and expectations of the work force. Having this understanding, management should then be able to develop and administer incentives that will predictably stimulate employee contributions. However, a long history of empirical research on the relationships among technological, social, and psychological factors and such contribution-related variables as morale, job satisfaction, and productivity has revealed an extraordinarily complicated picture. Inducements strategies based on what are now known to be simplistic and unrealistically generalized assumptions about human behavior and motivation have been discredited, but they have not been replaced by any broadly accepted and empirically supported alternatives. It is unlikely that the future will bring the "discovery" of a set of principles that tells managers how to design and operate a universally effective system of organizational inducements. Porter and Miles have described the situation in the following terms.

> Of all the problems that are faced by management, motivation must surely be ranked as one of the most intractable. For years, organizations—both business and non-business types—have attempted to find better ways of motivating employees or at least better ways of understanding how they are motivated. Likewise, for several decades, social scientists, particularly psychologists, have been proposing theories on the subject and carrying out innumerable research studies relating to it. After all of this time and effort on the part of both scholars and practitioners we still have at best only a hazy and far from firm grasp of motivation. In our opinion, there is no single theory relating to motivation that can be completely and unqualifiedly accepted as accounting for all the known facts, and there is no definite set of prescriptions that are unequivocally supported by research data.[8]

---

[8]Lyman W. Porter and R. P. Miles, "Motivation and Management," in J. W.

Another problem has to do with assumptions about the personnel management function that are implicit in bureaucratic structures and procedures. Existing theory and research on motivation suggest the need to gear inducements to specific conditions and to the characteristics of small groups and individuals. However, bureaucracies are designed to handle people in large groups or categories and to deal with them in depersonalized terms. Centrally administered, impersonally applied inducements are more appropriate from a bureaucratic standpoint than are nonroutinized methods geared to special situations and to each individual.[9] Although in theory the perfect incentives system would fully exploit the abilities and motivations of each employee, organizational constraints require that such maximization of contributions be sacrificed in order that complexity and variability can be held to levels that enable management to maintain *control* through programmed and broadly applicable sets of inducements. Accommodating the variability and complexity of human motivation would be an extremely expensive undertaking. Large, bureaucratic organizations accept adequate as opposed to maximum employee contributions because the investment in money, time, and expertise required for *fully* tapping the potential of the work force is not justified when viewed in relation to its capacity to increase contributions beyond levels achieved by less expensive means. In other words, if a set of relatively uncomplicated inducements that can be applied to large numbers of people on a routine basis generates *satisfactory* contributions, management will use it and allocate available resources elsewhere.[10]

Extrinsic inducements

The vast majority of today's formal organizations rely on *extrinsic* inducements. "Extrinsic motivation . . . comes through reward external to the job itself. It takes the form of some extrinsic drive reduction in hun[g]er, thirst, material reward, or others."[11] Pay,

---

McGuire (ed.), *Contemporary Management: Issues and Viewpoints* (Englewood Cliffs, N.J.: Prentice-Hall, 1974), p. 545.

[9]See Max Weber, "The Development of Bureaucracy and Its Relation to Law," in W. G. Runciman (ed.), *Weber: Selections in Translation*, E. Mathews, trans. (Cambridge: Cambridge University Press, 1978), pp. 341–354.

[10]See Herbert Simon, *Administrative Behavior*, 2d ed. (New York: Free Press, 1957), pp. 172–197.

[11]Debra W. Stewart and G. David Garson, *Organizational Behavior and Public Management* (New York: Dekker, 1983), p. 33.

working conditions, and fringe benefits are examples of material extrinsic inducements, and promotions, honors, and prestige of the nonmaterial category. Of course, money is the most visible and commonly understood extrinsic reward.

Using money as *the* basic extrinsic inducement is predicated on the assumption that people will work (make contributions) in order to acquire the money required to satisfy their needs and wants. To the organization, money is a very convenient inducement for at least three reasons. *First,* its use greatly narrows the range of human needs and desires that the organization must somehow meet directly. Money can be used for many purposes and, by rewarding people with it, organizations *externalize* the problem of having to understand and respond to much of the complexity of human motivation. The individual is left with the task of meeting his or her needs outside the organization. *Second,* money is subject to centralized administration and to standardized managerial accounting procedures. As such, it provides a "common denominator" for the calculation of organizational return on outlays for inducements. In some cases, these calculations take the form of measures of individual or group productivity, which may be used to make merit pay and bonus decisions.[12] *Third,* if it has clearly defined the behaviors it wants, management has in money a relatively unambiguous *reinforcer*.[13] The receipt of money can be made dependent on behavior understood to be organizationally functional. Although the concept of behavior reinforcement applies to all kinds of inducements, money has the practical advantages of serving many purposes and of being convenient to administer according to planned "schedules" that emphasize the connection between behavior and reward.[14]

Given the emphasis placed on extrinsic inducements in many societies, surprisingly little is known about the causal relationships between them and and performance in organizations.[15] Although research findings do allow some crude generalizations, important

[12]See Jesse Burkhead and Patrick J. Hennigan, "Productivity Analysis: A Search for Definition and Order," *Public Administration Review* 38, no. 1 (January–February 1978): 34–40; also Stewart and Garson, *Organizational Behavior*, p. 34.

[13]Skinner, *Beyond Freedom and Dignity*, pp. 56–95.

[14]See F. Luthans and R. Kreitner, *Organizational Behavior Modification* (Glenview, Ill.: Scott, Foresman, 1975); and Gary Yuki, K. N. Wexley, and J. O. Seymore, "Effectiveness of Pay Incentives under Variable Ratio and Continuous Reinforcement Schedules," *Journal of Applied Psychology* 56, no. 1 (February 1972): 19–23.

[15]See V. H. Vroom, *Work and Motivation* (New York: Wiley, 1964).

questions remain unanswered. This uncertainty places rather narrow limits on the assumptions management may confidently make about the impact of extrinsic inducements on individual, group, and organizational performance. However, the research evidence suggests that those concerned should be careful to distinguish between: (1) rewards that are "earned" by people primarily because of their *membership* in the organization or one of its subgroupings, and (2) rewards derived largely from *individual* effort.[16]

Membership based inducements (system rewards). Incentives systems designed to reward people by functional groups and hierarchical levels typically divide performance into two categories: satisfactory and unsatisfactory. Satisfactory performance leads to maintenance of membership in a group or hierarchical level, and membership is the basis for being rewarded. Within the "satisfactory" category, individual differences in performance are not considered in making decisions about pay and other benefits.[17] Within each category of employee, those rated satisfactory all get the same rewards. Since maintenance of membership is the basis for rewards, attention is concentrated on the standard of acceptable performance. These "system rewards," as Katz and Kahn call them, dominate the inducements strategies used by public and private employers. Accordingly, hourly rates, salary schedules, and standardized fringe benefits are hallmarks of the modern public organization.

A complaint frequently made about the inducements strategies of public agencies is that they encourage, indeed positively reward, mediocre performance. In fact, extrinsic system rewards have not been found to be particularly effective devices for promoting above average or exceptional performance.[18] Using a system reward approach, management may be able to improve *overall* performance by upgrading the basic criteria for maintenance of membership, but it should not expect to stimulate behavior much above that baseline. From an organizational standpoint, this may or may not be a problem, but it should be recognized.[19]

---

[16]See Katz and Kahn, *The Social Psychology of Organizations*, pp. 409–417.

[17]See John P. Campbell, M. D. Dunnette, E. E. Lawler, and K. E. Weik, *Managerial Behavior, Performance, and Effectiveness* (New York: McGraw-Hill, 1970).

[18]L. W. Porter and E. E. Lawler, III, *Managerial Attitudes and Performance* (Homewood, Ill.: Irwin-Dorsey, 1968).

[19]Campbell et al., *Managerial Behavior*, p. 347; also Daniel Yankelovich and J. Immerwahr, *Putting the Work Ethic to Work* (New York: The Public Agenda Foundation, 1983), pp. 26–27.

System reward approaches do have several positive features that make them attractive to management. First, they can be routinely applied to groups and can be centrally administered. Second, they are not unrelated to *organizational* performance—if the incentives offered are sufficiently attractive, raising minimum performance standards should result in increased across-the-board effort. Third, if pay, benefits, and working conditions exceed those of other organizations, recruiting qualified personnel should be easier. Fourth, attractive extrinsic inducements are usually associated with comparatively low turnover and absenteeism rates. Fifth, as a group, employees are more likely to support and protect an organization that, in their estimation, provides superior rewards. Therefore, in terms of the behavioral requirements listed earlier, system rewards can play a major role in satisfying the needs of organizations.[20]

Individualized inducements. In contrast with system rewards, individualized inducements are intended to tie rewards *directly*' to a person's performance or output. The emphasis is on differences between individuals. For example, each person in a work group is paid according to his or her performance in one or more task areas, which means that everybody in the group could be earning a different amount of money. In general terms, it is assumed that people are economically rational, will see the connection between performance and reward, and, if given the opportunity, will seek to maximize their rewards through productivity.

Yankelovich and Immerwahr go so far as to associate individualized incentives with American individualism, and they argue that a major reason for "declining" productivity in the United States is the "undercutting of the link between pay and performance." They say:

> This situation represents a sharp departure from the traditional American value of individualism. A central theme of our cultural heritage supports the idea that individuals will fail or succeed through their own efforts and hard work. When people receive equal rewards regardless of effort or achievement, the implicit message from management is: "We don't care about extra effort, so why should you?"[21]

---

[20]Katz and Kahn, *The Social Psychology of Organizations*, pp. 413–414; L. W. Porter and R. M. Steers, "Organizational Work and Personal Factors in Employee Turnover and Absenteeism," *Psychological Bulletin* 80, no. 2 (1973): 151–176.

[21]Yankelovich and Immerwahr, *Putting the Work Ethic to Work*, p. 26; see also

The most extreme form of individualized inducement is the "piece rate." Management assigns a cash value to each unit of output or service (e.g., a pair of shoes repaired, a social security claim processed, or a building inspected), and the worker's pay for a specified period is determined by multiplying the number of units "produced" by the unit value.[22] Under a modified piece-rate system, the worker is paid a basic wage to meet performance standards applied to the entire group or organizational function (a system reward) and receives an additional amount for each unit of output over and above the established norm. Alternatively, a bonus may be given as a reward for very good or outstanding performance.

Usually found in industrial, craft, and merchandising settings, pure piece-rate systems are not used in the U.S. public sector. Although comparatively rare, examples can be found of efforts in government to overlay system rewards with individualized incentives. Time off, educational opportunities, payment for unused sick leave, and voluntary overtime are sometimes used for this purpose. Recently, there has been renewed interest in using within-grade salary increases (in practice, usually a given for satisfactory performance coupled with seniority) as rewards for better-than-average to superior performance, in which case they truly become merit increases.[23] In fact, the Civil Service Reform Act of 1978 provides for merit pay for supervisors and managers in General Schedule Grades 13–15. This legislation also authorizes cash bonuses for high-performing members of the Senior Executive Service.[24]

These changes in inducements strategy at the federal level reflect the belief that system rewards, in and of themselves, are not capable of generating the superior levels of achievement required to meet the challenges now facing public agencies. Given the lack of in-depth research on the effects of individualized inducements on managerial personnel, the federal merit pay and bonus programs must be considered major experiments. Since existing evidence points to a positive association between individualized pay

---

Edgar H. Schein, *Organizational Psychology* (Englewood Cliffs, N.J.: Prentice-Hall, 1965), pp. 48–50.

[22]See E. E. Lawler, *Pay and Organizational Effectiveness* (New York: McGraw-Hill, 1971).

[23]See David W. Belcher, "Ominous Trends in Wage and Salary Administration," *Personnel* 41, no. 5 (September–October 1964): 42–50.

[24]Civil Service Reform Act of 1978, Title V.

incentives, other extrinsic rewards, and performance, there is room for cautious optimism.[25] Yet the research also makes clear that at least two conditions must be met if this relationship is to be realized in the work place.

The most obvious of these conditions is that it must be possible to isolate clearly and measure accurately individual contributions. Performance evaluation is far from an exact science, and in many cases it cannot be done with a precision that justifies using the results as the basis for making decisions about pay and other extrinsic rewards. In many organizations, responsibilities and work processes are so interdependent that they defy efforts to draw boundaries around a person's "job" and then measure his or her contributions separately from those of others. Under these circumstances, the injection of an individual-centered reward mentality might generate destructive interpersonal competition for organizational resources and produce feelings of inequitable treatment that could seriously undermine a group's capacity to perform. In such cases, rewarding group, as opposed to individual, performance might be a more logical strategy.[26]

The other condition is the individual's *real* ability to control his or her productivity. Organizational technologies and routines often afford little room for variability. Day-to-day output is, in effect, dictated by the overall pace of a coordinated set of activities, production processes, or procedures. On an assembly line, for example, workers must conform to a pace set either by management or under terms of a contract negotiated with a union. Much the same situation exists in many areas of nonindustrial activity where tasks are narrowly specialized and so interdependent that it is virtually impossible for people to play the "entrepreneurial" roles required by individualized inducements. To ask them to do so when they have little or no control over major aspects of their performance would be an invitation to frustration and suspicion about management's intentions.[27]

In a recent evaluation of monetary incentives used in state and

[25]John M. Greiner, H. Hatry, M. Koss, A. Miller, and J. Woodward, *Productivity and Motivation: A Review of State and Local Initiatives* (Washington, D.C.: Urban Institute Press, 1981), p. 112.

[26]See Lawler, *Pay and Organizational Effectiveness,* p. 278; W. F. Whyte, *Money and Motivation* (New York: Harper & Row, 1955); and Frederick Thayer, "The President's Management 'Reforms': Theory X Triumphant," *Public Administration Review* 38 (July–August 1978): 309–314.

[27]See Katz and Kahn, *The Social Psychology of Organizations,* pp. 335–338; E. L. Trist, G. W. Higgin, H. Murray, and S. B. Pollock, *Organizational Choice*

local governments, the Urban Institute concluded that cost savings and increases in efficiency are possible if relationships between pay and performance are clearly defined, objective performance criteria exist, and quality controls have been established. Piecework and shared savings plans appear to be the most consistently effective.[28] However, the Institute recommends caution because supporting research evidence is scarce, and formidable barriers to successful implementation are likely to exist (e.g., insufficient funds, legal restrictions on administrative discretion, constraining civil service rules, and contracts negotiated with employee organizations).[29]

The Institute's report goes on to recommend that state and local governments should give "serious consideration" to individualized and group-based monetary incentives, but only if they are willing to make the investments necessary to overcome existing barriers and to do the following.[30]

1. Construct "valid, comprehensive, and objective performance indicators."[31]
2. Actively involve workers, supervisors, and managers in the development of the plan.
3. Pilot test the plan before full-scale implementation, and carefully train supervisors in its administration.
4. Design and implement an evaluation process that permits top-level administrators to track its impacts on individual and organizational productivity.
5. Establish broadly agreed-upon performance standards that can be effectively administered.
6. Heavily involve top management in the decision-making processes regarding all of the above.[32]

Why organizations rely on system rewards. Studies of the federal experience with merit pay and bonuses reveal problems quite similar to those found by the Urban Institute on the state and local levels of government.[33] Technical and administrative difficulties

---

(London: Tavistock, 1963); and Greiner et al., *Productivity and Motivation*, pp. 100–102.

[28]Greiner et al., *Productivity and Motivation*, p. 112.

[29]Ibid., pp. 95–113.

[30]Ibid., p. 113.

[31]Ibid.

[32]Ibid., pp. 113–114.

[33]Bruce Buchanan, II, "The Senior Executive Service: How Can We Tell if It

have been significant, and political barriers have proven to be frustrating. In other words, the Institute's warning should be taken seriously: decisions regarding individual versus system rewards should not be made in isolation from organizational needs, constraints, and capabilities. Figure 3.1 explains why public organizations rely so heavily on system rewards and can be expected to continue to do so.

The probabilities associated with each YES-NO branch in the sequence of decisions outlined in Figure 3.1 will vary according to the nature of the work involved and the way in which the organization is structured to carry out its various functions. Anticipated social-psychological and material rewards and costs must also be considered. The answers to the questions will depend on opportunities and constraints confronting management. The appropriateness of management's choices depends on its ability to: (1) accurately diagnose situations, (2) evaluate the alternatives that exist, and (3) choose a course of action that has a reasonably high chance of producing a satisfactory (if not optimal) outcome. Note, however, that it only takes one NO to push management in the direction of a system reward strategy. Consequently, it should be anticipated that the odds will usually favor a decision to use system rewards.

Intrinsic inducements

An extrinsic inducements strategy assumes that the work to be performed need not be a *direct* source of need satisfaction. In contrast, a person is *intrinsically* motivated if he or she does something because it produces rewards in the form of feelings of competence or self-determination.[34] The reward flows from doing the work itself. The relationships between job satisfaction, performance, and the intrinsic rewards of jobs and their settings have been found to be highly complex. They cannot be combined in a simple

---

Works?" *Public Administration Review* 39 (May–June 1981): 349–358; Bernard Rosen, "Uncertainty in the Senior Executive Service," *Public Administration Review* 41 (March–April 1981): 203–207; James Perry, Carla Honzlik, and Jane Pearce, "Effectiveness of Merit Pay Pool Management," *Review of Public Personnel Administration* 2 (Summer 1982): 5–12; Buddy A. Silverman, "The Merit Pay System: A Prognosis," *Review of Public Personnel Administration* 2 (Summer 1982): 29–36; and Peter Ring and James Perry, "Reforming the Upper Levels of the Bureaucracy," *Administration and Society* 15 (May 1983): 119–144.

[34]See Edward Deci, *Intrinsic Motivation* (New York: Plenum Press, 1975).

FIGURE 3.1.
Outline of a Decision Tree Concerning the Choice of an Inducements
Strategy for a Specific Kind of Work

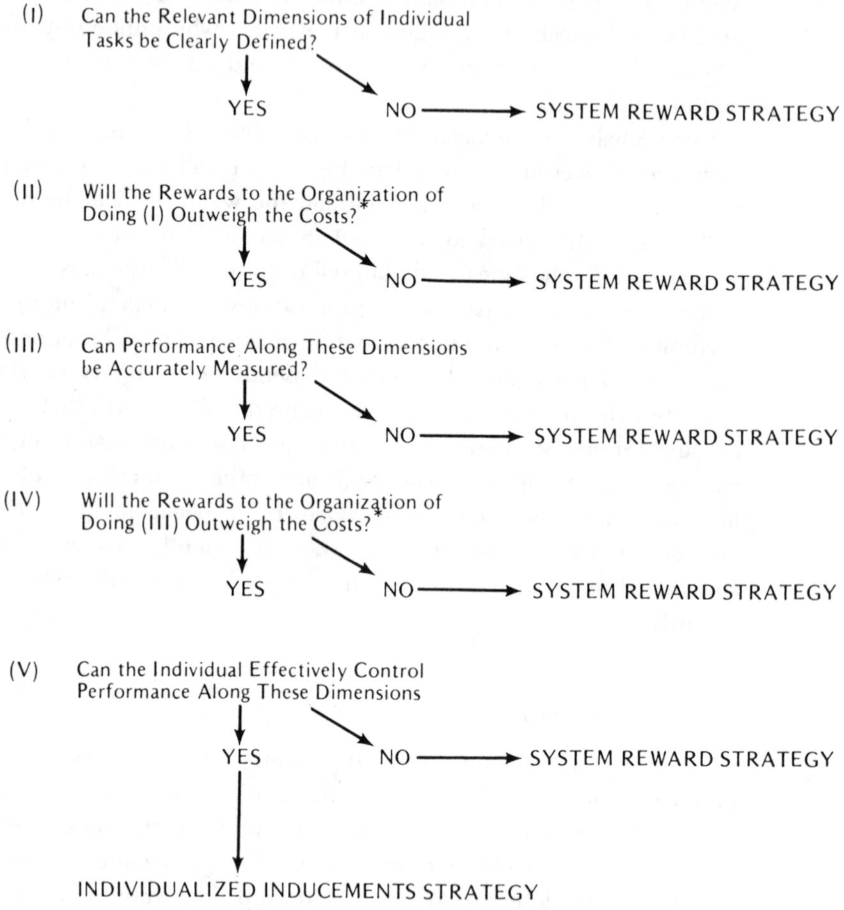

(I)   Can the Relevant Dimensions of Individual
Tasks be Clearly Defined?

          YES   NO ⟶ SYSTEM REWARD STRATEGY

(II)   Will the Rewards to the Organization of
Doing (I) Outweigh the Costs?*

          YES   NO ⟶ SYSTEM REWARD STRATEGY

(III)   Can Performance Along These Dimensions
be Accurately Measured?

          YES   NO ⟶ SYSTEM REWARD STRATEGY

(IV)   Will the Rewards to the Organization of
Doing (III) Outweigh the Costs?*

          YES   NO ⟶ SYSTEM REWARD STRATEGY

(V)   Can the Individual Effectively Control
Performance Along These Dimensions

          YES   NO ⟶ SYSTEM REWARD STRATEGY

INDIVIDUALIZED INDUCEMENTS STRATEGY

*The time frames used by public managers are, for political and budget-cycle reasons, often very short term. Calculations of this type usually involve questions of internal resource allocations *and* external contingencies such as client support, union attitudes, and other conditions in the task environment. Rewards and costs include social and psychological variables as well as economic factors.

"causal" model uniformly applicable to the different situations facing public management. Nevertheless, the research evidence is strong enough to justify saying that management should pay close attention to: (1) the social-psychological implications of how jobs are designed and interrelated, and (2) the impact of supervisory styles and group dynamics on performance. Equally important is an understanding of the basic needs that motivate human behavior in these two areas of organizational structure and functioning.

Human needs and intrinsic rewards. Probably the single most influential theory about human needs and their relevance to inducements strategies has been Abraham Maslow's need-hierarchy concept.[35] According to Maslow, needs fall into four basic categories: (1) physical safety and security, (2) love or supportive affective relationships with others, (3) self-esteem and recognition by others, and (4) self-actualization or the realization of one's capabilities and potential.[36] Maslow believed that people perceive and try to satisfy these needs in an hierarchical progression from safety-security (lowest) to self-actualization (highest). He also argued that once a need is satisfied it no longer motivates normal adults. Only self-actualization needs, in Maslow's view, are open-ended and never fully satisfied.[37]

Empirical tests of Maslow's theory have not substantiated his postulation that there is an hierarchical order of needs and that all normal individuals respond to and try to satisfy needs in a sequential manner.[38] It appears that "lower" needs do not have to be completely satisfied before "higher" needs become motivators, and studies of organizations have revealed that workers have different "mixes" of needs and also differ with respect to the intensity of particular needs. On the other hand, it has been established that many people do have strongly felt social and psychological needs *related to the nature of their work*.[39] This insight greatly broadens the range of potential inducements available to organizations, because it justifies management changes in adapting tasks

---

[35]A. H. Maslow, *Motivation and Personality* (New York: Harper & Row, 1954).

[36]Ibid., p. 82.

[37]For an example of Maslow's application of these concepts to management, see A. H. Maslow, *Eupsychian Management* (Homewood, Ill.: Irwin-Dorsey, 1965).

[38]See M. A. Wahba and L. G. Bridwell, "Maslow Reconsidered: A Review of Research on the Need Hierarchy Theory," *Proceedings of the Academy of Management*, 1973, pp. 514–520; C. P. Aldefer, *Existence, Relatedness, and Growth: Human Needs for Organizational Settings* (New York: Free Press, 1972); and Stewart and Garson, *Organizational Behavior and Public Management*, pp. 13–17.

[39]See *Work for America: Report of a Special Task Force to the Secretary of HEW* (Cambridge, Mass.: MIT Press, 1973); Yankelovich and Immerwahr, *Putting the Work Ethic to Work*, pp. 19–30; and Office of Merit Systems Review and Studies, *The Elusive Bottom Line: Productivity in the Federal Work Force* (Washington, D.C.: U.S. Merit Systems Protection Board, May 1982).

to the social-psychological needs of workers. Management determines how need-frustrating factors can be minimized and need-satisfying ones used to increase job satisfaction and provide incentives for better performance.[40]

■ JOB CHARACTERISTICS, JOB SATISFACTION, AND PERFORMANCE

Numerous studies have revealed a relationship between job content and satisfaction that exists in the case of a wide variety of jobs and at all levels of organizational responsibility. In the United States and other developed countries where for much of the population basic needs of safety and security have been met, the evidence suggests a trend toward greater interest on the part of workers in the social-psychological rewards that jobs can offer.[41] Broadly speaking, workers report a need for work that is intrinsically interesting, challenging, and personally meaningful. Opportunities for varied tasks, influence over how work is done, and autonomy or self-direction are also important needs for many.[42] Bearing in mind that people vary in the degree to which they have these needs, the overall pattern is for job satisfaction to be higher for jobs that offer these kinds of intrinsic rewards.

An instructive example of how intrinsic factors may be closely related to job satisfaction and performance is the PATCO strike mentioned in Chapter 2. In his analysis of the conditions leading to the strike, David Bowers points out that it took place even though the controllers were aware that they faced a determined, hostile administration. It was clear that a strike would bring firings

---

[40]See Rensis Likert, *The Human Organization* (New York: McGraw-Hill, 1967).

[41]There is a very large literature in this area. As examples, see F. Kilpatrick et al., *The Image of the Federal Service* (Washington, D.C.: Brookings, 1964); R. P. Quinn and L. Shepard, *The 1972–1973 Quality of Employment Survey'* (Ann Arbor; University of Michigan Survey Research Center, 1974); J. R. Hackman and E. E. Lawler, "Employee Reactions to Job Characteristics," *Journal of Applied Psychology* 55, no. 3 (June 1971); A. Campbell, P. E. Converse, and W. L. Rodgers, *The Quality of American Life* (New York: Russell Sage Foundation, 1976); L. E. Davis, "Job Satisfaction Research: A Post-Industrial View," *Industrial Relations* 10, no. 2 (1971); W. G. Scott and T. R. Mitchell, *Organization Theory: A Structural and Behavioral Analysis*, 3d ed. (Homewood, Ill.: Irwin, 1976), pp. 152–156.

[42]Hackman and Lawler, "Employee Reactions to Job Characteristics"; and A. P. Brief and R. J. Aldag, "Employee Reactions to Job Characteristics: A Constructive Replication," *Journal of Applied Psychology* 60, no. 2 (1975). Also R. Quinn, S. Seashore, R. Kahn, and others, *Survey of Working Conditions 1969–70* (Washington, D.C.: Government Printing Office, 1971); R. Blauner, *Alienation and Freedom: The Factory Worker and His Industry* (Chicago: University of Chicago Press, 1964); and Stewart and Garson, *Organizational Behavior and Public Management*, pp. 33–34.

and legal action against PATCO and its officials. The Reagan administration's actions, therefore, should have come as no surprise, and Bowers asks: "What Would Make 11,500 People Quit Their Jobs?"[43]

The "official" FAA explanation of the strike stressed extrinsic factors, including: (1) unreasonable wage demands, (2) peer pressure, and (3) a lack of discipline in the controllers' ranks. The FAA, in turn, was blamed for "overindulging" its employees, allowing unrealistic expectations regarding pay to spread, and entering into an unreasonably restrictive agreement with PATCO. However, Bowers disagrees, concluding that the central causes of the strike were management practices and working conditions.

Bowers' research revealed that before the strike morale was low, in part because FAA supervisors and managers were using highly autocratic styles in their dealings with the younger controllers who valued collaboration and participative decision making. Another important contributor was "burnout" caused by highly stressful working conditions. Burnout, aggravated by unsupportive management practices, generated very high levels of job dissatisfaction which, Bowers argues, made it easier to support and join a strike. In effect, many PATCO members "quit" by striking.

In Bowers' judgment, the "greatest labor relations disaster in the history of modern public administration" was the result of stressful jobs, supervisory styles that were inappropriate for the workforce, and management policies and practices geared only to extrinsic motives.[44] The controllers were not able to derive important intrinsic rewards from their work. Because a professional management should be expected to understand the importance of intrinsic as well as extrinsic rewards, Bowers believes that the FAA's administrators and supervisors must shoulder a large share of the responsibility for the strike and its consequences.

Against this background, there has been growing support for the idea that job design and supervisory styles should take into account factors relating to satisfaction and motivation.[45] Illustrations of this approach are Frederick Herzberg's widely known concept of job enrichment, Rensis Likert's participative group system, and Nor-

---

[43]David G. Bowers, "What Would Make 11,500 People Quit Their Jobs?" *Organizational Dynamics* (Winter 1983): 5–19.

[44]Ibid., 19.

[45]This does not mean that these variables should *replace* traditional technical-economic criteria. They should be *added* to the list of important considerations.

wegian and Swedish experiments with enlarged tasks and worker participation in industrial organizations.

Herzberg's Two-Factor Theory

Building on Maslow's concepts, Herzberg theorized that motivators fall into two general categories—those that are intrinsic and those that are extrinsic or "hygiene"-based. According to Herzberg, intrinsic factors include achievement, recognition, and meaningful responsibility. His research convinced him that improvements in intrinsic factors yielded higher levels of satisfaction and motivation. Extrinsic hygiene factors, he maintained, cause dissatisfaction when they fall below "acceptable" levels, but they are *not* positive sources of satisfaction. Thus, pay, quality of supervision, working conditions, and job security cannot "cause" satisfaction and motivate performance; however, if they do not meet worker expectations, they can cause dissatisfaction and perhaps a reluctance to perform. The message to managers was clear: If you want to motivate employees positively and improve job satisfaction, use job designs that emphasize intrinsic motivators. Extrinsic hygiene factors, although important, provided only a *foundation* upon which a structure of intrinsic *motivators* could be constructed.[46]

Herzberg's thesis is *intuitively* plausible, but studies designed to verify it have revealed that people respond differently to his intrinsic and extrinsic hygiene factors. Consequently, no *universal* pattern of responses can be presumed. The needs, attitudes, and expectations of individuals must be taken into consideration.[47] However, Herzberg's basic idea that satisfaction and performance may be enhanced through "enriching" jobs by adding diversity, increasing responsibility, and allowing greater participation in decisions has been very influential. Job enrichment experiments in a variety of occupational and organizational settings have overall produced a pattern of positive results.[48]

---

[46]F. Herzberg, *Work and the Nature of Man* (Cleveland: World Publishing Co., 1966); and F. Herzberg, "One More Time: How Do You Motivate Employees?" *Harvard Business Review* 46, no. 1 (1968): 53–62.

[47]See R. J. House and L. A. Wigdor, "Herzberg's Dual Factor Theory of Job Satisfaction," *Personnel Psychology* 20 (1967): 369–390; W. G. Scott and T. R. Mitchell, *Organization Theory*, 3d ed., pp. 118–120; and G. B. Graen and C. L. Hulin, "Addendum to an Empirical Investigation of the Two-Factor Theory of Job Satisfaction," *Journal of Applied Psychology* 52 (1968): 341–342.

[48]See W. J. Paul, K. B. Robertson, and F. Herzberg, "Job Enrichment Pays Off,"

For example, the Urban Institute believes that "job redesign still appears to be a promising strategy for improving government productivity and employee satisfaction . . . the distinguishing characteristic of job redesign, and job restructuring in particular, is its emphasis on humanistic treatment of employees as well as job efficiency."[49]

Likert's Participative Group System

Based on data collected during the 1950s on management practices and performance, Rensis Likert concluded that effective supervisors focused "their primary attention on the human aspects of their subordinates' problems and on endeavoring to build effective work groups with high performance goals.[50] Likert's research strongly supported the conclusion that the *work group* can be a central and major source of intrinsic rewards if the supervisor is able to develop a supportive social-psychological climate within the group. The emphasis here, therefore, is on the group's dynamics and leadership process. In general terms, Likert found that high satisfaction and productivity were associated with groups having the following characteristics:

1. Group members provided social-psychological support for one another.
2. Member identification with and loyalty to the group was strong.
3. Group decision processes were highly participative.
4. Supervision was general rather than close.
5. Group members were highly goal-oriented and mutually reinforced that orientation.

Supervisory styles and attitudes conducive to the emergence of these group characteristics included:

Harvard Business Review 47, no. 1 (1969); C. D. Jacobs, "Job Enrichment of Field Technical Representatives—Xerox Corporation," in L. E. Davis and A. B. Cherns (eds.), *The Quality of Working Life, Vol. II* (New York: Free Press, 1975), pp. 285–299; R. Jansen, "A Job Enrichment Trial in Data Processing in an Insurance Organization," in Davis and Cherns (eds.), *The Quality of Working Life, Vol. II,* pp. 300–315; and in the same volume, E. J. Bryan, "Work Improvement and Job Enrichment: The Case of Cummins Engine Co.," pp. 315–329.

[49]Greiner et al., *Productivity and Motivation,* p. 340.

[50]Rensis Likert, *New Patterns of Management* (New York: McGraw-Hill, 1961), p. 7.

1. An emphasis on supportive and helping relationships with subordinates.
2. Trust in the commitment and ability of group members.
3. Willingness to train and otherwise develop the skills of subordinates.
4. High expectations with regard to group performance.
5. Participative approaches to decision making with the supervisor concentrating on coordinating the planning and initiating of activities.

Thus, in addition to extrinsic inducements, the productive group provided opportunities for achievement, self-esteem, and psychological security. Accordingly, Likert urged that:

> The leadership and other processes of the organization must be such as to ensure a maximum probability that in all interactions and all relationships with the organization each member will, in light of his background, values, and expectations, view the experience as supportive and one which builds and maintains his sense of personal worth and importance.[51]

As prime sources of intrinsic rewards, work groups provide a potent mechanism for socialization to values regarding commitment to the organization and to standards of performance. If these values emphasize performance, the group may become a basis for high levels of productivity as well as satisfaction.[52] Cultivating, supporting, and reinforcing a positive performance orientation in the work group, therefore, is a major challenge for management. It is an especially important task because group norms are a double-edged sword—they can also promote alienation from organizational goals and restricted productivity.[53]

The Norwegian and Swedish Experiments

These experiments are significant because they are a rare example of an attempt to improve organizational performance and job sat-

---

[51]Ibid., p. 103.

[52]See A. K. Rice, *Productivity and Social Organization* (London: Tavistock, 1958); D. Cartwright and A. Zander (eds.), *Group Dynamics* (New York: Harper & Row, 1968), pp. 401–417; Paul Blumberg, *Industrial Democracy: The Sociology of Participation* (New York: Schlocken Books, 1968), pp. 70–138; and Stewart and Garson, *Organizational Behavior and Public Management*, pp. 43–72.

[53]See S. E. Seashore, *Cohesiveness in the Industrial Work Group* (Ann Arbor; University of Michigan Press, 1954).

isfaction through the coordinated design of intrinsically rewarding jobs, technological operations, and participatory decision processes. Careful attention was paid to the creation of working conditions that provided opportunities for: (1) challenging and varied work, (2) individual and group discretion, (3) personal and work team recognition, (4) self-development, and (5) upward mobility and other forms of career development.[54]

Following these general guidelines, major interventions were made in the areas of job design, production technologies, group powers and responsibilities, and the administration of pay incentives. Jobs were enriched *vertically* by giving workers the opportunity to participate directly in the making of decisions about such matters as output goals and quality control. Variety and challenge were also enhanced through *horizontal* enlargement or the adding of new functional responsibilities. In several cases (the best known being the Saab and Volvo factories), traditional assembly line technologies were extensively modified to permit the formation of permanent groups or teams having responsibility for the production of major subassemblies. Teams were also delegated significant control in the areas of work pacing and division of labor within the group. Also, an effort was made to reinforce these changes by establishing *group* performance as the criterion for above base rate and bonus pay.[55] From a social-psychological standpoint, all of these changes were designed to create supportive, participative, and personally rewarding groups with norms favoring high performance and commitment to organizational goals.

Evaluations of the Norwegian and Swedish experiments report some failures and instances where less than optimal results were obtained. Given the challenge to their traditional authority represented by increased worker participation, some managerial personnel felt threatened by the changes but most found the new arrangements acceptable. Assembly line workers responded the most favorably. Absenteeism and turnover were meaningfully reduced in the experimental plants. Efficiency and quality either improved somewhat or achieved levels identical to those in plants

---

[54]See E. Thorsrud, B. S. Sorenson, and B. Gustavsen, "Sociotechnical Approach to Industrial Democracy in Norway," in R. Dubin (ed.), *Handbook of Work, Organization, and Society* (Chicago: Rand McNally, 1976); and Alfred L. Thimm, "Union-Management Codetermination in Sweden," *Journal of Social and Political Studies* 4 (Summer 1979): 147–173.

[55]See Swedish Employers' Confederation, *Job Reform in Sweden* (Stockholm, 1975).

operated under traditional methods.[56] Generalizing these outcomes to nonindustrial settings, including the public sector, is a risky venture.

Nevertheless, Stewart and Garson observe that while participatory management faces administrative and political barriers in the public sector, American cultural values, workforce characteristics, organizational technologies in the public sector, and beliefs about its contributions tend to support and promote it as a motivational strategy.[57] In U.S. state and local governments, the Urban Institute found that experiments with participatory management were far from universally successful; however, its overall evaluation was favorable.

> Taken together, joint labor-management committees and other approaches to increase employee participation appear to represent a promising way to improve productivity and job satisfaction, on the basis of the limited documentary evidence available. They also appear to be particularly useful as a vehicle for introducing other motivational approaches, such as monetary incentives or job redesign.[58]

One conclusion does seem justifiable: *Redesigning jobs, technologies, and social relationships in organizations can result in significant improvements in management's capacity to offer work that is intrinsically rewarding and fosters job satisfaction.* There is also little evidence to support the assertion that changes of these kinds negatively affect individual, group, or organizational performance. There is reason to believe that if the performance-reward connection is appropriately structured by management, intrinsic as well as extrinsic inducements can be effective motivators of performance.

■ STRUCTURING THE RELATIONSHIP BETWEEN INDUCEMENTS AND CONTRIBUTIONS

There is little evidence to suggest that simply meeting the material, social, and psychological needs of people will somehow make them work harder or be more productive. For example, a large

---

[56]See S. Aguren, R. Hansson, and K. G. Karlsson, *The Impact of New Design on Work Organization* (Stockholm: The Rationalization Council SAF-LO, 1976); also, see Katz and Kahn, *The Social Psychology of Organizations*, 2d ed., pp. 716–749, for a general review.

[57]Stewart and Garson, *Organizational Behavior and Public Management*, pp. 154–160.

[58]Greiner et al., *Productivity and Motivation*, p. 337.

body of research on job satisfaction reveals almost no evidence to support the widespread assumption that job satisfaction *leads* to greater effort or better performance.[59] There is, in fact, no logical reason why job satisfaction should cause higher performance. As Scott and Mitchell put it:

> . . . there is no reason to believe that liking the job will prompt one to higher levels of effort. People are attracted to jobs for various reasons (the work conditions, the friendships, the supervision, and so on). They may find that all of these things can be obtained without extra effort, and indeed, this is the case in many organizations. It is true that some rewards may be lost such as a bonus or a promotion, but in many cases these incentives are not of utmost importance. The other incentives are typically not related to effort, and it should not be surprising, therefore, that overall job satisfaction is only slightly related to output.[60]

Accordingly, it makes little sense to conclude that survey data on the U.S. population showing roughly 90 percent of all workers "satisfied" means that all or even most of these people are being motivated to "produce."[61] Likewise, an Office of Personnel Management survey indicating that about 80 percent of federal employees are satisfied with their work reveals little about the extent to which federal "rewards" are stimulating performance.[62]

Expectancy Theory

What then, is the nature of the relationship between extrinsic-intrinsic rewards, motivation, and performance? An explanation derived from psychology called expectancy or instrumentality theory offers a plausible answer. According to expectancy theory, a person's motivation to behave in a particular way is a function of three factors: (1) the extent to which the individual believes that a certain behavior is possible, for example, getting to work on time; (2) the degree to which the behavior in question is seen to be likely to result in the attainment of some objective or outcome; and (3) the worth or value attributed to that outcome by the individual. "Expectancy" is the person's estimation of the probability that a behavior like getting to work on time is attainable. "Instru-

---

[59]See V. Vroom, *Work and Motivation*, especially Chapter 5.
[60]Scott and Mitchell, *Organization Theory*, 3d ed., p. 159.
[61]Ibid., pp. 154–155.
[62]Office of Personnel Management, *Survey of Federal Employee Attitudes*, 1979.

mentality," on the other hand, is the perceived extent to which the behavior (getting to work on time) can be associated with an outcome, for example, that coming to work on time will result in a pay raise. Expectancy theory predicts that the motivation to come to work on time should be a function of perceived expectancy and instrumentality,[63] and of the value given to the outcome—in this case, a pay raise.

Expectancy theory assumes that people are able rationally to calculate expectancies and instrumentalities and will behave accordingly. Management, on the other hand, must know what outcomes the individual values and be able to "motivate" by setting up conditions wherein: (1) expectancy is high, (2) highly positive instrumentalities exist, and (3) outcomes are valued. As an example, let us assume that management wants to set up an incentives system that motivates employees to come to work on time (desired behavior). First, it must consider the extent to which the workers believe that coming to work on time is an achievable objective (expectancy). If expectancy is, or can be made to be, high, then management must develop outcomes (incentives) highly valued by the employees, and then establish conditions under which coming to work on time is clearly and positively linked to these outcomes (instrumentality). If, from the employees' standpoint, expectancy is high, outcomes are valued, and instrumentality strongly positive, the theory predicts that a strong effort will be made to come to work on time (performance). (See Figure 3.2.)

Studies of motivation and performance in organizations tend to support the general outlines of expectancy theory.[64] However, the model requires information about changeable values and perceptions of individuals that from a practical standpoint would be extraordinarily difficult and expensive to obtain. It also assumes that everybody engages in rational, quasi-economic calculations before choosing a course of action.[65] Although it is probably true that most

---

[63]See V. Vroom, *Work and Motivation*, p. 18; and L. W. Porter and E. E. Lawler, III, *Managerial Attitudes and Performance*.

[64]See H. G. Heneman and D. P. Schwab, "Evaluation of Research on Expectancy Theory Predictions of Employee Performance," *Psychological Bulletin* 78, no. 1 (July 1972): 1–9; and T. R. Mitchell, "Expectancy Models of Job Satisfaction, Occupational Preference, and Effort," *Psychological Bulletin* 81, no. 12 (1974): 1053–1077.

[65]See G. R. Salancik and J. Pfeffer, "An Examination of Need-Satisfaction Models of Job Attitudes," *Administrative Science Quarterly* 22 (September 1977); and C. P. Alderfer, "A Critique of Salancik and Pfeffer's Examination of Need-Satisfaction Theories," *Administrative Science Quarterly* 22 (December 1977).

FIGURE 3.2.
The Basic Expectancy-Instrumentality Relationship

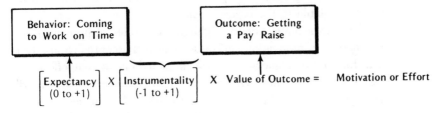

KEY: Value can run from 0 (none) to +1 (very high).

Expectancy (0 to +1) where 0 means no perceived probability that the behavior can be accomplished and +1 means a 100% probability.

Instrumentality (-1 to +1) where -1 means the behavior is seen to never lead to the outcome, 0 means no perceived relationship, and +1 indicates that the individual believes that the behavior always leads to the outcome.

people often try to make these calculations, Stewart and Garson point out that "critics suggest that expectancy theory defers too much to the nineteenth century ideal of the economic man . . . employees cannot be as knowledgeable about outcomes as the model assumes."[66] In the latter case, expectancy theory would neither explain motivation nor predict behavior. Nevertheless, expectancy theory does offer some useful guidelines for managerial thinking about structuring the relationship between inducements and contributions.

First, management should make a determined effort to state clearly and make highly predictable the connections between levels and types of performance and rewards. *Second,* an attempt should be made to understand, at least in general terms, the value groups in the organization place on outcomes of a material and nonmaterial nature. Even if this information on values cannot be obtained for the individual worker, making this attempt should increase the probability that inducements strategies are in general aligned with the values and needs of large segments of the membership. It may

[66]Stewart and Garson, *Organizational Behavior and Public Management,* pp. 25–26.

also promote the use of recruitment and selection criteria that result in the employment of persons who value highly the inducements available to the organization.

Third, expectancy theory highlights the roles of perceived and real ability in motivation and performance. Perceptually, ability is a factor in expectancy—does the person believe that effort will result in performance? Objectively, no amount of motivation will yield performance if ability does not exist.[67] This means that management must take into account the psychological and objective limits on the worker's physical and mental capacities. The contributions potentialities of people are not unlimited, and at some point incentives, no matter how attractive, will cease to have a positive impact on performance. It is, therefore, important that management identify these constraints and be prepared either to adapt to them or to intervene actively in order to improve the capabilities of the organization's human resource base.

Interventions of this type include: (1) upgrading recruitment and selection standards in such key areas as education, experience, and physical abilities; (2) providing training and other developmental opportunities so that employees are able to increase their skills and knowledges; and (3) the design of jobs that take full advantage of the workers' abilities. Equally important are investments in technological aids (e.g., computers, word processors, communications equipment, automated machinery, etc.) that enable people to improve performance.

Fourth, by focusing attention on how performance leads to rewards and on how rewards relate to need satisfaction, expectancy theory highlights the importance of perceived as well as actual equity in the allocation of rewards by management.[68] Since instrumentalities are perceptions of the probability that performance will lead to rewards, a belief or awareness on the part of the organization's members that rewards are not actually given on the basis of an accurate (unbiased) comparative evaluation of performance will seriously damage the psychological basis for motivation. Operationally, perceived equity also depends on clearly defined performance objectives and standards, broadly accepted and trusted performance evaluation procedures and instruments, *and* on the

[67]V. Vroom, *Work and Motivation,* p. 203.
[68]See E. E. Lawler, III, and L. W. Porter, "The Effect of Performance on Job Satisfaction," *Industrial Relations* 7, no. 3 (May 1968).

availability of reliable information about the actual distribution of intrinsic and extrinsic "income."[69]

Expectancy theory was developed and has been tested largely in a private sector context. However, Bruce Buchanan observes that the public sector environment presents special difficulties because goals are often unclear or contradictory, and objectives change often and quickly in a political setting.[70] Because effective implementation of expectancy concepts requires goal clarity and stability, applications in government may be difficult, if not impossible in some cases.[71]

■ THE ROLE OF THE PERSONNEL SPECIALIST

Personnel specialists have at least two general sets of responsibilities relating to internal extraction. They should be prepared to help line managers in isolating material and nonmaterial factors influencing motivation and performance in *public agencies*. This is essentially a *diagnostic and consultative role*. In addition, they must do everything possible to see to it that personnel policy and practices are: (1) consonant with existing knowledge about the nature and dynamics of human motivation and performance, (2) in alignment with the constraints and opportunities created by workforce and organizational characteristics, (3) effective instruments for the management of human resources. It could be said that a major responsibility of the personnel specialist is to see to it that technique *promotes* purpose and does not, as one observer put it, "triumph *over* purpose."[72]

On the basis of its findings, the Urban Institute recommends that personnel specialists concentrate on the following:[73]

1. Improving the performance appraisal systems used throughout the public sector. Accurate, well-documented measures of employee performance are the key to almost all incentives plans. Public management must have confidence in its appraisal data *and*

---

[69]See Katz and Kahn, *The Social Psychology of Organizations*, 2d ed., pp. 340–343.

[70]Bruce Buchanan, II, "Government Managers, Business Executives, and Organizational Commitment," *Public Administration Review* 34 (July–August 1974): 339–347.

[71]Ibid.

[72]See W. S. Sayre, "The Triumph of Technique over Purpose," *Public Administration Review* 8, no. 2 (Spring 1948).

[73]Greiner et al., *Productivity and Motivation*, pp. 417–420.

members of the organization must believe that they are being evaluated objectively and fairly.[74]

2. Identifying unnecessary barriers to innovation in existing civil service laws, rules, and procedures. New concepts and purposes require flexibilities such as those created by the experiments and demonstration projects authorized under Title VI of the U.S. Civil Service Reform Act.[75]

3. Design, implement, and carefully administer rigorous evaluations of new or modified motivational programs. Efforts should be made to show impacts (if any) on productivity, job satisfaction, and other areas relevant to organizational performance.[76]

The consultative and technical roles of the personnel specialist are carried out within the parameters set by the extent to which management is able to establish control over two kinds of variables: (1) the nature of the organization's human resource base, and (2) the social and technical characteristics of the organization.

Controlling the Human Resource Base

Organizations rely on more-or-less complicated sets of procedures to control the characteristics of their workforce and to facilitate the integration of the worker with the technical and social-psychological fabric of the organization.[77] Many of these techniques are within the traditional domain of personnel administration and are discussed in detail in other chapters. They include the following:

1. Analytic systems for job-task analysis and position management.
2. Recruitment procedures aimed at finding people and groups having "desirable" skills, attitudes, and expectations.
3. Selection methods and procedures designed to determine abilities and congruence with organizational norms.
4. Placement and career management policies intended to match people and jobs effectively.

---
[74]Lloyd G. Nigro, "Attitudes of Federal Employees Toward Performance Appraisal and Merit Pay: Implications for CSRA Implementation," *Public Administration Review* 41 (January–February 1981).

[75]Lloyd G. Nigro and Ross Clayton, "An Experiment in Federal Personnel Management: The Naval Laboratories Demonstration Project," in G. Ronald Gilbert (ed.), *Making and Managing Policy* (New York: Dekker, 1984), pp. 153–172.

[76]Ibid., pp. 165–168.

[77]C. Argyris, *Integrating the Individual and the Organization* (New York: Wiley, 1964).

5. Training programs for upgrading existing employee skills and adding new ones.
6. Performance evaluation systems devised to provide a credible basis for allocating rewards and taking other personnel actions.

In the final analysis, these and other techniques have one overriding purpose: to generate the administrative capacity needed to establish some degree of predictable control over key dimensions of the human resource base *and* thereby to increase the predictability of employee responses to organizational performance needs and inducements.

Controlling the Sociotechnical Nature of the Organization

It is highly unlikely that even the most sophisticated personnel system will produce anything close to complete organizational control over the physical, social, psychological, and skills attributes of the membership. Limitations are imposed by sociopolitical forces and values in the external environment, the availability of personnel having *all* or *most* of the desired characteristics, and the effectiveness of existing methods for predicting, controlling, and changing human behavior. Consequently, an organization must have some ability to adjust to constraints and to exploit opportunities through internal adaptations.

More specifically, organizations vary in the degree to which they are able to adjust their social and technological structures and processes. Social aspects of the organization include leadership and supervisory styles, decision-making processes, group dynamics, and the psychological "climate" of the work place. As Bowers observed in his study of the FAA's management practices, supervisors attempted to use autocratic controls and extrinsic inducements on a workforce oriented toward participation and intrinsic rewards. Technical factors relate to the functional technology of the organization—its administrative structure, the materials used, how they are processed, and the physical and mechanical procedures employed. Optimally, all of these variables should be conducive to high levels of motivation and performance and be adjusted to "fit" available human resources. Some organizations are relatively flexible in all or some of these areas and are able to adjust effectively to compensate for less-than-perfect control over values and skills of their human resources. Others are not very flexible and must rely on rather tight control over the nature of their memberships if they are to function effectively.

The social and technological dimensions of organizations are interrelated and each affects the other. A particular technology, such as an assembly line, may severely limit the ability of an organization to offer social and psychological inducements to its members. Other technologies do provide opportunity for intrinsic rewards and satisfaction of social-psychological needs. While technology does not *determine* how organizations will function socially, it is a powerful conditioning factor that must be recognized (as it was in the Norwegian and Swedish experiments described earlier).[78] Although the technologies of some public agencies are highly routinized or mechanized, most are not industrial in nature. The technologies found in law enforcement, education, medicine, and scientific research appear to function well under a variety of administrative and social systems. The problem for the vast majority of organizations is to find ways of blending technology and social arrangements into patterns that stimulate and sustain high levels of quality performance. Figure 3.3 suggests the broad outlines of the task confronting the modern manager and personnel administrator. Specialists are working in both control areas shown, but the broader perspective requires a capacity to see and deal with their interrelations, limitations, and potentials. Over the long run, the effective management of the inducements-contributions equation depends on a broad gauged capacity to manipulate the human resource base and sociotechnical variables in a *coordinated manner*.

Within the framework shown in Figure 3.3, there are at least four areas where personnel specialists can make important contributions.

First, personnel administrators can develop methods of more clearly defining and evaluating the technical (formal) and behavioral (informal) demands of positions. Job evaluation is a good example of how the formal aspects of positions can be clarified. Techniques for evaluating informal requirements are less developed but probably no less important. The evaluation of incentives is a closely related activity. Personnel administration has tended

---

[78]See David Silverman, *The Theory of Organizations* (New York: Basic Books, 1970), pp. 100–125.

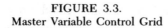

FIGURE 3.3.
Master Variable Control Grid

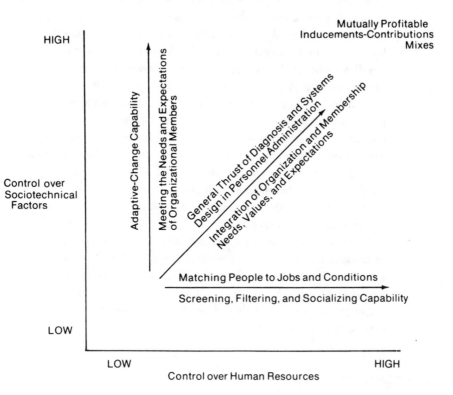

to focus on formal extrinsic incentives (wages and fringe benefits) and more attention should be given to informal intrinsic incentives and disincentives (social and psychological aspects) of specific tasks.

Second, personnel specialists have a continuing role in the design of systems to attract, select, and place employees who are most likely to perform satisfactorily and respond favorably to organizational inducements. Contemporary personnel administration is far more advanced in its capacity to screen and place employees on the basis of technical qualifications than it is in predicting responses to the social and psychological climates of organizations and their subunits.

Third, personnel administrators can take the lead in developing methods of monitoring relationships between employees and the organization. It has been proposed that supervisors conduct regular "audits" of employee perceptions and needs in order to detect and eliminate job-related dissatisfactions which can lower productivity and morale.[79] Such audits could aid management by pinpointing problems caused by working conditions and by identifying performance gaps attributable to the incentives structure of the organization.[80] The efficacy of incentives could be evaluated in the light of the motivational profiles of different groups of employees. Feedback obtained through such studies would provide a basis for the planning and execution of more effective policies.

Fourth, building on this diagnostic capability, personnel administrators can follow up by suggesting and helping carry out needed changes in the social and technical characteristics of organizations. This is essentially a systems design function. Trained personnel specialists could work with management to manipulate sociotechnical variables which are to some degree subject to administrative control with the objective of creating working conditions conducive to employee productivity.

Purposeful interventions are possible in these and other areas of organizational life. In sum, organizations are far from helpless or unchangeable. Given understanding, a willingness to experiment and change, and the necessary skills and resources, the ability of organizations to exploit the talents and energies of their members can be greatly enhanced.

BIBLIOGRAPHY

Blanchard, K., and Johnson, Spencer. *The One-Minute Manager*. New York: Morrow, 1982.

Glaser, Edward M. *Productivity Gains Through Worklife Improvements*. New York: Harcourt Brace Jovanovich, 1976.

Hackmon, J. Richard. "Is Job Enrichment Just a Fad?" *Harvard Business Review* 53 (September–October 1975).

Jung, John. *Understanding Human Motivation*. New York: MacMillan, 1978.

Kerr, Steven. "On the Folly of Rewarding A, While Hoping for B." *Academy of Management Journal* 18 (December 1975).

Lawler, Edward E., III, and Olson, Raymond N. "Designing Reward Systems for New Organizations." *Personnel* 54 (September–October 1977).

---

[79]Rensis Likert, "Measuring Organizational Performance," *Harvard Business Review* 36, no. 2 (March–April 1958): 41–49.

[80]Gerald Zaltman, Robert Duncan, and Jonny Holbek, *Innovations and Organizations* (New York: Wiley, 1973), pp. 2–3, 55.

National Center for Productivity and Quality of Working Life. *Employee Attitudes and Productivity Differences Between the Public and Private Sector*. Washington, D.C.: U. S. Civil Service Commission, 1978.

Peters, Thomas J., and Waterman, Robert H. *In Search of Excellence*. New York: Harper & Row, 1982.

Schein, Edgar. *Organizational Psychology*, 3d ed. Englewood Cliffs, N.J.: Prentice-Hall, 1980.

Steers, Richard M., and Mowday, Richard T. "The Motivational Properties of Tasks." *Academy of Management Review* 20 (October 1977).

Wahba, Mahmoud, and Bridwell, Lawrence. "Maslow Reconsidered: A Review of Research on the Need Hierarchy Theory." *Organizational Behavior and Human Performance* (April 1976).

4 The Career Concept

The role of career is vital in anyone's life because it connotes advancement and therefore success. Beyond the two words, "advancement" and "success," there is, however, much disagreement as to what constitutes a career system.

To some people, the most important characteristic of a career system is that it protect the employee's interests and tenure in his or her job. In its most extreme form, this means guaranteeing lifetime employment. More commonly, it means making promotion and other personnel decisions on the basis of seniority, and protecting the job holder in any one administrative unit from competition for advancement by "outsiders"—persons not employed by the governmental jurisdiction or, if so employed, holding positions in other administrative units. Of course, it also entails providing appeal rights that protect the employee from arbitrary disciplinary action by management but may make it very difficult to dismiss the employee for incompetence or misconduct.

Another concept of career is elitist, namely, that the best opportunities should be reserved for persons best prepared in terms of social background and/or education or of mental capacity and suitability as measured by some scheme developed by the employer. Elitist-based career systems either prevent persons lacking certain backgrounds or characteristics from competing for entrance into the civil service or from competing effectively for promotion to the higher posts.

To elective officials and the public, the mark of a true career service is responsiveness to the wishes of political leaders and the electorate. A widely held view is that career employees are not sufficiently responsive and that this is one of the worst features of civil service or merit systems. On the other hand, career officials maintain that all too often what political leaders mean by respon-

siveness is taking orders and not asking questions or making comments—in other words, the suppression of dissent.

Increasingly, management in government is devoting attention
to the development of special personnel systems for executives that
seek to spur performance by providing bonuses and other advantages not enjoyed by employees under the regular civil service
system. In return for these advantages, management gains greater
flexibility in moving the executive from job to job. Because of the
importance of the top executive jobs, career management for
higher executives is being stressed.

At the same time, upward mobility for employees in the lower
ranks is being emphasized. These employees are often locked into
"dead-end jobs" with no opportunity for advancement. In upward
mobility plans, organizations are restructured, jobs redesigned, career ladders established, and employees trained to fill the promotional positions so created. As only one example, in public
hospitals attendants are prepared to become laboratory technicians
and practical nurses to become registered nurses.

With these observations as a beginning, let us now turn to a
comparison of the British and United States civil service systems
with respect to career service. This comparison will show how in
both countries social structure and tradition have influenced concepts of governmental employment and advancement and how
greatly increased demands for public services have caused each
nation to reappraise its personnel practices and to make substantial
changes.

■ COMPARISON OF BRITISH AND AMERICAN SYSTEMS

In 1968, the British government, headed by Prime Minister Harold Wilson for the Labour Party, published the findings and recommendations of the Fulton Committee which had been
established to make a thoroughgoing reexamination of the British
civil service.[1] Wilson, whose training was as an economist and who
earlier had been employed in that capacity in the British government, had long been critical of the dominant role played by the
small elitist group at the top of the civil service known as the
administrative class. He believed it had a strong upper-class bias

---

[1]See *The Civil Service, Vol. 1, Report of the Committee 1966–68, Chairman Lord
Fulton* (London: Her Majesty's Stationery Office, Cmnd. 3368, June 1968).

and denied opportunities for persons with specialist training like economics to participate in shaping governmental policies. The most important recommendations of the Fulton Committee have not been implemented, but its report should be very useful to persons in other countries desirous of clarifying their thinking about how career systems should be structured. By structure of the civil service, we mean the arrangement of positions, the lines of promotion, and the policies governing movements from positions of lower to positions of higher responsibility. It is this structure that determines an employee's career opportunities; it can provide or deny such opportunities.

The Fulton Committee found that in Britain the structure of the civil service still reflected basically the same assumptions as those in a document prepared more than a century before—namely, the Northcote-Trevelyan report of 1854[2] which had led to the introduction of civil service in about 1870. Northcote and Trevelyan recommended a division of the service into intellectual and routine work: university graduates to be recruited for the former and nongraduates for the latter. They particularly had in mind filling the top administrative posts with the best products of the universities. The "routine" work was to be performed by persons of lesser education, and thus the tradition was established of recruiting persons with designated levels of education for beginning positions in the higher or lower civil service.

In later years, as the British government took on new functions, a greater variety of positions was created but always in conformance with the thinking of Northcote and Trevelyan. After World War I, the following classes of positions in descending order of importance were established: administrative, executive, and clerical. University graduates were recruited for the first, those who had completed secondary schools for the second, and those with a lower level of education for the third. When it became necessary to employ large numbers of specialists (scientists, engineers, architects, medical doctors, lawyers, and other professional workers), the same principle was followed of dividing each occupational group into higher and lower classes, for example in the case of scientists, scientific officer, experimental officer, and scientific assistant.

Since the background and preparation of the person were the

---

[2]Reprinted in *Public Administration* 32 (Spring 1954): 1–16.

guiding considerations in developing the class structure, that precise art known as position classification was not practiced. Under
position classification, duties and responsibilities are carefully analyzed, and only those jobs that are considered approximately equal
in duties and responsibilities are placed in the same class; there
is no greater heresy than placing unequal jobs in the same classes.
Such reasoning was farthest from the minds of Northcote and Trevelyan; indeed, in Western Europe the principle generally followed
has been classification according to rank or status of the person,
rather than detailed job analysis and ranking of positions according
to complexity of duties and level of responsibilities. In some cases,
the British placed members of the same occupation in different
classes, and they saw nothing wrong in sometimes giving the same
duties and responsibilities to employees in the lower and upper
levels of the *same* class.

But what disturbed the Fulton Committee more than anything
else was that careers in Britain were for the most part limited to
positions in the same class. If one started in one class, he or she
likely could obtain promotion only in that class. This was illogical
because, as just stated, not all positions in the same occupation
were placed in the same class and also because being employed
in one kind of work did not mean that one might not be qualified
for a different kind of work. Thus, if one were not a member of
the administrative class, there was very little opportunity to climb
to the top policymaking posts.

As a result, scientists and other persons with specialized professional training—often referred to as "subject matter" specialists in
the United States—had a very limited role in the British government no matter what their ability to serve in the policymaking
posts. The British had developed a cult of the all-rounder, someone
who does not concentrate in any one substantive area of government (e.g., housing, agriculture, labor), or, for that matter, in the
task of administration itself. British ministries were organized in
parallel hierarchies, one "administrative" and the other "specialist." For example, in a motorway construction organization, there
was an administrative division staffed with members of the administrative and executive classes, and a specialist division employing
engineers and other specialists. These two hierarchies were so separate that when representatives of each met together the confer-
ences were more like those between different agencies than
between members of the same organization. Although the spe-

cialists prepared the detailed project plans for the motorways, the decisions on routes, costs, contracts, and expenditures were made by the administrative division. The specialists questioned the ability of the "amateurs" in the administrative posts to make these decisions, and they resented being denied the opportunity to participate in policy decisions and to have access to the minister.[3] The Fulton Committee also found that upward movement *within* classes was too restricted. For example, although many promotions from the executive to the administrative class had been made during and after World War II, very few such promotions were presently taking place, contributing to the view of the administrative class as closed and undemocratic. Late entry (appointment of persons outside the civil service to the middle and top grades of a class) was uncommon, and there was very little movement of civil servants into commerce and other employments. Most civil servants spent their entire working lives in the civil service and subsequently had "little direct and systematic experience of the daily life and thought of other people."[4]

The entire service was still based on the "cult of the generalist" or "all-rounder" for the "great majority of recruits to the Administrative Class had taken their degrees in arts or humanities . . . mainly in history or classics."[5] Northcote and Trevelyan had argued that it was a much wiser policy to recruit young persons with first-class minds directly from the universities rather than individuals who had tried private employment and gained some work experience. Unlike the sponsors of the Pendleton Act in the United States, they did not believe in "practical" tests for public employment. Actually, by their time the amateur tradition had been firmly established in English life[6]; they simply applied it to a new scheme of competitive recruitment for the public service. The trouble, in Fulton's view, was that while society was now much more complex, the amateur approach persisted. In its extreme form, the civil servants felt themselves demeaned if they devel-

[3]*The Civil Service, Vol. 2, Report of a Management Consulting Group, Evidence Submitted to the Committee under the Chairmanship of Lord Fulton, 1966–68* (London: Her Majesty's Stationery Office, 1968), pp. 56–59, pp. 104–110.

[4]*The Civil Service, Vol. 1*, p. 12.

[5]Peter Kellner and Lord Crowther-Hunt, *The Civil Servants: An Inquiry into Britain's Ruling Class* (London: Macdonald and Jane's, 1980), p. 38. See also Lord Crowther-Hunt, "Mandarins and Ministers," *Parliamentary Affairs* 33, no. 4 (Autumn 1980): 373–399.

[6]See Ernest Barker, *The Development of Public Services in Western Europe, 1660–1930* (Hamden, Conn.: Archon Books, 1966), p. 32.

oped very detailed knowledge about a particular subject; indeed, they had to exercise care in this respect, for, if they showed such inclinations, they might be denied promotion. To be "promotable" one had to transfer frequently (every two or three years) to new posts in order to develop the knowledge of the government machine that is valued by superior officers.

Fulton's verdict was that by and large members of the administrative class did not have a proper conception of their responsibilities in the modern state which provides so many specialized services to its citizens. Not only did they fail to develop knowledge in depth of the programs to which they were assigned, but they were mostly interested in being "advisers on policy matters to people above them rather than in managing the administrative machine below them."[7] The work of administration was mostly assigned to members of the executive class; they were the managers of regional and local offices, and they generally were in charge of government accounting, negotiation and management of contacts, automatic data processing, organization and methods work, and departmental training. The responsibilities of government had grown so much that the top administrative positions required people who could manage very large blocks of work, who were administrators rather than advisers. The all-rounder approach had deemphasized specialized training in management, and there was very little such training for members of both the administrative and executive classes.

Fulton's Recommendations

Among Fulton's principal recommendations were the following:

1. The abolition of the multitude of classes and separate career structures and, on the basis of job analysis, fitting all jobs into a number of grades, each grade to have its own pay range. (This process was referred to by Fulton as "unified grading.")
2. Every qualified employee to be considered for every opening, regardless of their points of entry into the service.
3. Much more emphasis on personnel management and career planning for all employees.
4. Training for recruits in administrative work both in substan-

---

[7]*The Civil Service*, Vol. 2, p. 86.

tive activities of government, such as housing, education, social security, and in techniques of management, and
management training for specialists; also creation of a civil
service college to provide the training.
5. Considerable expansion of late entry.
6. More movement into and out of the civil service.

These recommendations were accepted by Wilson and his cabinet, and Wilson sought implementation without undue delay. The
most important recommendation was for unified grading, for without it specialists would continue to be kept in a subordinate role
and there would be no "open road" to the top of the civil service.
This would remain the virtually exclusive province of direct entrants with generalist backgrounds—predominantly graduates of
Oxford and Cambridge.

In January 1972 unified grading was adopted for about 800 positions at the top of the civil service, including the undersecretary
level, but since then it has not been extended to positions below
that level, nor does there appear to be any realistic prospect that
it will be. Unified grading, along with discarding the concept of a
generalist or all-rounder background as the best preparation for
administrators, has been defeated by an alliance of two strong
forces—key generalist administrators in the civil service and two
staff associations, the Society of Civil and Public Servants and the
First Division Association.

As Lord Crowther-Hunt, who served on the Fulton Committee,
recounts in detail in his jointly-authored book with Peter Kellner,
it was to members of the administrative elite that implementation
of the Fulton reforms was entrusted.[8] Even before Wilson's Labour
government was turned out, these officials opposed as "impracti-
cal" extension of unified grading to all levels of the service. They
saw complete unified grading for what it was—an end to the dom-
inance of the generalist. The Society of Civil and Public Servants
represented those in the executive grades (below the administrative class). While it favored expanded opportunity for promotion
of its members to the administrative class, like the First Division
Association which represented the generalist administrators, it
knew that unified grading would enable specialists to compete effectively for jobs in the executive and administrative lines of
progression.

---

[8]Kellner and Lord Crowther-Hunt, *The Civil Servants*, Chapter 4.

The former classes have been abolished and replaced by groups; for example, the administrative, executive, and clerical classes have been merged into a new administrative group. According to Hunt and Kellner, and other British authorities, this has been a cosmetic change only because the "Civil Service has remained a jumble of different categories of people with different pay structures, different career prospects, and *few chances to escape from the group each one belongs to.*"[9] (Italics ours) Even in the posts to which unified grading has been applied, specialists normally are placed only in administrative positions in their own disciplines or professions, for example, an economist as Director General of Economies and Resources. Very few are found in policy-making positions outside their specialties.[10] Fulton's recommendation was to integrate specialists and generalists and to assign both to administrative posts. The only change that was made was to permit more specialists to hold administrative jobs in the top grades. While the administrative class was abolished, this has been for title purposes only, and the "running of policy divisions is still almost exclusively the preserve of civil servants who have climbed the administrative, and therefore generalist ladder."[11]

Fulton intended that the composition of the administrative class substantially be changed by opening it to many more university graduates with course concentrations in subjects "relevant" to the problems of contemporary British government. In Great Britain the university output now is very different from what it was in the times of Northcote and Trevelyan and subsequent years. Most graduates are from the newer universities, and they do not concentrate on the arts and humanities. Before the Fulton recommendations, Oxbridge graduates (Oxford and Cambridge) held a high percentage of the positions in the administrative class. Fulton believed that in the recruitment of administrative recruits an important qualification should be university training in "relevant subjects," such as engineering, economics, and the social sciences. This preference for "relevance" was rejected by the government even before Harold Wilson lost office, and a disproportionate number of those successful in the competition for administration trainee still consists of Oxbridge graduates.[12] For example, "among appli-

---

[9]Ibid., p. 62.
[10]Ibid., p. 84.
[11]Ibid.
[12]Ibid., p. 121.

cants for entry . . . in 1979, 60 percent of successful candidates were Oxbridge, 24 percent of all candidates sitting the entrance examination were Oxbridge, and [only] 8 percent of all students were at Oxford or Cambridge. . . . Among successful 1979 candidates, 62 percent studied arts subjects, 30 percent a variety of social science courses, and 7 percent science and technology."[13]

Applicants for administration trainee positions must pass a qualifying written test and then survive the Civil Service Selection Board procedure, which consists of group discussions, written exercises, and individual interviews by assessors serving the Board. It should be pointed out that internal candidates with at least two years of experience in the civil service are eligible to compete for administration trainee positions along with university graduates. The assessors reach a consensus on which participants have qualified for going on to the final step in the selection process—an individual interview before the members of the Final Selection Board (it consists of representatives of the Civil Service Commission, the senior civil service, and an academic and an industrial or trade union official). The Board usually approves the marks given the applicants by the assessors.

While the assessors endeavor to safeguard against any personal bias in their rating of the candidates, the exercises and interviews administered are admittedly subjective, and critics of the entire process maintain that the assessors tend to view favorably persons like themselves. According to Hunt and Kellner, "Since most assessors are themselves past products of similar recruitment exercises, it would scarcely be surprising if they seek to recruit in their own image. To do otherwise would be to confess that the Civil Service might have been wrong to choose persons like themselves in the past."[14]

Two years after appointment, the administration trainees are evaluated on their performance and divided into a *fast* stream and a *main* stream. Those placed in the fast stream receive special training and are promoted more rapidly up the administrative hierarchy than those in the main stream. The critics say that the senior civil servants who decide in which of the two streams to place someone are by background also biased in favor of all-roun-

---

[13]Richard Rose, "The Political Status of Higher Civil Servants in Britain," February 1981, a paper prepared for a conference organized by the Centro de Investigaciones Sociologicas, Madrid, 15–18, December 1980, p. 10.

[14]Kellner and Lord Crowther-Hunt, *The Civil Servants*, pp. 136–137.

ders. Whatever the truth of this allegation, the reality is that most of those who move up in higher civil service are basically the same types as in the former administrative class.

The considerable increase in lateral entry that Fulton desired has not materialized, because the very small number of persons hired from outside the civil service for positions in grades above the entry level has not increased. Furthermore, the movement Fulton desired into and out of the civil service has not taken place. As Richard Rose writes, "There is virtually no mid-career movement from the civil service to nationalized industries, public corporations or local authorities or the health service and mid-career movement into the private sector is also slight."[15]

The Civil Service College still functions and is acknowledged to perform a useful training function but on a modest scale. During the first years after the Fulton report, there was an appreciable increase in management training throughout the British service, but in recent years budgetary cutbacks have reduced this training effort.

The purpose of this account of the Fulton Committee report, its recommendations, and the failure to put the major ones into effect has not, of course, been to expose the failures of the British. Fulton acknowledged that the British civil service has a distinguished past record, and personnel reform proposals have failed of implementation in the United States and in other countries. The objective rather has been to examine Britain's recent experiences in the light of conceptions of what constitutes a true career service.[16] If the essential element of such a service is an "open road to the top," it still does not exist in Britain.

■ AMERICAN EFFORTS TOWARD CAREER SERVICE

Although in passing the Pendleton Act in 1883 Congress modeled the new United States civil service system on that of the British, it rejected the division into higher and lower classes of work and did not tie in recruitment with educational attainment the way the British did. The importance of education was recognized, but Americans did not believe that the top administrative posts nec-

---

[15]Rose, "The Political Status of Higher Civil Servants in Britain," p. 15.

[16]See Felix A. Nigro, "What Has Happened to Fulton?" *Public Administration Review* 33, no. 2 (March–April 1973), and Anthony Sampson, *The Changing Anatomy of Britain* (New York: Random House, 1982). Chapter 10.

essarily were best filled by persons originally recruited directly from the universities. Everybody should have the chance to enter the public service no matter what the person's age, schooling, and other characteristics.

When Senator Pendleton introduced his bill, it contained a provision limiting outside recruitment to the lowest grade. This was so repugnant to the Senate that Pendleton proposed an amendment to delete, which was "accepted without even the formality of a roll call."[17] The British principle of appointment through competitive examinations was endorsed, but the idea of a closed service with entrance limited to the bottom rungs of career ladders was rejected.

At all levels of government in this country, there has always been a great deal of lateral entry to the intermediate and top grades, and maximum age limits have been very high or nonexistent. There also has been much movement between government and private employment in line with the country's history of mobility and its respect for the freedom of individuals to prove their ability to any employer. So much lateral entry, however, raised the question of how the career concept could be implanted in government if many employees did not spend all or the major part of their lives in the public employ. It was suggested that for many government employment was a mere episode, not a career.

Besides questioning the constant shuttling in and out of public service, there was much concern about the prevailing practice in government of recruiting for specific jobs rather than providing for a progression of increasingly more responsible positions. The Pendleton Act had set this precedent by its emphasis on "practical tests," which was fully in line with American pragmatism. There has always been flexibility in this pragmatism, however, and the sentiment for recruitment for careers, not individual jobs, gained support as the need to attract talent to the public service became evident.

With the advent of the New Deal in the 1930s, the times became more favorable for the career idea. Large numbers of college graduates were employed in the new agencies and programs, and the challenge of government employment grew throughout the nation. In 1935 the report of the Commission of Inquiry on Public Service

---

[17]Paul P. Van Riper, *History of the United States Civil Service* (New York: Harper & Row, 1958), p. 100.

Personnel was published. This commission, which held public hearings in various parts of the country, compiled voluminous testimony about poor personnel practices in government. It recommended that the public service, instead of being "minutely classified into pigeon holes, for which the civil service commission tries to find men who exactly fit each compartment," be divided into career ladders for which "young men are normally selected to start on the bottom rung." These ladders would "rise from different points depending upon the kinds of service" with "opportunity . . . provided for advance at different rates of speed and for transfer from one ladder to another."[18]

Although the commission recommended normal entrance to the bottom rungs, it did not propose a British-style closed service, since transfers between career ladders were to be encouraged, and both upward and horizontal mobility were to be guaranteed. Like many other Americans, its members were concerned that young people were not being attracted to public service as they were in Britain.

Prior to the New Deal, college graduates in professional fields such as agriculture, geology, engineering, and forestry had been entering government and making careers for themselves, but the public service generally was not promoting the career concept and making positive efforts to attract college students. Many Americans were impressed by the British administrative class because it reserved the administrative posts for college graduates and offered them the possibility of rising to the top career position, that of permanent undersecretary.

In the American public service, engineers, scientists, and other specialists usually obtained the administrative posts, but their preparation and outlook were considered too narrow. It was not argued that they should be denied the opportunity to compete for such posts, as in Britain. The concern was that the requirements of the administrative function as such were not being stressed, and management training programs for specialists or anyone else generally did not exist.

Teachers of government were generally unable to indicate to students any possibilities for administrative careers in government, and they were among the most anxious that such career patterns

---

[18]Commission of Inquiry on Public Service Personnel, *Better Government Personnel* (New York: McGraw-Hill, 1935), pp. 4–5, pp. 27–28.

be established. Increasingly, the need for generalists was being recognized, but in this context the term "generalists" did not mean all-rounders as described in the Fulton report. Syracuse University and a few other learning institutions pioneered with public administration programs, but the graduates of these programs were primarily employed in housekeeping staff services such as personnel and finance. Actually, these are management specialties, so generalist could be considered a misnomer in this sense. Nevertheless, these students were not graduates of the engineering, architectural, forestry, and other professional schools which had been supplying trained personnel for government. Universities also began to offer programs to broaden the outlook of graduates of these professional schools who had been promoted to administrative posts. Here the purpose (often stated) was to convert specialists into generalists, but again the intention was not to make them all-rounders. As the reader can readily see, much caution should be exercised with the use of the two words, "generalist" and "specialist."

The more recent period

Efforts by the United States Civil Service Commission to provide a clear route in government for college students were climaxed in 1955 by introduction of the Federal Service Entrance Examination, replaced in 1975 by a similar examination, the Professional and Administrative Career Examination (PACE). Thousands of positions were filled annually through PACE, which was open to all college majors except engineers, physicians, chemists, accountants, and a few other technicians. Practically all entrance level professional, administrative, and technical positions were filled through PACE and other competitions.

However, in the spring of 1982, the Office of Personnel Management terminated PACE, maintaining that this was the only action it could take because of the terms of a consent decree entered into by the Carter administration just before it left office. This court decree, discussed in detail in Chapter 10, settled a class action suit by minority group representatives charging that the questions in PACE failed to measure accurately ability for the job and that there was considerable adverse, discriminatory impact on black and Hispanic applicants.[19] Jobs formerly filled by PACE have

---

[19]See Senate Committee on the Judiciary, *P.A.C.E. Consent Decree: Equal Pro-*

been removed from the competitive service and are now filled through various alternative means not requiring competitive written examination.

Leading figures in public administration are bitterly critical of the consent decree and/or of OPM's decision to abolish PACE without continuing efforts to develop substitute examinations that could be acceptable under the decree. Former Civil Service Commission Chairman John W. Macy, Jr. put it simply, "How can we possibly have a career service if we don't have a professional entry test for college graduates?"[20] While it is true that because of budgetary reductions, the number of appointments made from PACE had dropped greatly, at least the entrance door for graduating college students remained partly open. With the end of PACE, it was slammed shut except for the technical jobs mentioned above not filled through that examination.

In 1978 the Carter administration started a presidential management internship program which has been continued by the Reagan administration. Under this program, 250 graduate degree holders in public management are appointed annually to two-year developmental internships, principally in federal agencies but also in state and local governments. Those who successfully complete their internships in federal agencies may be granted career service positions, a positive approach to attracting to the federal service capable young persons trained in public management. Of course, the limited number of internships provided under this program far from compensates for the loss of PACE from whose registers as many as 10,000 appointments were made annually in the 1970s.

Training programs for both new and existing employees are important, for career progress, and although the federal government had previously not accepted responsibility for providing such training, in 1958 it did so with passage of the Government Employees Training Act of 1958. Before 1958, personnel officers themselves sometimes told employees that they should "pay for their own training." President Lyndon Johnson's Executive Order 11348 of April 1967 increased the government's training commitment, for it required agencies to review *each* employee's training needs pe-

tection Issues, 97th Congress, 1st Session (Washington, D.C.: Government Printing Office, 1981).

[20]See Bernard Rosen, "A Disaster for Merit," *The Bureaucrat* 11, no. 4 (Winter 1982–83), and Chester Newland, "A Mid-term Appraisal—The Reagan Presidency, Limited Government and Political Administration," *Public Administration Review* 43, no. 1 (January–February 1983).

riodically in relation to career objectives. Considering the very large number of federal employees, this was a massive undertaking, as was a provision in the Equal Employment Opportunity Act of 1972 requiring the agencies to establish training and education programs for facilitating upward mobility of the thousands of employees in low-level jobs.

Before passage of the Civil Service Reform Act of 1978, a few agencies had good quality career development programs for executives, but many had not given high priority to such efforts. Title IV of the reform act requires the OPM to establish programs for the systematic development of senior executives, but the reductions in the OPM and agency budgets under the Reagan administration have held back progress in this training area.

With passage of the Intergovernmental Personnel Act of 1970 (IPA), the federal government began to provide financial aid and technical assistance to state and local governments for improving their training and other personnel activities. When this legislation was first considered in Congress, Senator Edmund S. Muskie said, "When we examined the potential of State and local governments to attract bright, young people for careers in public service, we found a discouraging picture. . . . Career development systems, including the chance for job mobility, in-service training, and promotions were minimal except in the larger jurisdictions."[21] This was in 1967; in 1962 the Municipal Manpower Commission had reported that "this country's local governments are doing little to develop the persons who must bear vital responsibilities."[22] These characterizations were for the country as a whole with its thousands of governmental units; there were jurisdictions which had made important progress in attracting college students to career service, but, in truth, as Muskie noted, they were and still are exceptions. Under the IPA, state and local governments receiving such assistance were able to improve training, examining, and other phases of their personnel programs, but because it believes the federal government should not intrude in such state and local matters these IPA grants have been terminated by the Reagan administration.

---

[21]Senate Subcommittee on Intergovernmental Relations, *Intergovernmental Personnel Act of 1967, Intergovernmental Manpower Act of 1967* (Washington, D.C.: Government Printing Office, 1967), p. 2.

[22]Municipal Manpower Commission, *Governmental Manpower for Tomorrow's Cities* (New York: McGraw-Hill, 1962), p. 73.

In recent years, civil service career system advocates in the United States have not recommended limiting entry to bottom rungs. Increasingly, in fact, the concept of careers has stressed mobility and lateral movement between levels of government and the private sector. It is recognized that provision for lateral entry in and of itself does not mean that government employment will be considered merely a temporary episode; it is pointed out that most federal government "professional and administrative personnel enter the system at a job level specified for recent college graduates or for those entering employment with higher degrees."[23] If career opportunities are provided in government, able young persons will be attracted to it and can be expected to spend much if not all of their lives in the public employ. Interestingly, there is concern in Britain that in terms of national needs its civil service may draw an unduly high proportion of young talent away from the private sector. This indicates the opposite danger—one not likely to occur in the United States.

■ THE QUESTION OF ELITES

Returning to the British and the Fulton report, let us consider the question of elites, mentioned at the beginning of this chapter but not yet discussed in detail.

Fulton believed that an important reason for the remoteness of the civil service from the community was the narrow social composition of the administrative class which predominantly was drawn from the higher social classes (measured by the father's occupation). A social survey of the civil service commissioned by the committee showed that, for the entire period since World War II, recruitment to the administrative class had *not* been from "a steadily widening social background."[24] A later inquiry (1969) into methods of selection for the administrative class found that candidates with lower social class backgrounds were "significantly less well represented among candidates than among the entire student population" and that the far greater representation of persons with middle class backgrounds was probably attributable to the "streaming influence of social and educational forces."[25]

---

[23]John W. Macy, Jr. *Public Service: The Human Side of Government* (New York: Harper & Row, 1970), p. 43.

[24]*The Civil Service*, Vol. 1, p. 12.

[25]*The Method II System of Selection, Report of the Committee of Inquiry, 1969* (London: Her Majesty's Stationery Office), p. 34, p. 82.

In his outstanding book, *Politics, Power, and Bureaucracy in France: The Administrative Elite*,[26] Ezra N. Suleiman emphasizes these same "streaming influences." Suleiman presents factual evidence showing that in Britain, France, Denmark, Germany, Spain, Turkey, India, and—despite its system of mass education—the United States, the higher civil service is composed mostly of persons with middle-class backgrounds who have had advantages not enjoyed by the general population.[27]

On their face, selection systems are objective because candidates take the same examination, but they do not enter the competition on an equal footing because of differing social backgrounds. Someone who has been able to go to Oxford or Cambridge, with their high quality education and long background in supplying recruits for administrative careers, has a definite advantage, just as those who have attended the "Big Three"—Harvard, Yale, and Princeton—stand a better chance of becoming assistant secretaries in U.S. federal agencies. On the background of the assistant secretaries, Suleiman refers to comprehensive research on 650 assistant secretaries who served in the administrations of F. D. Roosevelt, Truman, Eisenhower, and Kennedy.[28] Similar research on the backgrounds of a bigger sample of leading federal executives showed that they attended the best schools, and a study of over 10,000 federal executives revealed that "compared with the general population, most . . . come from the more highly placed occupational levels."[29] Suleiman's thesis is that what distinguishes administrative elites in Britain, the United States, and France is the quality of their education[30] and that "where occupational success depends on academic success it is also likely to depend on social origin."[31]

Of Britain, the United States, and France, administrative elitism is greatest in France because of its severely restricted educational system. Since 1945, when it was established, the Ecole Nationale d'Administration has supplied the members of the French higher

---

[26]Ezra N. Suleiman, *Politics, Power, and Bureaucracy in France: The Administrative Elite* (Princeton, N.J.: Princeton University Press, 1974).

[27]Ibid., p. 79.

[28]Dean E. Mann, *The Assistant Secretaries: Problems and Processes of Appointment* (Washington, D.C.: Brookings, 1965).

[29]David T. Stanley et al., *Men Who Govern* (Washington, D.C.: Brookings, 1967), and Lloyd Warner et al., *The American Federal Executive* (New Haven, Conn.: Yale University Press, 1963).

[30]Suleiman, *Politics, Power, and Bureaucracy in France*, p. 78.

[31]Ibid., p. 81.

civil service. Although the stated purpose of the reforms associated with creation of the ENA was to democratize and regionalize the higher civil service, it remains "strongly middle- and upper-middle class in composition."[32] The explanation is that no fundamental change was made in the French educational system.

Prior to 1945, the Ecole Libre des Sciences Politiques in Paris trained the administrative elite. Although the Ecole Libre was abolished and provincial Instituts d'Etudes Politiques established, it is the IEP in Paris that now supplies most of the entrants to the ENA. While the ENA also admits civil servants under 30 who have completed at least five years of service, the number of such persons enrolled is much smaller. Because they have full-time jobs, civil servants eligible for admission find it difficult to undergo the long preparation required for passing the entrance examination. The government "does not make adequate provision for them to prepare for the ENA examination, nor do these officials receive, on the whole, much encouragement from their peers or superiors."[33] Ann Stevens writes, "Recruitment to the ENA has been no more open to candidates from all sections of the country than has entrance to French universities, which have not achieved as wide a social-mix as have British universities."[34]

ENA graduates with the highest numerical ratings gain entry to the Grand Corps, which provides the best career opportunities. The system is so elitist that persons who miss the Grand Corps by one or two percentage points instead go into the Corps of Administrateurs Civils, which means resigning themselves "permanently to less prestigious and glorious careers."[35] There is no lateral entry and no promotion through the ranks. "The very idea of civil servants entering ENA by a special examination recognized the impossibility of climbing through the ranks. The reform closed all other avenues of promotion to the top and opened a path only to those who had overcome the most stringent academic requirements."[36]

If administrative elitism is based on ability, with all segments of society able effectively to compete for positions in the higher civil service, then the sole issue—but always a difficult one—would be

---

[32]Ibid., p. 55.
[33]Ibid., p. 62.
[34]Ann Stevens, "The Role of the Ecole Nationale d'Administration," *Public Administration* 56 (Autumn 1978): 287.
[35]Suleiman, *Politics, Power, and Bureaucracy in France*, p. 96.
[36]Ibid.

the accuracy of the measures of ability. The American tradition of egalitarianism has reduced "social and educational streaming" by comparison with many other countries, but some groups are more privileged than others, and this is reflected in the composition of the U.S. higher civil service. A high priority is more adequate representation of minority groups and women in the highest career posts.

■ THE CONCEPT OF A SENIOR EXECUTIVE SERVICE

If efforts to create and maintain a career service are to be successful, programs must be established for assuring the retention of able senior executives. For that reason, in recent years much attention has been given to the establishment of special personnel systems for executives. As mentioned in Chapter 1, the Civil Service Reform Act of 1978 provided for a Senior Executive Service (SES) in the federal government, and similar systems are functioning in several state governments.[37]

The rationale for having an SES is that traditional civil service systems lack the flexibility, reward systems, and other attributes essential for effective utilization of the services of senior officials, for providing them with the inducements that will make them want to continue their careers in the government, and for assuring their responsiveness to political direction.

In the case of the federal government, for long it had been recognized that it lacked an effective system for determining future needs for executives, providing career development plans for them, utilizing their services most advantageously, and rewarding them in proportion to the quality of their work. Comparison frequently was made with private companies that make substantial investments in career management programs for executives. The second Hoover Commission (Commission on Organization of the Executive Branch of the Government, 1955)[38] had recommended a senior civil service, a plan supported in general outline by President Eisenhower but not implemented because of opposition in Congress, and President Nixon's bill for a federal executive service

---

[37]See Arthur L. Finkle, "Senior Executive Service: The State of the Art," *Public Personnel Management* 10, no. 3 (Fall 1981).

[38]Commission on Organization of the Executive Branch of the Government, *Personnel and Civil Service* (Washington, D.C.: Government Printing Office, 1955), pp. 37–44.

failed of enactment by Congress.[39] Although these plans differed from the SES in some respects, the objective was the same: institute a sound, imaginative system for improving executive performance and thus the effectiveness of government programs.

"Sound" included assuring adherence of career executives to the directives of the administration in power and to the orders of the *noncareer* officials under whom they served. Career officials are appointed and hold their positions under the civil service system; noncareer officials are selected through political channels (e.g., by the President or an agency head), and they do not have the tenure of career officials. The very highest segment of federal noncareer officials, included for pay purposes in what is known as the Executive Schedule, consists of cabinet members, other agency heads, undersecretaries, assistant secretaries, bureau heads, members of boards and commissions, and similar officials at the top of an agency. Below them, in the highest ranks of the General Schedule, there is an intermingling of noncareer and career officials with no consistent pattern agency by agency as to which level and kinds of positions are noncareer and which career.[40]

While career officials heavily outnumber noncareer officials in the General Schedule, the number of noncareer positions is substantial and in recent decades has increased, dangerously so in the opinion of observers like James L. Sundquist, who writes, "Indeed, the so-called political level at the top of the government has been progressively extended over the past quarter century, both laterally and downward, in the process that has come to be called 'politicization' of the civil service."[41] During the Senate debate on the Civil Service Reform Act, Stevens of Alaska commented, "The desire of a new President to use a broom and sweep the office clean has always emerged—always."[42] Stevens and others believe recent administrations, both Democratic and Republican, have intensified politicization by indiscriminate "sweeping out" of holdover career officials suspected of political disloyalty to the new administration.[43]

---

[39]See "Documentation, The Federal Executive Service," *Public Administration Review* 31, no. 2 (March–April 1971): 235–252.

[40]See Hugh Heclo, *A Government of Strangers: Executive Politics in Washington* (Washington, D.C.: Brookings, 1977), pp. 36–41.

[41]James L. Sundquist, "Jimmy Carter as Public Administrator: An Appraisal at Midterm," *Public Administration Review* 39, no. 1 (January–February 1979): 7.

[42]*Congressional Record*, August 24, 1978, SI 4274.

[43]Heclo, *A Government of Strangers*, pp. 71–81.

Certainly, there is much distrust between career and noncareer officials, as documented in Hugh Heclo's book, *A Government of Strangers: Executive Politics in Washington*. Heclo states that career officials' "power does not typically derive from refusing to do what their superiors want," but rather from "withholding positive help." This "bureaucratic veto," writes Heclo, "is a pervasive constant of government, for without higher civil service support almost nothing sought by political executives is likely to take effect."[44]

During his presidential campaign Carter said, "The greatest need facing the United States today is for a well-managed structure of government—one that is simple, efficient, and economical."[45] His interest in sound management could be expected to make him support such a managerial reform as a senior executive service. But he had also made many statements critical of Washington and the "bureaucracy." Watergate and the record of the Nixon administration in subverting the civil service system were very recent events. Thus, it was not surprising that when Carter proposed the SES there was much fear of "more politicization."

The Senior Executive Service as Enacted by Congress

As enacted by Congress, which made certain amendments to Carter's bill as originally submitted to Congress, the principal features of the SES are:

(1) It includes all managers above GS-15 and below Level III of the Executive Schedule, a total of about 7,000. There are two categories of SES positions: *career-reserved* and *general*. Career-reserved positions may be held only by career officials; general positions may be occupied by career or noncareer executives. No more than 10 percent of SES positions may be held by noncareer executives, and the number of career-reserved positions may not be less than the number of SES positions which at the time of passage of the legislation were in GS 16–18 and were filled by competitive selection. These restrictions on the numbers and placement of noncareer executives are intended to protect against further politicization.

(2) Those in SES positions when the legislation was passed could choose whether or not to become SES members; if they decided

[44]Ibid., p. 172.
[45]*Congressional Record*, August 24, 1978, SI 4278–9.

to do so, no review of their qualifications was necessary. Future candidates for SES positions would have to undergo qualifications review in accordance with OPM regulations.

Under these regulations, each agency establishes the qualification standards for its SES positions and appoints an executive resource board made up of agency employees to recruit and evaluate SES candidates. OPM evaluates the managerial qualifications of candidates, utilizing for this purpose qualification review boards the majority of whose members must consist of career managers.

(3) SES executives are untenured and if they receive one unsatisfactory performance rating they must be transferred to another SES position or be removed from the SES. They must be removed from the SES if they receive two unsatisfactory performance ratings within a five-year period or two less than fully satisfactory ratings within three years. However, if removed they are guaranteed placement in a continuing career position equivalent to at least a GS-15. There is no appeal right except for an informal hearing before an official designated by the Merit Systems Protection Board but MSPB is not authorized to overrule the removal action.

(4) Intended to compensate for the lack of tenure, SES members have much better salary possibilities than those under the regular civil service system. Rank is in the person, not the position, and agency heads may pay any salary within a very broad pay band, extending from the lowest rate for GS-16 to the rate for Executive Level V, the rate at which pay has been capped by Congress far below the salaries paid executives in the private sector. Provision is made for performance awards (bonuses) of up to 20 percent of base salary and also for extra pay for those given the honorary rank of meritorious executive or distinguished executive. Originally, bonuses could be given to 50 percent of eligible executives, but Congress, because of what it believed to be abuses, quickly reduced this to 25 percent and OPM then to 20 percent.

(5) SES executives may be moved by their superiors from position to position within their agencies and may appeal such reassignments to the Merit Systems Protection Board only on grounds that the transfer was ordered for discriminatory reasons, such as punishment for "whistle blowing."

(6) Agencies are required to establish SES candidate development programs, as well as to provide further management training for SES members.

Experience with the SES has now been sufficiently long to make conclusions as to whether it has succeeded or failed, and in what respects. More than 98.5 percent of the 7,000 eligible executives did elect to join. Apparently, many had decided that the SES as finally legislated did not present the risks they feared, but it was also true that someone electing to stay out of the SES damaged his or her prospects for advancement because all executive positions filled in the future were to be in SES.

Considering the opinions of SES members themselves, there is strong evidence that they think the SES has failed to fulfill its major objectives. A survey of 300 career executives made by the Federal Executive Institute Alumni Association showed that 44 percent believed the SES had had a negative effect on improving government operations, 40 percent that it had had no effect, and only 16 percent that it had had a favorable effect. Only 20 percent considered that the SES candidate development programs were working well, 34 percent believed they were not working well, and 46 percent ventured no opinion. A report published in September 1981 by the Merit Systems Protection Board showed that 45 percent of the respondents to a questionnaire survey of 979 career executives believed that bonuses were given to management favorites, rather than being based on merit.[46] A two-year study by researchers Peter Smith Ring and James L. Perry, based on questionnaire responses by employees in grade levels 13 and above in five federal agencies, concluded that "virtually none of the major objectives of the architects of the SES are being perceived as met."[47]

A survey by the Department of Health and Human Services of its SES members reports more favorable findings, for example, that 68 percent of the respondents said they would join the SES again, but 38 percent said the SES had made it less likely that executives would express their real views.[48] In late 1983, the General Accounting Office reported that despite certain problems the SES was making progress in achieving its goals. The GAO said agencies had greater flexibility in utilizing their executive resources, management operations were being improved, it was easier to deal

---

[46]Rosen, "A Disaster for Merit," 11.

[47]Peter Smith Ring and James L. Perry, *Reforming the Upper Levels of the Bureaucracy: A Longitudinal Study of the Senior Executive Service* (Irvine, Calif.: Graduate School of Management, University of California, August 1982).

[48]House Subcommittee on Post Office and Civil Service, *Civil Service Oversight*, 98th Congress, 1st Session (Washington, D.C.: Government Printing Office, 1983), p. 527.

with ineffective managers, and greater emphasis was being placed on executive development programs. The two principal difficulties were the continuation of the legislative pay cap on executive salaries and the discontent over the reduction in the number of SES members eligible for bonuses. As to political manipulation, the GAO found most of these charges unsubstantiated and that there had been no systematic abuse of the authority to transfer SES members to different positions and geographical locations.[49]

In evaluating the SES, a distinction must be made between inherent defects in its underlying theory and conditions in government not attributable to SES that have lowered the morale of federal workers. Continuation of the pay cap is an important, perhaps the most important, part of this external situation. When maximum executive salaries are increased very little over a long period of years during which the cost of living has gone up greatly, it is understandable why the SES, based largely on financial incentives, should lack credibility with its intended beneficiaries. If career executives believe that the quality of those in political policy-making positions from whom they receive direction has declined—as many do so believe—this is another reason for the lack of confidence in the ability of an SES to improve government operations. Furthermore, while the GAO may be correct that there is no systematic abuse of the discretion given department heads, as the Health and Human Services survey demonstrates, there can be an inhibiting effect on exercise of the right career officials consider so essential to their role in government—to express frank opinions to their political superiors.

Certain assumptions about SES were made by its supporters that were much too optimistic, and others were made the soundness of which can be questioned. The optimism was in believing—or hoping—that conditions external to SES would not damage its chances to be successful. Pay, for example, was not even dealt with in the Civil Service Reform Act, and the possibility, some would say likelihood, that leading political figures, including Presidents, would continue to make disparaging statements about the "bureaucrats" and lower their morale was brushed aside in the enthusiasm for obtaining some legislation on civil service reform.

---

[49]*Summary Statement of Charles A. Bowsher, Comptroller General of the United States before the House Subcommittee on Post Office and Civil Service on An Assessment of the Impact of the Senior Executive Service* (Washington, D.C.: General Accounting Office, November 7, 1983).

As to the theoretical foundations of SES, the research of Ring and Perry shows that, while the pay cap is of great concern to SES members, many do not place the importance on financial incentives considered so enticing by the authors of the Reform Act. As commented on in Chapter 1, because of the element of politics the governmental environment is different from that of business and this political element makes risky the adoption of some of the flexible personnel practices of the private sector. Certainly, the federal SES has been a valuable experiment, and there are sound features of SES plans in government, such as rank in the person, mobility of executives, and special incentives for executives, subject to safeguards against political manipulation.

BIBLIOGRAPHY

America's Unelected Government: Appointing the President's Team. New York: Ballinger/Harper & Row, November 1983.

Finkle, Arthur. "Senior Executive Service: The State of the Art." *Public Personnel Management* 10, no. 3 (Fall 1981).

Heclo, Hugh. *A Government of Strangers: Executive Politics in Washington*. Washington, D.C.: Brookings, 1977.

Huddleston, Mark. "Foreign Systems, Familiar Refrains: Civil Service Reform in Comparative Perspective." *Review of Public Personnel Administration* 2, no. 2 (Spring 1982).

Kellner, Peter, and Lord Crowther-Hunt. *The Civil Servants: An Inquiry into Britain's Ruling Class*. London: Macdonald and James, 1980.

Nigro, Felix A. "Two Civil Service Systems: Alike Yet Different." *Good Government* 90, no. 2 (Summer 1973).

———. "Public Personnel Administration: From Theodore Roosevelt to Ronald Reagan." *International Journal of Public Administration* 6, no. 1 (March 1984).

Ridley, F. F. *The British Civil Service: Recruitment, Promotion, Remuneration, Politics*. University of Liverpool, Department of Political Theory and Institutions. Contains four reports prepared from 1980–1983.

Suleiman, Ezra N. *Politics, Power, and Bureaucracy in France: The Administrative Elite*. Princeton, N.J.: Princeton University Press, 1974.

The Civil Service, Vol. 1, Report of the Committee 1966–68,

Chairman: Lord Fulton. London: Her Majesty's Stationery Office, June 1968, CMND 3638.

Zimmerman, Virgil B. "Public Personnel Administration Outside the United States." In *Handbook on Public Personnel Administration and Labor Relations*, edited by Jack Rabin, Thomas Vocino, W. Bartley Hildreth, and Gerald J. Miller. New York: Dekker, 1983.

5 Collective Bargaining in Government

The first of these two chapters on collective bargaining describes its rapid development in the public service, provides a brief description of public employee organizations, and discusses peculiar features of the government environment and how they affect labor relations. Essentially, this chapter provides background material for Chapter 6 which describes collective bargaining systems in government and analyzes the impact of bilateralism on personnel policies and procedures. We use the terms "employee organization" and "union" synonymously because in common usage today "union" no longer refers only to private sector organizations of workers.

Collective bargaining is a "method of determining terms and conditions of employment by *negotiation* between representatives of the employer and union representatives of the employees. The results of the bargaining are set forth in a *collective bargaining agreement*. Collective bargaining, which determines terms and conditions of employment for all workers in a *bargaining unit,* is to be distinguished from individual bargaining, which applies to negotiations between a single employee and the employer."[1]

In the history of the United States, collective bargaining is relatively new. The first private sector unions emerged in the latter part of the 18th century and had to struggle with a hostile environment. Many courts considered unions criminal conspiracies, and it was not until 1842 that this "conspiracy doctrine was given a fatal blow." In that year, the Massachusetts Supreme Court "held

---

[1]Robert E. Doherty, *Industrial and Labor Relations Terms: A Glossary*, 4th ed. rev. (Ithaca, N.Y.: New York State School of Industrial and Labor Relations, Bulletin 44, 1979), p. 7.

that combinations of workers were not illegal per se, nor were their efforts to improve their condition, unless illegal means were used."[2] However, the judges differed in their determinations as to whether or not the means employed by the unions were legal, and they generally held that strikes, boycotts, and picketing were illegal. Employers had little difficulty in obtaining court injunctions to stop such actions by the unions, and employers could legally enter into "yellow dog" contracts with the workers whereby the latter agreed as a condition of employment not to join unions.

With the formation of the American Federation of Labor in 1886, the unions began to gain strength, but it was not until the Great Depression in the 1930s that labor was able to obtain major legislative protection. In 1932, the Norris-La Guardia Act was passed. It greatly restricted the use of federal injunctions in labor disputes and made yellow dog contracts unenforceable in court. In 1926, the Railway Labor Act had provided for collective bargaining in the railroad industry, but other workers in interstate commerce still lacked legal collective bargaining rights. In 1935, with passage of the National Labor Relations Act (Wagner Act), private workers in interstate commerce were granted such rights, and the nation's policy as embodied in this legislation now was to encourage unionization and collective bargaining. Coverage of public employees was not even considered because the constitutionality of the Wagner Act was considered dubious to begin with because of states' rights. Besides, "public sector labor relations had *never* been an element of the story" behind passage of the legislation.[3] In 1947, because of numerous post-World War II strikes and the belief that labor had gained too much power, Congress passed the Labor-Management Relations Act (Taft Hartley Act). This legislation—an amendment of the Wagner Act—placed certain limitations on the unions and strengthened the employers' position somewhat but in no way changed the basic policy of requiring employers to bargain collectively with representatives of the unions selected by employees in majority vote secret elections.

By the 1960s—when unionization began to increase greatly in

---

[2]Walter J. Gershenfeld, "Public Employee Unionization—An Overview," in Public Employment Relations Service, *Portrait of a Process: Collective Negotiations in Public Employment* (Fort Washington, Pa.: Labor Relations Press, 1979), pp. 4–5.

[3]James Gross, "Why Public Employees Were Left Out of the National Labor Relations Act," in *Selected Proceedings of the 27th Annual Conference of Association of Labor Relations Agencies* (Fort Washington, Pa.: Labor Relations Press, 1979), p. 92.

the public service—collective bargaining already had a long history in the private sector. The picture was very different in the public sector. Ida Klaus wrote in 1959 that although many governmental units permitted their employees to organize and gave organizations of employees some role in the determination of conditions of employment no level of government had adopted a "thoroughgoing and systematic code of labor relations at all comparable in fundamental policy, basic guarantees and rights, and procedures for their enforcement, with those of prevailing labor-relations laws in the private sector."[4] As the reader knows from Chapter 1 of this book, since 1959 collective bargaining has become a reality at all levels of government although it is not found in some state governments and in many local jurisdictions.[5]

■ REASONS FOR SPREAD OF COLLECTIVE BARGAINING IN PUBLIC SERVICE

Many reasons have been given for the sudden, rapid rise of collective bargaining in government, but none is more important than the markedly changed perceptions and attitudes of public employees. During the Depression years, they perceived themselves as having certain advantages over private workers, particularly as concerned job security. In the post-World War II years, the private sector expanded, jobs were plentiful, and compensation generally kept pace with changes in the price level. At the same time, many private employers improved annual leave, sick leave, medical, and other benefits. Pay adjustments in government generally were slower and smaller, and government workers considered themselves disadvantaged by comparison.

As labor authority Gus Tyler has written, in the 1960s public employees were in much the same position as mass production workers in the 1930s: "numerous, needed, and neglected." There were many more white-collar than blue-collar workers in the nation's workforce, and government had become the biggest growth

---

[4]Cited in B. V. Schneider, "Public Sector Labor Legislation: An Evolutionary Analysis," in Benjamin Aaron, Joseph R. Grodin, and James L. Stern (eds.), *Public Sector Bargaining* (Washington, D.C.: Bureau of National Affairs, 1979), pp. 191–192.

[5]See also Farouk K. Umar and Roy V. Kirk, "Legal Context of Public-Sector Labor Relations," in Jack Rabin, Thomas Vocino, W. Bartley Hildreth, and Gerald J. Miller (eds.), *Handbook in Public Personnel Administration and Labor Relations* (New York: Dekker, 1983), pp. 297–317.

industry of all. Public employees realized that they were a "major presence," and they decided that they no longer would tolerate a status inferior to that of private workers.[6]

Noneconomic motives also caused public employees to support collective bargaining. With the expansion of governmental programs, many public agencies had increased greatly in size, and relationships between management and the employees had become very impersonal. Many employees had little or no contact with the top managers of their agencies; to them management was remote and insensitive to their needs. As public employee leaders often stated, collective bargaining—giving employees an effective voice in the determination of personnel policies—was essential for recognizing the "dignity" of the government worker. Many public employees, particularly professional workers, had long been concerned about the quality of public services and desired an opportunity to participate in determining program policies. Collective bargaining provided them with that opportunity because employment conditions and program policies are very closely related, for example, class size in the public schools and participation of nurses in patient treatment teams. The paternalism of the public employer was rejected because no matter what its benefits to the worker it denied them participation.

Whereas most public employees had considered that it was inappropriate, even improper, for them to join unions and to support collective bargaining, many of them now saw matters differently. In the private sector, unionization has most of its strength among blue-collar workers, although in recent years the unions have made some progress in organizing white-collar workers. In government, most employees are white-collar workers, including very large numbers of professionals. Yet, despite the long-held belief that white-collar workers disdain unions, many thousands of them have joined public employee unions and strongly support collective bargaining. Undoubtedly, pragmatic considerations of self-interest have influenced public employees in this matter. Initially, many had reservations about collective bargaining when it began to make inroads in the public service. But when it became clear that because of unionization and collective bargaining some government

---

[6]See Gus Tyler, "Why They Organize," in Felix A. Nigro (ed.), "A Symposium: Collective Bargaining in the Public Service, A Reappraisal," *Public Administration Review* 32, no. 2 (March–April 1972): 99.

workers had materially improved their compensation and other conditions of employment, then other public employees became more receptive to unions and joined them.

For quite a few years now, the percentage of union membership in the nonagricultural labor force has declined despite the creation of millions of new jobs. Most of these new jobs have been created in the service industries such as government, transportation, trade, education, health care, public utilities, finance, insurance, and real estate. Because of automation and other factors, thousands of jobs have been eliminated in the mass production industries. In their organizing efforts, private sector unions now encounter strong competition from nonunion employers, as in the energy fields, the construction industry, and some white-collar occupations and professions. In general they find it difficult to attract substantial numbers of new members to make up for the shrinkage of blue-collar jobs.

Accordingly, the AFL-CIO affiliated and other unions have concentrated more effort on organizing public employees at all levels of government—an effort in which they have achieved significant successes. Several years ago the AFL-CIO established a public employee department to provide services to the some 33 AFL-CIO unions that have members in the public sector. At the outset of the increased unionization in government, many public officials identified unions as being mostly responsible for this puzzling new phenomenon. This exaggerated labor's role for, as Tyler states, public employees were ripe for unionization. They were not simply pawns of outside forces.

Competition between employee organizations for new members also contributed to the growth of collective bargaining in government. When independent organizations like the National Education Association (NEA) saw that labor-affiliated organizations like the American Federation of Teachers, AFL-CIO, were gaining new members and winning important contract gains in terms of better salaries and other conditions of work, they decided to support collective bargaining despite a long history of aversion to methods used by "labor." Private sector unions also competed among themselves to obtain new members in government, since every union wants to build its strength.

As unionization expanded in government, political leaders—always interested in increasing their electoral support—strengthened their relationships with public employee leaders. Union alliances with mayors and other elective officials contributed to union momentum in organizing public services. Employee organizations supply numerous workers from their memberships who labor diligently and effectively in political campaigns and, as noted in Chapter 1, union political action committees provide much financial support for candidates in elections.

Removal of Legal Obstacles

Another significant reason for the greatly increased collective bargaining activity in government has been removal of certain legal obstacles—particularly the sovereignty doctrine. As this doctrine was long construed, the government as sovereign employer could not be compelled to accept any obligation it shunned or to continue to respect a commitment if it later decided it could not or should not. The public employer would be ceding its sovereignty if it entered into a collective agreement with an employee organization, and, even if it were so imprudent as to do so, it was justified in reneging on the agreement.

The sovereignty doctrine originated in the English common law precept that the king could do no wrong and that no individual could sue the state without its consent. Legal scholars pointed out that while government was unique in possessing sovereignty it had voluntarily waived it in many cases. For example, public agencies entered into many contractual agreements with private parties which in theory the government could fail to respect but in practice did not. As one writer wrote, sovereignty "was a meaningless legislative circumlocution" because "a right which will never be exercised is the equivalent of no right at all."[7] If it had been considered correct to forget sovereignty and allow government to be sued by persons with just claims, why was it improper to share decision making with employee organizations?

It was also stressed that under democratic governments sovereignty resides in the people, so if the public's elected representatives passed laws authorizing collective bargaining for public employees, they could not be said to be violating sovereignty. Union leaders claimed that public officials often invoked the sov-

---

[7]Wilson R. Hart, *Collective Bargaining in the Federal Civil Service* (New York: Harper & Row, 1961), p. 43.

ereignty argument as an excuse for not wanting to bargain collectively with the employees. As more and more legislatures passed laws providing for collective bargaining in government, it was evident that the concept was developing that while government had ultimate coercive power it could and should as it found desirable agree to certain controls on its discretion. In relatively few years, the sovereignty doctrine was redefined in this manner and no longer functioned as a strong deterrent to the institution of collective bargaining programs.

The right of federal employees to join unions was established with passage of the Lloyd-La Follette Act in 1912. This legislation prohibited the removal or reduction in rank or compensation of any postal employee for joining any organization not affiliated with an outside body imposing an obligation to engage in or support a strike against the United States. Although it mentions only postal employees—at the time the ones mainly involved in confrontations with administrators—it was later held by extension to protect organization rights of all federal employees.

However, many state and local governments with court sanction refused to allow all employees, or certain kinds of them, to organize or affiliate with outside organizations. Since 1968, however, as explained in Chapter 15, the federal courts have held that the First Amendment to the federal Constitution protects the right of public employees to form and join unions. Thus, this obstacle to unionization of public employees has been removed, although as is pointed out in Chapter 15, the courts do not recognize a constitutional right of public employees to bargain collectively with the public employer or to strike.

Lack of Confidence in Civil Service Systems

Many public employees turned to unions and collective bargaining because they had lost confidence in traditional merit systems. There were many reasons for their disillusionment with civil service: inadequate pay and benefits; management controlled grievance systems; and no effective employee voice in the determination of personnel policies. Merit system administrators who were confident that long-service civil service employees would reject unionization were very much surprised when many of them welcomed it instead. Indeed, union leaders persuaded many employees that the collective bargaining contract would give them more job security, arguing that civil service systems were often manipulated by the politicians.

As will be pointed out in Chapter 6, an accommodation has been worked out between civil service and collective bargaining systems. In many jurisdictions, the two systems have been fused, and the merit principle has been strengthened, not weakened. Many traditional civil service systems lost out in the competition with collective bargaining because employees preferred bilateralism to unilateralism and paternalism.

■ COLLECTIVE BARGAINING IN GOVERNMENT SINCE THE 1960s

There have been two distinct stages in the collective bargaining movement in government. The first stage—1960 to the beginning of the recession in 1973—was one of passage of many state collective bargaining laws, of introduction of collective negotiations in the federal service through executive order, and of numerous union victories in winning substantial concessions at the bargaining table. It was one also of unprecedented work stoppages by government workers, a period during which many public employee organizations that previously had rejected the strike weapon now asserted the right to strike if necessary—and did strike.

These were also years during which much of the public sympathized with poorly paid government employees who withheld their services, for example, teachers and then the some 200,000 postal workers who went out on strike in 1970. The rate of increase in public employee union membership was very great, union financial resources grew as a result, and the unions were able to increase their expenditures for lobbying and political action. Much concern was expressed by taxpayer and other groups that public employee unions had amassed too much power in detriment to the public interest.

This initial period was also one in which it quickly became obvious that most public employers were poorly equipped to deal with the unions. When in states without collective bargaining laws for public employees, union organizers presented themselves and made certain requests, public officials often made mistakes because they did not know in detail what the constitutional and legal rights of the employees were. In states that passed laws authorizing collective bargaining, personnel offices and line officials often lacked expertise in bargaining and other dealings with the unions.

Another explanation given for the early successes of the unions is that public employers lacked sophistication in labor relations matters and did not offer strong resistance to union demands. Actually, some public sector unions themselves did not believe they were sufficiently prepared for bargaining with public officials, so in many jurisdictions it was a period of inexperience on both sides. The need for labor relations training programs in government and for pooling of efforts by governmental jurisdictions in labor relations matters was recognized, and soon state leagues of municipalities and other existing organizations of public employers became active in this area. New organizations were also formed to provide informational, training, consulting, and other services, such as the Labor Management Relations Service of the United States Conference of Mayors.

The Period from 1973 to the Present

Labor authority Tim Bornstein identifies the years 1962–1972, roughly, as the great growth period of public employee unionism. During these years, the economy expanded, there was a high level of employment in the private sector, and governmental functions grew. The recession that began in 1973—the deepest economic decline since the Great Depression of the 1930s—ended the period of phenomenal growth and continuous successes of the public employee unions. While most of them did not suffer great losses in membership, their ranks did not increase at the same rapid rate, and they generally were unable to win as substantial salary increases and other concessions at the bargaining table. Governmental revenues had fallen sharply, and management negotiators were in a much better position to resist union demands.

Taxpayer attitudes changed markedly. As Bornstein states, previously elected public officials had been the target of taxpayer hostility; now they shared this role with public employees and their unions.[8] The opinion was widely held that the unions had exacted oversized settlements that had contributed to the serious financial difficulties of cities like New York. To much of the public, pay of teachers, police, fire fighters, nurses, and other public employees had improved so much that it was time for the public employer

---

[8] Tim Bornstein and John T. Conlon (eds.), *Proceedings, Public Sector Labor Relations: At the Crossroads* (Amherst, Mass.: School of Business Administration, U. of Mass., 1977), pp. 36–37, p. 34.

to be very firm at the bargaining table. Whether the union wage and other demands were unreasonable is, of course, a matter of opinion. What is indisputable is that much of the public viewed the employee unions negatively to such a point that pollster Louis Harris in effect advised politicians to run against the unions.

Since the number of new states passing public worker collective bargaining legislation had declined greatly, some public employee leaders intensified their efforts to obtain federal legislation mandating *all* state and local governments to establish collective bargaining programs. Bills providing for such mandating had been introduced in Congress, and for a time it appeared that such legislation might be approved. Union leaders maintained that uniformity throughout the country in public sector relations was essential, whereas many state and local government officials opposed federal mandating as an infringement on state and local autonomy. Of course, those favoring collective bargaining for public workers supported the legislation, and those who did not approve of collective bargaining opposed it.

In June 1976, the U.S. Supreme Court by a five-to-four vote ruled in *National League of Cities et al.* v. *Usery* that Congress did not have the power under the commerce clause to extend to state and local governments the minimum wage and overtime pay provisions of the Fair Labor Standards Act of 1938. The Court majority maintained that the power of a state to determine the compensation and hours of its employees was essential to its "separate and independent existence" and that extension of the Fair Labor Standards Act meant supplanting the policy choices of state officials with respect to how to structure pay scales in state employment.

This decision was widely interpreted to mean that the Court would rule unconstitutional federal mandating of collective bargaining. The bills providing for such mandating were based on the power of Congress to prevent interruptions to interstate commerce caused by labor unrest (the same justification as for the Wagner and Taft-Hartley Acts). After the decision in *National League of Cities* v. *Usery*, there was not much consideration of the mandating bills in Congress, but many observers believed the real reason was the public hostility towards increased spending and higher taxes which are associated with public employees and the unions. The recession ended but was quickly succeeded by the "taxpayer's revolt" and the Proposition 13 mentality. By the end of the 1970s, the unions were fighting hard to prevent passage of new state constitutional and other limitations on taxes and public expenditures. Union leaders railed against the "meat axe" approach of legislative bodies in reducing expenditures and eliminating jobs of public employees. In February, 1985, the Supreme Court reversed the decision in *National League of Cities* vs. *Usery* but it remained unlikely that Congress would approve federal mandating of collective bargaining.[9]

Yet, while the union movement in government slowed after 1973, the decade of the 1970s was one in which collective bargaining in government solidified itself and came more and more to resemble collective bargaining in the private sector. As Bornstein writes, in the 1960s public employee unions "strained to keep their distance from private sector unions" and "even rejected the vocabulary of private sector labor relations." For example, the NEA used the term "professional negotiations" instead of collective bargaining and did not want to be called a union. During the 1970s, however, "the most refined teachers organizations" called themselves " 'unions'—with pride." Attitudes of many public managers also changed. Whereas in the 1960s they "resisted the idea of collective bargaining in government," in the 1970s they learned how to deal with the unions at the bargaining table. Comments Bornstein: "Public sector negotiators have learned well from the private sector that there are 10,000 ways to say 'no' to a union's demands without bargaining in bad faith. And they have learned the ultimate lesson from private sector management: Never blink an eye at a union's strike threats; talk softly and carry a big strike contingency plan."[10]

In the 1980s another recession and the decreased federal aid to state and municipal governments combined to increase the difficulties of the public employee unions in making major gains at the bargaining table. Yet two large industrial states, Illinois and Ohio, passed comprehensive bargaining statutes for their public employees, and elsewhere in the nation there was no indication that the continuation of collective bargaining in government was threatened

---

[9]"Excerpts From Court Opinion and Dissents on States' Power," *New York Times*, February 20, 1985.

[10]See Tim Bornstein, "Legacies of Local Government Collective Bargaining," *Labor Management Relations Service Newsletter* 11, no. 2 (February 1980): 3–5. The LMRS Newsletter is published monthly by the United States Conference of Mayors, Washington, D.C.

seriously. Labor authority Jeffrey B. Tener makes the following observations: (1) government is no longer the high growth industry it was from "World War II until the 1970s"; (2) there has been a substantial downward trend in federal, state, and local expenditures; (3) "fiscal restraints on public employers and related issues" will be the "dominant issues for public sector management and unions throughout the decade"; (4) public sector union membership "will not increase very much," keeping in mind that the "education sector is already highly organized and most of the other easier to organize public employees in the larger employing organizations have already been organized."[11] Besides pressing for increases in compensation to offset inflation, public employee unions are concentrating on protecting job security by opposing layoffs, subcontracting of public services to private businesses, and further cutbacks in government programs.

■ PUBLIC EMPLOYEE ORGANIZATIONS

There are many employee organizations active in the public sector, and they can be classified in several different ways. Some function at just one level of government, others at two or more. Some are organized on craft or occupational lines, others are analogous to private sector industrial unions and include in their memberships workers of many different kinds. We will generally follow Jack Steiber's classification,[12] concentrating our discussion on the organizations in each classification that represent the largest numbers of public employees.

1. *Mixed unions,* those with members both in government and in the private sector. Most of their members are in private establishments, but in recent years some have substantially increased their membership in public agencies.
2. *All public or mostly public unions,* those with all or most of their members in government. Some of these unions are affiliated with the outside labor movement; the others are in-

---

[11]*Labor Management Relations Service Newsletter* 13, no. 2 (March 1982): 6.

[12]Jack Steiber, *Public Employee Unionism: Structure, Growth, Policy* (Washington, D.C.: Brookings, 1973), pp. 1–14. Our research in the mid-1980s showed that Steiber's listing of the unions with the greatest membership under this classification remains correct.

dependent. We are not including in this category police officer and fire fighter organizations. They are listed as classification (5) below.

3. *Professional associations,* organizations that draw the bulk of their membership from those in a particular profession and are not affiliated with labor.

4. *Independent associations of state and local government employees* (not including police and fire fighter associations). These organizations have members in many different kinds of work, and they operate on a statewide or local basis. Most were established between 1920 and 1950—well before the spread of collective bargaining in government.

5. *Police and fire fighter organizations.* This classification overlaps some of the preceding ones, but the purpose of this last category is to give a complete account of the kinds of organizations, large and small, that represent fire fighters and police, both of whom have been very active in collective bargaining.

The Mixed Unions

This category includes a diversity of unions, as a group functioning at all levels of government.[13]

Those with the strongest representation in state and local government are the Service Employees' International Union (SEIU), the International Brotherhood of Teamsters, the Amalgamated Transit Union (ATU), the Communication Workers of America (CWA), and Laborers' International Union (LIU). All are AFL-CIO affiliates except for the Teamsters. The largest organization in this category in the federal service is the Metal Trades Council, AFL-CIO, made up of several national craft unions. There are many other mixed unions, such as the Transport Workers Union of America, National Hospital Union, International Union of Operating Engineers, the International Brotherhood of Electrical Workers, and the International Chemical Workers Union, all AFL-CIO.

---

[13]It is very difficult to obtain accurate figures on union memberships. Unions are not prone to understate their memberships, and the number of their members fluctuates because of changes in employment and other factors. Our figures are based on telephone and other inquiries to the unions themselves, publications on labor relations in government, and other sources. The Bureau of Labor Statistics for budgetary reasons has terminated publication of its *Directory of National Unions and Employee Associations*.

The SEIU has a public sector membership of about 320,000, and it is in government that it has made most of its membership gains in recent years. It has many members in California state and local government, in 1984 gaining as an affiliate the California State Employees Association. It also recently added as an affiliate the formerly independent National Association of Government Employees (NAGE), which has a membership of about 40,000, and represents about 66,500 federal employees. The teamsters have about 57,000 public employee members, the ATU about 50,000, the CWA about 45,000, and the LIU 7,000 in state and local government. (The LIU has about 38,000 mail handler members in the U.S. Postal Service.)

All Public or Mostly Public Unions

The largest organization of this type is the American Federation of State, County, and Municipal Employees, AFL-CIO. It now has about 1 million members, most of whom are in state and local governments. A small number is in the federal government and in quasi-public and nonprofit organizations. Its membership includes public workers of all kinds although by its own decision it does not admit teachers.

AFSCME started in 1936 as a small union dedicated to advancing the cause of merit systems in state and local governments. When the late Jerry Wurf became its president in 1964, AFSCME changed its orientation, aggressively reached out for new members, enthusiastically endorsed collective bargaining, and achieved remarkable membership gains and successes at the bargaining table.

Another large predominantly public union is the American Federation of Teachers (AFT), AFL-CIO. AFT has increased its membership tenfold from 1960 and now has about 450,000 teacher members. It also has members in nonteaching classified positions as well as registered nurse members, making its total strength about 650,000. AFT several years ago started organizing nurses in direct competition with the American Nurses Association. Most of its public membership is in the elementary and secondary schools, principally in very large cities, but in recent years it has enrolled many members in colleges and universities where it now represents more faculty and staff than NEA. The success of its largest affiliate, the United Federation of Teachers, in winning the collective bargaining election in New York City in 1961 gave a great impetus to collective bargaining in the public schools. The election was the first in a large metropolitan school district, and the UFT negotiated a comprehensive contract that was unprecedented by comparison with then existing AFT local and NEA affiliate teacher agreements.

Other large mostly public unions are found in the federal service. We will mention first those outside the postal service; in each case they have members in many different kinds of work in a number of agencies. The largest is the American Federation of Government Employees (AFGE), AFL-CIO, which has a membership of about 220,000, and represents about 685,700 workers in exclusive bargaining units. The National Federation of Federal Employees (NFFE) originated in 1917 as an AFL-CIO affiliate but left the AFL-CIO in 1931 because of disagreements with the craft unions. It represents about 136,600 employees, but its membership has declined from some 100,000 in 1970 to about 40,000. The National Treasury Employees Union (NTEU), another independent union, started in the Internal Revenue Service, spread to the entire Treasury Department, and has recently expanded its jurisdiction to include employees in other federal agencies. Its membership has increased from about 25,000 in 1969 to some 63,000, including approximately 2,000 outside the Treasury Department, and it represents about 100,500 federal workers.

AFGE and NTEU are now considered the two most influential of these three organizations. NTEU, the fastest growing federal employee union, has a large legal staff and has won significant victories in its court challenges of government actions and its representation of employees in grievance proceedings and court cases.[14]

The American Postal Workers Union (APWU) and the National Association of Letter Carriers (NALC), both AFL-CIO, have about 249,000 and 200,000 members respectively. The APWU was created in 1971 as the result of a merger between the AFL-CIO Postal Clerks, the independent National Postal Union, and three smaller AFL-CIO postal unions. The NALC was established in the late 19th century and was one of the first affiliates of the AFL-CIO. Both NALC and APWU are very strong unions, both at the bar-

---

[14]See M. J. Fox, Jr. and Marvin Judah, "National Treasury Employees Union: Description of a Federal Employee Union," *Journal of Collective Negotiations in the Public Sector* 9, no. 1 (1980).

gaining table and in lobbying with Congress. The Postal Reorganization Act of 1970 granted postal employees collective bargaining rights, including the right to negotiate compensation, and placed them under the jurisdiction of the National Labor Relations Board.

Professional Associations

By far the largest organization of this kind is the National Education Association (NEA) with a membership of about 1,100,000. Because of pressures from its membership and the strong competition offered by AFT after the latter's collective bargaining victory in New York City in 1961, NEA in 1962 officially adopted collective negotiations. Since then it has participated in many collective bargaining elections and is in fact as much involved in collective bargaining and strikes as AFT. It has rejected merger with AFT largely because of the AFT's affiliation with AFL-CIO. NEA's public school membership is greatest in suburban and rural areas.

The American Nurses Association (ANA) with a membership of about 165,000 was the first professional association to adopt collective bargaining. In 1946, it approved its Economic Security Program which is "committed to the use of collective bargaining as one of the most effective means of assuring nurses' right to participate in the implementation of standards of nursing employment and practice."[15] ANA's membership is open to registered nurses both in private and public employment, and it represents public sector nurses at all levels of government.

In recent years, independent associations of other kinds of professional workers have been formed that function as collective bargaining representatives in negotiations with public employers. Examples are house staff organizations of medical interns and residents and associations of legal aid attorneys.

Independent Associations of State and Local Government Employees

Discussing state associations first, they were established for a number of reasons. In some cases, the objective was to "provide some type of unified general representaion for government employees." In others, the motivation was to support a particular cause or em-

---

[15]See Jacquelyn Gideon, "The American Nurses Association: A Professional Model for Collective Bargaining," *Journal of Health and Human Resources Administration* 2, no. 1 (August 1979).

ployee benefit. For example, several were organized to initiate or protect a civil service system, others to start or safeguard an existing retirement system or to provide insurance benefits.

Most of them restrict their membership to state government employees, but in recent years the number of state associations also admitting local government employees has increased. Most of the state associations are federated with the Assembly of Government Employees (AGE), which was established in 1952 and estimates its membership as between 250,000 and 275,000.

AGE strongly supports merit systems. Like most of its constituent state associations, it did not welcome collective bargaining in government largely because it believed that such unions as AFSCME aimed at completely replacing civil service with collective bargaining agreements. After collective bargaining laws had been passed in a number of states, AGE faced the choice of accommodating to the new public policy or of recommending that its member state associations not compete with the "unions" in the collective bargaining elections. It chose to accommodate and compete, and many of its member associations have now been engaging in collective bargaining for many years.

Turning to the local associations, they were organized for the same reasons as those given above for the state associations. The total membership of local associations not included in national and state associations has been estimated as around 300,000. Most local associations also did not originally support collective bargaining, but some now serve as bargaining agents. An increasing number of the state and local associations, to add to their bargaining power, have affiliated with AFSCME and other AFL-CIO affiliates, a trend that is likely to continue.

Police and Fire Fighter Organizations

Police officers are represented in several different kinds of organizations. A small number are members of AFSCME or of one of the mixed unions that admit police (e.g., the Teamsters and SEIU). One police organization, the International Brotherhood of Police Officers based in New England, is affiliated with NAGE. There are also many local police associations not affiliated with any national organization. Finally, the remainder are members of three loose national organizations of police: The Fraternal Order of Police (FOP), the International Union of Police Associations (IUPA), and the National Association of Police Officers (NAPO).

The members of FOP, which was established in 1915, are regularly appointed or full-time law enforcement officers of all ranks who are employed in local and state governments and in the federal service. FOP does not consider itself a union, but some of its lodges engage in collective bargaining and have taken militant stands. IUPA and NAPO were formed after dissolution of the International Conference of Police Associations (ICPA) in 1978. The member organizations of ICPA (state and local associations of police) split over the issue of affiliation with the AFL-CIO. One segment of ICPA formed IUPA and applied for an AFL-CIO charter which was granted in 1979. The remaining segment formed NAPO and, as an independent "police only" organization, is ICPA's successor.

The International Association of Fire Fighters (IAFF), to which the great majority of the nation's fire fighters belong, is an affiliate of the AFL-CIO. It has about 172,000 members, most of them in cities and towns but some also in state governments and the federal service. The IAFF, which was established at the end of World War I, has the longest continuous experience in dealing with local-level labor-management relationships of any of the public employee unions. It has vigorously pursued collective bargaining agreements in most cities of any size.

■ LABOR RELATIONS IN THE GOVERNMENT ENVIRONMENT

Although labor relations in government has moved closer to the private sector model, there remains the fundamental difference that what happens in government is the public's business and that decisions in government are made through the political process. As Clyde W. Summers writes, "Government is not just another industry . . . in private employment collective bargaining is a process of private decision making shaped primarily by market forces, while in public employment it is a process of governmental decision making shaped ultimately by political forces."[16] Public em-

---

[16]Clyde W. Summers, "Public Employee Bargaining: A Political Perspective," in David Lewin, Peter Feuille, and Thomas A. Kochan, *Public Sector Labor Relations: Analysis and Readings* (Glen Ridge, N.J.: Thomas Horton and Daughters, 1977), p. 44.

ployees and their unions are part of these political forces as are political leaders, elective officials, pressure groups, the media, and the numerous taxpayers and voters. Unlike private workers, public employees may be able to vote out of office employers with whose labor relations policies they are dissatisfied.

However, there also is taxpayer retaliation over the size of the public payroll, and taxpayers hostile to public employees may vote out elective officials considered too easy with the unions. As Summers points out, in the typical governmental jurisdiction public employees are only a small part of the total number of voters. The rest of the voters are purchasers and users of the employees' services, and "they want to maximize services and minimize costs." Thus, public employees are at a disadvantage in the budget-making process, but this is balanced by collective bargaining because it provides special procedures that "insure that their interests receive adequate consideration in the political process."[17]

Other authorities believe public employees are not disadvantaged without collective bargaining and that with collective bargaining they have gained excessive power. These authorities stress that in the private sector market constraints moderate union demands. Union leaders know that if wage costs become too high the employer may have to close down or move and the workers will lose their jobs. They also are aware that consumers may refuse to buy the product if they find the price too high and instead will purchase substitute products or those made by firms with lower-paid nonunion labor. Public agencies cannot close down and they usually are the only suppliers of the particular service. According to these authorities, collective bargaining makes this situation worse for the public employer because the employee unions may have the political strength to force acceptance of many of their demands.[18]

Theories of collective bargaining in government are important for identifying potential imbalances between the public employer and the unions, but assumptions as to power possessed by each side should be checked against the facts. Research on public employee union political power is not voluminous, and the most complete study—a *UCLA Law Review* project—was made in the early 1970s. However, that was during the period of early great suc-

---

[17]Ibid., p. 46.
[18]See Harry Wellington and Ralph K. Winter, Jr., *The Unions and the Cities* (Washington, D.C.: Brookings, 1971).

cesses by the unions, yet the basic finding was that except for a few places like New York City "the problem of union power seems more an emergent possibility than a present reality."[19] The recession followed and the unions lost political power in New York and other big cities that they have not regained because of financial stringencies in government. All the same, unions remain in the political arena, and the "emergent possibility" still concerns many people.

The Management Structure in Government

As Milton Derber writes, "The private employer is readily identified as an entity, and the line of management responsibility for bargaining is usually clear and direct. But in the public sector responsibility is generally divided or shared, and the formal responsibility often differs from the actual."[20] This explains why when collective bargaining began to spread in government the question soon arose, "Who is the management?" Note this statement.

> In coming to grips with the concept of collective bargaining in public service, one of the most difficult problems is to find management and, having found it, to clothe it with the authority it needs to play the part. In a public service setting, managerial authority tends to be divided between a legislature and an executive, between politicans and bureaucrats, between independent commissions and operating departments. Because badly dispersed, it tends to lack substance and definition and almost, at times, to disappear in a forest of checks and balances. One could almost sustain the thesis that collective bargaining has been slow to establish itself in public services because employee representatives have been unable to identify individuals with whom they could really deal.[21]

In a private company, the management fully controls spending decisions, but in government there usually is a separation between the fund recommending and the fund approving groups. The exceptions are agencies like the New York Port Authority whose

---

[19]"Project: Collective Bargaining and Politics in Public Employment," *UCLA Law Review* 19, no. 6 (August 1972).

[20]Milton Derber, "Management Organization for Collective Bargaining in the Public Sector," in Aaron, Grodin, and Stern (eds.), *Public Sector Bargaining*, p. 81.

[21]Douglas Love, "Proposals for Collective Bargaining in the Public Service of Canada: A Further Commentary," in Gerald C. Somers (ed.), *Collective Bargaining in the Public Service, Proceedings of the 1966 Annual Spring Meeting, Industrial Relations Association* (Milwaukee, Wis., May 6–7, 1966), p. 28.

board of directors does not have to go to any legislature for the money to meet labor contracts, but this is rare. Even when the legislature delegates to the executive branch the authority to set pay scales, it does not relinquish its control of the purse and may refuse to make the necessary funds available.

A local school board may not have to get its budget approved by the city council, but, if it wants to increase expenditures beyond the estimated yield of the school tax, it must present the issue to the residents of the community in a special referendum. Furthermore, since there is a limit to the money which can be raised locally, it may be impossible for school boards to pay better salaries without an increase in state support. Many state and local government functions are now financed substantially with federal grant funds, but, when they negotiate with the unions, state and local officials often do not know how much federal aid they will receive and can only estimate how much it will be. These uncertainties place them in the risky position of committing funds they may not receive. To protect themselves, they sometimes give the unions low estimates of the anticipated state or federal aid. These are some but by no means all the ways in which management authority in government is dispersed.

Summarizing the research on the subject, Kearney writes that "unionization and collective bargaining lead to centralization of management structure."[22] Before collective bargaining, responsibility for making decisions on compensation and working conditions typically is divided among several officials. When collective bargaining replaces unilateral decision-making by management officials, negotiations between the unions and different officials become cumbersome and the public looks to one elective official, the chief executive, for leadership in labor relations. Accordingly, the power of the executive branch in determining conditions of work gains at the expense of the legislature, and within the executive branch responsibility for labor relations is centralized under the chief executive.

In state and local governments, the labor relations function often is assigned to the personnel director or else a separate office of labor relations is established. In some jurisdictions, an office of

---

[22]Richard C. Kearney, "Monetary Impact of Collective Bargaining," in Rabin, Vocino, Hildreth, and Miller (eds.), *Handbook on Public Personnel Administration and Labor Relations*, p. 381.

labor relations has been created that combines the labor relations and personnel functions. In small local jurisdictions and state agencies, part-time consultants often are hired to represent management at the bargaining table.

When there is one office responsible for labor relations and another for personnel, close coordination between the two is essential because those in the labor relations office negotiating union agreements should be thoroughly familiar with personnel laws, regulations, and problems. When the functions are combined in one office, but there is a separate staff for labor relations and another for personnel, similar coordination is needed. Whatever the allocation of responsibilities for personnel functions, those negotiating the contracts should be in close touch with line officials in the operating departments and obtain their ideas about contract provisions. Unfortunately, coordination between labor relations and personnel staffs and sufficient consultation with line officials often have been lacking.

In the federal service, in most cases the labor relations function has been assigned as an additional function to the personnel office, although in a few agencies there is a separate office of labor relations. In the regional offices of federal agencies, labor relations has been added to the regional personnel office's function. There is no government-wide bargaining with the unions, and the Office of Personnel Management serves as management adviser to the agencies on labor relations.

■ SUPERVISORS AND COLLECTIVE BARGAINING

In the private sector, with the exception of a few skilled craft unions such as those in printing, construction, public utilities, and the maritime industry, supervisors from the foreman level up are typically excluded from bargaining units. This is in part because the NLRA excludes supervisors from bargaining rights and protections and in part because most employers have strongly insisted supervisors must be regarded as part of management. Historically, in the industrial establishments where the private sector unions developed strength and gained collective bargaining rights, the workforce consisted mostly of production and maintenance employees with few clerical workers.

In government, the workforce is predominantly white- rather than blue-collar, and there are numerous levels of supervision. From their inception, the employee associations admitted to membership both supervisory and nonsupervisory employees. In fact, supervisors often were primarily responsible for creation of the associations, and many of them have held office in them. Most of the mixed, all public or predominantly public, and other public employee unions previously mentioned admit lower-level supervisors, many of whom also have occupied leadership positions in the union. Thus, when collective bargaining programs were established in government, many public employee leaders objected to the prohibition on having supervisors in the same bargaining unit as nonsupervisory employees. Most state collective bargaining laws contain such a prohibition as well as the same definition of supervisor as in the National Labor Relations Act.

The reason for the private sector precedent of not having supervisors in the same bargaining unit as nonsupervisory workers is conflict of interest. Supervisors and nonsupervisory employees have opposed, not common, interests. Supervisors represent management; the union represents the workers. Since the bargaining unit is supposed to represent persons with common interests, having them both in the same bargaining unit does not make sense. Either the supervisors will permeate the unit with the management point of view, thereby undermining the collective bargaining rights of the workers, or the supervisors will side with the nonsupervisory employees, undermining management's position.

The public employee leaders who see nothing wrong in having supervisors in the same unit believe the conflict of interest argument lacks validity in government. One of their principal arguments is that the actual supervisory authority possessed by many persons holding supervisory positions in public agencies is limited. In his study of the independent state associations, Jerry Lelchook writes, "Most associations view the supervisor in public service as simply one link in a chain of command, with no real discretional authority."[23] Morris Slavney and George R. Fleischli state that "supervisors in public employment usually perform unit work and frequently do not enjoy the same degree of autonomy in the exercise of supervisory authority as do supervisors in the private sector,

[23]Jerry Lelchook, *State Civil Service Employee Associations* (Washington, D.C.: Government Printing Office, 1973), p. 27.

whose actions are not governed by statute and ordinances or subject to review by political bodies. In fact, many positions in government which are identified as supervisory by job title are more in the nature of promotion based on increased ability, longevity, and level of responsibility."[24]

In occupations such as nursing, teaching and police and fire services, it is emphasized that there is a strong common interest linking together all workers. About the American Nurses Association, Steiber writes:

> The association argues that the educational backgrounds and working values of all registered nurses are much alike. Responsibility to the patient transcends concepts of rank. While supervisors may advise and assist, each nurse "directs" her own practice. Moreover, nurses change jobs frequently, moving up and down in the hierarchy without thought of how their "careers" are being affected. Few possess supervisory authority in the industrial sense, and those alien standards should not be applied in determining appropriate bargaining units for nurses.[25]

In police and fire services, the common bond of mission is stressed, and it is pointed out that fire fighters "work, eat, and sleep together for periods of 24 hours." As to police, Slavney and Fleischli state that "most do not exercise significant supervisory authority with sufficient frequency to be deemed supervisors." Furthermore, many "do not have any occasion to exercise supervisory authority, even though other personnel in the same or lower rank do have occasion to do so."[26] In fighting fires, all ranks perform the same tasks as necessary; the lieutenant who mans a hose is not considered to be invading bargaining unit work.

Most collective bargaining statutes in government do not specify which individual positions are to be considered supervisory and to be excluded from the bargaining unit. This determination is made by the administrative agency that decides the bargaining unit, and some of these agencies examine closely into the duties of positions with supervisory titles and exclude from the unit only those positions in which real supervisory authority is exercised. However, there remain frequent disagreements between management, the

[24]Morris Slavney and George R. Fleischli, "The Uniformed Services," in Public Employment Relations Services, *Portrait of a Process*, p. 412.

[25]Steiber, *Public Employee Unionism*, p. 147.

[26]Slavney and Fleischli, "The Uniformed Services," p. 416, p. 413.

unions, and the administrative agency that makes the bargaining unit decisions as to which positions are supervisory.

Although many employees with supervisory titles in government do not exercise supervisory authority, in some jurisdictions almost all levels of supervision in certain departments have been included in the same bargaining unit as nonsupervisory employees. Cases commonly cited are in police and fire departments. When this happens—and it occurs largely because of pressures of the employee organizations in the particular line of work—there is little left in the department to represent the management point of view.

The Question of Collective Bargaining Rights for Supervisors

Under the Taft-Hartley Act, organizations of supervisors do not have collective bargaining rights. Employers may bargain collectively with such organizations, but they are not required to do so and almost none do. Most public worker collective bargaining laws also do not grant collective bargaining rights to supervisors. However, some of the state laws do.

The rationale for not giving supervisors collective bargaining rights is that they are part of the management team and as such should share common interests with the top management group that determines personnel policies. Also, if supervisors are given bargaining rights, they may sympathize with strikes of rank-and-file workers. When such strikes occur, management may need to use supervisors to perform essential work of the striking employees, and the supervisors may refuse to do so or do so half-heartedly. It is contended that through consultations with supervisory organizations top management can determine the salary and other needs of supervisors and arrive at mutually satisfactory agreements.

This reasoning is not accepted by many supervisors in both private and public sectors. In the public sector particularly they often have many differences of opinion with the top management group and feel disadvantaged in comparison with employees who have collective bargaining rights. Because of their pressures at the bargaining table, these employees often get better or speedier treatment as far as salary increases are concerned than supervisors. Whatever the desirability or undesirability of giving supervisory workers in government bargaining rights, it is clear that many public employers give inadequate attention to the pay and other needs of supervisors.

BIBLIOGRAPHY

Aaron, Benjamin; Grodin, Joseph; and Stern, James L., eds. *Public Sector Bargaining*. Washington, D.C.: Bureau of National Affairs, 1979.

Bureau of National Affairs. *Government Employee Relations Report*. Weekly publication. Washington, D.C.

ILR Press. *Books, Monographs, and other Publications*. Ithaca, N.Y.: Cornell University, New York State School of Industrial and Labor Relations, 1984. Brochure listing publications in private and public sector labor relations.

Journal of Collective Negotiations in the Public Service. Quarterly published by Bayard Publishing Company, Farmingdale, New York.

Labor Management Relations Service Newsletter. Published monthly by Labor Management Relations Service, Washington, D.C.

Lewin, David; Feuille, Peter; and Kochan, Thomas A. *Public Sector Labor Relations: Analysis and Readings*. Glen Ridge, N.J.: Thomas Horton and Daughters, 1977.

Nigro, Felix A. *Management-Employee Relations in the Public Service*. Washington, D.C.: International Personnel Management Association, 1969.

Public Employment Relations Services. *Portrait of a Process: Collective Negotiations in Public Employment*. Fort Washington, Pa.: Labor Relations Press, 1978.

Rabin, Jack; Vocino, Thomas; Hildreth, W. Bartley; and Miller, Gerald J., eds. *Handbook on Public Personnel Administration and Labor Relations*. New York: Dekker, 1983.

Steiber, Jack. *Public Employee Unionism: Structure, Growth, Policy*. Washington, D.C.: Brookings, 1973.

Tyler, Gus. *The Political Imperative: The Corporate Character of Unions*. New York: Macmillan, 1968.

6 The Bilateral Input—The Unions

In this chapter, we provide an overview of the impact of public employee unions on personnel policies and practices. Subsequent chapters present in more detail the effect of collective bargaining on compensation, examining, and other phases of the personnel operation.

If we think in terms of a public personnel policymaking universe in the United States, there are several possibilities, namely, jurisdictions with (1) no civil service or collective bargaining systems; (2) civil service but no collective bargaining; and (3) both civil service and collective bargaining. In the third situation, there usually is or has been much concern that collective contracts not violate the merit principle. In the second situation, public management often fears that collective bargaining will become a reality in the jurisdiction at some future date, and it is apprehensive about survival of the merit principle in that eventuality. Because it is so important an issue, we will pay particular attention to the relationships, conflicts, and possible incompatibilities between civil service and collective bargaining systems. This issue hinges on the definition of "merit principle." As indicated in Chapter 1, there are many critics who believe that civil service systems have failed to carry out the merit principle.

■ THE MERIT PRINCIPLE, CIVIL SERVICE, AND COLLECTIVE BARGAINING

The early civil service commissions concentrated on giving examinations, preparing employment registers, certifying the names of eligibles from these lists to the hiring departments, and keeping central records. Beginning early in the 20th century, another important duty was added: preparation and administration of position classification and compensation plans. Then, as concepts of the personnel function broadened, central personnel agencies assumed responsibilities in other areas such as employee benefits, safety, suggestion systems, training, and grievances. Important as it was, the examining function became only one of a number of personnel activities.

Which personnel functions are essential to realization of the merit principle? This is a key question in determining the respective jurisdictions of civil service and collective bargaining systems, for some authorities believe civil service agencies now carry out many activities that are *not* essential to the merit principle and, therefore, are proper matters for collective bargaining. Actually, as civil service agencies assumed these new responsibilities, they often tended to think of them as not part of the core merit system. Preparation of the salary plan is one example: The purpose was equal pay for equal work, but somehow that was not "merit." "Merit" was giving examinations, ranking the successful candidates in order of their scores, and keeping partisan political and other nonmerit-related factors out of the examination and appointment process.

There is no agreement today on which functions are essential to the merit principle. Generally, there is consensus that the examining and ranking of candidates for original appointment or promotion are essential to merit, but opinions vary as to the other functions. In practice, civil service systems have retained the examining and ranking responsibility, but quite a few other personnel activities are often completely under collective bargaining (e.g., compensation) or partially so. As later chapters will show, the actual personnel decision, such as the transfer, promotion, or layoff of a particular employee, usually is not determined by collective bargaining, but the standards and procedures that are followed *are* so determined.

Civil service systems are provided for by provisions of state constitutions, state statutes, and local government charters and ordinances. In the United States, there have been very few examples of civil service agencies administering collective bargaining programs.

■ ELEMENTS OF A COLLECTIVE BARGAINING SYSTEM

In state and local governments, collective bargaining systems are based on state statutes or local ordinances except in those few cases where they have been provided for by executive order. (See the appendix to this chapter at the end of this book for excerpts from one example, the Public Employe Relations Act of the State of Pennsylvania.) However, in numerous state and local jurisdictions although collective bargaining is not authorized by law or executive order, it takes place on a de facto basis and has been sanctioned by the courts. In these governments, public management has, because of union pressures and/or its own desires, decided to bargain collectively with union representatives, and the courts have ruled valid the collective bargaining agreements entered into under these arrangements. However, in some states the courts have held that public employers cannot bargain collectively with employees "in the absence of enabling legislation." This was the decision of the Virginia Supreme Court in *Commonwealth of Virginia* v. *County Board of Arlington County* (1977).[1] With passage of the Civil Service Reform Act of 1978, collective bargaining in the federal service is now on a statutory basis.

In the discussion that follows, to avoid repetition, when we say "legal authorization," this refers to collective bargaining laws, or ordinances, or executive orders.

The Labor Relations Agency

In state and local governments, the collective bargaining program often is administered by a new agency, usually a board or commission, or by an existing agency responsible for regulating collective bargaining in the private sector (usually also a board or commission). Where collective bargaining is provided for by local government ordinance, the administering agency typically is a board or commission established by the same ordinance. In state governments, appointments of board or commission members are made by the governor, in a majority of cases with confirmation of the state senate.[2] Labor relations in the federal service are regu-

---

[1] Joel A. D'Alba, "The Nature of the Duty to Bargain in Good Faith," in Public Employment Relations Services, *Portrait of a Process: Collective Negotiations in Public Employment* (Fort Washington, PA.: Labor Relations Press, 1979), p. 156.

[2] See Robert D. Helsby and Jeffery B. Tener, "Structure and Administration of Public Employment Relations Agencies," in Public Employment Relations Services, *Portrait of a Process: Collective Negotiations in Public Employment*, pp. 31–49.

lated by the Federal Labor Relations Authority (FLRA), whose three members are appointed by the President with Senate confirmation.

Bargaining Agents and Units

With very few exceptions, the bargaining is between representatives of management and of the *exclusive bargaining agent*, which is the union that has majority support within the particular *bargaining unit*. The criteria to govern the determination of units are specified in the legal authorization, and one of the principal functions of the administering agency is to decide what the unit will be when management and the union disagree about what positions it should include. Generally, units are established on the basis of type of work performed or function (e.g., fire fighters, blue-collar workers) or organizational location (e.g., a field office).

If many bargaining units are established, this means that the number of contract negotiations is correspondingly large for an agreement must be negotiated with the majority union in each unit. Besides increasing the workload for management officials responsible for the negotiations, a multiplicity of units improves the chances of the unions to "whipsaw," that is, use a favorable agreement in one unit to press for the same or better terms in another unit. While in government management tends to prefer bigger units rather than a scattering of small ones, neither management nor the unions invariably support larger or smaller units. Each party develops its strategy in the light of what unit size suits its needs best in a given situation. If management is faced by a powerful union, or unions, it may try to divide union power by seeking several small units. Similarly, unions may want larger units if they believe this would increase their bargaining strength.

The administering agency interprets the bargaining unit criteria stated in the legal authorization. One of these criteria may be efficiency of government operations, which standard may influence it to rule in favor of a larger unit in order to reduce the number of negotiations and to assure that units are big enough to encompass the level at which management officials are authorized to make personnel decisions for employees in the unit, for example, a field office, rather than a few employees in a particular field location.

Furthermore, management and the union may disagree about

which positions are supervisory. The definition of a supervisory position set forth in the collective bargaining statute may be detailed, but no matter how detailed there are frequent disagreements over whether the supervision exercised is such as to justify excluding it from a nonsupervisory bargaining unit. As stated in Chapter 5, some statutes do grant collective bargaining rights to supervisors, but the question remains whether a position really is supervisory and should be contained in a bargaining unit of supervisors. Every position included in a unit increases the power of the majority union, and if an entire class of positions with many jobs in the class is ruled to be supervisory and therefore ineligible for inclusion in the unit, the union suffers a significant loss. Conversely, management may endeavor to reduce union strength by persuading the public employment relations board or commission that certain jobs are supervisory and thus should be excluded from the unit. Suffice it to say that in jurisdictions with collective bargaining, an important question in public personnel administration is the precise definition of supervisor.

Public Employee Rights

Also specified in the legal authorization are public employee rights, it being expressly stated that employees have the right to form, join, and participate in employee organizations for the purpose of conferring and bargaining collectively with management. The right of employees *not* to join may or not be stated. If it is omitted, this usually means that union or agency shop agreements may be negotiated. Under the union shop, employees must join the majority union within a specified time period, often 30 days, or forfeit their jobs. Under the agency shop, the employees need not join the union, but to retain their jobs, they must pay the equivalent of the union dues. This payment is in return for services provided by the exclusive bargaining agent which is required to represent the interests of all persons in the bargaining unit, whether or not members of the majority union.

Usually also specified is that employees have the right to be represented by the majority union in grievances over the terms and conditions of employment, or to refrain from exercising such right. Further specified is that the unit member may elect to present his or her own grievance to the public employer on an individual basis, but the settlement of such grievance may not be inconsistent with the terms of the collective bargaining agreement and the union must be given reasonable opportunity to be present at any meeting called to resolve such grievance.

Management Rights and Bargaining Scope

Personnel administration is, of course, a management function, and management in any organization wants to be able to manage its personnel resources without interference. The reality is that management in contract negotiations yields some of its rights, sometimes important ones, in return for union concessions. Of course, it seeks to retain as many management rights as possible; as for the unions, while they usually do not press for contract clauses changing the organization's mission or purpose, they do try to negotiate as much as possible of personnel policy and procedure.

A management rights clause often is included in the legislative authorization to specify the rights that may not be bargained away. Generally enumerated are the following rights: to direct the work of employees and to hire, promote, assign, and transfer them; to demote, suspend, discharge, or otherwise discipline employees for proper cause; to lay off employees because of lack of work or for other legitimate reason; and to determine the organization, methods, means, and personnel by which work operations are to be conducted. Such management rights clauses are repeated in the agreements reached wtih the union, but a reading of the entire contract often shows that management has accepted limitations on the exercise of certain of these rights, for example, it agrees to follow certain steps in the grievance procedure provided for in the agreement.

Since the public employment board or commission rules on the interpretation of what each of these enumerated rights actually means, it can readily be seen why its role is so important. Does the right to determine the organization and methods of work operations mean that management may unilaterally decide the classification level of individual positions? The Federal Labor Relations Authority interpreted the word "organization" to include individual positions and duties, thus the agencies are not required to negotiate over job content.[3]

---

[3]Paul A. Krumsiek, "Contract Negotiation and the Classification Specialist," *Public Personnel Management* 11, no. 1 (Spring 1982): 32.

In the private sector, scope of negotiations is defined briefly in the National Labor Relations Act (NLRA) to include wages, hours, and conditions of employment. The National Labor Relations Board has established three categories of issues, (1) those that may not be bargained because contrary to law, for example, that only union members may be employed (the closed shop); (2) those that must be bargained (mandatory issues); and (3) those that may be bargained if management agrees to do so (permissive subjects). The NLRA defines the mandatory issues very briefly as "hours, wages, and terms and conditions of employment," and it is the province of the NLRB and ultimately the courts to decide what these words mean. Over the years the NLRB and the courts have interpreted them to include "paid vacations, holidays, merit increases, incentive-pay plans, Christmas bonuses, pensions, group health and accident insurance, stock purchase plans, and, under certain circumstances, the rental of company houses and the price of meals in company cafeterias."[4]

Although they are not bound by NLRB precedents, public employee relations boards or commissions in practice generally have followed this three-fold classification of issues. In government, the existence of civil service laws, state educational codes, special legislation covering the pay of blue-collar workers, and other legislation—federal, state, and local—that must be observed by the public employer makes many issues nonnegotiable that may be bargained in the private sector. The legal authorization in government usually circumscribes the negotiations by providing that subjects already covered by existing laws—particularly civil service statutes—may not be negotiated.

However, this often does not mean that the issue may not be discussed at the bargaining table or that contract clauses may not be negotiated that conflict with provisions of existing law—provided that the clause may not be made effective unless the conflicting provision of law is changed. The public employer agrees to try to get the local governing body or state legislature to change the law. The unions have maintained, and justifiably so, that some laws and regulations, such as those of civil service commissions, are not sacred, and that the collective bargaining process can play

---

[4]Donald E. Cullen, *Negotiating Labor-Management Contracts* (Ithaca, N.Y.: Cornell University, New York State School of Industrial and Labor Relations, 1951), p. 46.

a constructive role in prodding legislators to make desirable changes. So long as the lawmakers have the final say, the democratic process and the public interest are protected.

Rulings of the labor relations agency and of the courts as to which issues are mandatory or permissive vary from state to state. For example, class size may be ruled negotiable in one state but not so in another. Professional employees in government tend to define as working conditions affecting them directly many matters that the public employer believes are policy questions it must unilaterally decide in order to fulfill its responsibility for carrying out the program mission. Based on their analysis of numerous court decisions, Walter J. and Gladys Gershenfeld "conclude that courts have tended to be more concerned with preserving those rights that it believes management must possess to carry out its public duties and responsibilities under enabling statutes than with providing a safety valve for employees. The courts appear to be likely to rule borderline issues as nonmandatory, but they do provide some flexibility for employee organizations by making the *impact* of management action on wages, hours, and working conditions negotiable."[5] (Italics ours)

Impact bargaining expands the area of mandatory negotiations for the unions at the same time that it protects management rights. In personnel matters, it means that management retains its right to make program decisions, such as whether or not to have a reduction-in-force. Unless there is a nonlayoff clause in the collective agreement—and there are very few examples of such clauses in government—management can proceed with the layoff as it finds necessary but it must negotiate with the union about any action the union believes necessary to lessen impact. For example, the union may request that in filling future openings for the same kinds of positions as those held by the employees laid off they receive first consideration. As another example, if class size may not be negotiated, because of the impact of having so many pupils, the union may request an extra amount in the teachers' pay for each additional pupil.[6] Of course, management is not compelled to grant these requests but it cannot say they are nonnegotiable.

---

[5]Walter J. Gershenfeld and Gladys Gershenfeld, "The Scope of Collective Bargaining," in Jack Rabin, Thomas Vocino, W. Bartley Hildreth, and Gerald J. Miller (eds.), *Handbook of Public Personnel Administration and Labor Relations* (New York: Dekker, 1983), p. 349.

[6]Ibid., p. 348.

Unfair Labor Practices

Actions of management officials and the employee organization are constrained by what are known as unfair labor practices, by either party. Commonly, in the legal authorization such practices by the *employer* are defined to include: (1) interfere, restrain, or coerce the employees in the exercise of their collective bargaining rights; (2) dominate, interfere, or assist in the formation, existence, or administration of any employee organization; (3) encourage or discourage membership in any employee organization by discrimination in hiring, tenure, or other terms and conditions of employment; (4) discourage or discriminate against any employee because he has joined the union or filed a grievance under the collective bargaining agreement; and (5) refusing to negotiate with the union in good faith. Unfair practices by *employee organizations* include: (1) interfere with, restrain, or coerce employees in the exercise of their bargaining rights; (2) interfere with, restrain, or coerce a public employer in the selection of its representative for the purposes of negotiations or the adjustment of grievances; (3) refuse to negotiate in good faith with the employer.

The parties file their unfair labor practice charges with the labor relations agency which investigates and, if it finds a charge sustained, orders the party in violation to terminate the practice and, in the case of dismissals for union activity, to reinstate the employee with back pay. These orders may be appealed to the courts which then make the final decision.

This bare listing of unfair labor practices does not reveal the complexities, complexities with which both parties should make their representatives familiar. For example, a derogatory statement about the union and its leadership made before union members by a management official could lead to an unfair labor practice charge by the union. Unless management negotiators are aware of which overt acts the labor relations agency considers evidence of lack of good faith bargaining, such as putting off interminably meeting with the union bargaining team or refusing to meet with it at all, they may be found guilty of an unfair labor practice.[7] Collective bargaining adds a whole new dimension to public personnel administration—some instruction for managers, supervisors, and em-

---

[7]Schlomo Sperka, "Unfair Labor Practice Remedies and Judicial Review," in Public Employment Relations Services, *Portrait of a Process: Collective Negotiations in Public Employment*, p. 317.

ployees in the different aspects of labor relations becomes a necessity.

Grievances and Grievance Arbitration

The legal authorization in some cases requires, and in many cases authorizes, the parties to negotiate grievance procedures, usually with arbitration as the final step for settling the grievance. Chapter 14 is devoted to grievances and appeals; the grievance procedure and binding arbitration are mentioned here because of the relevance of binding arbitration to the relationship between collective bargaining and civil service. When an arbitrator decides whether or not an employee has been discharged for just cause, he or she, and not the civil service commission, applies the merit principle to the particular case, in other words, did the discharge violate the merit principle?

Approval of Agreements

The role of the legislative body in the approval of agreements after they are negotiated by the parties varies. In many municipalities, agreements must be approved by the local governing body (e.g., county or city council). In most school districts, approval of the agreement by the school board is required. In some state governments, the legislature must ratify the agreement, but in most states this is not the case. Of course, in every jurisdiction the legislature is responsible for voting the funds to finance the contracts and so may exercise a veto power. Management officials presenting the proposed agreement must be prepared to explain in detail its implications, in fiscal terms and anticipated impact on management rights. In the federal government, agreements take effect when approved by the agency head.

Impasse Resolution

One of the advantages of legally authorized collective bargaining programs is that they establish procedures and machinery for settlement of bargaining deadlocks (impasses). The administering agency is responsible for seeing to it that these procedures are followed and for providing the services of mediators, factfinders, and, in some cases, arbitrators to help resolve the impasse.

Mediation usually is the first step in the impasse procedure. The mediator meets with the parties, separately and jointly, and tries to bring them together on a settlement. If mediation fails, the next step often is factfinding, a semijudicial procedure in which both sides present documentation, such as cost-of-living data and information on what other employers are paying for comparable positions, and have witnesses testify in support of their recommended terms. The factfinder analyzes the evidence presented at the hearing and issues a report with his or her findings and recommendations for a settlement. If these are not accepted by the parties, in some jurisdictions they may elect to go to binding arbitration. Arbitration, too, is a semijudicial proceeding conducted in the same way as factfinding. Arbitration may be compulsory by law, as it is for fire fighters and police in about 20 states.

In both factfinding and arbitration, care and thoroughness are required in preparing documentation and witnesses. The jurisdiction's personnel office has much of the responsibility for collecting and preparing tables, charts, and other visual presentations of wage and other data. This adds still another dimension to public personnel administration; developing expertise in preparing for factfinding or arbitration and effectiveness in building management's case.

Local Agency Option

Some state laws provide a local agency option, which means that local governing bodies may opt out of the state law if they establish collective bargaining systems of their own that are in substantial conformity with the state law. The New York statute has such a provision, but very few local governments have exercised this option because of the financial and other advantages of having a state agency provide representation election, impasse resolution, and other labor relations services.

This brief discussion of collective bargaining programs leaves out many important other parts of such programs, but the purpose has been to focus on aspects with particular relevance to relationships with civil service and to the question of compatibility with the merit principle.

■ IMPACT OF COLLECTIVE BARGAINING ON PERSONNEL
ADMINISTRATION

Let us turn now to a discussion of the impact of collective bargaining on the total personnel program. In so doing, we will refer
to pertinent elements of collective bargaining programs just
presented.

Minority and Individual Rights

Some merit system administrators, as well as other critics of collective bargaining in the public service, believe that the principle
of "exclusivity" violates both minority and individual rights. "Exclusivity" means that only the majority union is authorized to negotiate terms and conditions of employment with management.
Where an exclusive bargaining agent has been recognized, minority unions and individual employees may not bargain with management on such terms for themselves. Indeed, if management
makes separate deals with them, it is guilty of an unfair labor
practice.

The objection is that if collective bargaining means recognition
only through a group then the individual is denied the right to
speak for himself or herself, and, furthermore, "The right of representation of more than one group is equally fundamental to a
merit system in representative government."[8] In government, just
as in the private sector, the exclusive bargaining agent is required
to represent the interests of *all* members of the bargaining unit,
not only in its negotiation of contract terms but also in its representation of employees in grievance cases. Employees can, if they
prefer, represent themselves in grievances, without any intervention by the majority union, but resolution of the grievance must
be consistent with the terms of the collective bargaining contract
and a designated representative of the majority union usually is
given the opportunity to be present during adjustment of the
grievance.

The courts have ruled that if exclusivity is provided for by law
it is legal and, further, that there is no violation of constitutional
rights. In an illustrative decision, it was stated:

---

[8]Felix A. Nigro, *Management-Employee Relations in the Public Service* (Washington, D.C.: International Personnel Management Association, 1969), p. 90.

> Application of the majority rule concept strengthens the right of the
> individual employee to obtain fair and equitable terms of employ-
> ment. It brings the collective strength of all the employees in the
> unit to the bargaining table and thus enhances the chances of ef-
> fectuating their community purposes and serving the welfare of the
> group. The employee who votes against the representative chosen
> by the majority or who exercises his privilege not to join the or-
> ganization of the representative suffers no constitutional infringe-
> ment of his basic freedom of contract right because of the exclusivity
> principle.[9]

Union leaders maintain that having exclusive bargaining agents
stabilizes labor relations and, in government, strengthens the merit
principle because strong unions can and do press for improvements
in personnel policies and practices. Without exclusivity, interunion
rivalries necessitate spending much time and effort on defeating
(and outpromising) the opposition, with consequent inability to
concentrate on getting the employer to improve working conditions. Objections to exclusivity were heard mostly during the first
years of the spread of collective bargaining in government; today
they are heard less frequently. Of course, those who are opposed
to collective bargaining also are against exclusivity.

Protests about the union and agency shops are still voiced with
intensity by some groups and individuals, although many merit
system administrators and other public officials apparently no
longer regard these shops as having the potential completely to
destroy the merit principle.

Several of the state collective bargaining laws authorize the
union or agency shop. Both are prohibited in the federal service
by Title VII of the Civil Service Reform Act of 1978. Some unions
are concentrating on obtaining the agency shop since the opposition to it may be less because union membership is not required.
In civil service systems, any requirement for filling or holding a
job not related to ability to do that job is a violation of the merit
principle. Although employee leaders have argued that union
membership or payment of dues reflects merit, this contention has
generally not been convincing outside union circles.

In practice, however, dire predictions as to the damage union
or agency shops would inflict on merit systems have not proved
correct. With very few exceptions, those interested in jobs under

[9]Russell A. Smith, Harry T. Edwards, R. Theodore Clark, Jr., *Labor Relations
in the Public Service: Cases and Materials* (Indianapolis: Bobb-Merrill, 1974), p.
361.

civil service have not failed to apply because of a union or agency shop nor have many of those already holding merit system positions refused to join the union or pay the equivalent of the union dues. One explanation is disenchantment with merit systems and skepticism that they really carry out the merit principle. If the union wins improved salaries and better working conditions, why be concerned about having to join or pay the union dues?

In *Abood* v. *Detroit Board of Education* (1977), the United States Supreme Court upheld the constitutionality of the agency shop in the public sector. This case originated as a class action suit by some teachers in Detroit who wanted an agency shop clause negotiated with the Detroit Board of Education invalidated. They charged that they were "forced to pay for political activities of the union with which they disagreed and in which they had no voice."[10] In a previous decision, the Court had ruled that Congress had the power to pass legislation authorizing the union shop for railroad workers in interstate commerce. In another decision, it held that prohibiting enforcement of a union shop agreement because some workers complained that their dues money was being expended for political purposes was "an unnecessarily harsh remedy." Arrangements could be made whereby a proportion of the complaining member's dues money equal to the proportion represented by the union's expenditures for political purposes to the union's total budget could not be spent by the union for political purposes or would have to be refunded if so spent.

In *Abood*, since public sector workers were the complainants, the Court directly dealt with the constitutional issue. The Court upheld the constitutionality of agency shop agreements in government (and thereby that of union shop agreements), provided that the dues money was used for customary union activities such as collective bargaining but not for political or ideological activities to which a nonunion member objected. Although the majority decision is not precise on how this principle is to be made effective, it does establish that the employee must first make known to the union his or her opposition to a union activity.

The *Abood* decision means that for the time being opposition to the union and agency shops will have to be concentrated on legislators and, because of their role in recommending legislation, on

---

[10]Robert H. Wilde, "Abood versus Detroit Board of Education," *Journal of Collective Negotiations in the Public Sector* 7, no. 3 (1978): 214.

chief executives. There is no constitutional right to the union and agency shops, just as there is none to collective bargaining.

Uniform Position Classification and Salary Plans

One of the tenets of civil service has been that there should be uniform position classification and salary plans. The positions of all employees in a jurisdiction should be classified in accordance with common standards, and salary scales and benefits should be the same for all workers in the same job classification. If this principle of uniformity is violated, the classification plan loses integrity and employees do not receive equal pay for equal work. Much of the legitimacy of civil service systems has derived from their role in enforcing this principle of uniformity in position classification and salary plans. There has been much skepticism that classification and salary plans are as objective as claimed, but until collective bargaining the principle of uniformity itself was little questioned.

Collective bargaining, at least potentially and often in practice, works against uniformity. With more than one bargaining unit, which is often the case, it is possible that the salary scale negotiated for a given job classification in one unit may be lower or higher than that negotiated for the same or similar classification in another unit. Decisions on salary scales made through the bargaining process depend on the relative power of the unions and management, not on an objective weighing of the worth of each job classification in terms of the duties, responsibilities, and qualification requirements of the positions. In standard position classification and salary plans, each job classification, after comparison with other kinds of work within the jurisdiction, is assigned to one of the grades in the salary plan. This is a ranking process because the higher the grade, the higher the salary scale. The scales themselves are based on comparisons with pay by private and other public employers for the same job classifications.

Actually, uniform classification and compensation plans have been bent, because shortages of some kinds of workers often make it necessary to pay them higher salaries than the duties and responsibilities of their positions warrant. Yet this is compromise, not an abandonment of the principle of uniformity—this is the justification made by many merit system administrators.

Unions view this matter differently. They see their objective as improving pay, thus promoting equity, not inequity. Although contract settlements may provide disparate pay and benefits for the same job classifications, still the levels of such pay and benefits are better than before the bargaining, and, in the long run, contract negotiations should eliminate any disparities. As to benefits, in some jurisdictions—notably New York City—the unions bargain jointly with management, thus assuring uniformity. Thus, in the union view there is nothing about the collective bargaining process per se that makes uniformity impossible.

Like other aspects of the disagreement between unions and civil service supporters as to what "merit" means, this debate is endless. The reality is that pay and benefits increasingly are being determined through collective bargaining, a process that is very different from "scientific management."

■ CONTRACT ADMINISTRATION

Under civil service, supervisors are considered key figures in maintaining the quality of personnel administration, since they have the most direct contact with rank-and-file employees. Supervisory training is emphasized in progressive personnel systems but nowhere is supervision so continuously monitored as under collective bargaining, and herein may lie the greatest positive impact of collective bargaining on public personnel administration. Grievance arbitration clauses are now very common in the public sector, and the supervisor is expected to be so skilled in dealings with subordinates as to remove many causes for discontent and keep formal grievances to a minimum. Of course, supervisors carry out higher management directives which often cause the grievances, but still supervisors' ineptness in dealing with subordinates accounts for a large percentage of the grievances.

Because of their mission within the union, union stewards, who are elected by the membership, often are more diligent than management and the personnel office in detecting supervisory deficiencies. Of course, they are oriented towards ferreting out "mistakes by the boss," but they may execute this policing role well because they are strategically situated in the management-worker relationship. Located at the work place where supervision functions, stewards can have intimate knowledge of the work activities conducted and of the problems involved for both management and the worker. Stewards sometimes are overzealous and some may be so antagonistic towards management that supervisors have some cause for considering them "troublemakers," but the capable, conscientious steward is a "troubleshooter" and can be a problem solver for both the union and management.

The late Nathan Wolkomir, former president of the National Federation of Federal Employees, maintained that stewards and other union officials performed much work that the personnel office should have been doing or was unable to do. Wolkomir meant investigation of grievances and calling management's attention to personnel problems of which it was not aware, and certainly union representatives are very busy in this area. Whatever the personnel office should have been doing, under collective bargaining an effective union unquestionably participates in everyday personnel administration. Even though the scope of bargaining and/or of grievance arbitration may be limited, the union and its representatives frequently will check on supervisory performance and management's obligations under the contract.

In a 1976 comprehensive mail survey of personnel directors or their equivalents in municipal and county governments, 61 percent of the respondents agreed with the statement that collective bargaining forces efficiency on management.[11] Similarly, one of the findings in a recent study (based on interviews with 81 management and 61 union officials at 20 federal government bargaining units) was that "both parties thought that steward oversight was a key element in guaranteeing uniform and equitable treatment of employees in terms of personnel policies and practices."[12]

Nearly three-quarters of the respondents in this latter study believed that supervisory performance had improved "since labor-management agreements came on the scene at national government installations." Further, "Repeatedly it was stressed by interviewees that supervisors now had to pause and think before they acted, had to document and develop a rationale for their actions, had to organize and plan the work-week in a more systematic, impartial manner."[13] Interestingly, management was a "little more sure than union officials that supervisory performance had im-

[11]Lloyd G. Nigro and John DeMarco, "Personnel Managers' Attitudes and Beliefs Concerning Collective Bargaining, Training, and Affirmative Action," p. 7. Paper delivered at 1978 annual meeting of International Personnel Management Association, New Orleans, October 1978.

[12]George T. Sulzner, *The Impact of Labor-Management Relations upon Selected Federal Personnel Policies and Practices* (Washington, D.C.: Government Printing Office, 1979), p. 36.

[13]Ibid., p. 40.

proved while agreements have been in effect."[14] Eighty-four percent of the respondents concurred that "administration of collective agreements opened up the personnel management process and has taken 'some of the mystery out' of personnel management." They attributed this "to the greater involvement in the process by program managers, supervisors, stewards, and other union officials and the employees themselves."[15]

More recent research has not contradicted the findings in these two studies that collective bargaining has in many ways been a constructive force for improvement in public personnel administration. Besides the criticism mentioned in Chapter 1, that collective bargaining is very time-consuming, many public officials dislike the adversarial nature of the bargaining process and believe that some settlements place serious restrictions on management's ability to control work operations and the workforce. In a survey of the opinions of public personnel professionals at all levels of government, Ross and Pugh found that, although a substantial majority of the respondents disagreed that collective bargaining contracts are an effective way of ensuring a more productive workforce, 46 percent disagreed and 26 percent agreed that employee associations/unions are a serious detriment to the effectiveness of the public service.[16]

■ ASSESSMENT OF THE UNION IMPACT

Based on what has been said above and other information, what summary can be given of the union impact on public personnel administration? A number of points can be made:

1. In most jurisdictions with both civil service and collective bargaining, an accommodation, although often uneasy and subject to many tensions, has been reached between the two systems. Collective bargaining partly replaces the civil service system, but civil service commissions are not limited to recruitment and examinations. They generally retain control over promotions, transfers, reductions-in-force, performance evaluation, and other aspects of the in-service personnel program, but in all or many of these areas standards and pro-

---

[14]Ibid., p. 43.
[15]Ibid., p. 34.
[16]Joyce D. Ross and Daniel L. Pugh, "Profile of the Public Personnel Administrator," *Public Personnel Management* 12, no. 3 (Fall 1983): 240.

cedures for effectuating employee status changes are governed by contract provisions.

2. With few exceptions, contract provisions do not supersede civil service laws. In many places, contract clauses that conflict with the civil service law are negotiated, subject to approval and enactment into new law by the governing body. This is particularly true in local governments.

3. Whether or not contract provisions violate the merit principle is a matter of opinion since what is "merit" to one person may not be to another. Generally, there is no convincing evidence that collective bargaining has stripped the merit principle from civil service systems. In any event, the merit principle is not consistently applied in civil service systems; for example, undue emphasis on seniority in many such systems predates collective bargaining.

4. The potential does exist that collective bargaining may substitute policies and practices that could not reasonably be equated with the merit principle, but management need not accept such bargaining demands.

5. There is growing evidence that the introduction of collective bargaining has stimulated improvements in personnel policies and practices.

6. Although not discussed in this chapter, unions carry out other activities besides collective bargaining that protect and advance employee interests and often improve personnel administration. Examples are representing union members in court actions, negotiating with administrative officials to stop certain policies or to moderate their impact on the employees, and lobbying with legislators. Of course, through these activities unions sometimes place obstacles in the way of good personnel administration.

BIBLIOGRAPHY

Burpo, John. *Police Unions in the Civil Service*. Washington, D.C.: Public Administration Service, 1979.

Hanslowe, Kurt L.; Dunn, David; and Eastling, J. *Union Security in Public Employment: Of Free Riding and Free Association*. Ithaca, N.Y.: New York State School of Industrial and Labor Relations, Cornell University, 1978.

Kearney, Richard. "Monetary Impact of Collective Bargaining." In

Handbook on Public Personnel Administration and Labor Relations, edited by Jack Rabin, Thomas Vocino, W. Bartley Hildreth, and Gerald J. Miller. New York: Dekker, 1983.

Lelchook, Jerry, and Lahne, Herbert J. *Collective Bargaining in Public Employment and the Merit System*. Washington, D.C.: Government Printing Office, 1971. Publication of Labor-Management Services Administration, U.S. Department of Labor.

Nigro, Felix A. "Collective Bargaining and the Merit System." In *Unionization of Municipal Employees*, edited by Robert Connery and William V. Farr. New York: Academy of Political Science, Columbia University, 1970.

Stanley, David T., with the assistance of Carole L. Cooper. *Local Government under Union Pressure*. Washington, D.C.: Brookings, 1971.

Sulzner, George T. *The Impact of Labor-Management Relations upon Selected Federal Personnel Policies and Practices*. Washington, D.C.: Government Printing Office, 1979.

Zeidler, Frank. *Management's Rights under Public Service Collective Bargaining Agreements*. Public Employee Relations Library, 59. Washington, D.C.: International Personnel Management Association, 1980.

7 Equal Employment Opportunity and Affirmative Action

In Chapter 1, equal employment opportunity, affirmative action, and court decisions relating thereto were discussed briefly. In this chapter, these subjects are treated in detail, and in Chapter 8 the concept of representative bureaucracy is analyzed.

Equal employment opportunity (EEO) means the absence in hiring and employment practices of discrimination on the basis of race, color, religion, sex, or national origin, age, or handicapped condition. EEO is required by the Equal Employment Opportunity Act of 1972, which amends Title VII of the Civil Rights Act of 1964, and by the Age Discrimination Employment Act and the Rehabilitation Act, both passed by Congress in 1973. Some state and local governments also have EEO legislation. Affirmative action is the instrumentality for achieving equal employment opportunity. Specifically, "Affirmative action is a good faith effort by an employer to achieve equal employment opportunity by developing and implementing results-oriented procedures."[1] In its *Affirmative Action Guidelines* issued in January 1979, the Equal Employment Opportunity Commission (EEOC) states, "The term affirmative action means those actions appropriate to overcome the effects of past or present practices, policies, or other barriers to equal employment opportunity."[2] Thus, affirmative action is a remedial concept that requires the "employer to analyze and then correct its

---

[1]Karen Ann Olsen, *Equal Employment Opportunity and Affirmative Action: A Guide for Mayors and Public Officials Prepared by Labor-Management Relations Service* (Washington, D.C.: United States Conference of Mayors, 1979), p. 17.

[2]Equal Employment Opportunity Commission, "Affirmative Action Guidelines," Part XI, *Federal Register* 44, no. 14 (January 15, 1979): 4422.

own recruitment, hiring, promotional, and other employment practices that appear to have had a disparate effect on the employment of persons protected by the federal statutes just referred to."[3]

As Thomas Sowell points out, the principle behind affirmative action is that a "court order to 'cease and desist' from some discriminatory practice may not be sufficient to undo the harm already done, or even to prevent additional harm as the result of a pattern of events set in motion by the prior illegal activity." Affirmative action as a remedial concept predates the Civil Rights Act of 1964 and applies to many questions besides rights of minorities and women. For example, the National Labor Relations Act of 1935 not only provided for cease and desist remedies against employers that engaged in antiunion activities but also for affirmative action by the employer, such as reinstatement of unlawfully discharged workers with back pay and posting of notices in "conspicuous places" to the effect that the employer would discontinue such illegal practices. "Had the employer merely been ordered to 'cease and desist' from economic (and physical) retaliation against union members, the *future* effect of its *past* intimidation would have continued to inhibit the free-choice elections guaranteed by the National Labor Relations Act."[4]

Affirmative action may be voluntary on the part of the employers or required by court order, law, or executive order. When undertaken voluntarily by the employer, affirmative action is intended to protect against possible charges of discriminatory employment practices and to avoid litigation over such matters. Affirmative action on the part of employers was first required by Executive Order 11246 issued in 1965, the employers being federal government contractors and subcontractors. In 1969, President Nixon's Executive Order 11748 required affirmative action by federal agencies to achieve equal employment opportunity in recruiting and hiring and in their personnel practices in general.

The Civil Rights Act of 1964 did not require affirmative action plans, but EEOC in its *Guidebook for Employers* (1974) stated, "The certainty of increased legal action, and consistent record of

[3]Bonnie G. Cebulski, *Affirmative Action Versus Seniority: Is Conflict Inevitable?* (Berkeley, Calif.: Institute of Industrial Relations, University of California, 1977), p. 3.

[4]Thomas Sowell, " 'Affirmative Action' Reconsidered," *Public Interest* 42 (Winter 1976): 48.

court-required affirmative action to remedy discrimination found under Title VII, emphasize the advantage to you, as an employer, of instituting an effective affirmative action program voluntarily and speedily."[5] In the EEOC's 1979 "Affirmative Action Guidelines," it states that "each person subject to Title VII should take voluntary action to correct the effects of past discrimination and to prevent present and future discrimination without awaiting litigation."[6] EEOC issued these guidelines to make clear that it approved of voluntary affirmative action plans that were "race, sex, or national origins conscious in order to achieve the Congressional purpose of providing equal employment opportunity."[7] As the reader will recall from Chapter 1, EEOC's position in this matter was sustained later in 1979 by the U.S. Supreme Court's decision in *United Steelworkers of America* v. *Weber*, but that the Reagan administration disagrees with this decision and believes that both voluntary and legislatively required affirmative action programs calling for remedial hiring ratios are illegal and unconstitutional.

■ GOALS, TIMETABLES, AND QUOTAS

This is the logical point at which to discuss the controversial question of goals, timetables and quotas.

Goals and timetables were first used by an EEO enforcement agency in 1968. In that year, the Labor Department's Office of Federal Contract Compliance Programs (OFCCP) required contractors to develop "specific goals and timetables for the prompt achievement of full and equal opportunities." In May 1971 the Civil Service Commission issued a policy statement encouraging the use of goals and timetables in federal employment in:

> . . . problem areas where progress is recognized as necessary and where such goals and timetables will contribute to progress, i.e., in those organizations and localities and in those occupations and grade levels where minority employment is not what should reasonably be expected in view of the potential supply of qualified

---

[5]U.S. Equal Employment Opportunity Commission, *Affirmative Action and Equal Employment: A Guidebook for Employers, vol. 1* (Washington, D.C.: Government Printing Office, 1974), p. 13.

[6]U.S. Equal Employment Opportunity Commission, "Affirmative Action Guidelines," *Federal Register*, January 19, 1979, p. 4426.

[7]Ibid., p. 4425.

members of minority groups in the work force and in the recruiting area and available opportunities within the organization.[8]

Controversy quickly developed that the goals were in effect quotas of minority employment that had to be achieved within given time periods and that such quotas were prohibited by Title VII of the Equal Employment Opportunity Act of 1964. As this controversy intensified, in March of 1973 the commission, the EEOC, the Justice Department, and Labor's Office of Federal Contract Compliance Programs issued a joint memorandum, relevant portions of which appear below:

> A quota system, applied in the employment context, would impose a fixed number or percentage which must be attained or which cannot be exceeded; the crucial consideration would be whether the mandatory numbers of persons have been hired or promoted. Under such a quota system, that number would be fixed to reflect the population in the area, or some other numerical base, regardless of the number of potential applicants who meet necessary qualifications. If the employer failed, he would be subject to sanctions. It would be no defense that the quota may have been unrealistic to start with, that he had insufficient vacancies, or that there were not enough qualified applicants, although he tried in good faith to obtain them through appropriate recruitment methods. . . .
>
> A goal, on the other hand, is a numerical objective, fixed realistically in terms of the number of vacancies expected, and the number of qualified applicants available in the relevant job market. Thus, if through no fault of the employer, he has fewer vacancies than expected, he is not subject to sanction, because he is not expected to displace existing employees or to hire unneeded employees to meet his goal. Similarly, if he has demonstrated every good faith effort to include persons from the group which was the object of discrimination into the group being considered for selection, but has been unable to do so in sufficient numbers to meet his goal, he is not subject to sanction.
>
> Under a system of goals, therefore, an employer is never required to hire a person who does not have qualifications needed to perform the job successfully; and an employer is never required to hire such an unqualified person in preference to another applicant who is qualified; nor is an employer required to hire an unqualified person in preference to a better qualified person, provided that the qualifications used to make such relative judgments realistically measure the person's ability to do the job in question, or other jobs to which he is likely to progress. . . . Unlike quotas, therefore, which may

---

[8]Elliot Zashin, "Affirmative Action, Preferential Selection and Federal Employment," *Public Personnel Management* 7, no. 6 (November–December 1978): 383–384.

call for a preference for the unqualified over the qualified, or of the less qualified over the better qualified to meet the numerical requirement, a goal recognizes that persons are to be judged on individual ability, and therefore is consistent with the principles of merit hiring.[9]

As is exemplified by these quoted statements, it is easy to establish in theory the differences between goals and quotas. As stated in Chapter 1, political pressures to achieve the goals may have the effect of converting them into quotas, and some people believe this is what happens.

In imposing remedial numerical hiring ratios, the courts do provide for giving priority in appointments and promotions to less qualified candidates over more qualified ones. The court orders the employer to "establish separate eligibility lists for white males and for women and/or minorities. Candidates are then selected from these separate eligibility lists in the ratio ordered by the court for a given period of time or until a given representation of women and/or minorities is achieved in the job classifications covered by the court order."[10] The creation of two employment lists instead of one means that a male with an examination rating higher than that of a woman or minority person may be passed over repeatedly and may never be appointed. As discussed in Chapter 1, the justification for the remedial hiring ratio is to correct present and past patterns of discrimination, a consideration of social justice.

Pros and Cons of "Quotas"

At this point in this book, we would like to summarize the arguments made for and against remedial hiring ratios. These arguments are *legislative, constitutional, merit-related, philosophical,* and *moral.*

Legislative

Against: There is express language in the Civil Rights Act of 1972 banning employers from granting preferential treatment to any individual or any group because of their race, color, religion, sex, or national origin, "on account of an imbalance which may exist"

---

[9]Memorandum—"Permissible Goals and Timetables in State and Local Government Employment Practices," March 23, 1973.

[10]Olsen, *Equal Employment Opportunity and Affirmative Action,* p. 22.

in the employment of such persons as compared with the total or percentage of such persons "in any community, state, section or other area, or in the available work force in any community, state, section, or other area."

For: As stated by Justice Brennan in *Weber* (see Chapter 1), the legislative history of the Civil Rights Act of 1964 and its Amendment in 1972 clearly establishes that Congress meant to authorize affirmative action plans as a means of achieving the goal of equal employment opportunity. Why would Congress have passed this historic legislation to redress discrimination without having in mind means of making it effective? And, as Brennan said, if Congress was opposed to affirmative action plans, why did it not forbid them in the legislation?

Constitutional

Against: The Fourteenth Amendment to the federal Constitution prohibits state and local governments from depriving any person of equal protection of the laws. Remedial hiring ratios deny equal protection of the laws to persons who are not appointed because preferential treatment is given to someone else.

For: Equal protection of the laws must be viewed in broad historical and social context. There is nothing in the Constitution that says that equal protection does not encompass providing redress for a class of individuals that for decades has been denied equal rights in employment, even though the means of redress does some injury to the rights of persons not in that class.

Merit-related

Against: The only permissible basis for employment under merit systems is capacity to do the job, with the candidates ranked according to their ability as measured by competitive examination. No one with a higher ranking should be passed over for someone with a lower one. Admittedly, civil service testing is imperfect, but it generally does distinguish between the lesser and the better qualified.

For: A meritorious civil service system is one that provides adequate representation in the public service for all segments of society. Besides, there is the example of veterans preference, still firmly in place at all levels of government. Why is preference justifiable for veterans but not for other classes of persons that deserve special treatment?

As Drew S. Days, III, professor of law at Yale University, states, "We have a societal attraction, at least since World War II, to testing as the most effective way to determine who is qualified and who is unqualified. That . . . is a false assumption, unless one is looking at people at the very top and the very bottom. There is a great middle section in which, even though there may be 20 percentage points between one score and the others, as a practical matter, those people will perform more or less equally."[11]

Philosophical

Against: The state should not use its coercive powers to violate individual rights even when this occurs in the process of improving the condition of deprived classes of persons. In the opinion of Robert Nozick of Harvard's Philosophy Department, equality of opportunity violates the principle that the state may not help one citizen at the expense of another. He favors a "minimal state, limited to the narrow function of protection against force, theft, fraud, enforcement of contracts, and so on."[12] In such a minimal state, a legal requirement for remedial hiring ratios obviously has no place.

For: In a state, based on justice, no advantage is permitted to some persons at the expense of others, and inequalities are justified "only if they result in compensating benefits for everyone, and in particular for the least advantaged members of society."[13] Remedial hiring ratios are a just means of providing such compensating benefit.

Michael Walzer, professor of social service at Princeton University, opposes the coercion of state-imposed equality, but he also opposes a minimal state. He writes: "Just as we could not adopt a system of preventive detention without violating the rights of innocent people, even if we weighed fairly the costs and benefits of the system as a whole, so we can't adopt a quota system without violating the rights of candidates." Walzer stresses that the blacks' history of "slavery, repression, and degradation" prevented them

---

[11]*New York Times,* December 11, 1983.

[12]Robert Nozick, *Anarchy, State, and Utopia* (New York: Basic Books, 1974), p. ix.

[13]William Goodman, "New Panel Appears to Narrow Idea of Civil Rights," *New York Times,* February 2, 1984.

from developing the "neighborhood culture and communal institutions" that would have enabled them to qualify for jobs in the numbers that they could have "under conditions of freedom and social equality." Therefore, such remedial efforts as "open search and selection programs, extensive recruiting," and "serious efforts to discover talent even when it isn't conventionally displayed" are necessary although he thinks that the long-term solution is a "significant redistribution of wealth and resources (for the sake, say, of a national commitment to full employment)."[14]

Moral

Against: It is morally wrong to "use discrimination to cure discrimination." (The quoted words are those of William Bradford Reynolds, Assistant Attorney General in the Reagan Administration.)[15]

Under remedial hiring ratios, a minority group member or a woman who has not been discriminated against is employed instead of a better-qualified white male who has no personal responsibility for previous discrimination against minorities and women. Two wrongs—one against minorities and women as a class and the other against the white male—do not make a right.

Furthermore, the minority person or the woman ends up by "being more disadvantaged" from the psychological standpoint than "if they'd been treated based on their own individual merit."

For: The white male is not treated unfairly because he has had advantages in developing employment qualifications denied minority persons and women. If one reads Supreme Court decisions carefully, the Court has recognized the reality that "a wrong that's based on race cannot be recognized without recognizing race in the process."[16]

The contention of the Reagan administration that the benefits of affirmative action and the remedies should be limited to "individual, identifiable victims of proved discrimination" is fallacious. Consider the example of school desegregation: "Case law does not require a black child to come forward to show that the child was the victim of discrimination and therefore had a right to go to a

---

[14]Michael Walzer, *Spheres of Justice* (New York: Basic Books, 1983), pp. 153–154.
[15]*New York Times,* December 11, 1983.
[16]Ibid.

desegregated school. What the Supreme Court said was that all black children, indeed all children, have a right to go to a desegregated school."[17]

As this discussion of pros and cons shows, there are many arguments on both sides. Considering the element of practicability, it is contended that affirmative action cannot succeed in the foreseeable future if reliance is placed simply on building up the candidate pool of disadvantaged persons, the stated policy of the Reagan administration. Even with expanded hiring in government instead of the present retrenchment, equal employment opportunity goals cannot be achieved on more than a token basis without remedial hiring ratios. As pointed out in Chapter 1, the reduced employment opportunities for all job seekers in the present economy and the competition of other ethnic minorities besides blacks explain much of the concern about "quotas." Of course, only the United States Supreme Court can resolve this personnel policy issue.

■ COMPONENTS OF AN AFFIRMATIVE ACTION PLAN

In all its details, what is an affirmative action plan? The EEOC, OPM, and other federal agencies enforcing equal employment opportunity requirements have published material on this subject to guide employers. Because of the importance of this matter, we reproduce in its entirety in the appendix to this chapter at the end of this book the major components of an affirmative action plan as contained in orders of the U.S. Labor Department's Office of Federal Contract Compliance Programs (OFCCP). This same material appears in a publication of the United States Conference of Mayors, *Equal Employment Opportunity and Affirmative Action: A Guide for Mayors and Public Officials* (1979).[18]

As the reader analyzes this appendix, he or she finds that it logically begins with the issuance of a written EEO policy and "affirmative action commitment," and the assignment of responsibility to a top official to carry out the program. Next is the utilization survey to determine the existence and extent of underutilization of women and minority persons, followed by the development and implementation of specific programs to eliminate

---

[17]Ibid.
[18]Olsen, *Equal Employment Opportunity and Affirmative Action.*

discriminatory barriers and correct underutilization. These specific programs include goals and timetables to increase utilization. To determine the effectiveness of implementation, a vital component is a monitoring system (audits and reports) to evaluate progress in each aspect of the total affirmative action plan.

Underutilization is determined by comparing the "percentage of available qualified" persons in the relevant labor market "with those currently employed by the organization" in the particular occupational category. The sources for obtaining labor market statistics are identified, and it is stressed that the utilization survey should include an analysis of the availability within the organization of promotable, trainable, and transferable persons.

A frequent question is, what happens if collective bargaining agreement(s) entered into by the employer with union(s) conflict with the organization's EEO policy? The answer is clearly stated: The conflicting contract provisions are illegal and must be renegotiated if employer and union(s) are to protect themselves from law suits.

Basically, the items included in the monitoring or auditing requirements for determining EEO progress are very similar to the checklists used in periodic evaluations by employers of their personnel programs. The important difference is that under EEO there are legal sanctions against the employer if its EEO program is not implemented properly. Periodic evaluations of the employer's personnel programs are made by the enforcement agencies, and if violations are found and conciliation fails, court remedies are available. Throughout the history of EEO and AA, there have been many complaints that enforcement is lax, and such charges have been made against the Reagan administration because of changes in policies it has made in this area. These charges are vehemently denied by administration officials.

The reader will note the comprehensiveness of the audit requirements, to the point that social and recreational programs are included. Special attention is necessarily given to the maintenance of records. Particularly important are applicant flow records to identify applications from minorities and women. (Fairfax County, Virginia, won a discrimination suit entered against it by the Justice Department by proving from its applicant records that the relevant labor market for employees in the lower salary brackets was northern Virginia, not the entire Washington, D.C., metropolitan area as claimed by the Justice Department. Because of transportation problems, applications for Fairfax County jobs from central city residents in Washington, D.C., were far less than those from northern Virginia. The court agreed that no prima facie case of discrimination against blacks from the District of Columbia had been established.)

Note also the requirement for "affirmative action records" to determine possible disparate effect of decisions on layoff, recall, demotion, discipline, discharge, seniority, transfer, training, and career development.

The questions posed under "Recruitment" reflect the concept of positive recruitment, that concept being applied comprehensively to attraction of minority candidates and women. The points to be investigated under "Minimal Job Qualifications" and "Selection Procedures" cover in detail requirements for job relatedness. To improve validity of recruitment and selection methods, desirability of using women and minority group members as recruiters, reviewers of applications, and interviewers is indicated.

Under "Wages and Benefits," discriminatory treatment of women in pay, job classifications, fringe benefit, and disability allowances is probed. The questions under this heading pinpoint where in the past women often have been given discriminatory treatment now prohibited by law and court decisions. Under "Social and Recreational Programs and Other Employment Conditions," monitoring of the work environment to assure that it is free of intimidation and other harassment based on sex, color, creed, age, disability, religion, or national origin is emphasized.

As to goals and timetables to correct underutilization, both long-range and short-range targets are to be included in the affirmative action plan.

■ AFFIRMATIVE ACTION AND SENIORITY

In recent years, as governments have had to reduce force for budgetary reasons, preference in order of layoff for minority group persons has become a controversial issue. Just as with remedial ratios, the Reagan administration considers preferential layoff policies illegal, unconstitutional, and in fact reverse discrimination.

The Civil Rights Act provides in Section 703(h) of Title VII:

> Notwithstanding any other provision in this title, it shall not be an unlawful employment practice for an employer to apply . . . dif-

ferent terms, conditions, or privileges of employment pursuant to a bona fide seniority or merit system . . . provided that such differences are not the result of an intention to discriminate.

The last hired, first fired rule has long been provided for in many private sector collective bargaining agreements, and in government length of service is the most important factor in determining the order of layoff in a majority of jurisdictions.

Exactly what Congress meant by a bona fide seniority system is unclear from the legislative history. Many unions maintain it meant to "immunize neutral seniority systems from attack even if such systems tended to perpetuate the effects of past discriminatory employment practices." Civil rights groups and black union members contend that "Congress could not have intended to permit the continuation of employment practices that institutionalized the effects of past discrimination."[19]

In *Franks* v. *Bowman* (1976), the U.S. Supreme Court ruled that an employment seniority system that perpetuates discrimination suffered by an employee *after* passage of the Civil Rights Act of 1964 must be altered and retroactive seniority granted and that Section 703(h) does not prohibit such remedy. The plaintiffs were black truck drivers who until 1972 were restricted to "local, less well-paying runs" and barred from the "more desirable and remunerative long distance runs" which were reserved for white drivers. The black drivers had applied for the long-haul jobs but their applications had been rejected. The Court maintained that there was nothing in the legislative history of Section 703(h) to indicate that it was "intended to modify or restrict relief otherwise appropriate once an illegal discriminatory practice occurring after the effective date of the Act is proved—as in the instant case, a discriminatory refusal to hire." Congress had vested the courts with broad discretion to provide relief from illegal discrimination, and an award of both retroactive back pay and seniority since the date of rejection of the black drivers' applications for the longer-haul jobs was appropriate. The Court stressed that seniority rights were very important, noting that in the case being reviewed they "determined not only layoff and recall but also who was the highest bidder for either scarce or the best driving jobs." The Court made clear that "it was the hiring practices, not the seniority system,

---

[19]Robert N. Roberts, " 'Last Hired, First Fired' and Public Employee Layoffs: The Equal Employment Opportunity Dilemma," *Review of Public Personnel Administration* 2, no. 1 (Fall 1981): 31.

that were unlawful. The decision merely required that the plaintiffs be granted a rank whereby they would obtain the benefits inherent in the system, namely competitive status to bid for limited benefits as well as noncompetitive, remunerative benefits such as vacations."

In *Teamsters* v. *United States* (1977), the Court ruled that the "literal terms of Section 703(h) and its legislative history demonstrates that the act was not meant to be applied retroactively." (This case also dealt with short- and long-run drivers.) Accordingly, a bona fide seniority system that perpetuates pre-1964 act discrimination is legal, and retroactive back pay and seniority rights may not be granted. However, the Court reiterated the ruling in *Franks* v. *Bowman* that seniority systems continuing postact discrimination were illegal. It also dealt with an issue not resolved in the prior case: whether those who had *not* applied for the long-run jobs because of the discriminatory practices could also be granted relief. The Court ruled that such relief could also be granted this latter category of employees since they must have been deterred from applying because of the futility of doing so in view of the employer's discriminatory practices. The case was remanded to the district court for it to determine the "actual relief to be granted . . . whether the individual plaintiff either was or would have been an applicant, whether the applicant was qualified and therefore would have been hired but for the unlawful practices, and whether and when vacancies in the long-haul positions had occurred."

While *Franks* v. *Bowman* and *Teamsters* v. *United States* are private sector cases, the federal courts have followed them as precedents in deciding public sector conflicts between seniority systems and affirmative action.

In *Chance* v. *Board of Examiners* (1972), decided by a federal circuit court of appeals, the district court in which the case had originated had approved a rule providing ethnic quotas in layoffs so as to maintain existing minority-white ratios. The positions were those of supervisors in the New York City public schools, and the controversy was over how to "measure seniority for minority employees recently placed" in these positions in the event of layoffs. Under the rule approved by the district court, three seniority lists were to be maintained, and "no person from either the black or Puerto Rican list could be laid off in any one school district unless the percentage of the group in that district exceeded the percentage of the employees of the same group in the citywide school system." This meant that in order to adhere to this ratio, white supervisors with more seniority "could be laid off before junior minority employees."

The appeals court ruled that "to lay off in such a manner would amount to 'constitutionally forbidden reverse discrimination.' " However, it approved the granting of "constructive seniority" to individual employees "denied promotion because of a test since invalidated as discriminatory." Specifically, the court approved the "education board's offer to grant such employees a fictional date of employment which would be the mean (average) appointment date of those people who did pass the examination."

In *Acha* v. *Beame* (1972), the same appeals court ruled that if employees can prove in court that "but for the employer's discriminatory hiring practices" they would have been employed early enough to gain enough seniority to protect them from layoff, then laying them off would violate Title VII. Before 1973, the New York City police department had "hired females only as 'policewomen,' for which there was a quota of 1.34 percent of the total police force . . . " After 1973 a single classification of police officer for males and females was established with the same entrance test, "but hiring continued to be based on a sex quota, four men being hired for every one women." The number of women police officers had increased to 2.6 percent of the force by June 1975 when 4,000 police officers were laid off because of the city's financial crisis. As the result of the city's "facially neutral seniority rule, 73.5 percent of the females on the force were laid off as compared to 23.9 percent of the males."

The district court had ruled that the city acted legally in applying its seniority rule and "that to do otherwise would constitute unlawful preferential treatment on the basis of sex." The appellate court reversed this decision but limited relief to those persons who "themselves were the victims of discrimination by the [city]. In outlining the the kind of proof the district court might consider adequate in making individual determinations of discrimination, the court suggested that the individual show she had filed an application, written a letter complaining about the hiring policy, or 'expressed a desire to enlist,' but was 'deterred' by the city's known discriminatory practices."

In 1973, as the result of a court suit, the city of Detroit had modified hiring practices that discriminated against women; however, it had continued a civil service rule providing for layoff in accordance with length of service in a particular classification such as sergeant in the police department. Until 1970, women had been eligible only for positions in the police department's women and children's section, "thereby limiting the number of vacancies as well as the number of sergeant positions available to women." After 1973, 100 women had been hired in the police department and 18 promoted. In July of 1976, Detroit laid off 1,280 employees including 600 police officers, the layoffs affecting women more adversely than minorities or males because of the seniority by rank rule. All 100 of the newly hired women were to be laid off, and all 18 of those who had been promoted were to be demoted in accordance with this rule.

The U.S. district court hearing the suit enjoined the layoffs and demotion of the women in the police department because it did not think the seniority system was a bona fide one inasmuch as it perpetuated the effects of past discrimination. "The newly promoted women in the police department had longer service in the department but less seniority in the rank of sergeant than the men because prior to the court-ordered affirmative action plan they had been eligible for promotion only in the segregated women's department." [20]

The seniority controversy came to a head in 1982 when an appeals court upheld a district court requiring that when the Boston school system reduced force, it had to maintain the existing proportion of black teachers regardless of seniority. In 1974, the district court had found the Boston School Committee guilty of intentional segregation in the employment and assignment of teachers, and in 1975 it ordered that one black teacher be hired for every white teacher hired until black teachers constituted 20 percent of the teachers in the school system. Whereas the percentage of black teachers was only 5.4 percent in 1974, by 1981 it had risen to 19.09 percent. Layoffs became necessary for budgetary reasons, and the School Committee petitioned the court to allow it to disregard the seniority provisions of its contract with the teacher union. Not only did the court grant this request, it also required that, when the school system recalled teachers to fill future openings created by retirements, resignations, and reassignments or by new recruitment because of improved finances,

---

[20]See Cebulski, "Affirmative Action Versus Seniority: Is Conflict Inevitable?" for a detailed discussion of these cases.

black teachers had to be given absolute recall reemployment preference until the 20 percent goal was achieved. Albert Shanker,
president of the American Federation of Teachers, wrote: "This is
new legal turf. While the federal courts have previously imposed
racial hiring quotas in cases where general racial discrimination has
been determined, and while they have granted retroactive seniority, and thus job protection, to *individuals* who were found to
be victims of earlier discrimination—they have never required that
innocent employees of one racial group be let go, regardless of
seniority, to make room for less senior (or even new) employees
of another racial group."[21]

The Supreme Court declined to hear this appeal, but later in
1982 the Justice Department filed a Friend of the Court brief con-
testing a district court order requiring that in layoffs of black and
Hispanic members of Boston's Police and Fire Departments, the
existing percentage of minority group members in both departments had to be preserved, seniority notwithstanding. Because the
whites who had been laid off were later rehired, the Supreme
Court declared the case moot.

In June of 1984, in *Memphis v. Stotts,* the Supreme Court did
rule on the legality under Title VII of the Civil Rights Act of 1964
of court orders setting aside the normal seniority rights of non-
minority employees.[22] In 1980, under a district court-approved
consent decree the City of Memphis had adopted a goal of increasing minority representation in the Fire Department to about
the same proportion of blacks as in the labor force of Shelby
County, Tennessee. The court decree said nothing about layoff policy in relation to this goal, and in May of 1981 the City announced
that it would make layoffs, following the rule of last hired, first
fired. The district court issued an order, affirmed by the appeals
court, requiring the City not to apply a seniority policy if such
action would result in a decrease in the percentage of black employees in the Fire Department. In some cases, so as to comply
with the district court order, nonminority employees were laid off
or reduced in rank. However, all white employees laid off were
reemployed only one month after layoff, and others who were demoted were offered their old positions.

Voting six-to-three, with Justice White writing the majority opin-

---

[21]Albert Shanker, "Teachers in Boston Laid Off by Race," *New York Times,* June
20, 1982.

[22]*Memphis* v. *Stotts,* 52 LW 4764 (1984).

ion, the Supreme Court ruled that the case was not moot since the district court's order remained in effect and would have to govern future reductions-in-force. Furthermore, noted White, the dismissed employees had lost a month's pay and seniority that had not been restored. The Court majority held that the district court's order constituted an improper modification of the original consent decree since that decree made no mention of layoffs at all. Reaching the heart of the preference question, White stated that the congressional debates on Title VII made clear that relief could only be provided to those who themselves have been the victims of illegal discrimination. Further, there had been no finding that the blacks protected from layoff had been victims of discrimination nor had awards of retroactive seniority been made to any of them. White cited *Teamsters* v. *United States* (previously referred to in this chapter) as clearly establishing the Court precedent that mere membership in a class (minorities) was insufficient to warrant a seniority award and that each individual had to prove that the discriminatory practice had an effect on him or her.

Writing for the Court minority, Justice Blackmun rejected the majority's opinion that the case was not moot. It had been the previous practice of the Court in similar cases, he said, simply to erase the orders of the lower courts, thus eliminating any continuing effects from the orders of those courts. The minority justices flatly disagreed with White's statement that to obtain relief the individual would have to demonstrate that he or she had been the actual victim of discrimination. In its past decisions the Court had made a distinction between relief for an individual and relief for a class of persons, and all the federal courts of appeals had ruled that race-conscious affirmative relief is appropriate under Title VII. Finally, the minority justices maintained that the legislative history of the Civil Rights Act of 1964 and of its amendment in 1972 abundantly makes clear that Congress intended for race-conscious remedies to be provided. Blackmun points out that when Congress amended the Civil Rights Act in 1972, it added language authorizing the federal courts to order any "equitable relief" they believe necessary.

The Civil Rights Act of 1964, as amended in 1972, does contain a provision on bona fide seniority systems. It says nothing specifically about preferential treatment of minorities through the use of hiring ratios. The decision in *Memphis* v. *Stotts* does not deal with "quotas" for appointment or promotion, yet inevitably deductions are being made as to how the Court will rule at some future time on remedial hiring or promotion ratios. In the majority opinion, White does quote a statement by the Republican sponsors of the Civil Rights Act of 1964 in the House of Representatives to the effect that Title VII would not "permit the ordering of racial quotas in business or unions." The minority justices quote various evidences that Congress in approving the legislation did want and expect race-conscious remedies to be employed as necessary. The speculation will, of course, continue until the Supreme Court finally decides this question.

BIBLIOGRAPHY

Bureau of National Affairs. *EEO in Public Safety Agencies*. Washington, D.C.: 1982.

Cebulski, Bonnie G. *Affirmative Action versus Seniority: Is Conflict Inevitable?* Berkeley, Calif.: Institute of Industrial Relations, University of California, 1977.

Golden, Michael Evan. *A Dialogue on Comparable Worth*. Ithaca, N.Y.: New York State School of Industrial and Labor Relations, 1983.

Goodman, Carl. "Equal Employment Opportunity: Preferential Quotas and Unrepresented Third Parties." *Georgetown Law Journal* 44, no. 4 (May 1976).

Nigro, Lloyd G., ed. "A Mini-Symposium: Affirmative Action in Public Employment." *Public Administration Review* 34, no. 3 (May–June 1974).

Olsen, Karen Ann. *Equal Employment Opportunity and Affirmative Action: A Guide for Mayors and Public Officials*. Prepared by Labor Management Relations Service. Washington, D.C.: United States Conference of Mayors, 1979.

Public Personnel Management 10, no. 4 (Winter 1981). Special issue on affirmative action.

Rosenbloom, David. *Equal Employment Opportunity: Politics and Public Personnel Administration*. New York: Praeger, 1977.

Stewart, Debra W. "Assuring Equal Employment Opportunity in the Organization." In *Handbook on Public Personnel Administration and Labor Relations*, edited by Jack Rabin, Thomas Vocino, W. Bartley Hildreth, and Gerald J. Miller. New York: Dekker, 1983.

Stewart, Debra W., and Garson, David G. *Organizational Behavior and Public Management*. New York: Dekker, 1983.

U.S. Commission on Civil Rights. *Nonreferral Unions and Equal Employment Opportunities*. Washington, D.C.: Government Printing Office, 1982.

8 Public Personnel and Representative Bureaucracy

Over the past 25 years, economic, social, and political forces in the United States have combined to produce heavy pressure on public employers to eliminate long-standing barriers to the hiring and career development of minorities and women. Those who make and administer public personnel policies are expected to support the goal of a "representative" public workforce. Laws requiring equal employment opportunity ii the public as well as private sectors, and the affirmative action pro͵rams designed to implement them, have had a major impact on public personnel practices. Equal employment opportunity (EEO) and affirmative action were discussed fully in Chapter 7. In this chapter we examine the *concept* of representative bureaucracy and its implications for public personnel administration. We will be dealing with these questions: What relationship is there, if any, between the socioeconomic backgrounds of civil servants and the political behavior of public bureaucracies? Would the policies of public agencies staffed by minorities and women be more "responsive" to the needs and interests of these groups? More broadly, does "representative bureaucracy" support democratic institutions and values? These questions suggest that representative bureaucracy is a concept with ramifications extending well beyond the now generally accepted need to assure equality of opportunity for minorities and women.

■ THE CONCEPT OF POLITICAL REPRESENTATION

The idea of representative bureaucracy has its roots in Western political theory and philosophy. With respect to U.S. institutions, the concept of representative *government* may be traced directly to the political theory of 17th-century England and, of course, to the American and French Revolutions. In Hanna F. Pitkin's words:

> Representation had become one of the traditional "rights of Englishmen," worth fighting for; with the American and French revolutions it was transformed into one of the "rights of Man." Thus representation came to mean popular representation, and to be linked with the idea of self-government, of every man's right to have a say in what happens to him. And that is how it became embodied in our institutions.[1]

Historically, political theorists have concentrated on executive, legislative, and judicial institutions as means of representation; bureaucratic organizations have only recently drawn attention. However, the first step toward an understanding of what is implied by the term representative bureaucracy is to attempt to clearly define what is meant by *representation*. For many, a representative is someone who *acts for* an individual or group. Alternatively, representation may be seen as *standing for* the population or groups and individuals within it. Generally speaking, U.S. governments operate on the "acting for" model; however, concepts of representative bureaucracy tend to mix it with the "standing for" idea.

The "Acting for" Concept of Representation

In general terms, this interpretation stresses that representatives are persons *authorized* to act on behalf of others. This authority may be derived from any one or a combination of sources, including divine right, popular election, appointment, custom, law, and force of personality (charisma).[2] In democracies, political authority is balanced by *accountability*. In other words, representatives are empowered to act for others, but they are also restrained and made responsive by a variety of electoral, judicial, and institutional processes. In liberal democracies such as the United States, representative government is conceived of as a structure for articulating and balancing different interests. Elected representatives are ex-

---

[1]Hanna F. Pitkin, *The Concept of Representation* (Berkeley, Calif.: University of California Press, 1967), p. 3.

[2]Max Weber, *The Theory of Social and Economic Organization*, Talcott Parsons, ed. (New York: The Free Press, 1947), pp. 120–145.

pected to act for a variety of groups or factions with overlapping as well as conflicting interests, and the need to satisfy these groups encourages compromise and discourages radical or extreme positions.[3] Responsiveness and accountability to constituencies are also promoted by regular elections and other means of removing incumbents from elective or appointive office.[4]

The "Standing for" Concept of Representation

In contrast to the "acting for" approach, the "standing for" concept is largely passive in its definition of the representative's behavior. Emphasis is placed on the creation of legislative bodies composed of persons who in their social origins and occupations mirror the composition of the general society. According to Pitkin, "In political terms, what seems important is less what the legislature does than how it is composed."[5] With respect to decision making, a passively representative legislature is supposed to provide "information" about attitudes and interests throughout the society that may be useful to the *executive*. In effect, the legislative body does not initiate action, it reacts to initiatives taken by the executive. At best, the legislature has the formal power to limit executive action and to block policies that run counter to the interests of a majority of legislators. At worst, it is a powerless "debating society." The framers of the U.S. Constitution, especially Alexander Hamilton, argued that a "mirroring" legislature could exist only if required by the Constitution. Otherwise, the electorate would, in its wisdom, select those who would be most effective and responsive as active representatives.[6]

The rise of the modern administrative state, the emergence of large public bureaucracies, and the expansion of bureaucratic power and discretion have raised serious questions about the extent to which today's bureaucrats are accountable and responsive to the popular will. In the United States, and many other countries, public administrators have been given broad authorizations to interpret legislative intent and to act in the "public interest."

---

[3]Robert A. Dahl, *Pluralist Democracy in the United States: Conflict and Consent* (Chicago: Rand McNally, 1967).

[4]Alexander Hamilton, "Federalist No. 35," *The Federalist Papers* (New York: Washington Square Press, 1964), pp. 76–82.

[5]Pitkin, *Representation*, p. 61.

[6]Hamilton, "Federalist No. 35," pp. 79–80.

However, many fear that this power may not be adequately limited by traditional "external" methods such as regular elections, laws, administrative procedures, budgets, and legislative oversight.[7] If external controls are not effective, officials may escape accountability and use their resources and expertise to promote "special interests," including their own.[8] Proponents of representative bureaucracy suggest that it is (or can be) an important *internal* source of popular control.[9]

It is posited that a representative bureaucracy promotes an internal diversity of opinions and interests that greatly improves the likelihood of broadly responsive public policies. However, among those who accept this general proposition, there is disagreement over *how* representative bureaucracy leads to greater accountability and responsiveness. Some believe that representation in the organization must be of the active variety, but others favor the passive model.

Those taking the "acting for" point of view believe that the civil service should be made up of people drawn from the ranks of politically significant and legitimate interest groups within society. Their reasoning is that public agencies staffed in this manner should be responsive to the values and needs of these groups. It is also assumed that domination over public policy by any one group will not take place because those acting for different and rival interests will "check" and restrain each other; negotiation and compromise will produce policies that are acceptable (if not optimal) to all or most of the interests concerned.[10] In other words, popular control and accountability are achieved not primarily by elections and other external mechanisms but rather because civil servants will be "psychologically responsible" as a result of their socialization in the values and interests of the groups from which they come.

Samuel Krislov, following the above line of reasoning, sees the central functions of representation as: (1) allowing broadly based

---

[7]Herbert Kaufman, "Fear of Bureaucracy: A Raging Pandemic," *Public Administration Review* 41, no. 1 (January–February 1981): 1–9; Reinhard Bendix, *Higher Civil Servants in American Society* (Boulder, Colo.: University of Colorado Press, 1949).

[8]Phillip J. Cooper, *Public Law and Public Administration* (Palo Alto, Calif.: Mayfield Publishing Co., 1983), pp. 213–232.

[9]Bendix, *Higher Civil Servants*.

[10]J. Donald Kingsley, *Representative Bureaucracy: An Interpretation of the British Civil Service* (Yellow Springs, Ark.: Antioch Press, 1944).

and balanced presentation of viewpoints within public agencies, and (2) assuring that differing and conflicting interests will be considered when decisions are made and policies formulated.[11] J. Donald Kingsley concluded, " . . . if the essence of responsibility is psychological, the degree to which all democratic institutions are representative is a matter of prime significance. No group can safely be entrusted with power who do not themselves mirror the dominant forces in society . . . "[12]

Kingsley was the first writer to propose an "acting for" concept of representative *bureaucracy*. His frame of reference was the British civil service; he stressed the need for that nation's bureaucracies to be actively representative of its social, political, and economic elites. Those looking at the issue from a U.S. point of view, as might be expected, have taken a far more pluralistic and egalitarian position. Norton E. Long, for example, has asserted that the federal government's agencies are actually *more* representative than are the Congress and the chief executive. According to Long, the federal bureaucracy effectively acts for legitimate interests not fully attended to by legislators and the president because it has a more "democratic" membership as concerns such characteristics as social origin and economic class.[13] Others, while accepting the "acting for" approach, reach conclusions different from Long's. They argue that the U.S. civil service is representative only in the dominant class sense described by Kingsley.[14]

Other theorists put forward a largely passive approach to the question. They reject the active orientation, primarily on grounds that it subverts the equal employment opportunity built into the merit principle and encourages partisan activity by the civil service. Paul P. Van Riper and Frederick C. Mosher see passive representation as providing an internal sociological source of information about the range of societal norms and interests needed to make policies that are in the public interest (or, more likely to be in the public interest than those made by unrepresentative bodies). Both also believe that proportional sociological representation gives symbolic affirmation to the democratic value of equal op-

---

[11]Samuel Krislov, *Representative Bureaucracy* (Englewood Cliffs, N.J.: Prentice-Hall, 1974), pp. 64–66.

[12]Kingsley, *Representative Bureaucracy*, p. 282.

[13]Norton E. Long, "Bureaucracy and Constitutionalism," *American Political Science Review* 46, no. 3 (September 1952): 808–818.

[14]Gideon Sjoberg, Richard A. Beymer and Buford Farris, "Bureaucracy and the Lower Class," *Sociology and Social Research* 50, no. 3 (April 1966): 325–337.

portunity.[15] Mosher offers the following definition of passive representation:

> The passive (or sociological) meaning of representativeness concerns the sources of origin of individuals and the degree to which, collectively, they mirror the total society. It may be statistically measured in terms, for example, of locality or origin and its nature (rural, urban, suburban, etc.), previous occupation, father's occupation, education, family income, family social class, race, and religion.[16]

In these terms, the function of representative bureaucracy presumably is similar to that of legislative "standing for." Administrative policymakers must continuously work with civil servants who by their presence symbolize and "inform" them about a wide (representative) spectrum of values and interests in the society. Passive representation may also become active if sociological, ethnic, or racial groups within the bureaucracy see policies as having a strongly negative impact on their counterparts in the population. Consequently, at least in theory, passive representation effectively moderates and limits the exercise of executive power.

In practice, both the active and passive concepts of representation rely heavily on socioeconomic, racial, ethnic, and gender variables as measures of representativeness. Both approaches also tend to assume that these characteristics are valid indicators of the content of preentry *socialization* experiences and, therefore, of postentry values and attitudes. At this point, the passive model concentrates on the informational and constraining effects of sociological representation. In contrast, the active representation model posits that attitudes lead to advocacy-related behaviors which, in turn, have an influence on the policy outputs of public agencies.[17] Figure 8.1 shows the hypothesized chain of events, and the differences between the two models.

■ WEAKNESSES IN THE THEORY OF REPRESENTATIVE BUREAUCRACY

Although it is intuitively plausible and a great deal of research needs to be done on the topic before a final judgment can be made,

---

[15]Paul P. Van Riper, *History of the United States Civil Service* (New York: Harper and Row, 1958), and Frederick C. Mosher, *Democracy and the Public Service* (New York: Oxford University Press, 1968).

[16]Mosher, *Democracy and the Public Service*, pp. 12–13.

[17]Raymond Barton, "Roles Advocated for Administrators by the New Public Administration," *Southern Review of Public Administration* 3, no. 4 (March 1980).

FIGURE 8.1.
Active and Passive Representative Bureaucracy: Linkages Between
Group Origins and Bureaucratic Responsiveness

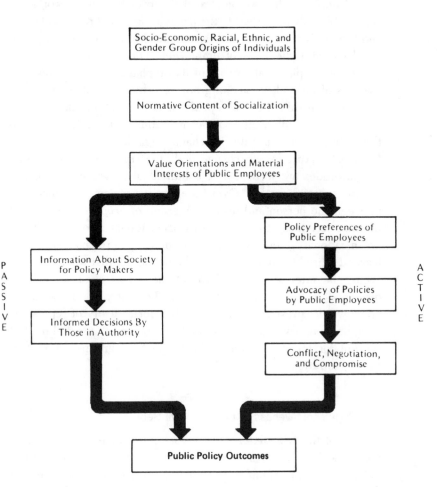

there are several reasons why the "theory" of representative bureaucracy should not be accepted uncritically. First, it is reasonable to ask whether or not the basic assumption that *internal* representativeness is necessary in order to maintain control over bureaucratic behavior can be supported. Existing (or new) external controls may be enough to assure responsiveness and accountability, thereby undermining the political "need" for representative bureaucracy, be it passive or active.[18] Second, power and influence

---

[18]Kenneth J. Meier, "Representative Bureaucracy: An Empirical Analysis," *Amer-*

is not distributed evenly throughout bureaucracies; coalitions of bureaucratic elites control major areas of the policy-making process.[19] Therefore, the sociological makeup of the entire workforce is probably only important to the passive concept of representation, and then only if it is assumed that the decisionmakers actually deal regularly with the mass of employees. On the other hand, the active model places almost all of its emphasis on the representativeness of the policy-making group, the higher civil service.

Third, it is difficult to accept the necessary assumption that attitudes toward policy alternatives are acquired *prior* to entry into the public service and do not change significantly over a career. Obviously, attitudes do change and, perhaps more importantly, new attitudes are formed as the individual moves from one reference group to another. Over time, the psychological connections between the person and his or her *group of origin* may very well become secondary to those with organizational associates. If the organizational reference group becomes a primary source of learned attitudes, there is at least the possibility that when conflicts occur, the interests or standards of the *group of origin* will be discarded or seriously compromised. Postentry socialization, in other words, presents a major problem for a theory of representative bureaucracy that sees the public employee as a sort of neutral conduit for the expression of the interests of groups external to the organization.

The Representativeness of the U.S. Civil Service

Studies of the U.S. federal service are illustrative of how data on sociological and other measures of representativeness can produce different interpretations. Kenneth J. Meier, in an analysis of the data collected by a number of researchers reported that *in the aggregate* the federal workforce was highly representative. Using a summary measure of inequality or representativeness called the Gini Index (R), Meier found the following:

1. With regard to father's occupation ordered by status, federal

ican Political Science Review 69, no. 2 (June 1975), and Kenneth J. Meier and Lloyd G. Nigro, "Representative Bureaucracy and Policy Preferences: A Study in the Attitudes of Federal Executives," *Public Administration Review* 36, no. 4 (July–August 1976).

[19]Hugh Heclo, *A Government of Strangers* (Washington, D.C.: Brookings Institution, 1977).

employees were very close to the general population (R = .12).

2. Educationally, federal employees closely resembled the society at large (R = .11).

3. Age-wise, they were also quite representative (R = .11).

4. Income was at some variance with that of the overall population (R = .25). This is to be expected since federal pay practices tend to upgrade lower-level and blue collar employees while greatly underpaying executives in comparison to the earnings of their counterparts in the private sector.[20]

Using the civilian labor force (CLF) as the standard for comparison, government statistics actually reveal slight overrepresentations of minorities and women. Table 8.1 shows the extent of minority and female participation in the federal workforce as of late 1982.

It is figures like these that have led some observers to describe the U.S. civil service as "representative" and, by implication, "re-

TABLE 8.1
Minority and Female Participation in the Federal Workforce*

Race/Ethnic Group	% Workforce	% Male	% Female
White	75.9	48.3	27.6
		(46.2)	(35.0)
Black	15.5	7.0	8.5
		(5.1)	(5.0)
American Indian/ Alaskan Native	1.7	.9	.8
		(.3)	(.2)
Asian/Pacific Islander	2.4	1.6	.9
		(1.0)	(.8)
Hispanic	4.5	3.0	1.5
		(3.8)	(2.4)

*Nonpostal civilian employees
Effective September 30, 1982
Figures in parentheses are for the entire civilian labor force (CLF) in the United States. Total minority workforce representation in the 1982 CLF was 18.6 percent. The percentage of women in the CLF has been increasing rapidly, and is probably around 40 percent as of this writing.
Source: *Affirmative Employment Statistics,* OPM Compliance and Investigations Group, Office of Workforce Information (Washington, D.C.: U.S. Office of Personnel Management, September 30, 1982).

[20]Meier, "Representative Bureaucracy: An Empirical Analysis": 531–534.

sponsive."[21] However, these data are somewhat deceptive because they do not control for level of responsibility, agency, or type of work being done. Meier, for example, found that representativeness declined rapidly as one moved up the hierarchy.[22] As Tables 8.1–8.4 indicate, minorities and women are concentrated in the lower levels of the grade structure, are unevenly distributed among federal agencies, and minorities tend to be overrepresented in blue collar jobs.

Studies of the higher U.S. civil service have shown that this influential administrative elite is not sociologically representative of the general population. Federal SES and executive personnel "are predominantly white, male, well-educated professionals from upper-middle class urban families."[23] A 1980 study by Russell

TABLE 8.2
Nonpostal Civilian Employment in Executive Branch Departments and Selected Independent Agencies

Department	Total	% Minority	% White	% Female	% Male
Agriculture	137,008	12.7	87.3	31.9	68.1
Commerce	36,637	20.4	79.6	43.9	56.1
Defense	950,975	22.0	78.0	33.1	66.9
Education	5,902	39.2	60.8	55.5	44.5
Energy	17,376	16.2	83.8	35.5	64.5
HHS	143,247	35.1	64.9	64.5	35.5
HUD	14,296	32.3	67.7	48.2	51.8
Interior	72,041	30.5	69.5	32.2	67.8
Justice	57,011	25.7	74.3	38.0	62.0
Labor	18,575	28.0	72.0	43.4	56.6
State	10,967	16.4	83.6	38.9	61.1
DOT	61,033	15.5	84.5	20.2	79.8
Treasury	123,274	26.6	73.4	52.7	47.3
EPA	9,379	19.4	80.6	34.1	65.9
GSA	32,210	39.9	60.1	37.3	62.7
MSPB	308	36.0	64.0	57.8	42.2
NASA	22,623	12.6	87.4	23.9	76.1
OPM	7,245	29.7	70.3	61.9	38.1
VA	231,300	29.4	70.6	52.7	47.3

Effective September 30, 1982
Source: *Affirmative Employment Statistics,* OPM Compliance and Investigations Group, Office of Workforce Information (Washington, D.C.: U.S. Office of Personnel Management, Sept. 30, 1982).

---

[21]Long, "Bureaucracy and Constitutionalism," and Van Riper, *History of the U.S. Civil Service.*

[22]Meier, "Representative Bureaucracy: An Empirical Analysis": 533–535.

[23]Meier and Nigro, "Representative Bureaucracy and Policy Preferences": 462.

TABLE 8.3
Federal Employment of Minorities: White Collar vs. Blue Collar Jobs*

	% White Collar Jobs	% Blue Collar Jobs
Total**	78.5	20.6
Black	72.6	26.8
Hispanic	68.1	31.1
Asian and Pacific Islander	69.9	29.5
American Indian and Alaskan/Native	73.8	25.6
White	80.4	18.3

*Nonpostal civilian   Effective September 30, 1982
**Total = 1,991,507
Source: *Affirmative Employment Statistics,* OPM Compliance and Investigations Group, Office of Workforce Information (Washington, D.C.: U.S. Office of Personnel Management, September 30, 1982), p. 5.

TABLE 8.4
Employment of Minorities and Women by Grade*

Grade	% Minority	% Black	% Hisp.	% A/PI	% AI/AL	% Fem.	Total
1	50.6	37.3	8.5	2.6	2.2	75.4	6,195
2	39.7	28.8	6.4	1.7	2.8	72.3	23,233
3	34.3	23.5	5.5	2.1	3.2	75.8	94,353
4	31.8	22.1	5.0	1.8	2.9	77.2	179,788
5	29.1	20.6	4.6	2.1	1.7	71.5	202,101
6	28.8	21.4	4.0	1.8	1.5	73.7	94,034
7	24.1	16.3	4.5	2.1	1.2	56.1	138,506
8	24.5	19.0	3.2	1.5	.9	52.9	30,305
9	20.2	11.7	4.4	2.5	1.7	42.8	160,191
10	18.3	11.1	4.8	1.5	.8	42.2	28,797
11	16.3	9.3	3.4	2.4	1.2	28.1	170,655
12	13.0	7.2	2.6	2.3	.8	16.8	170,332
13	10.3	5.8	2.0	1.9	.7	11.2	113,111
14	8.8	4.7	1.7	1.7	.6	8.3	59,979
15	8.7	3.7	2.0	2.7	.4	7.3	36,696
SES & Exec.	7.2	4.3	1.6	.7	.6	9.2	7,803

*Nonpostal civilian employees
Effective September 30, 1982
Source: *Affirmative Employment Statistics,* OPM Compliance and Investigations Group, Office of Workforce Information (Washington, D.C.: U.S. Office of Personnel Management, September 30, 1982).

Smith revealed a very similar pattern on the state level.[24] It is hard to conclude, therefore, that bureaucratic accountability and responsiveness are being achieved through sociological representa-

[24]Russell L. Smith, "Representative Bureaucracy: A Research Note on Demographic Representation in State Bureaucracies," *Review of Public Personnel Administration* 1, no. 1 (Fall 1980).

tiveness in the higher levels of public agencies. In fact, if the "active" version of the theory of representative bureaucracy is predictive with respect to the connections among origins, attitudes, and behaviors, there should be major differences between the policy preferences of those running government organizations and those of the public. However, this sharp contrast does not seem to exist. Contrary to the predictions of the theory of representative bureaucracy, attitudes in the higher civil service appear to be similar to those of the general population. At least, this seems to be the case for the federal service.[25] In other words, knowing the ethnic, racial, and sociological origins of members of administrative elites may tell us very little about their attitudes and preferences with regard to most public policies.[26]

There is, on the other hand, evidence to suggest that agency affiliation is a better predictor of attitudes than social origin. Given that most high level career civil servants have spent many years working in their agencies, it is not surprising that they express policy preferences which favor the programs they administer. Since many public agencies are dependent on organized interest groups or clientele for political support and, accordingly, have long histories of being highly responsive to these groups, it is also not surprising that the degree to which policy priorities are shared with the general public tends to break down when agency affiliation is taken into account. What emerges is a pattern of bureaucratic *pluralism* (agencies tied to specific interests) that *aggregates* into an attitudinally "representative" higher civil service. Although further research is needed, at this point it seems reasonable to expect that knowing the administrator's current organizational affiliation is more important than knowing his or her race, ethnicity, or socioeconomic group of origin.[27] Apparently, socialization to agency values and perspective tends to overcome beliefs and attitudes associated with the individual's *group of origin*.[28] However, it should be noted that the very small percentages of women and racial minorities at the highest levels of the civil service makes it very difficult to predict what impact they might have if fully represented.

[25]Lloyd G. Nigro and Kenneth J. Meier, "Bureaucracy and the People: Is the Higher Federal Service Representative?", *The Bureaucrat* 4, no. 3 (October 1975).
[26]Meier and Nigro, "Repre?entative Bureaucracy and Policy Preferences": 466.
[27]Nigro and Meier, "Burea?cracy and the People": 304; see also Samuel Krislov and David H. Rosenbloom, *Representative Bureaucracy and the American Political System* (New York: Praeger, 1981), pp. 31–73 and 75–107.
[28]Meier and Nigro, "Representative Bureaucracy and Policy Preferences": 467.

The early 1980s, for example, have witnessed the emergence of a "gender gap" on political issues and candidates.

■ IMPLICATIONS FOR PUBLIC PERSONNEL ADMINISTRATION

In the form outlined above, the concept of representative bureaucracy appears to be inadequate as a prescription for using personnel policies and methods to achieve more effective political control over public bureaucracies. Although the available evidence is far from complete and more research needs to be done before the case can be declared "closed," there is now little reason to believe that making the higher civil service demographically or sociologically representative would produce greater responsiveness.[29]

Nevertheless, the relatively strong association between policy preferences and agency affiliation suggests that the concept of active representation may be a useful guide to the evaluation of public personnel practices *if the agency and its interest group clientele are treated as the primary agents of socialization*. If, in fact, Kingsley's psychological responsibility is to specific agencies and to programs favored by agency clientele (as opposed to the administrator's group of social origin), then responsiveness to the broad range of societal interests may be at least in part a function of: (1) the organizational structure of the executive branch, and (2) the personnel policies and procedures applied to the higher civil service.

The first point to be made is that active representation is probably best understood as a primarily *interagency* or interorganizational unit process as opposed to an intergroup phenomenon. Thus the focus of analysis becomes the departments, bureaus, agencies, and other units of the administrative system. To rephrase Kingsley: No executive branch organization can safely be entrusted with power that does not contain the range of administrative agencies (and influential bureaucratic elites) necessary to allow the active representation of most if not all significant societal interests. Second, if agency elites are important "vehicles" of representation, then the extent to which personnel practices support as well as

---

[29]Orville G. Brim, Jr., "Socialization Through the Life Cycle," in Orville G. Brim and Stanton Wheeler (eds.), *Socialization After Childhood* (New York: Wiley, 1966), pp. 3–32; Herbert Kaufman, *The Forest Ranger* (Baltimore, Md.: Johns Hopkins Press, 1960); Emmette S. Redford, *Democracy in the Administrative State* (New York: Oxford University Press, 1969); and Kenneth J. Meier, *Politics and Bureaucracy* (North Scituate, Mass.: Duxbury Press, 1979).

limit this role for the elites must be considered. More specifically, to what degree are high-level administrators encouraged or permitted to build strong long-term loyalties to a specific agency and its programs? Also, do personnel rules and regulations "protect" administrators who actively promote agency interests, even if these run counter to those of hierarchical superiors and elected executives?

The Agency Socialization Model of Representative Bureaucracy

Like the group of social origin approach, the agency socialization model of representative bureaucracy predicts that attitudes and policy preferences are often translated into decisions about what policies to promote and to implement. The major difference is that it makes agency elites central elements of executive branch responsiveness and accountability. Figure 8.2 sets forth the basic components of the agency socialization model.

The pattern of relationships shown in Figure 8.2 does not conform to the hierarchical or "top-down" structure of political policymaking and administrative roles assumed to exist in the so-called overhead democracy system of government. At least in theory, "vertical" or overhead democracy assigns the representative function to legislatures and elected executives, leaving neutral implementation to the public bureaucracy. However, a more accurate description of how governments in the U.S. operate must include a very strong "horizontal" component. In a still quite accurate description of the federal personnel system, Herbert Kaufman noted that:

> The operation of the government in each policy area devolved upon clusters of administrative agencies, congressional committees, and interest groups . . . agencies . . . began to function almost autonomously, behaving less like parts of a large team than as individual, independent establishments. With the end of the spoils system, the civil service had been growing steadily into a corps of specialists who outlast political officers. The politicians come and go; the civil servants remain. The transients are amateurs, laymen; the permanent body is expert. In relations between the two groups, it was often the political officers who felt themselves at a disadvantage, psychologically, factually, technically. Political control declined somewhat in force; some agencies went into virtual freewheeling and others partially so.[30]

---

[30]Herbert Kaufman, "The Growth of the Federal Personnel System," in Francis

FIGURE 8.2.

The Agency Socialization Model of Representative Bureaucracy

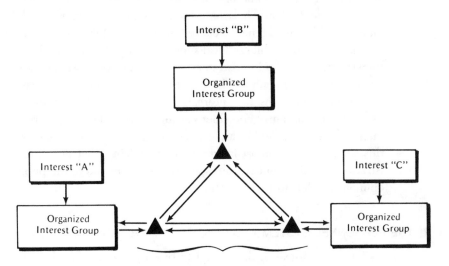

Inter-Agency Conflict, Cooperation, Negotiation, and Compromise Through Successively Higher Levels of the Executive Hierarchy

Policies and Program Priorities Responsive to Interests A, B, and C

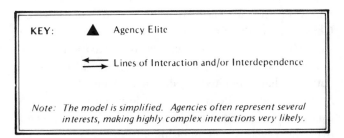

KEY: ▲   Agency Elite

         ⇄   Lines of Interaction and/or Interdependence

Note: The model is simplified. Agencies often represent several interests, making highly complex interactions very likely.

For the federal government, and for many state and local governments, the reality of public administration is one of a fragmented, pluralistic, often loosely articulated structure of executive departments, independent agencies, and regulatory bodies—each

E. Rourke (ed.), *Bureaucratic Power in National Politics*, 2d ed. (Boston, Mass.: Little, Brown, 1972), pp. 272–273.

actively transacting with relevant interest groups, legislative actors, and other agencies, some of which are likely to be on other levels of government. This "horizontal" environment provides a solid foundation for the agency socialization model. Here, responsiveness is not always to hierarchical superiors, even Presidents. Using their power bases, administrators will not always passively carry out the political agenda of the elected executive, especially when that agenda threatens the interests of agency clientele or upsets established programs. For chief executives and their appointees, intent on establishing hierarchical control over "the bureaucracy," this situation leads amost inevitably to complaints that the administrative establishment is "unresponsive" to them and to the public opinion that led to their election.

■ THE PERSONNEL SYSTEM AND CONTROL OF THE BUREAUCRACY

As Kaufman indicates, the administrative arrangements, rules, and procedures of the federal personnel system contributed in part to conditions that fostered and encouraged agency-level resistance to efforts at hierarchical control by elected and other "political" executives. Many Presidents cited the commission system and the insulation of the personnel system from executive direction as a major factor in their inability to fully implement the policy objectives of their administrations. In fact, a major reason for the passage of the Civil Service Reform Act (CSRA) in 1978 was the Congress's willingness to accept President Carter's argument that the old system was frustrating efforts to achieve more responsive government. Chief among the practices listed as requiring extensive reform were: (1) a merit system that overprotected employees at the expense of managerial capacity and flexibility, (2) agency-based career patterns that promoted loyalty to the agency and responsiveness to its clientele while providing little incentive to look to the chief executive for policy leadership, and (3) lack of executive control over the rewards and punishments necessary to control the behavior and performance of civil servants.

Merit Protections

The merit system, designed in large measure to protect public employees from undue partisan influence and coercion, deliberately places obstacles in the way of those trying to exert political discipline over the bureaucracy. While employees are expected to be "neutral," merit protections and procedures have made it difficult to hire, transfer, discipline, or fire career personnel for reasons that appear to be partisan. This point was made strongly in the so-called "Malek Manual" prepared during the Nixon administration as a guide to "getting around" the system:

> . . . because of the maze of rules and regulations with regard to the hiring and firing of Federal employees, the executive is more often than not frustrated with its ability to insure a loyal chain of command. Yet the executive is answerable to the electorate, every four years, for its management of the Government. . . . The record is quite replete with instances of the failures of program, policy, and management goals because of sabotage by employees of the Executive Branch who engage in the frustration of these efforts because of their political persuasion and their loyalty to the majority party of Congress rather than the executive that supervises them. And yet, in their own eyes, they are sincere and loyal to their Government.[31]

Given the American experience with the Nixon administration's efforts to bypass the federal merit system and to install a pervasive structure of political "clearances" for government jobs, one wonders how strongly its leaders believed in majoritarian rule. It is also absurd to equate the executive branch with the government. The executive branch is one part of a system of shared and diffused powers. The legislative and judicial branches have strong and legitimate claims on the loyalties of public administrators, and they have on many occasions joined with them to block or to modify executive policy initiatives. However, by 1978, many believed that the executive branch's capacity to function was threatened by an overly protective personnel system that provided a shield behind which agency administrators could build very powerful coalitions with interest groups and legislative committees. The establishment of the Office of Personnel Management (OPM), the creation of the Senior Executive Service (SES), and the streamlining of disciplinary and appeals procedures under the CSRA, while not eliminating basic protections against partisan manipulation, do represent major steps in the direction of increasing executive control over the higher federal civil service.

---

[31]*The Bureaucrat* 4, no. 4 (January 1976): 430–431.

Career Patterns

Another major contributing factor was the typical career followed by those reaching the highest positions in the federal service. The vast majority have pursued a career within a single agency. Historically, interagency mobility has been limited, especially for those above General Schedule (GS) pay grade 13 or 14. A 1979 OPM survey of federal employees revealed that during the previous 10 years fully 78 percent had *never* made an interagency move.[32] Between 1965 and 1969, only 5 percent of supergrades (GS 16–18) moved from one agency to another.[33] Prior to the creation of the SES, the federal personnel system—tied to job classifications and position descriptions—discouraged voluntary as well as planned movement of senior level personnel among agencies. Over the years, the result has been the emergence of highly stable, deeply entrenched groups of senior administrators who have had little or no meaningful management experience in more than one agency.[34] Since most high level administrators have entered the federal service at relatively low levels and worked their way up to leadership positions over a 15- to 25-year period, conditions have been ideal for strong socialization to a *single agency or program perspective*.

The greatly increased mobility and expanded lateral entry provisions of the CSRA as it applies to the SES allow the executive to move SES personnel from agency to agency in a way that may, over time, weaken ties to specific agencies while promoting a point of view that emphasizes loyalty to the SES and the President. It is still too early to determine if such a change is taking place; however, if it does, the CSRA will have had a major impact on the balance of power in the federal policy-making process. In other words, the roles played by administrative elites in representing interests will probably shift strongly in the direction of those associated with the President and his or her party.

Control Over Performance Evaluations and Incentives

Performance appraisals are discussed in some detail in Chapter 11. However, it is worth noting here that prior to implementation of

---

[32]Office of Personnel Management, *Federal Employee Attidude Survey,* 1979.

[33]Thomas E. Schism, "Employee Mobility in the Federal Service," *Public Administration Review* 34, no. 3 (May–June 1974).

[34]Heclo, *A Government of Strangers.*

the CSRA there was no strong incentive to use performance evaluations as an *executive* goals setting and control mechanism in the federal bureaucracy. The performance appraisal and merit pay provisions of the Act are designed to place supervisors squarely at the center of an effort to establish stronger hierarchical control over the behavior of federal employees, including the higher civil service.[35] In fact, while promoting the CSRA, President Carter and then Civil Service Commission Chairman Alan Campbell argued that it would greatly increase responsiveness to executive as well as congressional mandates because managers could use its performance appraisal and merit pay features to effectively "motivate" and discipline federal workers. Under the "old system," over 95 percent of performance ratings given were "Satisfactory" or better, and pay raises were largely a matter of seniority within grade.[36] Carter, and other Presidents before him, believed that he needed more control over the performance evaluation and incentives systems than that offered by the Commission model created under the Pendleton Act.

Taken in combination, the performance appraisal, merit pay, and SES components of the CSRA provide the chief executive and his or her deputies considerable *direct* control over the pay and career prospects of administrators. If this leverage is used effectively (see Chapter 3 on motivation), the higher federal service should become more "responsive" to the chief executive. If this is indeed the outcome, it should provide at least a partial counterweight to the forces that favor an agency model of responsiveness. One possible way to evaluate the impact of the CSRA on agency socialization would be to monitor the relationship between agency affiliation and policy preferences, paying particular attention to the degree to which these preferences reflect the "policy agenda" of the elected executive.

■ IS REPRESENTATIVENESS DESIRABLE?

As we have pointed out above, personnel policies may have a major impact on the behaviors of higher civil servants, especially with regard to the question of representation in its active sense. We have also noted that existing research evidence tends to suggest

---

[35]Barry Dean Karl, *Executive Reorganization and Reform in the New Deal* (Cambridge, Mass.: Harvard University Press, 1963).
[36]According to Civil Service Commission and OPM reports and documents.

that proportional representation of women and minorities on all levels of public bureaucracy would not by itself create an administrative establishment more responsive to societal values. The higher federal service, while not demographically representative, appears to be fairly representative of the general public in its policy preferences. Agency elites tend to support policies that favor their organizations and programs. Often, chief executives are frustrated in their attempts to exercise hierarchical control because career administrators derive much of their power from strong "horizontal" coalitions with legislative committees and interest or clientele groups, and the protections offered by civil service laws, regulations, and procedures.[37]

It is somewhat ironic that President Carter engineered the passage of the first major legislation on the federal civil service since the Pendleton Act only to see it became a tool in the hands of a new administration committed to radically different policies. What practical effect the CSRA has had on the Reagan administration's capacity to discipline the higher federal service is a question that has not been explored systematically, but there is little doubt about its commitment to a sustained effort to establish hierarchical control. While most public administration as well as corporate management thought emphasizes the control needs of executives and, therefore, tends to see the organizational world in "vertical" terms, active representation of client interests keyed to agency socialization probably articulates a broader range (not a complete range) of societal interests than would a tightly hierarchical system of control by an elected chief executive who is necessarily oriented to majority opinion. Responsiveness *up* the chain of command is certainly to be valued in managerial-administrative terms, and personnel policies that enhance such responsiveness should be given careful consideration. However, a multiplicity of channels among bureaucrats, legislators, and interest groups provides a level of "horizontal" responsiveness that should not be undervalued. Chief executives may be expected to want personnel arrangements that strengthen their control over the day-to-day operations of the bureaucracy. Given their administrative responsibilities and political objectives, a strongly executive-oriented personnel management

---

[37]Graham T. Allison, *The Essence of Decision: Explaining the Cuban Missile Crisis* (Boston, Mass.: Little, Brown, 1971); Ronald Randall, "Presidential Power versus Bureaucratic Intransigence: The Influence of the Nixon Administration on Welfare Policy," *American Political Science Review* 73, no. 3, 1979.

program is a normal and entirely legitimate desire. Nonetheless, the executive branch *is not* the government, and those concerned about personnel administration as a contributor to democracy and bureaucratic responsiveness to a broad range of minority interests should pause to consider the virtues of personnel systems that in certain important respects limit executive power.

Finally, what importance should be given to demographic or passive representation? It is possible that passive representation serves an important political function by psychologically constraining and informing those who make and implement public policies. Although it would be difficult to clearly establish such an impact, it might exist. Far more significant, we suspect, is the symbolic role of a demographically representative public bureaucracy.[38] The effort to achieve a representative bureaucracy communicates the idea that the United States is truly committed to the values of equal opportunity and socioeconomic mobility on the basis of effort and ability. This affirmation of the rule of law and the dignity of the individual is reason enough to seek demographic representativeness on all levels of government in the United States.

BIBLIOGRAPHY

Bendix, Reinhard. *Higher Civil Servants in American Society*. Boulder, Colo.: University of Colorado Press, 1949.

Dahl, Robert A. *Pluralist Democracy in the United States: Conflict and Consent*. Chicago: Rand McNally, 1967.

Kingsley, J. Donald. *Representative Bureaucracy: An Interpretation of the British Civil Service*. Yellow Springs, Ark.: Antioch Press, 1944.

Krislov, Samuel. *Representative Bureaucracy*. Englewood Cliffs, N.J.: Prentice-Hall, 1974.

————, and Rosenbloom, David H. *Representative Bureaucracy and the American Political System*. New York: Praeger, 1981.

Mosher, Frederick. *Democracy and the Public Service*. New York: Oxford University Press, 1968.

Pitkin, Hanna F. *The Concept of Representation*. Berkeley, Calif.: University of California Press, 1967.

Suleiman, Ezra N. *Politics, Power, and Bureaucracy in France: The Administrative Elite*. Princeton, N.J.: Princeton University Press, 1974.

---

[38]Murray Edelman, *Political Language* (New York: Academic Press, 1977).

9 Job Evaluation and Pay: Pressures and Conflicts

There are many technical aspects of the preparation and maintenance of job evaluation and pay plans, questions which must, of course, be satisfactorily resolved by personnel administrators. We will not go into these technical problems in any detail; a number of books and many articles are available for anyone seeking this kind of information.[1] Rather we will concentrate on job evaluation and pay in terms of their impact on relationships between employees and management. Above all, the public policy implications of job evaluation and pay decisions will be stressed.

■ JOB EVALUATION

Job evaluation is the process of comparing individual positions and ranking them in value for pay purposes. Whatever the method employed, it results in the assignment of each job to a pay level or grade, the term commonly used. Job evaluation is based on *job analysis*, which is essential not only for establishing pay distinctions but also for providing detailed information required for recruitment, examination, performance evaluation, and other phases of the personnel program.

In the public services of the United States, the most common method of job evaluation is *position classification*. In this approach, all positions considered approximately equal in duties, responsibilities, and qualification requirements are placed in the same *class* of positions. The same examination is used in filling vacancies in the class, and the same salary range applies to all positions in the

---

[1]Harold Suskin (ed.), *Job Evaluation and Pay Administration in the Public Sector* (Washington, D.C.: International Personnel Management Association, 1977).

class. Hundreds and even thousands of jobs may be determined by the position classification analysts to belong in the same class (e.g., messenger or beginning clerk), or the class may consist of only one position (e.g., budget director). Classes are aligned internally on the basis of comparisons with the other classes. Obviously, the budget director class is much higher than that of a beginning clerk, and clerks performing more responsible duties are placed in higher classes than beginning clerks, such as senior clerk. Classes are also aligned on the basis of *external* comparisons, that is, comparisons with private sector rates for comparable duties and responsibilities.

Each class of positions is assigned to a pay grade, the number of which varies from jurisdiction to jurisdiction, depending upon whatever number is considered necessary to reflect significant work differences in the salaries paid. Some state and local governments have dozens of pay grades; the federal government has 18 grades in its General Schedule for white-collar employees (members of the Senior Executive Service are compensated under a different plan, described in Chapter 4 and to be discussed again later in this chapter).

Other methods of job evaluation of a quantitative nature and widely used in the private sector are increasingly being adopted in government.[2] Position classification is based on an evaluation of the job as a whole. While all important aspects of a job are considered, no attempt is made to assign point values in accordance with judgments as to the degree to which a job possesses each of certain ranking factors such as skills required, degree of responsibility, complexity of the work, and analytical and creative ability. In point rating schemes, each factor is defined, and various degrees of each factor are described in "narrative form, varying from the lowest to the highest degree of the factor. . . . Point values are assigned to each degree. A position is evaluated by selecting the appropriate degree on each factor and assigning the point value for that degree. . . . The worth of a position is determined by totaling the points assigned to each factor. This total can be converted to a dollar amount, a grade, or a skill level."[3]

Another method, a version of which was adopted by the federal government and has been implemented for close to half the white

---

[2]Ibid., pp. 130–174.
[3]Ibid., p. 21.

collar positions, is based on factor comparisons, whereby key jobs are chosen and "ranked under each factor from the strongest to the weakest position with respect to that factor. Point values are assigned to each position for each factor. . . . An individual position is evaluated by comparing it with the key jobs factor by factor. If the position is considered to be of equal value with a key position on a particular factor, the point value for the key job is assigned. . . . The points thus selected for each factor are totaled and converted to a dollar amount, a grade, or a skill level." Factor comparison differs from point rating in that comparisons are made with a key job, factor by factor, rather than with a "narrative definition of a degree." An important reason for adopting factor comparison is that many employees find comparisons with key jobs easier to understand and more acceptable.[4]

The Experience with Position Classification

The historic contribution of position classification was to bring relative order out of a chaotic situation of misleading job titles, grossly inequitable pay for the same kind and level of work, and blind recruitment and examination procedures owing to lack of detailed knowledge of job content. Adoption of position classification and accompanying compensation plans, beginning with the first decades of the 20th century, constituted a new, important stage in development of merit systems because it ended legislative juggling of pay rates for individual employees in order to reward political supporters. Position classification also gained wide support as an administrative reform, reflecting basically the same thinking as scientific management which placed great emphasis on the breakdown of the job as basic to the introduction of more efficient methods. Rationality characterized both position classification and scientific management, and it was this rationality that constituted a big selling point for position classification. It was businesslike.

The element of subjectivity

Actually, position classification has always been a subjective process, which is true of all forms of job evaluation including the quantitative ones. Some jobs are easy to classify, for example, those of

---

[4]Ibid., pp. 21–22.

messengers, but in many lines of work, differentiations as to levels of difficulty and responsibility are hard to make. This is particularly true in "clerical, fiscal, social service, medical, scientific, and administrative classes."[5]

Critics of the personnel function in government maintain that, far from being a scientific process, it is a mysterious one, and decisions by position classifiers often are given as examples. The contention is that the classifier decides the classification of an individual position on the basis of "hunch," not irrefutable evidence and conclusions about the job. Whatever the truth in this contention, classification analysts obviously are no more infallible than other kinds of workers, and they do misclassify some positions. For example, an audit conducted several years ago by the Office of Personnel Management of the classification of white-collar jobs by agency personnel offices revealed that about 11 percent of these jobs may be overgraded and about 3 percent undergraded. Although much of the overgrading was attributable to pressures by operating officials who for one reason or another wanted higher salaries for the employees, still some of the erroneous grading was due to error by the classifier.[6]

Because the process is subjective, classifiers themselves disagree. The quantitative methods of job evaluation are said to be more objective than position classification, but still they call for "several exercises of unscientific human judgments at each stage of value determination before the final scientific and arithmetic whole is reached."[7] The factors employed in evaluating jobs under the quantitative plans are essentially subjective, particularly such factors as skill, effort, initiative, complexity, judgment, adaptability, and aptitude for learning. Others such as responsibility for work of others, responsibility for policy formulation, and supervision exercised are less subjective, but there are frequent ambiguities and disagreements with respect to them also.[8] The fact that there are many subjective elements in job evaluation and other personnel processes does not mean that they are worthless. The challenge is to reduce the element of subjectivity and arbitrary judgment to the extent possible.

---

[5]Ibid., p. 99.

[6]*A Federal Position Classification System for the 1980's*, Report of the Classification Task Force (Washington, D.C.: Office of Personnel Management, 1981), p. viii, p. ix.

[7]Suskin, *Job Evaluation and Pay Administration in the Public Sector*, p. 127.

[8]Ibid., p. 136.

Failure to consider the person

Conversely, classification analysts are criticized for too much objectivity because they base their determinations on the duties and responsibilities of the position, not the qualities of the person occupying it. Better prepared and more efficient workers do not understand why the analyst is not swayed by these factors in deciding whether or not to recommend a higher classification for their positions. The classifier is not concerned with how much work the employee turns out and how well he or she does it. The relevant question to the classifier is whether the duties and responsibilities of the employee fit the class of positions to which the employee's job is presently assigned or have grown so much as to justify placing the position in a higher class. The employee may have more education and professional training than his or her coworkers, but, if the duties and responsibilities are not different, the classifier will recommend disapproval of the requested reclassification. The same holds for efficiency; that does not count either to the position classifier. Of course, it counts when decisions are made by the employees' supervisors on salary increases, but these usually are small in amount because salary scales in government are narrow (the spread between minimum and maximum rates is not great). Besides, the usual practice is for within-grade increases to be granted automatically (upon completion of a given time period) to almost all employees, the mediocre as well as the good ones.

Rank classification. Rank classification was mentioned in Chapter 4 in comparing the British and United States personnel systems. It takes into account the background, qualifications, and abilities of the employee and is not geared as is position classification to assuring equal pay for equal work. In the American environment, rank classification has generally been viewed as alien although it has a long history in the military and in a few organizations like the Foreign Service. The only concession that classification analysts would make was that if employees through their ability and efforts made their jobs more responsible, then reclassification was proper but only because the jobs had changed sufficiently.

For some kinds of positions, however, the rank principle has been tolerated as a practical necessity. A good example is secretarial positions because pressures are intense to give higher classifications to secretaries of higher executives, no matter that they may be doing less difficult and responsible work than secretaries of officials lower in the organization. A classification expert once said that "secretarial jobs are the most sacrosanct of the sacred cows!"[9] Classification analysts make recommendations that may or may not be approved by their superiors in the personnel office, and agency heads or their designated representatives can and do veto some recommendations of the personnel office.

Position classifiers have also long acquiesced in the rank principle for certain kinds of professional jobs, such as in the social work field. Unless supervisory responsibilities are assigned, caseworkers normally perform the same general type of work. Some will have invested in a two-year program of training at a graduate school of social work whereas others will have an undergraduate degree only. The incentive to obtain the graduate training is to earn more, and so pressure is brought on the classifiers to take the qualifications of the person into account. It is argued that the caseworker with the superior training does a more effective job of interviewing and serving the needs of welfare clients than the person without such advanced preparation. Because of this pressure, classifiers often agree to two levels of social workers because otherwise they would be held responsible for discouraging the employment and retention of better trained social workers. Similarly, the skill of trial lawyers varies so greatly that classification analysts often decide to follow the recommendations of the head of the legal department for, if they do not, they bring on a storm of opposition by placing in the same class the position of the weakest and of the most effective trial lawyer.

In recent years, there has been much support for application of the rank principle to high-level professional and executive jobs. It is maintained that there are many intangible factors of creativity, drive, and leadership, the possession or absence of which makes for success or failure in these positions. The long-cited example of the private sector, where there is a wide spread in the pay of executives depending on their performance, has now had impact, and, as the reader knows from Chapter 4, position classification is not followed in the federal government's Senior Executive Service. However, according to a Classification Task Force of OPM and agency personnel experts, "in most agencies and in the regulations

---

[9]Julius Eitington,"Why Classify Secretarial Positions?" *Personnel Administration* XV, no. 5 (September 1952): 33.

governing the system issued by OPM," rank-in-person is a "misnomer" for the SES because "the criteria for assigning SES pay rates are either non-existent or have no direct connection with either the accomplishments and performance of the individual or the importance of that individual's job to the organization."[10]

In the United States, possibilities of adopting the rank principle—or loosening position classification tenets—for middle- and lower-level jobs appear small. The objection is that this change would create the same chaos and salary inequities that existed prior to the adoption of position classification plans. Employees and unions are very much concerned with preserving the hard-earned victory of "equal pay for equal work." Tradition has a strong role in these matters. One of the reasons why the British have not extended unified grading to positions below the undersecretary level (see Chapter 4) is that civil servants in that country have not been "paid strictly according to the jobs they do, but rather according to their *rank* in a class."[11]

Grade Creep

Since the newspapers have published many articles about "grade creep," this term is fairly well known, certainly in government circles. "Grade creep" refers to the rise in the *average* grade of all employees in a jurisdiction. Much of this increase is attributable to the employment of large numbers of professional, administrative, and technical employees needed to carry out new kinds of frequently very complicated programs. But some of the "grade creep" is also the result of overgrading in order to pay someone more, often to meet outside offers, compensate for inflation, or to give special treatment to an employee for one reason or another. As the result of grade creep, taxpayers become irate over the increase in the government's salary bill, and critics of the personnel office deride it for not living up to its claims about maintaining equal pay for equal work.

There is, of course, no justification for blown-up job descriptions and payment of higher salaries to employees whose level of work and performance do not merit it. Yet much of the overgrading

---

[10]*A Federal Position Classification System for the 1980's*, p. 29.

[11]M. J. Flores and J. B. Heath, "The Fulton Report: Job Evaluation and the Pay Structure," *Public Administration* 48 (Spring 1970): 15–22.

occurs because the classification and salary plans are tied together in what sometimes appears to be an inextricable knot. Jobs are assigned to relatively narrow classes, and the latter are then placed in crowded pay grades which usually cannot be changed without authorization of the legislative body which often delays in acting to raise pay. In such a situation, pressures are enormous to place positions in higher grades in order to obtain higher pay for the incumbents. Consequently, the classification plan is distorted by numerous such reclassifications and new inequities created because some employees do not succeed in getting their positions reclassified.

Grade distortion of this type occurs even when the legislature delegates to the executive branch the responsibility for changing the salary scales. As recent history in the federal service shows, chief executives seeking to control inflation may be unwilling to grant increases sufficiently high to make the pay fully comparable with that in the private sector. Furthermore, the process of making surveys of private sector rates is time-consuming, and by the time such studies are completed and new compensation scales adopted, private pay has already changed, even substantially.

Of course, even when job evaluation does not apply, as in the federal government's SES, the chief executive could delay in changing the broad bands of pay for the employees involved, so inequities of the same type could be created. However, rank classification does not pretend to provide equal pay for equal work, and, as already noted, it has been applied to relatively few workers. The solution, of course, is to provide a mechanism for prompt pay revision in government to maintain full comparability with private rates, but this is very difficult to achieve. As we shall see later in this chapter, there is much criticism that federal salaries are too high compared to private pay, and there is much disagreement over the correct measures of comparability.

Narrow classes and inflexibility

Narrow rather than broad classes of positions have characterized American classification plans. Narrow classes contain a restricted range of duties requiring specialized qualifications whereas in broad classes there are wide ranges of tasks that a worker with a general background can be trained to perform. Narrow classes have resulted from the historic emphasis upon recruitment to fill particular positions, the duties of which candidates are expected to be able to perform without extended on-the-job training. The early classification plans were very specialized, but, in recent years in some but hardly all jurisdictions, very narrow classes have been consolidated into broad ones, a process sometimes referred to as broadbanding.

As the example of New York City illustrates, a huge number of narrow classes, each requiring a different examination, not only impedes management flexibility in the utilization of personnel resources but also restricts employee opportunities for promotion. In late 1977, New York City had 2,800 job titles in 240 occupational groups, compared with a few hundred titles in 22 occupational groups in the federal government. Since then the number of job titles in New York has been greatly reduced through broadbanding. Previously, as one example of how very narrow classes reduce productivity, each member of a highway repair crew occupied 1 of 11 specialized job titles and performed a "limited, specific set of duties; therefore some members had to stand by idly while others performed their particular parts of the total job." The 11 titles were replaced by 3 titles, and a crew member now performs "all aspects of street maintenance work rather than merely a particular phase of the operation," and the productivity of the crews increased substantially.

Promotional progress is impeded by narrow classes because to progress up the hierarchy the employee must pass the examination required for each of many different classes. Thus, when the city broadbanded its clerical classes, reducing the number of titles from 58 to 8, clerical workers and district council 37 of the American Federation of State, County, and Municipal Employees welcomed the change.

Broadbanding has disadvantages; it is more difficult to prepare examinations for a wide range of duties, and employees recruited with general backgrounds must be trained to carry out the specialized tasks to which they may be assigned.[12] Yet the prevalence of narrow classes and their limitations are evidenced in the fact that in quite a few jurisdictions broadbanding is now part of civil service reform.

---

[12]Peter Allan and Stephen Rosenberg, "New York City's Approach to Civil Service Reform: Implications for State and Local Governments," *Public Administration Review* 38, no. 6 (November–December 1978): 582, 583.

The Politics of Job Evaluation

Personnel practitioners and writers in the field of public personnel administration are criticized for not having perceived or explained that job evaluation is a political process. Politics in this context refers to overgrading, grade creep, yielding to operating officials on the classification of individual positions, and in general to the bargaining that takes place in classification decisions. Classification analysts also are viewed by some critics as dishonest when they approve job classifications they know are too high.

It is true that the literature of job evaluation does not emphasize these "political" aspects but instead the technical problems. That personnel experts have not been aware of these "politics," however, is impossible to believe because they are very much involved in the negotiation process on grades and know intimately from their own daily experiences what pressures are exerted. Some classification analysts do yield too easily to these pressures, but classifiers have recommendatory powers only, and actually they are often disliked by operating officials who find them far too inflexible. The failures are largely systemic ones, caused by the relationships between the classification and compensation plans just described and by the fundamentally subjective nature of classification decisions.

Position Management

Since they are not independent agents, classifiers do not create or restructure jobs, except as their help is sought by operating officials, and the latter have the final say in such matters. In the United States, job evaluation and organization and methods (O&M) work are seldom assigned to the same persons. O&M usually is the responsibility of a separate organization unit that may or may not work closely with the personnel office.

The traditional self-concept of classification analysts is that they photograph the position as it is and that it is not their responsibility to recommend changes in administrative organization and structuring of individual jobs. This has changed somewhat in recent years, although in practice not to a great extent, because of the assignment of responsibilities to classifiers in what is called "position management." This term has not been precisely defined, but generally it covers "a wide spectrum of management concerns about efficiency and effectiveness—from the organization of work and allocation of numbers of positions to full utilization of people."[13]

In position management matters, the role of the agency personnel staff is advisory to the agency head, but, although advisory, it does cast personnel technicians in a new, unaccustomed role. Some of them have not felt comfortable in this capacity because they "are not at all sure that they have definitive answers."[14] Certainly, the information that personnel workers gather about faulty administrative structure and poor design of individual jobs should be made available to those agency officials who decide how the work is organized. An advisory role in position management makes the position classifier more than a photographer of the position; he or she can contribute to better structuring of the work. Job restructuring obviously is a policy matter, as when certain tasks are separated out in order to provide jobs for minority group workers. But decisions to restructure are made by elective officials and agency heads, not by the classification analyst, and rarely does he or she provide the initiative.

Union Role in Job Evaluation

In most public jurisdictions, the establishment of job evaluation standards and the classification of individual positions both remain management prerogatives and are not negotiable under collective bargaining programs. Unions have concentrated on improving pay and fringe benefits, but this does not mean that they are content to leave job evaluation completely to management. Some unions have pressed for making the classification of individual positions subject to negotiation and binding arbitration, and in some places they have been successful in this endeavor.

Most public officials are opposed to having classification decisions made through collective bargaining. They believe that management will be unable to manage effectively if it cannot itself determine the job evaluation plan and the classification of individual positions. To classification analysts in government, bargaining in these areas is anathema, because they consider the process of

---

[13]John D. R. Cole, "Position Management and Classification," *Civil Service Journal* 17, no. 1 (July–September 1976): 9.

[14]Ibid., 12.

evaluating and ranking jobs a strictly technical question, one not to be decided through the pull and haul of negotiations.

In the federal service, under Title VII of the Civil Service Reform Act of 1978, negotiations may not cover job evaluation and individual job classifications for either white- or blue-collar workers. In the postal service, job evaluation is subject to negotiation as provided in the Postal Reorganization Act of 1970, but in practice the "preexisting pay structure and job evaluation plan has been left largely unchanged."[15]

In some state and local governments, the scope of negotiations includes job evaluation. In Hartford, Connecticut, establishment of new classes of positions is subject to union negotiation and disputes over the classification of individual positions to binding arbitration. This change was sought by the "city manager and the personnel director, more than the union" because they wanted to decrease the authority of the personnel board (previously it decided classification appeals).[16] Then Hartford director of personnel, Robert D. Krause, whose merit credentials are very strong, believed that the State Board of Mediation and Arbitration, which arbitrated the classification disputes, upheld "merit factors as much as the city's personnel board, if not more."[17]

Discussion of job evaluation and compensation plans is difficult to separate because job evaluation is the basis for pay grade determination. When jurisdictions adopt collective bargaining, they often are unable to maintain a unified job evaluation and pay plan. This happens when there are several bargaining units; no one union wins the representation election in all the units, and thus the jurisdiction must bargain with a number of different unions. In any one unit, the union bargaining with management naturally concentrates on doing all it can to improve the status of members of the union in the unit—although the contract gains negotiated may create inequities for employees doing the same kind and level of work in the other units. As the result of this bargaining unit by

---

[15]Anthony F. Ingrassia and Charles Feigenbaum, "The Union Impact on Job Evaluation and Pay Administration," in Suskin, *Job Evaluation and Pay Administration in the Public Sector*, p. 530. See also B. Virginia Comella, "Labor Relations and the Federal Personnel Specialist," *Public Personnel Management* 9, no. 2 (March–April 1980): 103.

[16]Ingrassia and Feigenbaum, "The Union Impact," p. 545.

[17]Sterling Spero and John M. Copozzola, *The Urban Community and Its Unionized Bureaucracies: Pressure Politics in Local Government Labor Relations* (New York: Dunnellen, 1973), pp. 206–207.

unit, separate job evaluation and pay plans eventually are created for each unit; the grading and pay are equitable *within* each bargaining unit, but not *between* bargaining units.[18]

■ COMPENSATION

Compensation includes pay, fringe benefits, and monetary payments such as shift differentials. The money value of fringe benefits is computed in determining total compensation.

In both private and public sectors, compensation is an area of much disagreement between management and the employees. In government, there is the additional complication of disagreements between the executive and legislative branches over pay policy.

Further, since the government environment is a political one, there are strong pressures and various stratagems by unions and employees—such as the "end run" to the legislature to get pay and benefits higher than those recommended by the executive branch. The political climate influences the pay decisions of executive branch officials and of legislators, and in general the political climate has been much less favorable than it was in the late 1960s and early 1970s to substantial increases in pay for public employees.

Inflation has added greatly to the difficulties in resolving conflicts over employee pay because understandably workers are much concerned about appreciable declines in their buying power and in their standards of living. While research has shown that for some workers compensation is not everything—or most of what they value in their jobs—it has also established that employees of all kinds become dissatisfied if pay is not adequate to meet their needs.[19] Public employees believe they should receive the same percentage increases that private workers get to compensate for rises in the cost of living, but since the government is their employer they often get less.

In one area—merit pay for executives—present public dissatisfaction with governmental performance has had the beneficial effect of permitting experimentation that legislators might otherwise have rejected. Paying "oversize" raises to some employees

---

[18]Ingrassia and Feigenbaum, "The Union Impact," p. 548.
[19]George Strauss, "Workers: Attitudes and Adjustments," in Jerome M. Rosow (ed.), *The Worker and the Job: Coping With Change* (Englewood Cliffs, N.J.: Prentice-Hall, 1974).

and denying increases to others or giving them very small ones generally has not been popular with legislators. Because it is so closely related to performance evaluation, merit pay is discussed in Chapter 11, "Performance Appraisal and Merit Pay."

■ COMPENSATION POLICIES IN GOVERNMENT

As Henry Parris states concisely, there are three possible approaches to fixing compensation of public employees: (1) to pay as little as possible so as to relieve pressure on the taxpayer; (2) to pay enough more than the private sector to set a good example; or (3) to pay rates comparable with those in the private sector.[20] In both Britain and the United States, the third policy is the one now generally followed as a matter of principle. Often the rates are not comparable because a jurisdiction lacks the necessary financial resources or sets higher priorities for other spending programs. Also, while the objective may be to achieve full comparability, the methods used in making surveys of external salary data may be technically deficient, and the new compensation schedules adopted result in underpaying or overpaying certain kinds of workers.

In the United States, until recent years it was not generally accepted that government should pay comparable salaries for white-collar workers. Indeed, it was considered "normal for public servants to make a financial sacrifice."[21] The payment of prevailing wages for blue-collar workers does have a long history, going back as far as 1862 in the federal service. In that year, Congress passed a statute directing the Navy Department to relate pay rates in the shipyards "as nearly as is consistent with the public interest, to prevailing private industry rates in the immediate vicinity" of the Navy yards.[22] Many state and local governments also adopted the prevailing rate standard for setting blue-collar pay.

A characteristic of government pay is "compression," which occurs as the difference between the top and the bottom rates in the salary schedules narrows. Two forces—peculiar to the government environment—are largely responsible for compression. First, leg-

---

[20]Henry Parris, *Staff Relations in the Civil Service* (London: Allen & Unwin, 1973), p. 81.

[21]Elmer B. Staats, "Experience of the Federal Government in Maintaining Equivalency with Private Sector Pay." Paper presented at the Conference on Public Employment, Syracuse University, October 26, 1972, p. 9.

[22]Raymond Jacobsen, "Efforts to Resolve Problems in Federal Compensation," in Suskin, *Job Evaluation and Pay Administration in the Public Sector*, p. 470.

islative compensation often places a ceiling on executive branch pay since the legislators do not relish approving top pay in the executive branch higher than their own salaries. Politically, as any newspaper reader knows, lawmakers tread carefully when it comes to raising their own pay because of strong opposition by newspaper editorial writers and community groups.

Second, when authorizing changes in base pay, legislators tend to be more generous—sometimes much more so—with those in the lower ranks. The lower-paid employees are more numerous and often exert strong political pressure. Executives, in contrast, are much smaller in number and represent fewer potential votes; besides, legislators often sympathize more with the "underdog." This picture has changed somewhat as more legislators become concerned about the need in government for high-quality executives, but pay compression remains a serious problem at all levels of government.

Until the 1960s, the policy of determining pay and fringe benefits in government through collective bargaining was very limited. By 1983, collective bargaining was authorized by law or executive order in 40 states and the District of Columbia for some or all of their employees, and with very few exceptions the scope of bargaining includes compensation. In the federal service, pay and fringe benefits of federal nonpostal employees may not be bargained because they are prescribed by law and thus not negotiable under Title VII of the Civil Service Reform Act of 1978. However, as provided in the Postal Reorganization Act of 1970, pay and fringe benefits of postal workers are determined through collective bargaining. The impact of collective bargaining on compensation is discussed later in this chapter.

■ RECENT DEVELOPMENTS IN THE FEDERAL SERVICE

Controversies and difficulties in setting employee compensation are illustrated by the experience in the federal government where proposals for substantial changes in existing policies have been made.

White-Collar Workers

The comparability principle was first established by Congress for white-collar workers in the Federal Salary Reform Act of 1962 which provided that "federal salary rates shall be comparable with private enterprise salary rates for the same levels of work."[23] White-collar pay was so far behind that in 1967 Congress passed another law authorizing the President without requirement of congressional approval to bring federal pay up to private rates, "as nearly as practicable," in two big pay adjustments.[24]

In the Federal Pay Comparability Act of 1970,[25] Congress delegated to the President the salary-fixing authority for General Schedule and Foreign Service employees. Most federal white-collar jobs are under the General Schedule which consists of 18 grades, GS 1–18. The President is assisted by an agent he designates, presently the director of the Office of Personnel Management, the director of the Office of Management and Budget, and the Secretary of Labor, acting jointly.

The legislation also established a Federal Employees Pay Council and an Advisory Committee on Federal Pay. The council consists of five members from three employee organizations representing substantial numbers of General Schedule employees. There are three members of the advisory committee, all from outside the government. The President appoints them after reviewing recommendations from the director of the Federal Mediation and Conciliation Service and "other interested parties" of persons noted for their impartiality and knowledge of labor relations and pay policy.

Every year the Bureau of Labor Statistics conducts a national survey of private sector professional, administrative, and technical pay (PATC Survey). The President's agent instructs BLS as to which jobs to include in the survey and the establishments to be surveyed, and OPM and BLS jointly maintain job descriptions for each of the various work levels in the occupations surveyed. Each work level is so defined that it may be compared with grade levels in the General Schedule. BLS data collectors visit the establishments included in the survey, identify the jobs that match the BLS-OPM job descriptions, and collect the salary data. Because the Federal Pay Comparability Act of 1970 states that the comparability is to be with private enterprise, jobs in state and local governments are not covered in the survey.

[23]Public Law 87-973, 97th Congress.
[24]Section 212, Postal Revenue and Federal Salary Act of 1967, Public Law 90-206, 90th Congress, H. R. 7977.
[25]Public Law 91-656; Subchapter 1 of Chapter 53 of Title V, United States Code.

The agent consults with the Federal Employees Pay Council and with other representatives of federal employees on industry coverage, survey jobs, and the method of comparing federal and private pay rates, but the agent is not required to change its decisions as the result of these consultations. After reviewing the completed survey data, the agent sends a report to the President presenting the survey findings and giving its recommendations as to the size and form of the pay adjustment needed to maintain comparability. The agent includes in this report the views and recommendations of the Federal Employees Pay Council and of other unions not represented on the council. The Advisory Committee on Federal Pay, after reviewing the agent's report and studying the views of the council and of other employee representatives, submits an independent report to the President. The President then adjusts the pay rates, the changes to be effective on or after October 1 of the applicable year, but, if he believes it inappropriate to make the adjustments recommended by the agent because of "national emergency or economic conditions affecting the general welfare," he sends an alternative plan to Congress. This plan goes into effect within 30 days of transmittal unless either house passes a resolution of disapproval.

The Presidents have made frequent use of their authority to submit alternative plans providing for substantially less than full comparability increases, the justification being the need to control inflation and to keep down the costs of government. The effect of recent presidential alternative plans has been to widen greatly the gap between federal white-collar pay and the salaries paid for comparable work in the private sector. In 1984, the agent's survey showed that federal salaries were below private rates by an average of 18.28 percent, ranging from 17.01 at the GS-5 level to 21.66 at GS-15. President Reagan's alternative plan, not vetoed by Congress, provided for a 3.5 percent pay raise, instead of an average comparability raise of 18.3 percent that otherwise would automatically have gone into effect. Surveys have shown that the federal government greatly underpays its career executives in the top GS grades (16–18).

Uniform nationwide pay scales

General Schedule salary scales are uniform throughout the nation, for example, a GS-5 is paid within the same salary scale no matter where the position is located geographically. In determining GS pay scales, comparisons are made with the average rates paid in the private sector for the nation as a whole, rather than with locality rates. Bureau of Labor Statistics data show that in clerical and technical occupations there are "wide variations in pay between various geographic areas" and that "in some areas private sector pay is up to 20 percent above the national average, while in other areas pay is as much as 20 percent below the national average."[26] As a result of making comparisons with average nationwide private rates, the federal government underpays in some areas and overpays in others, sometimes by as much as 10 or 15 percent.

Private sector salaries for professional and administrative positions also vary by geographic area, so the federal government often also underpays or overpays for these positions depending on the location.[27]

Pay compression in the higher grades

There has been much compression in the salary scales at the top of the General Schedule. This compression, in the extreme form it has manifested in recent years, is largely attributable to a provision of law that provides that the top GS salary cannot exceed that of level V in the Executive Schedule. This latter schedule establishes the pay for the very highest management and policymaking positions in the federal service, such as cabinet secretaries, other agency heads and their principal deputies, undersecretaries, assistant secretaries, chairpersons and other members of regulatory commissions, some bureau heads, general counsels, and certain other noncareer officials. Practically all these posts are created by statute, and appointments to many of them are made by the President, for some positions with Senate confirmation. There are five levels in the Executive Schedule, each carrying a single annual rate.

In the statute it passed in 1967 authorizing the President to bring federal pay up to private rates, Congress also provided for establishment of a Commission on Executive, Legislative, and Judicial Salaries to make recommendations every four years to the Presi-

---

[26]A Federal Position Classification System for the 1980's, p. 33.
[27]Ibid., p. 34.

dent on the salaries of members of the House and Senate, federal judges, and incumbents of positions in the Executive Schedule. Members of the Commission are appointed every fourth fiscal year, three by the President, two by the President of the Senate, two by the Speaker of the House, and two by the Chief Justice of the Supreme Court. It is this same law that limits top GS pay to level V [lowest level] of the Executive Schedule. After considering the Commission's proposals, the President includes his own recommendations on executive, legislative, and judicial salaries in his next budget message to Congress, and the rates recommended go into effect unless within 30 days either house of Congress enacts legislation disapproving them in whole or part.

From 1969 to late 1975, because of the link between GS and Executive Schedule pay—and because Executive Schedule pay could be changed only once every four years—pay compression in the top GS grades increased greatly. Although the creation of the Commission on Executive, Legislative, and Judicial Salaries was intended to make it easier for Congress to raise its own pay, Congress has found it difficult politically to legislate the pay increase recommendations of the Commission.

In the summer of 1975 President Ford approved legislation providing that in the future members of Congress, judges, and Executive Schedule officials would receive annually the same increase granted GS employees under the comparability legislation. When the first such annual adjustment was made in October of 1975, this closed a period of six years during which there had been no increase in congressional, judicial, and executive pay. However, since then Congress has often deferred these annual adjustments or approved less than the comparability increases received by GS employees. Thus, the total situation can be summarized as one in which GS pay, already too low, particularly in the top grades, cannot exceed level V of Executive Schedule pay, and Executive Schedule pay increases have been deferred or been small.

Criticisms of white-collar comparability procedures

Principal criticisms of the methods used by OPM and BLS for determining white-collar comparability rates are: (1) jobs in state and local governments and in nonprofit organizations are not included in the PATC Survey; (2) the minimum establishment size (in terms of number of workers employed) for inclusion in the survey is set too high or too low, depending on the point of view of the critics; (3) "some jobs that are surveyed have relatively low employment levels in both the federal government and private industry, while other more populous jobs are omitted."[28]

When it passed the Federal Salary Reform Act of 1962, Congress excluded comparisons with jobs in state and local governments largely because it believed that salary data from this segment of the work force (then 6.1 million) "would be outweighed by private enterprise data."[29] Because state and local government employment has more than doubled since then, this argument no longer is valid, particularly since certain kinds of jobs not included in the PATC Survey are found in abundance in state and local governments (e.g., nurse, police officer, fire fighter, and social worker). In many small state and local governments, pay is substantially lower than that in the federal service, which explains the unions' objection to including them in the PATC Survey.

Nonprofit employment (e.g., health services, noncommercial educational, scientific, and research organizations, and educational and social services) has been excluded by administrative determination, but review of the legislative history of the 1962 legislation suggests that this was not the intention of Congress.[30] The nonprofit sector is now also very large and includes many kinds of jobs not included in the PATC Survey, such as in the health care occupations, a large area of federal white-collar employment. Union objection to including not-for-profit organizations in the PATC Survey is that they "traditionally pay lower wages than profit organizations."[31] Since the larger private establishments pay the higher rates, the employee unions also object to what they consider too low minimum employment cutoff points. Conversely, employer and other groups concerned about federal payroll costs believe the cutoffs should be even lower.

Blue-Collar Workers

Prior to 1968, the prevailing rate criterion for fixing the wages of the federal government's now some half-million trade, craft, and

---

[28] *Staff Report of the President's Panel on Federal Compensation* (Washington, D.C.: Government Printing Office, 1976), p. 89.

[29] Ibid., p. 76.

[30] Ibid., pp. 77–78.

[31] Ibid., p. 80.

labor employees was applied so poorly that in some local areas federal agencies paid different rates for the same occupations. This situation was corrected in July 1968 when the Civil Service Commission implemented a Coordinated Federal Wage System (CFWS). This system provided for a "common set of policies and operating procedures" covering "grade structures, occupational standards, survey coverage, labor organization participation, and other matters."[32] In 1972, Congress enacted the principal features of the CFWS into law—but also included certain provisions in this legislation that have resulted in paying blue-collar wages that are widely believed to be much too high.

Under the 1972 legislation, OPM prescribes uniform national job-grading standards and criteria to be followed by the agencies in the definition of wage areas, basic design of the local wage surveys, determination of industry and job coverage, and establishment of the grade structure of wage schedules. OPM is advised by an 11-member Federal Prevailing Rate Advisory Committee, consisting of 5 members representing the agencies, 5 representing the unions, and a full-time chairperson appointed by the OPM director. The local wage surveys are conducted by "lead agencies," that is, those with large numbers of blue-collar jobs in the area, frequently the Department of Defense. Each lead agency has an agency wage committee made up of two management members, two union members, and a chairperson appointed by the lead agency. This committee advises the lead agency on design of local surveys, review of survey data, establishment of local wage schedules, and related matters. Finally, there are local wage survey committees in each area, consisting of one union and one management member and a third person appointed by management, that oversee the conduct of the local surveys. As the Federal Wage System (FWS) functions in practice, there is "significant union influence" because there is a "real effort to achieve consensus."

The statutory features of FWS that are held responsible for causing payment of excessive rates are:

1. The "Monroney Amendment" which requires that if there is an insufficient number of comparable positions in the local area, the lead agency must obtain wage data from outside the area and consider the outside as well as the local data in constructing the wage schedules. Use of out-of-area data has

---

[32]*Staff Report of the President's Panel on Federal Compensation*, p. 107.

often resulted in payment of higher rates than those paid for the same work by private employers in the area.

2. The law prescribes five steps for each grade in a FWS regular nonsupervisory schedule. The first step provides 96 percent of the prevailing rate for the particular grade, the second step, 100 percent, and the third, fourth, and fifth steps, 104, 108, and 112 percent, respectively, of the second step. Because most federal blue-collar workers progress to the top of their grade in a relatively short time, this ensures that the wages of most of them are substantially above local prevailing rates.

3. The statute requires payment of night shift differentials substantially higher than those paid by private employers.

4. Since it requires that prevailing rates be based on private employer rates in the area, state and local governments are excluded from the wage surveys. Yet these governments employ many blue-collar workers in the local areas surveyed.

The Carter and Reagan Administration Proposals

In 1979, President Carter sent to Congress a comprehensive plan for federal compensation reform.[33] The Carter plan was not acted upon by Congress, nor did Congress act upon proposals of the Reagan administration in 1981 similar in some respects to the Carter recommendations but different in others.[34]

Both Carter and Reagan recommended (1) broadening the pay comparability process for both white- and blue-collar employees to include fringe benefits (such as retirement and health and life insurance) as well as pay; (2) compensating most white-collar workers on a locality basis; (3) including state and local governments in the compensation surveys for white- and blue-collar workers; (4) eliminating the Monroney amendment and the five-step wage scales for blue-collar workers, and modifying night differential rates for these workers so as to make them consistent with industrial practices. A significant difference in the Reagan plan is that it provided for paying 94, rather than 100 percent of the comparability rates for white-collar employees.

---

[33]*Federal Employees Compensation Reform, Message from the President of the United States,* House Document No. 96142, 96th Congress, 1st Session (Washington, D.C.: Government Printing Office, 1979).

[34]*Federal Pay Comparability Act of 1981* (Washington, D.C.: Office of Personnel Management).

The Reagan administration believes that such "attractive" features of federal employment as job security, job mobility, and portability of benefits are worth 6 percent in total compensation, calculated on the judgment of senior officials. The General Accounting Office concluded that the administration had not proved that these differences do exist between federal and nonfederal employment. For example, GAO stated, "The freedom to move and retain benefits when changing jobs or locations is certainly not unique to Federal employment."[35] GAO also interprets the comparability legislation to require that determinations be based on factual evidence, rather than opinions of officials.

The justification for including fringe benefits in the pay comparisons is that they constitute a substantial part of total compensation. The Reagan administration believes federal fringe benefits taken as a whole are superior to those provided in the private sector, and that total federal compensation is higher. The unions disagree that the benefits and pay are higher. The Congressional Budget Office has issued a report concluding that "federal compensation programs are at best a mixed bag when compared to those offered by large private firms." The CBO states that "while the federal retirement system is slightly more generous than the average private sector pension when combined with social security, federal workers trail the private sector in health and life insurance benefits and in paid time-off for vacations, holidays, and sick leave." CBO further found that while the government was ahead in workers' compensation, educational assistance, and severance pay, corporations were more generous with bonuses, employee parking, and various profitsharing and stock options.[36]

■ COMPENSATION PRACTICES IN STATE AND LOCAL GOVERNMENT

Prior to the Federal Salary Reform Act of 1962, some state and local governments had more progressive pay policies in some respects than the federal government. Their governing bodies reviewed pay rates annually or biennially and authorized adjustments considered necessary to make the rates more competitive. In a few

---

[35]*Proposal to Lower the Federal Compensation Comparability Standard Has Not Been Substantiated*, Report by the Comptroller General of the United States, Washington, D.C., January 26, 1982.

[36]"CBO: Feds Trail Industry on Most Fringe Benefits," *Federal Times*, April 4, 1983.

states, like California and Michigan, the legislature had delegated to the executive branch the authority to make revisions in the pay scales, and in some state and local jurisdictions executive pay was higher than in the federal service. For the country as whole, however, state and local government pay has been less adequate than in the federal government.

The biggest change has been determination of pay and fringe benefits through collective bargaining in many state and local governments. Because of collective bargaining, pay for some occupations such as police, fire fighters, teachers, and nurses has improved substantially; furthermore, jurisdictions facing the threat of possible introduction of collective bargaining have often acted more promptly to improve compensation. However, contrary to widespread belief, the impact of collective bargaining has not been to increase compensation greatly for all kinds of public employees. Summarizing the research on this subject to date, Daniel J. B. Mitchell writes:

> At the least, it can be concluded that unions and collective bargaining may raise pay in the public sector and influence working conditions. The magnitude of the effect may be large in some cases, small in others, and is sometimes nil. This finding is not very different from the general conclusion of comparable literature on private sector unionization. Despite the special features of public sector labor relations, there does not appear to be justification for the viewpoint that unionization must inevitably lead to a looted treasury.[37]

In some state and local governments, collective bargaining has contributed to increasing pension costs substantially. These costs are largely future, distant ones of which taxpayers are not fully aware, which is why some elective officials may decide to make more concessions in the fringe benefit than in the wage area. In New York City some union contracts have provided for the city to make special annuity fund payments to several employee organizations—payments in addition to those made by the city to the retirement systems for the particular employees. In some juris-

---

[37]See Daniel J. B. Mitchell, "Collective Bargaining and Wage Determination in the Public Sector: Is Armageddon Really at Hand?" *Public Personnel Management* 7, no. 2 (March–April 1978). Similar conclusions are reached by Richard C. Kearney in his comprehensive review of research on compensation of municipal and state workers, and teachers and college faculty, "Monetary Impact of Collective Bargaining," in Jack Rabin, W. Bartley Hildreth, Thomas Vocino, and Gerald J. Miller (eds.), *Handbook on Public Personnel Administration and Labor Relations* (New York: Dekker, 1983).

dictions, some long-service public employees receive benefits that in terms of net disposable income provide, together with social security, a larger income in retirement than they received when employed.

It is not surprising that efforts, sometimes successful, have been made by public management to remove pensions from the scope of negotiations. However, as Arvid Anderson, head of New York City's Office of Collective Bargaining, points out, if pensions are removed from the bargaining table, disputes about them are transferred to the legislature and unlimited pension bills are filed. Furthermore, the unions retaliate by increasing the "pressure for bargaining on wages and other fringe benefits which, in turn, will result in increased pension costs for present employees under existing formulas, thereby resulting in no reduction in employment costs."[38]

■ COMPARABLE WORTH

In the past several years, much controversy has developed over comparable worth—the principle that "jobs that are approximately of the same worth should be compensated equally"[39] even though market rates, for example, are higher for electricians than for licensed practical nurses. Worth to the employer is based on analysis of the duties, responsibilities, and qualification requirements of the position. A job evaluation study made for the state of Washington assigned the job of registered nurse a much higher total point score for the requirements of the job than the score given truckdrivers. The difference in the inherent difficulty of the two positions is indicated by the point scores for mental demands—122 for the nurse and 10 for the truckdriver. (The truckdriver job, of course, has higher skill requirements than that of routine positions such as messenger.) The comparison between registered nurses and truckdrivers was made to demonstrate that female jobs (those predominantly filled by women) are compensated lower than male positions (those held mostly by men).[40]

About 80 percent of the women in the U.S. workforce are con-

---

[38]Statement of Arvid Anderson, Chairman, Office of Collective Bargaining, New York City, June 21, 1973, before Select Committee on Pensions, New York State.

[39]Keon S. Chi, "Comparable Worth: Implications of the Washington Case," *State Government* 57, no. 2 (1984): 34.

[40]Tamar Lewin, "A New Push to Raise Women's Pay," *New York Times*, January 1, 1984.

centrated in 20 of the Labor Department's 427 job categories. Women working full time earn about 62 cents for every dollar earned by men. Women's groups, with strong support by some unions and some political leaders and elective officials, maintain that occupational segregation characterizes the workforce, with women segregated into low-paying, dead-end jobs. Women, they claim, do not take these low-paying jobs of their own free will; rather from early life on they are socialized by community concepts that it is appropriate for "girls" to look for "female jobs," like clerk, waitress, nurse. Since female jobs in the private sector are undervalued, when governments make outside pay surveys as the basis for setting their pay scales, they simply duplicate the bias against women. Comparable worth would not dispense with job evaluation; rather it would reform job evaluation and pay-setting practices to eliminate undervaluation and underpayment of women's jobs.

Opponents of comparable worth, such as the business community in general, dispute that there is occupational segregation of women. They say that the true condition is occupational *concentration*, which results from the free choice of women to plan their lives differently from men.

According to this explanation of why women are found predominantly in low-paying jobs, many women look forward, not to an uninterrupted work career but to one in which they will leave the workforce for substantial periods of time for marriage and child-rearing. With such plans, they find it inadvisable to invest in the training required for filling higher-ranking jobs. Although there is bias by some employers against women, it is not discrimination that explains the occupational concentration—rather it is the life role aspirations of most women. If eventually a majority of the women in the workforce are persons who deviated from this pattern and sought the same careers as men, then the occupational concentration would end. That is the solution which should be sought by women's groups, not comparable worth. In fact, if comparable worth were adopted, women would decide to continue in the lower jobs rather than trying to qualify themselves for higher ranking ones.[41]

From the practical standpoint, disbelievers in comparable worth

[41]See Michael Evans Gold, *A Dialogue on Comparable Worth* (Ithaca, N.Y.: Cornell University, New York State School of Industrial and Labor Relations, 1983).

stress their view—a widely-accepted one—that the public money-value of a job cannot be based on a philosophical concept of inherent worth, but only on open market forces of supply and demand. Not to go by these market rates would mean staggering expenditures to raise the compensation of women in low-paying jobs, no matter how justified by job evaluation considered alone. Comparable worth could even mean lowering pay for some male jobs—a practical impossibility in occupations where qualified workers are in very short supply.

The Present Situation

In December of 1983 a U.S. district court in the state of Washington ruled that in setting pay the state government had been guilty of sex discrimination under Title VII of the Civil Rights Act of 1964.[42] Actually, Washington had been the first state to initiate a comparable worth study (it did so in 1974), and the results of that study were used by the court to justify its decision. The court found intentional discrimination because there was a difference of about 20 percent in compensation for mostly male and mostly female job classifications with the same job evaluation point scores. The judge ordered the state to pay thousands of women employees the salaries they were entitled to under a comparable worth plan adopted by the state but only partially implemented. The suit was brought by the American Federation of State, County, and Municipal Employees, one of the organizations that strongly supports comparable worth. The decision has been appealed, but as this is written the appeal has not been resolved.

The significance of *AFSCME et al. v. State of Washington* is that it was the first decision finding any employer liable under the Civil Rights Act for failure to pay employees according to the comparable worth of their jobs. Since then comparable worth suits have been brought against several state, county, and municipal governments, and comparable worth studies are being carried out in many state and local governments. Demands for comparable worth adjustments are being made at the bargaining table; in 1981 the City of San Jose, California, settled a nine-day strike over this issue by agreeing to provide $1.5 million in pay equity increases for

---

[42]*AFSCME et al. v. the State of Washington et al.* (1983), No. C82-465T, The United States District Court for the Western District of Washington.

female employees. The state of Minnesota agreed to pay $22 million to raise women's pay, based on a 1982 study that found that rates for women were unduly low in comparison with those for men's jobs.

The comparable worth debate encompasses some key policy issues that divide employers, elective officials, political parties, women's organizations, and even the unions, the last because some unions with large male memberships show little enthusiasm for improving women's pay. From the political standpoint, the women's vote is very much in the picture, and comparable worth also is part of affirmative action for women. Job evaluation and pay-setting criteria are involved, and fresh approaches in these areas of public personnel administration are being sought. In its multiple facets, comparable worth is a highly important and interesting area in the current consideration of personnel policies.

BIBLIOGRAPHY

A Federal Classification System for the 1980s, Report of the Classification Task Force. Washington, D.C.: Office of Personnel Management, 1981.

Description of Selected Systems for Classifying Federal Civilian Positions and Personnel. Washington, D.C.: General Accounting Office, July 13, 1984.

Ganschinietz, Bill, and McConomy, Stephen. "Trends in Job Evaluation Practices of State Personnel Systems." *Public Personnel Management* 12, no. 1 (Spring 1983).

Gold, Michael Evans. *A Dialogue on Comparable Worth*. Ithaca, N.Y.: Cornell University, New York State School of Industrial and Labor Relations, 1983.

Kearney, Richard C. "Monetary Impact of Collective Bargaining." In *Handbook on Public Personnel Administration and Labor Relations*, edited by Jack Rabin, Thomas Vocino, W. Bartley Hildreth, and Gerald J. Miller. New York: Dekker, 1983.

Penner, Maurice. "How Job-Based Classification Systems Promote Organizational Ineffectiveness." *Public Personnel Management* 12, no. 3 (Fall 1983).

Reickenberg, Neil E., ed. "Special Issue: Comparable Worth." *Public Personnel Management* 12, no. 4 (Winter 1983).

Suskin, Harold, ed. *Job Evaluation and Pay Administration in the*

Public Sector. Washington, D.C.: International Personnel Management Association, 1977.

Staff Report of the President's Panel on Federal Compensation. Washington, D.C.: Government Printing Office, 1976.

Treiman, Donald J. *Job Evaluation: An Analytic Review, Interim Report to the Equal Employment Opportunity Commission*. Washington, D.C.: National Academy of Sciences, 1979.

Women, Work, and Wages: Equal Pay for Jobs of Equal Value. Washington, D.C.: National Academy Press, 1981.

10 Selection

As indicated in Chapter 1, the present period is one of intensive scrutiny of public service selection methods to assure that they are job-related and do not discriminate on the basis of race, color, sex, religion, or national origin. In this chapter, we will discuss in order: traditional selection methods; assessment centers, which we consider the most innovative approach of recent years; the methods of determining validity; the detailed requirements for making selection methods more job-related, as embodied in the Uniform Guidelines on Employee Selection Procedures of the Equal Employment Opportunity Commission, the Office of Personnel Management, and the Departments of Justice, Labor, and Treasury; and eligible lists and certification of names from such lists. The selection methods described in the present chapter are used both in promotional and entrance examinations.

■ TRADITIONAL MEASUREMENT DEVICES

In traditional selection procedures several measures of capacity to perform satisfactorily in the job are usually utilized. As Albert P. Maslow writes, "There are few cases in which a candidate's performance on a single measurement procedure controls the hiring decision."[1] Technically, all measurements of capacity are considered "tests," although some do not involve taking a pen or pencil test. The combination of tests used varies, depending on the requirements of the job being filled. Some jobs require certain abilities, others do not. Since different tests measure different things, efforts are made to include in the assortment of tests administered (test battery) the best available combination of tests for measuring

---

[1]Albert P. Maslow, *Staffing the Public Service* (Cranbury, N.J., 1983), p. 37.

all the required abilities. The measurement devices usually are selected from among the following:

1. Minimum qualification requirements.
2. Evaluation of training and experience.
3. Written tests.
4. Performance tests.
5. Oral examinations.
6. Background investigations.

Each test is weighted in accordance with the civil service agency's determination as to the relative importance of the qualifications it measures. Ideally, the precise weights should be determined only after thorough research on the relationship of given qualities to job success in the particular position. Very often, however, funds and time have not been available for such research, and personnel technicians have had to use their best judgment. The minimum qualifications are not weighted, and neither is the background check; as the latter is usually employed, it is qualifying or disqualifying only.

Every selection device should possess *validity*, meaning that it accurately measures what it is intended to measure. In civil service selection, what is assessed are the knowledges, skills, abilities, and other worker characteristics deemed necessary or important for performing a particular job. If a careful job analysis is not made, tests may be chosen that lack validity for the particular job, although they may be valid for other positions. "*Job analysis* is the process of systematically collecting, processing, analyzing, and interpreting important information about a specific position. . . ."[2] The information collected includes detailed data on the duties and responsibilities of the job and on the knowledges, skills, abilities, and other characteristics required to perform the job satisfactorily.

Selection devices should also possess *reliability*, meaning consistency. Reliability is a measure "of the degree to which chance factors affect . . . scores."[3] A test is reliable if the same persons taking it on different occasions make the same relative scores. Many factors affect reliability, such as the physiological or psychological state of the test taker, variations in the conditions under

---

[2]Personnel Research and Development Center, U.S. Office of Personnel Management, *Job Analysis for Selection: An Overview*, August 1979, p. 1.

[3]Vernon R. Taylor, *Test Validity in Public Personnel Selection* (Chicago: International Personnel Management Association, n.d.), p. 2.

which the test is administered or graded, and the number of items.[4] Obviously, a test cannot be valid unless it is reliable.

Minimum Qualifications

The purpose of minimum qualifications of education, training, and experience is to eliminate from consideration all persons whose background is such that they probably would not be able to pass the examination. There is no point in grading papers of obviously unqualified persons, but if a minimum qualification is not necessary for job success (e.g., a high school diploma), then persons who might be able to do the job satisfactorily are denied a chance to compete.

Graduation from high school has often been required for jobs such as "janitors, truck drivers, and machine operators where no valid justification could be offered."[5] Public employers must now be prepared to offer such valid justification, because the courts are striking down minimum qualifications that are arbitrary and unrelated to the particular job.[6] Demonstrating the validity of any kind of selection device is far from easy, as will be shown later in this chapter, but the attempt must now also be made in the case of minimum qualifications whereas previously reliance on personnel technicians' "best judgment" sufficed. Minimum requirements are often made more flexible by providing for substitution of education for experience up to a certain point, and vice versa, and by including the catch-all phrase, "or any equivalent combination of training and experience."

Some minimum qualifications for civil service such as residence and age may be fixed by law and may reflect social policy. The personnel agency has no discretion in application of these qualifications beyond determining whether or not to press for changes in the law.

Evaluation of Training and Experience

For positions beyond the beginning level, although a written, and often an oral, examination is given, either or both these tests may

---

[4] See American Psychological Association, *Standards for Educational and Psychological Tests and Manuals* (Washington, D.C., 1966), p. 26.

[5] John W. Gibson and Erick P. Prien, "Validation of Minimum Qualifications," *Public Personnel Management* 6, no. 6 (November–December 1977): 447.

[6] Maslow, *Staffing the Public Service*, p. 55.

not measure *all* the abilities, skills, knowledges, and personal characteristics required for successful job performance. In such case, an evaluation of training and experience often is included in the test battery.

For various reasons, neither a written nor an oral examination may be included in the battery, and the evaluation of training and experience constitutes the entire examination. This is known as an *unassembled examination* (candidates do not assemble together in one place to take a written test). Suitable written tests may not be available, or it is recognized that many qualified persons will not apply for government jobs if they have to take a written test. Unassembled examinations are often used in the federal service, in some cases for beginning jobs, and some use is made of them in state and local governments. Evaluation of training and experience, plus an oral examination, is common at all levels of government.

The valid way to evaluate training and experience is to determine first the work behavior, knowledges, skills, and abilities needed for success in the job. Once this has been accomplished through job analysis, candidates are ranked by trained examiners according to the extent to which they possess these behaviors, knowledges, skills, and abilities. This means that training and experience are not valued for their own sake but rather for what the candidate has gained from them. Some people learn more than others from exposure to the same training and experience, and the quality itself of the training and experience varies greatly. A degree from one educational institution in a particular field may be known to offer much more to students than the same degree in another institution. Relative length of experience cannot be presumed to establish valid differences between the capacities of the candidates, but, unfortunately, in the past some civil service agencies have assumed that the candidate with more years of experience was the better qualified one.

Many personnel experts believe that the best method of evaluating training and experience is the job element method. *Job elements* are knowledges, skills, abilities, and personal characteristics determined to constitute significant requirements for workers in the particular jobs. Candidates are rated in accordance with various "evidences" considered acceptable for demonstrating competence in the different job elements. For example, ratings on the job element Knowledge of the Theory of Electronics are based on such evidence as: "verified experience in mathematical analysis requiring electronic theory *or* outstanding record in advanced theory courses *or* score of 85–100 on theory test." This evidence is given the highest point value for the job element; other evidences are assigned lower point values or none at all.[7]

Rating of training and experience often is a cooperative undertaking of personnel specialists and operating officials (subject matter experts). "Personnel specialists can contribute a knowledge of rating techniques as well as of career staffing concepts and methods, while the subject-matter experts can assess the relative value of certain types of experience for their particular jobs."[8]

Written Tests

According to Maslow, "At least three of every four public jurisdictions use tests." Usually the tests employed are intended to measure job knowledge or skills, and little use is made of "traditional aptitude tests, of the kind used for college admission, for example, to predict trainability or performance."[9] The personnel agency may itself construct the test or purchase one from consulting or other organizations such as the International Personnel Management Association.

For the test to be valid, the questions in it must sample and measure adequately all the basic skills and knowledges required for successful performance in the job. Obviously, for this objective to be attained, the test and how it is administered must reflect a high level of professional competence. Since most public jurisdictions are small and lack the financial resources to employ test specialists, it is very difficult for them to achieve the highest standards in test use. Because of the stringent validity requirements to be discussed later in this chapter, some jurisdictions are discontinuing use of written tests but it is usually more difficult to prove the validity of other selection devices like the evaluation of training and experience or the oral interview.

The form of written test most commonly used is multiple choice; since the answers are machine scored, many people refer to them as "objective." Of course, all tests have degrees of subjectivity

---

[7]Albert P. Maslow, "Evaluating Training and Experience," in J. J. Donovan, *Recruitment and Selection in the Public Service* (Washington, D.C.: International Personnel Management Association, 1968), p. 253.

[8]Federal Personnel Manual Letter 335-13, *Guidelines for Evaluation of Employees for Promotion and Internal Placement,* December 31, 1979, p. 6.

[9]Maslow, *Staffing the Public Service,* p. 150.

since the determination of the abilities and knowledges to be sampled, as well as the preparation of scoring keys, is the work of humans who, no matter how expert, are fallible. Little use is made of essay-type examinations because time and other constraints make it impossible to include enough essay questions to obtain the broad sample of the candidate's abilities and knowledges required, whereas dozens and hundreds of items can be included in multiple-choice tests. It is also much more time-consuming to grade essay responses, and readers will evaluate the answers differently which can cause low rater reliability.

Written tests have long been criticized, often by older persons who believe such tests give an advantage to persons completing their schooling or who have completed it not too long ago. There has been much criticism in recent years that written tests measure verbal abilities rather than ability to do the job and that the vocabulary and concepts used make it very difficult for persons with deprived backgrounds to understand the questions and pass the tests. Many jurisdictions have reviewed written test items carefully and changed them in the effort to eliminate such vocabulary and concepts, but many test experts maintain that written tests are the most appropriate measurement device for certain purposes and can be prepared in such manner that they are valid and fair to minorities.

Performance Tests

Performance test refers to a "wide variety of tests, principally those which are not heavily dependent on intellectual skills," such as tests to determine whether the candidate has the "necessary physical and/or psychomotor skills for a job."[10] Common examples are stenographic and typing skills tests and tests of ability to operate certain vehicles, machines, and other equipment.

Many jurisdictions are switching to performance tests for manual jobs since such tests readily meet validity requirements and also have much acceptability with candidates. However, if there are large numbers of candidates, performance tests are costly because of the pieces of equipment required and the element of wear and tear. If valid written tests are available, a decision may be made

---

[10]Lynette B. Plumlee, *A Short Guide to the Development of Performance Tests* (Washington, D.C.: U.S. Civil Service Commission, 1945), p. 1.

to use them instead of performance tests because of this cost factor. The real problem has been the failure to give sufficient attention to the possibility of using performance tests, but many jurisdictions are now replacing written tests with performance tests. Since most public service jobs are not of the manual type, the limitations are apparent.

Oral Examinations

When referring to the evaluation of candidates for entrance or promotion, the terms "oral examination" and "interview" are often used synonymously. Interview may also mean the interview that a selecting official has with persons whose names are certified from eligible lists. Such persons have passed the battery of tests, and the selecting official is given a choice from among a certain number of names. Our reference here is to an oral that constitutes a *weighted* part of the total examination. The weight assigned varies with the importance given, as the result of job analysis, to the worker characteristics that the oral is intended to measure.

Oral examinations are used to evaluate the candidates' content knowledge of the job, skills, and work backgrounds, in lieu of a written test or as a supplement to it, or may be employed principally to evaluate personality characteristics. Many selection authorities believe that the oral should be confined to the latter use because "job skills and knowledge and the relevance of past education and work experience are best measured by other techniques."[11] The greatest use of the oral examination has been for positions at intermediate and higher levels, although it is often included in test batteries for entrance level positions. In some cases, for example, for promotions in the federal service, the interviewers (members of evaluation panels) combine interview results with other measures of the candidates' qualifications in determining the final ranking of the candidates. As with other parts of the test battery, the oral examination should be used only if it produces important evaluative information not obtainable sufficiently from other measurement devices. The validity of written personality tests is doubtful since, for one thing, the questions may be transparent and the candidate readily deduces the appropriate answer (fudging).

---

[11]Maslow, *Staffing the Public Service*, p. 148.

As previously noted, all tests are subjective to some extent, but in the oral examination there is much opportunity for subjective and biased judgments by the interviewers. To deal with this problem, oral examinations should be "well planned in terms of the behaviors and responses to be observed, the evaluation standards to be applied, and the procedures for conducting"[12] the examination, and the examiners should record their observations in a standard manner. Training of the interviewers is particularly important because the expertise of the interviewer greatly affects the validity of the ratings. Including members of minority groups on interview panels contributes to validity because it prevents cultural bias in the evaluation of minority group candidates.

Many of those who lack confidence in written tests prefer the oral or at least believe they do. Many other persons predict that if orals completely replaced written tests the complaints about subjectivity of the examining process would be even greater, and some say the oral is so inherently subjective that this would eventually mean the end of the merit principle in selection.

The oral often is not included in the test battery because of the expense. The interviewers are personnel office staff members or operating officials on salary, or outside consultants receiving fees, and sometimes there are travel and subsistence expenses of the interviewers and perhaps for the interviewees. It is often said in partial justification of omission of the oral that the selecting officials do interview the eligibles who are referred to them. The ideal solution is to alter financial priorities and invest the necessary financial and other resources in a weighted oral, but, because of the budgetary pressures, such a reordering of priorities is not likely.

The group oral performance test

The panel interview is the most common form of oral, but there is another type—the group oral performance test.

In the group oral, candidates are assembled in small groups, and a topic is assigned for discussion. Civil service examiners are seated in the room but not at the conference table. They study closely how the candidates *perform* during the discussion, observing their personal characteristics and how they interact with the other can-

---

[12]Federal Personnel Manual Letter 335-13, *Guidelines for Evaluation of Employees for Promotion and Internal Placement*, p. 8.

didates. Advocates of the group oral maintain that it shows how the candidates "think on their feet" and that since the examiners listen only they have more time to observe the candidates.

However, the group situation is an artificial one, and the candidates may or may not conduct themselves with the same degree of effectiveness, or lack of same, in a real administrative situation. The attention of the examiners may be so frequently distracted from one candidate to another that they really have less opportunity to size up each person than in the panel interview. Furthermore, the examiners may measure each participant against the quality represented by the particular group rather than against the requirements of the position. In such case the candidate fails to impress or shines, depending upon the verbal skills, maturity, and other characteristics of the persons in the group. Because each has advantages, some jurisdictions use both a panel-type interview and a group oral, the candidates' scores on both being averaged.

The origins of the group oral are worth noting, since it was first used in the 1920s by German psychologists to improve selection methods in the military services. During World War II, it was adopted by the British Army and the U.S. Office of Strategic Services. In this country, it is now used both in entrance and promotional competitions.

Background Investigations

The background investigation may consist of a routine reference check by mail, perhaps supplemented by telephone inquiries, or it may be carried out by investigators who visit with previous employers and others who have direct knowledge of the candidate's preparation, work experience, abilities, and personal qualities. Because of financial limitations and time pressures, civil service agencies have generally not made thorough background checks except for positions such as those in police departments, but even in these cases the checking is often far from thorough.

The neglect of this phase of the selection process is regrettable because those who have supervised candidates on previous jobs, have worked with them as colleagues and subordinates, or have known them for substantial periods of time can supply far more information about them than can be obtained in any interview. One of the findings of an intensive New York City-Rand Institute study of the employment histories of the more than 2,000 police officers appointed in 1957 was that "the rating of candidates by Police Department background investigators was a good predictor of later performance. . . . In general, the men they rated 'excellent' turned out to be well above average, and many of those termed 'poor' or 'disapproved' were later found to be departmental discipline problems."[13]

■ ASSESSMENT CENTERS

Reviewing the traditional selection devices just discussed, only two kinds—performance tests for jobs requiring physical and/or psychomotor skills and the group oral performance test—simulate actual work behavior. Even when a weighted oral is given, candidates are under observation for relatively brief periods of time, often 20 minutes to a half hour, and the same is true of the group oral for it usually does not exceed an hour. Written tests of mental ability do not indicate how candidates use their mental capacities in given situations whereas simulations usually do. This does not mean that written tests and the other traditional selection devices should be eliminated completely. Rather it means that in making selection and promotion decisions for some kinds of jobs, it may be highly desirable to substitute simulations for one or more of the traditional selection methods or to supplement them with simulations. This brings us to the discussion of the assessment center method, mentioned at the beginning of this chapter.

The word "center" is explained by the fact that some of the first uses of this method took place full-time at certain locations, but "assessment center" now means any evaluation procedure whereby the ability of individuals to function effectively in a particular job (target job) is measured by multiple methods under standardized conditions. The multiple measures are usually individual and group exercises but also often include background interviews of the assessees by one of the assessors and mental ability or other pen-and-pencil tests. A frequent, but not exclusive, use of assessment centers, which usually last several days, has been to aid in selection for or promotion to supervisory and executive positions and in selecting participants in training programs to prepare persons for such jobs. A related purpose is to provide employees completing

[13]Bernard Cohen and Jan M. Chaiken, *Police Background Characteristics and Performance* (Lexington, Mass.: Heath, 1973), pp. 83, 123.

assessment programs with feedback information on their performances during the exercises that will aid them in planning their
career development programs. The centers may last only a couple
of hours, but usually the duration is several days.[14]

While the assessment center approach can be traced back to the
work of German psychologists in the early 1900s, it was during
World War II that assessment centers were first used in the United
States, specifically in the Office of Strategic Services (OSS) to select
spies and guerrilla fighters.[15] British War Office Selection Boards
had been using a program of psychological-psychiatric assessment,
and an OSS official returning from London suggested that OSS,
which had recruited "large numbers of misfits from the very beginning," adopt a similar approach.[16] After World War II, OSS-
type assessment centers were "essentially abandoned in the United
States except for some intelligence gathering activities by the Central Intelligence Agency," but the British Civil Service Selection
Board (CSSB) continued to use the assessment process in selecting
members of the administrative class.[17] Frequently referred to as
the "extended interview process," the CSSB attempted to "obtain
as much evidence as possible about each candidate, both from his
previous record and from studying his performance during the two
days of extended interview" which included "cognitive tests, analogous tests, group exercises, and personal interviews."[18] Some use
was also made of the assessment approach in Australia for selection
to military college and in South Africa for identifying supervisory
potential for operations in gold mines.

In the early 1950s, the American Telephone and Telegraph Company pioneered with long-term research on the effectiveness of
assessment centers in identifying potential for success in supervisory and managerial jobs, and this research showed that "strong
relationships existed between predictions made at the assessment
center and subsequent career progress."[19] Within the Bell System,

[14]Maslow, *Staffing the Public Service*, p. 145.

[15]Joseph L. Moses, "The Assessment Center Method," in Joseph L. Moses and
William C. Byham (eds.), *Applying the Assessment Center Method* (New York:
Pergamon, 1977), pp. 9–10.

[16]Donald V. MacKinnon, "From Selecting Spies to Selecting Managers—the OSS
Assessment Program," in Moses and Byham (eds.), *Applying the Assessment Center
Method*, p. 14.

[17]Moses, "The Assessment Center Method," p. 9.

[18]E. Anstey, "The Civil Service Administrative Class: Extended Interview Selection Procedure," *Occupational Psychology* 45 (1971): 201.

[19]Moses, "The Assessment Center Method," p. 10.

beginning in 1958, assessment centers were employed to select first-level foremen and determine capacity for high-level management jobs. Other private companies established assessment centers, and the technique spread to the Canadian national government and then to the U.S. public services, the first federal agency to use assessment centers being the Internal Revenue Service in 1968. By 1975, most major federal agencies were making some use of assessment centers, usually as part of the process for selection and development of managers and supervisors. The State Department uses one-day assessment centers as an important part of its annual examinations to fill entry positions in the foreign service.

In 1969, only 12 American organizations, mostly private, had assessment centers, but since then the number has grown greatly. Assessment centers in state governments began in 1972 in Illinois and soon thereafter on a major scale in Wisconsin. The first use in cities was in police and fire departments to aid in making promotion decisions. In early 1980, results of a questionnaire survey of 208 state and local jurisdictions by the Assessment Services Division of the International Personnel Management Association showed that close to half of the 156 jurisdictions responding had employed the assessment center method, principally for selection and promotion of police officers but also for assessment of candidates for a variety of other positions such as fire fighter, librarian, social worker, personnel assistant, traffic engineer, civil engineer, foremen, and managers.[20] Furthermore, since this questionnaire survey was made, the use of assessment centers has continued to increase. Professional organizations of those interested in assessment centers have been formed, there are several meetings of an International Congress on the Assessment Center Method, and many organizations including private consulting firms now offer research, consulting, and other services to governments on the assessment center method.

While there definitely is a trend in government toward adoption of the assessment method, it cannot be said the assessment centers are replacing traditional selection methods on a wholesale basis. For some kinds of positions—generally nonsupervisory, nonmanagerial—assessment centers are not necessary since traditional se-

---

[20]Louise F. Fitzgerald, "The Incidence and Utilization of Assessment Centers in State and Local Governments" (Washington, D.C.: International Personnel Management Association, 1980).

lection processes, particularly when improved, are adequate. A serious limitation on the use of assessment centers is the question of cost, to be referred to again later.

Assessees and Assessors

The usual ratio between assessees and assessors is two or three to one.[21] During the first stages of adoption of assessment centers, nomination by supervisors was the method used for selecting the assessees, but increasingly employees are being allowed to nominate themselves. The latter method protects against charges of favoritism and discriminatory practices by management in selecting participants, and it prevents the complaint sometimes made that participation was pressured by management and therefore involuntary.

The assessors usually are line management officials employed by the same organization who are familiar with the requirements of the target job. They often occupy positions one level above the target job, and may themselves have been assessment center participants and thus already have a knowledge of the assessment method. If members of minority groups or women are represented among the assessees, the assessors frequently include one person from the particular minority group or one woman. Assessors receive training, to be described later, and their services are drawn upon as needed, sometimes on a rotating basis.[22] Care is taken to assure that no assessor is personally acquainted with an assessee, but, if this cannot be avoided, "assessors who know particular assessees can be scheduled to avoid any direct interaction with them."[23]

The "Dimensions"

Just as with any other selection method, the assessment process should be preceded by thorough job analysis to establish clearly the duties of the position and the qualities required by incumbents. The term "dimension" is commonly used in referring to these qualities. Since the requirements of supervisory and mana-

---

[21]Maslow, *Staffing the Public Service*, p. 145.
[22]William C. Byham, "Assessor Selection and Training," in Moses and Byham (eds.), *Applying the Assessment Center Method*, p. 96.
[23]Ibid., p. 100.

gerial positions are not exactly the same in all organizations, the dimensions vary so that job analysis should be peculiar to the target position. As an example, the dimension "oral communication skills" is defined as follows: To what extent can this individual effectively present an oral report to a small conference group? Similarly, for the dimension "reaction to pressure," the definition is: functions in a controlled, effective manner under stress." As a final example, "problem analysis" is described as "effectiveness in seeking out pertinent data and in determining the source of a problem."[24]

The Exercises and Other Assessment Techniques

The most common exercises are the *in-basket exercise* and the *leaderless group discussion*. In the in-basket exercise, the participant is presented with a packet of letters, memoranda, reports, and other materials that normally would be found in the incoming box on the manager's desk. The candidate, who is provided with selective background information on this incoming material, prepares a written report explaining how he or she would dispose of each item in the in-basket and then usually is interviewed by one of the assessors who asks detailed questions about *why* the candidate chose a particular solution to a problem.

Following is an example of a leaderless group discussion with assigned roles:

> Each of six assessees in a group is given a description of a fictitious subordinate he or she is recommending for a promotion. The descriptions are formulated so that the candidates are about equally qualified. The assessees study their candidate descriptions, and each is then allowed five minutes to make a pitch for the candidate the assessee is sponsoring. After all six assessees are heard, a period of free discussion is followed by a rank-ordering of the job candidates by the assessees from the most deserving to least deserving. Assessors observing the group (each assessor commonly observing two assessees) judge the assessees on ability to sell their candidates and what they have done to aid the group in reaching a decision.[25]

[24]See *Assessment Center Approach: A Comprehensive Summary* (Springfield, Ill.: State Department of Personnel, 1972), pp. 47–48, and National Institute of Law Enforcement and Criminal Justice, Law Enforcement Assistance Administration, United States Department of Justice, *Police Selection and Career Assessment* (Washington, D.C.: Government Printing Office, 1976), pp. 56–57.

[25]Lois A. Crooks, "The Selection and Development of Assessment Center Techniques," in Moses and Byham (eds.), *Applying the Assessment Center Method*, p. 75.

As another example, a newspaper reporter describes one of the
group exercises administered in a State Department assessment
center:

> . . . After a lunch break, the candidates [for entry level foreign
> service officer] were divided into groups of six and instructed to
> determine which agricultural, education and urban-aid programs an
> embassy in a theoretical country should fund from a $50,000 budget.
> The aim of the exercise was to uncover leadership skills and the
> ability to establish good working relationships.
>
> Minutes before the exercise was scheduled to end, the candidates
> were suddenly informed that "Budget Director David Stockman has
> gone berserk again, and so instead of $50,000 to spend, you have
> only $38,000." Most groups speedily compromised and eliminated
> or severely cut projects that did not virtually guarantee a return of
> good will for the United States.[26]

Role-playing exercises may also be included, for example, the
assessee plays the role of a supervisory official who meets with an
irate member of the public complaining about some treatment he
or she has received from the agency. Or the assessee, presented
with certain facts and/or allegations about a subordinate's misconduct, must hold a disciplinary interview with that employee. Often
one of the assessors plays the role of the person interviewed.

Another exercise is individual problem analysis and then oral
presentation of recommendations for dealing with the problem to
peers, superiors, or agency clients. The assessee is given detailed
information on a complex problem, expected to research the problem, develop alternative solutions, and select what he or she believes to be the best alternative, and then in the oral presentation
convince the audience that it *is* the best alternative, fielding questions from the audience.[27]

Some of the exercises described above are videotaped, and the
tapes are viewed by the assessors at the time and place they find
most convenient. Hypothetical situations for the assessees to analyze sometimes are also videotaped for better presentation of the
problem, with the opportunity to rerun the tape as desired. For
example:

---

[26]B. Drummond Ayres, Jr., "A New Breed of Diplomat," *New York Times Mag-
azine*, September 11, 1983.

[27]Crooks, "The Selection and Development of Assessment Center Techniques,"
p. 75.

In this exercise, candidates view a videotaped segment showing two patrol officers handling a domestic dispute. The tape is stopped at specific points and the candidates evaluate the performance of the two officers with instructions to indicate how they would have acted if they were the officers in this situation. After the tape is shown, candidates as a group discuss the officers' performance and try to achieve a consensus on the effectiveness of the performance of the officers in the videotaped segment.[28]

The background interview of the assessee by one of the assessors, previously referred to, is intended to measure the extent to which the candidate possesses the dimensions for the target job. Candidates are not ranked on the basis of this interview; ranking takes place after all evaluation methods used in the assessment center have been administered. Pencil-and-paper and other tests are employed when considered appropriate (e.g., verbal reasoning test).

Training of Assessors

William C. Byham, a leading authority on the assessment method, states that there is no agreement on the content and length of assessor training programs. Assessor training ranges from several hours to several weeks but typically lasts several days. Byham outlines a complete program of assessor training that indicates how with well-trained assessors the assessment method can provide much more intensive scrutiny of candidates than under traditional selection procedures.

Byham stresses the importance of careful training of assessors in the meaning of target job dimensions and in how to categorize behavior under each dimension. This is best accomplished by making the statement of the dimensions short and clear and by providing the assessor-trainee with "examples of observable behavior related to each dimension." For the dimension, "Use of delegation, ability to use subordinates effectively and to understand where a decision can best be made," a good example of observable behavior is, "Believes most decisions should be made at the lowest level by the people directly involved." A poor example is, "Delegated eight items to Rogers, but no items to Smith or Jones."[29] Assessors also require training in rating assessees on each dimension "according

---

[28]*Police Selection and Career Assessment*, p. 63.
[29]Byham, "Assessor Selection and Training," pp. 105–106.

to the observed behavior." The most common rating device for this purpose is a five-point continuum showing the degree to which the assessee possesses the dimension. The usual criterion for these ratings is comparison with "successful individuals at the target level for which the assessment center is designed."[30] Thus, assessees are not compared with one another, and an assessee's evaluation does not depend upon the chance factor of the qualities of the other assessees.

Assessors should also be trained "in the process of coming to a group consensus on each of the dimensions and an overall rating." The reference here is to group meetings of the center assessors at which they analyze all assessor reports on individual candidate dimensions, agree upon the proper rating of the candidate on each dimension, and then determine an overall rating for each candidate. Byham writes, "The last major portion of most assessor training programs is devoted to a mock assessor discussion where assessors practice reaching decisions on dimension ratings and in making overall judgments."[31]

Assessors are also trained in interviewing and in role playing, and they are provided with an observer manual that includes complete instructions on their responsibilities with respect to each exercise or other assessment technique.

The Question of Cost

For a center that lasts several days no matter what the variation in the cost estimates, the process obviously is not an inexpensive one. Since a small number of candidates is assessed intensively with a low ratio of assessees to assessors and several exercises and other assessment methods are utilized, the cost factor inherently is appreciable. Some assessment centers have closed down because of the expense.

Costs should be measured against benefits. If the assessment method is appreciably more valid than traditional devices for selecting and promoting supervisors and executives, the benefits far outweigh the costs. One poor supervisor or executive not weeded out through indiscriminate traditional selection methods can cause very substantial damage to the organization both in money and

---

[30]Ibid., pp. 108–109.
[31]Ibid., p. 113.

other costs. Consider, for example, the negative impact on employee morale. Cost comparisons, imprecise as they necessarily are, should be made when considering using the assessment method instead of traditional procedures.

■ TEST VALIDITY

The methods of determining validity generally accepted by test experts are: (1) criterion-related validity; (2) content validity; and (3) construct validity. These three validation strategies are described by the American Psychological Association in its *Standards for Educational and Psychological Tests and Manuals*.[32] The term "test" includes all selection methods used to make employment decisions such as interviews, written tests, and evaluations of training and experience.

In *criterion-related validity*, test scores are compared with criteria of job performance. In one method, after individuals have been on the job for some time the scores they made on an entrance test are compared with measures of job performance. In another method—known as concurrent validity—a proposed new test is tried out on existing employees, and their ratings on this test are compared with measures of their job performance.

In *content validity*, the test is constructed to constitute a representative sample of the duties or abilities, skills, and knowledges necessary or desirable for successful job performance. Examples are written job knowledge tests appropriate for the kind of work and level of responsibility involved and performance tests in which the actual duties are performed, as in typing and in welding.

In *construct validity*, the test is intended to measure an underlying human trait or characteristic (e.g., intelligence) that is important for successful job performance.

A test for a legal position provides an example of the difference between content and construct validity. Such a test has content validity if it asks questions about specific provisions of law with which the incumbent must be familiar. It has construct validity if it accurately measures "ability to read and interpret material of the same complexity as that in which laws are written. It is hypothesized that it would test ability to read and understand the laws."[33]

[32]American Psychological Association, *Standards for Educational and Psychological Tests and Manuals*, pp. 12–24.
[33]Taylor, *Test Validity in Public Personnel Selection*, p. 5.

In *Griggs* v. *Duke Power Company* (1971), the U.S. Supreme Court ruled that if a test has an adverse effect in terms of race, color, religion, or national origin, and if its validity has not been demonstrated, its use constitutes unlawful discrimination under Title VII of the Civil Rights Act of 1964.[34] Since the Equal Employment Opportunity Act of 1972 amended this legislation to extend coverage to "governments," "governmental agencies," and "political subdivisions," this ruling now applies both to the private and public sectors.

Disagreements Between the Enforcement Agencies on Selection Guidelines

During the late 1960s and the early 1970s, the Equal Employment Opportunity Commission, the Department of Labor, and the Civil Service Commission each issued guidelines on selection procedures. Labor's responsibility was to secure compliance with Executive Order 11246 requiring contractors and subcontractors of the federal government, as well as contractors and subcontractors under federally assisted construction contracts, to follow nondiscriminatory employment policies. Under another executive order, the Civil Service Commission was responsible for the equal employment opportunity program in the federal service. It also was responsible for monitoring compliance by state and local agencies receiving grants under the Intergovernmental Personnel Act of 1970 with the requirement contained in that legislation that they follow nondiscriminatory employment policies.

Unfortunately, the EEOC, Labor, and Civil Service Commission guidelines differed in the requirements placed on employers for demonstrating job-relatedness of selection methods. The Equal Employment Opportunity Act of 1972 established an Equal Employment Opportunity Coordinating Council (EEOCC), consisting of the Secretary of Labor, the chairpersons of the Equal Employment Opportunity Commission, the U.S. Civil Service Commission, the United States Civil Rights Commission, and the Attorney General. This council was to develop and implement "agreements, policies, and practices designed to maximize effort" and to eliminate conflicts, duplication, and inconsistencies in the functioning of the various federal agencies responsible for implementing and

---

[34]401 U.S. 424 (1971).

enforcing "equal employment opportunity legislation, orders, and policies."[35] The Attorney General was made a member because the Justice Department is responsible for any legal action taken against public employers for discriminatory employment practices. The U.S. Civil Rights Commission has an advisory role in advancing the cause of equal employment opportunity.

The EEOCC tried without success to get agreement on uniform selection guidelines. The principal problem was disagreement between EEOC and the Civil Rights Commission on the one hand and the Civil Service Commission, Labor, and Justice on the other. In late 1976, the latter agencies agreed upon and adopted certain guidelines,[36] but the Civil Rights Commission and EEOC were opposed, and EEOC retained its own guidelines adopted in 1970.[37] The following were principal points of disagreement between EEOC and the Civil Service Commission, Labor, and Justice:

1. The EEOC guidelines did not define *adverse impact* (on members of a race, sex, or ethnic group) but indicated that its existence would be determined by comparing the "rates at which different applicant groups pass a particular selection procedure."[38]

    The other three agencies' guidelines (known as the Federal Executive Agency Guidelines) defined adverse impact as a "substantially different selection rate . . . which works to the disadvantage of members of a racial, sex, or ethnic group," and the following rule-of-thumb was provided: "If the selection rate for a group is within 4/5 or 80 percent of the rate for the group with the highest rate, the enforcement agency will generally not consider adverse impact to exist." For example, if there are 120 applicants of whom 80 are white and 40 black and the employer selected 42 whites and 18 blacks, the selection rate for blacks is 18/40 or 45 percent, and that for whites 42/80 or 52.5 percent. Since the selection rate for blacks compared with that for whites is 45/52.5 or 85.4 per-

[35]Public Law 92-261, 92nd Congress, H. R. 1746, March 24, 1972.

[36]"Questions and Answers on the Federal Executive Agency Guidelines on Employee Selection Procedures," Part VI, *Federal Register* 42, no. 14 (January 21, 1977).

[37]Equal Employment Opportunity Commission, "Guidelines on Employee Selection Procedures," *Federal Register* 35, no. 149 (August 1, 1970).

[38]*Report to the Congress by the Comptroller General of the United States, Problems with Federal Equal Employment Opportunity Guidelines on Employee Selection Procedures Need to be Resolved* (Washington, D.C.: February 1978), p. 13.

cent, "the difference in impact would not be regarded as substantial in the absence of other information."[39]

2. The EEOC guidelines required validation of every part (component) of the total examination for filling a position (e.g., written test, evaluation of training and experience) if that component had an adverse impact. This meant making investigations of adverse impact for all examination components even when the examination as a whole did not have an adverse impact.

   The FEA guidelines stated that adverse impact was to be determined first for the "overall selection process for each job category." If no such adverse effect was found, there was no obligation to validate the selection components. If adverse impact were found, then each selection component would have to be analyzed for adverse impact and validated if adverse effect was discovered and the employer wanted to continue to use the component.[40]

3. Whereas the EEOC guidelines expressed a preference for criterion-related validity, the FEA guidelines pointed out that "generally accepted principles of the psychological profession do not recognize such preference, but contemplate the use of criterion-related, content, or construct validity strategies as appropriate."[41] In small jurisdictions, usually not enough people are tested or hired in single job classifications to give a statistical sample sufficiently large for studies comparing applicants' scores with measures of their performance after some time on the job. In large jurisdictions, the sample is usually big enough only in "relatively few classifications."[42]

4. EEOC guidelines required that employers, in validating a selection procedure, demonstrate that an alternative selection method with less adverse impact than the one it proposes to use does not exist. The objection to this requirement was that it could mean an endless "cosmic" search for alternatives with less adverse effect. The FEA guidelines provide that while conducting a validity study the employer should attempt to find and apply procedures that have as little adverse impact as possible. However, once the effort had been made and the

---

[39]"Questions and Answers on the Federal Executive Agency Guidelines," p. 4052.
[40]Ibid., p. 4053.
[41]Ibid., p. 4055.
[42]Taylor, *Test Validity in Public Personnel Selection*, p. 10.

chosen procedure had been shown to be valid, the employer did not have to search further for alternative procedures.

5. EEOC guidelines required tests to be validated for each minority group so as to assure that differential rejection rates based on the tests were relevant to performance on the jobs in question. The FEA guidelines recommended that, when criterion-related studies were made of a test that had an adverse effect on any one racial, ethnic, or sex group, data be compiled separately for all groups to determine "test fairness."[43]

After long, extensive negotiations, in August of 1978 the EEOC, the Civil Service Commission, Labor, and Justice reached agreement on Uniform Guidelines on Employee Selection Procedures. In the following month, the Department of Treasury—whose Office of Revenue Sharing is responsible for monitoring compliance by state and local governments receiving revenue sharing funds with antidiscrimination requirements contained in the revenue sharing legislation—also adopted the uniform guidelines.

In general, the uniform guidelines follow FEA guidelines closely. The uniform guidelines provide that if there is no adverse effect for the overall selection process in most circumstances there is no obligation to investigate adverse effect for the examination components. (This has been commonly referred to as the "bottom line standard.") No preference is expressed for criterion-related validity. When making validity studies, employers are expected to make a "reasonable effort to become aware of suitable alternative selection procedures and methods of use which have as little adverse effect as possible, and to investigate those which are suitable." An alternative selection procedure with lesser adverse impact must be used only if the "evidence shows that its validity is substantially the same or greater for the same job in similar circumstances."[44] Finally, the uniform guidelines provide that test fairness be investigated generally at the same time as a criterion-related study is made or as soon as possible thereafter.

As Maslow stresses, the Uniform Guidelines are not regulations but their "impact is substantial and persuasive" because the Supreme Court has said that as the administrative interpretations of

---

[43]"Adoption of Questions and Answers to Clarify and Provide a Common Interpretation of the Uniform Guidelines on Employee Selection Procedures," *Federal Register* 44, no. 43 (March 2, 1979), p. 12003.
[44]Ibid.

the enforcing agencies they are entitled to "great deference."[45] The ultimate determinations as to test validity requirements and whether or not an employer has met them are made by the Supreme Court, and no matter what the decisions of the enforcement agencies the individual may sue in court.

In *State of Connecticut et al*. v. *Winnie Teal et al*. (June 1982),[46] the Supreme Court dealt with the "bottom line" standard. In *Teal*, the appellant, a black, had failed the written test and thus been disqualified from taking the other components of the examination (the successive hurdles approach followed by some personnel agencies). Since the examination as a whole resulted in no disparate effect on the blacks taking it, the State of Connecticut asserted the "bottom line" defense. The Supreme Court ruled that the Equal Employment Opportunity Act was intended to protect individuals from discrimination, consequently the fairness of the written test to the *individual* candidate had to be established no matter what the adverse impact on the black applicants as a *group*. The minority justices warned that the majority's opinion could discourage financially-pressed local governments from validating any tests at all and might induce them to adopt the simple solution of quota hiring. In other decisions, the Supreme Court and the lower courts have not followed other parts of the guidelines uniformly. For example, the data they have accepted on what constitutes a "substantially different rate of selection" has varied.[47]

Apart from the question of cost, the uniform guidelines have been criticized as professionally unsound in some respects, unclear in many others, and requiring excessive, unnecessary record keeping, and it appears likely that the enforcing agencies will revise the guidelines before too long. In any case, the reality is that from a long previous history of relatively little test validation, public personnel agencies were suddenly thrust into a new era of much community expectation of massive, quick validation of selection procedures. However, the guidelines make clear that, "in determining whether to institute an action against a user [employer] on the basis of a selection procedure which has adverse effect and has not been validated, the enforcement agency will take into account the equal employment opportunity posture of the user . . . and the progress which has been made in carrying out any affirmative

---

[45]Maslow, *Staffing the Public Service*, p. 51.
[46]Ibid., p. 53.
[47]Ibid., p. 52.

action plan." If the employer can demonstrate that it has for a substantial period of time been "utilizing in the job or groups of jobs in question the available race, sex, or ethnic groups in the relevant labor force, the enforcement agency will generally exercise its discretion by not initiating enforcement proceedings based on adverse action in relation to the applicant flow."[48] Obviously, it will be many years before public employers can meet the full requirements of the uniform selection guidelines. However distant the ideal, clearly test validation is now fully established as a central element on public personnel agendas.

One reason for the growing interest in the assessment center method is that "it lends itself to validation based on 'content validity,' " and "basing a selection instrument on content validity allows an organization to put it into operation more rapidly than procedures requiring other forms of validity." Byham states that typically organizations initially base assessment center validity on the content of the program administered and then, after the center has been functioning for some time, make criterion-related studies comparing the evaluations of persons on assessment center measures with their performance after completing the assessment center program and returning to their jobs.[49] While research on assessment centers is as yet not extensive, studies are cited showing a higher validity for the assessment method than the traditional selection procedures. However, most of this research has been on content validity, and there have been very few criterion related validity studies of assessment centers. The findings show that, "although assessment center ratings have higher validities than do written tests, a program that includes both test data and assessment ratings is even more effective."[50]

The Politics of Test Validity—The Case of PACE

To test experts, the validity question is a technical one although, of course, like specialists in other professions their conclusions and recommendations may be affected significantly by their views on social policy. The controversy over public service selection meth-

[48]"Adoption of Questions and Answers to Clarify and Provide a Common Interpretation of the Uniform Guidelines on Employee Selection Procedures," *Federal Register*, no. 4 (March 2, 1979), p. 12201.

[49]Byham, "Assessor Selection and Training," p. 34.

[50]Maslow, *Staffing the Public Service*, p. 145.

ods and written tests in particular is basically one over social objectives, and clearly there is a "politics of test validity." Our example will be PACE, already briefly discussed in Chapter 4. It will be recalled that there was a class action suit challenging the validity of PACE, that the Carter administration entered into a consent decree to settle this suit, and that in mid-1982 the Reagan administration discontinued PACE.

In hearings before the House Subcommittee on Civil Service in 1979, then OPM Director Alan K. Campbell testified that thorough research by OPM had established the validity of PACE.[51] The first step had been to identify the abilities or constructs important for successful performance in PACE jobs and to decide how they would be measured. Twenty-seven PACE occupations accounting for about 70 percent of PACE hires during the early 1970s were selected for intensive analysis.

Senior level supervisory employees in these occupations prepared lists of the duties of the jobs in these 27 occupations, assessed the relative importance of these duties, and rated the required knowledges, skills, abilities, and other characteristics according to their importance for successful job performance. These ratings provided one basis for identifying the abilities to be measured by the written test. The other basis was a comprehensive review of "hundreds of tests whose construct validity had been explored in diverse settings."

The OPM researchers matched the knowledges, skills, abilities, and other characteristics identified in the 27 PACE occupations with those identified in these earlier tests, and they wrote examination questions similar to those in the earlier tests. After the PACE written test was prepared and administered, OPM made criterion-related validity studies that showed a positive relationship between test scores and job performance measures of persons already in PACE positions, such as social security claims examiners (an example of concurrent validity research).

The abilities found necessary for successful performance in PACE jobs included:

(1) *Verbal:* to understand and interpret complex reading materials where precise correspondence of words and concepts makes effective oral and written communication possible.

---

[51] House Subcommittee on Civil Service, *Professional and Administrative Career Examination* (Washington, D.C.: Government Printing Office, 1979), pp. 5–55.

(2) *Judgment:* to make decisions or to take actions in the absence of complete information and to solve problems by inferring missing facts or events to arrive at the most logical conclusion.

(3) *Induction:* to discover underlying relations or principles in specific data by formation and testing of hypotheses.

(4) *Deduction:* to discover implications of facts and reason from general principles to specific situations as in developing plans and procedures.

(5) *Number:* to perform arithmetic operations and to solve quantitative problems where the proper approach is not specified.

Those who brought the class action suit challenging PACE's validity maintained that tests based on these five constructs were much too general in character to measure the ability to succeed in all of 118 different occupations, each with a different work content. Further, they questioned the technical soundness of the OPM validity research on PACE. That PACE had a disparate effect on blacks and Hispanics is clear. Data collected by OPM on the April 1978 administration of PACE showed that 8.5 percent of whites taking the test received unaugmented scores of 90 or above, whereas the percentages of blacks and Hispanics who took the test receiving such scores were 0.3 percent and 1.5 percent respectively. (Unaugmented score means without veterans preference points. Very few appointments were made of persons with a score of less than 90.[52]) Other administrations of PACE have also shown adverse impact on blacks and Hispanics.

How the courts would have ruled on the validity of PACE no one can say. That the Carter administration entered into a consent decree to settle the suit rather than going to court, is evidence to opponents of preferential hiring that the decision was a political one and that Carter had yielded to minority group pressures.

The consent decree was signed on January 9, 1981, just two weeks before Ronald Reagan assumed office. The new administration strongly opposed the decree and was able to negotiate modifications of it with the court, including elimination of a requirement that the government continue affirmative action efforts until blacks and Hispanics comprised at least 20 percent of

---

[52]William C. Valdes, *The Selection of College Graduates for the Federal Civil Service: The Problem of the "PACE" Examination and the Consent Decree* (Washington, D.C.: National Academy of Public Administration, n.d.), p. 6.

all incumbents at the GS-5 level and higher levels in the entire job category on a national basis. As OPM Director Donald Devine later said, the new administration had wanted to withdraw from the terms of the decree but had regretfully concluded that the matter was in the "hands of the court, beyond the power of the government unilaterally to bar."[53] In previous chapters of this book, the strong opposition of the Reagan administration to preferential hiring has been discussed; its opposition to the court decree was an early statement of its position on this issue.

The principal terms of the modified decree are:

(1) OPM was to phase out use of PACE and permanently eliminate its use for competitive entry no later than three years after the effective date of the decree (January 18, 1982).

(2) Applicants for PACE occupations were to be selected through alternative examining procedures based on the requirements of the particular occupation.

(3) If these alternative procedures resulted in adverse impact on blacks and Hispanics, as such impact is defined in the Uniform Selection Guidelines, the government would have to demonstrate, under validation theories approved under Title VII of the Civil Rights Act, the Uniform Guidelines, and the decree, that the procedure was job-related. Adverse impact is defined under the decree to exist if the selection rate for minority applicants who are hired in a job category is less than 80 percent of the selection rate for white applicants who are hired.

(4) Agencies were to make "all practicable efforts" through recruiting and special programs to eliminate adverse impact from the interim use of PACE or from alternative procedures.

(5) The court (U.S. district court for the District of Columbia) was to retain jurisdiction of the case for five years after the implementation of an alternative examining procedure for each occupation.

Before the decree was signed, the Carter administration had started a plan for the agencies to "develop separate job-related examinations for specific occupations as a substitute for the PACE written test."[54] The two largest users of PACE, the Social Security

---

[53]Ibid., p. 12.
[54]Ibid.

Administration and the Defense Department, began work on alternative examinations during the last year of the Carter presidency, SSA for claims representative and Defense for four large occupational categories. Written tests were not a part of these alternative examinations. SSA rated the candidates on the basis of evaluation of training and experience and a structured personal interview; Defense relied exclusively on evaluation of training and experience. SSA and Defense both found the results disappointing, SSA finding that "many of those selected did not do well on the job" and Defense that the "quality of the candidates selected was not only much lower than their prior experience with PACE, but unacceptably low." Furthermore, while these alternative examinations did "reduce adverse impact on minorities they . . . created adverse impact on women."[55]

Several reasons were given by the Reagan administration for discontinuing PACE and placing positions formerly filled through PACE in the excepted (noncompetitive) service: (1) there were no alternative written tests and other merit selection procedures available, (2) reductions in federal employment would result in substantially fewer appointments from outside the service, and (3) the cost of developing validated competitive examinations consistent with the decree would be prohibitive.[56]

PACE positions were filled not only through the PACE written examination but also through promotion and transfer of persons already in the federal service. Emphasis had been given to upward mobility programs that enabled minority group and other employees to move up into PACE jobs. In 1979, OPM estimated that PACE positions were being filled 35 percent through the PACE examination and 65 percent through various non-PACE entry methods.[57] The budgetary reductions of the Reagan administration have substantially reduced opportunities for federal employment but, according to a thorough study by William C. Valdes, Senior Research Associate for the National Academy of Public Administration, agencies such as Defense, the Internal Revenue Service, and SSA have anticipated much need for external hiring during the life of the consent decree.[58]

For an administration intent on reducing the costs of govern-

---

[55]Ibid., p. 13, p. 15, p. 34.
[56]Ibid., pp. 26–27.
[57]Ibid., p. 5.
[58]Ibid., pp. 27–28.

ment, the expense entailed in validating alternative selection methods obviously is a big deterrent. According to OPM Director Donald J. Devine, 28.5 years of staff time and $750,000 were expended on the research and development of PACE, including construct validation studies that lasted from January of 1973 through August of 1977. The writing and trying out of questions during this period required about 43 additional staff years and a cost of $737,700.[59]

Valdes found little evidence that OPM "is engaged in a serious effort to develop alternative selection procedures," and he quotes a statement by the OMP General Counsel indicating that OPM's intention was "to allow *Luevano* [the class action suit] to sink of its own weight."[60] It seems clear that the Reagan administration, which dislikes the consent decree and finds it much too difficult to comply with, is following a political strategy of biding its time until the jurisdiction of the court ends in September of 1987.

The administration's opinion of the court decree is shared by many persons and groups. The issue is not a purely politically partisan one between Republicans and Democrats or one between conservatives and liberals. Among those testifying against the consent decree before a Senate subcommittee was a representative of the National Law Committee, Anti-Defamation League of B'nai B'rith who said, "It appears to stand for the proposition that if the numbers are wrong, you go back and redo it, and if it doesn't work, then you go back and redo it, and do it again—until the numbers are right."[61] Basically, the disagreement is between two different value systems each of which commands support in society: one favoring preferential hiring as redress for past discrimination against certain *groups* (minorities and women) and the other against what it considers to be reverse discrimination against *individuals*. (This same clash was discussed in Chapter 7 of this book.)

Under present OPM policy, agencies must obtain its prior approval for hiring from outside the government for entry level professional and administrative positions, and this approval is very difficult to obtain. Those persons who are hired from the outside

---

[59]Senate Committee on the Judiciary, *P.A.C.E. Consent Decree: Equal Protection Issues* (Washington, D.C.: Government Printing Office, 1981), p. 23.

[60]Valdes, *The Selection of College Graduates for the Federal Service*, p. 35, p. 31.

[61]Senate Committee on the Judiciary, *P.A.C.E. Consent Decree*, p. 67.

are not given career status and can be promoted or reassigned only
to PACE positions in the GS 5/7 job series for which placement
in the excepted service has been "determined to be appropriate."
In other words, they are locked into the noncompetitive service
and can only obtain appointments in the competitive service by
taking and passing a civil service examination for another position.
Some agencies have suggested to "candidates qualified and interested in professional and administrative positions that they apply
instead for clerical jobs for which examinations are available with
the hope that it may be possible to later promote them internally
to a competitive status PACE trainee job."[62] This is a deplorable
situation to those who supported the long, eventually successful
effort to obtain a main avenue federal entrance examination for
college students.

In external hiring to former PACE positions candidates must
meet the OPM minimum qualifications for the job, and there is
no requirement for the agencies to rate or rank candidates. Valdes
found that college placement offices were given "almost no information" concerning job opportunities for specific entry level positions now in the excepted service and "the delays and frustrations
involved in attempting to locate and be considered for positions
impel well qualified candidates to pursue other options."[63]

Many of those opposed to the consent decree believe, notwithstanding, that OPM was not justified in terminating PACE and
virtually giving up the effort to develop valid alternative examination procedures. Some of these critics think that written tests
could be developed that would satisfy the court that the intentions
of the consent decree were being met. Above all, they fear that
the political strategy of the Reagan administration on *Luevano* may
do permanent serious damage to opportunities for careers in the
federal service for graduating college students.

It is appropriate to finish this discussion with a quotation from
a National Research Council committee report issued in 1982:

> The committee has found no evidence of alternatives to testing that
> are equally informative, equally adequate technically, and also eco-
> nomically and politically viable. . . . Society has many goals. Pro-
> ductivity is one. Equity is another. . . . Americans have long valued
> pluralism and have considered it a benefit to society to encourage

[62]Valdes, *The Selection of College Graduates for the Federal Service*, p. 26, p.
28.
[63]Ibid., p. 36.

diversity. These fundamental goals exist in a state of tension that can become outright conflict as is illustrated by the conflict about ability testing. . . . It is essentially a political problem that must be threshed out in an open political process in which all interested parties participate.[64]

■ ELIGIBLE LISTS AND CERTIFICATION

A distinctive characteristic of civil service systems is that candidates who pass entrance or promotional examinations are placed on eligible lists where they are ranked in order of composite examination scores. When hiring officials have openings to fill, they request the civil service agency to certify names of eligibles from these lists in the order specified in the civil service law and regulations.

Until recent years, the "rule of three" (the three highest-ranking eligibles) was by far the most common one for certifying names from eligible lists. Historically, this rule emerged as a device for protecting the merit system but at the same time granting some discretion to appointing officers. The assumption was that examination scores would reflect real differences in capacities to do the job and that three was a reasonable number of names to certify for each opening. To certify more names would increase the risk that appointing officers would select on a political basis. Some jurisdictions were so concerned about political contamination that they adopted the "rule of one," and a few state and local governments still have such a rule.

Although the rule of three is still a very common one, many jurisdictions have abandoned it and are certifying more names— sometimes quite a few more and even the entire eligible list. Furthermore, indications are that many other jurisdictions will liberalize certification procedures. Very often eligibles are separated by very small differences in examination scores, sometimes by decimal points only. A dozen or more candidates may have scores within a range of two or three points. Furthermore, there often are tie scores with many persons sometimes having identical scores.

Restrictive certification rules are also held responsible in part for preventing appointment of more minority group members and women. The Carter administration's civil service reform bill would

---

[64]Ibid., pp. A-25–26.

have replaced the rule of three with selection from seven names, largely to improve the chances of minority groups and women to obtain appointments, but Congress did not approve this proposal. The National Research Council report just quoted above suggests the "goals of efficiency and representativeness might be brought into workable balance by altering the decision rule (ranking and the rule of three) that determines how test scores are used. This might be in the form of a weighting formula that recognizes high ability, ethnic diversity, and other socially valued considerations in selecting from the portion of the applicant population that has demonstrated the threshold level of ability or skill necessary to successful performance."[65]

Certification in rank order from eligible lists is only one part of a traditional civil service employment process that some persons predict will be greatly modified. They believe that use of written tests will terminate and that appointments will be made on the basis of evaluation of training and experience and interview. Candidates who are found satisfactory based on qualifications' review and interview will be placed in broad categories, such as excellent, well-qualified, and qualified. Names of those in the highest group will be sent first to hiring officials, but they could also request names of persons in the other quality groups. Many changes have already been made in traditional civil service practices, so this prediction may come true at some future time. Meanwhile, the uniform selection guidelines permit ranking on registers if there is evidence of validity of the selection procedure upon which the ranking is based.

■ PROBATIONARY PERIOD

From the selection standpoint the probationary period is the last stage in the sifting process; no matter how much effort is put into making preemployment tests valid, they may not screen out some candidates who lack the ability to perform satisfactorily in particular jobs. Since performance depends so much on motivation, interest, and response to factors in the work environment, probation gives supervisory officers the opportunity to evaluate new employees in daily work situations over a period of time and to ap-

---

[65]Ibid., p. A-27.

prove for permanent status only those whose services have been satisfactory. Probationary employees usually do not have appeal rights. If unsatisfactory workers are not separated at this stage, it generally is much more difficult to remove them later.

Probation marks the beginning of management's opportunity to benefit from its investment in recruiting the new employee, and management increases that investment with appropriate work assignments and training for the recruit. To the recruits, probation is a test not just of themselves but also of the employer: If the employer fails to offer them effective guidance and stimulus, they may quit or, if they remain, work without enthusiasm.

In practice, only a tiny percentage of appointees—sometimes less than 1 percent—is weeded out as unsatisfactory during or at the end of probation. This has traditionally been the case, despite such schemes to prod supervision as requiring the appointing officer 10 days before the end of the trial period to certify in writing to the personnel office that the employee's services have been satisfactory, in the absence of which certification all salary payments to the employee are suspended. The appointing officer perfunctorily complies by rating the employee satisfactory. Supervisors do not relish making decisions which require the termination of a subordinate's employment, and they will not make effective use of the probationary period when they know other supervisors are not doing so. The personnel office cannot step in and make this kind of determination because this would usurp the functions of program managers.

If the probationary period is not allowed to become a dead issue, the question of its length is important. Usually the duration is the same for all positions, but in some jurisdictions it is variable, depending upon the kind of position. The reasoning is that for some kinds of work it takes longer to decide whether the individual meets the job requirements. In any case, the length of the probationary period usually does not exceed one year. Normally, decisions as to the retention of probationary employees are based on supervisory ratings, but in some lines of work (e.g., the U.S. Foreign Service) special panels or boards interview the employee at the end of the probationary period, review the entire employment record, and make recommendations to agency heads for retention or separation. In most public agencies, permanent status is routinely approved.

BIBLIOGRAPHY

American Psychological Association. *Standards for Educational and Psychological Tests and Manuals*. Washington, D.C.: 1966.

Cronbach, Lee. "Selection Theory for a Political World." *Public Personnel Management* 9, no. 1 (January 1980).

Donovan, J. J., ed. *Recruitment and Selection in the Public Service*. Washington, D.C.: International Personnel Management Association, 1968.

Educational Testing Service. *An Investigation of Sources of Bias in the Prediction of Job Performance: A Six-Year Study*. Princeton, N.J.: 1972.

Lopez, Felix M., Jr. *Personnel Interviewing: Theory and Practice*. New York: McGraw-Hill, 1965.

Maslow, Albert P. *Staffing the Public Service*. Cranbury, N.J.: Basswood Plaza, 11C, 1983.

Moses, Joseph L., and Byham, William C., eds. *Applying the Assessment Center Method*. New York: Pergamon, 1977.

Mussio, Stephen J., and Smith, Mary K. *Content Validity: A Procedural Manual*. Washington, D.C.: International Personnel Management Association, 1973.

Office of Intergovernmental Personnel Programs, Office of Personnel Management. *How to Develop Job-Related Selection Procedures: A Handbook for Small Local Governments*. Washington, D.C.: 1979.

Primoff, Ernest S. *How to Prepare and Conduct Job Element Examinations*. Washington, D.C.: Personnel Research and Development Center, Office of Personnel Management, 1975.

Schroder, William B., ed. *Measuring Achievement: Progress Over a Decade*. San Francisco: Jossey-Bass, 1980.

Thorndike, Robert L., and Hagen, Elizabeth P. *Measurement and Evaluation in Psychology and Education*. 4th ed. New York: Wiley, 1977.

Wigdor, A., and Garner, W., eds. *Ability Testing: Uses, Consequences, and Controversies*. Washington, D.C.: National Academy Press, 1982.

Valdes, William C. *The Selection of College Graduates for the Federal Civil Service: The Problem of the "PACE" Examination and the Consent Decree*. Washington, D.C.: National Academy of Public Administration, n.d.

11 Performance Appraisal and Merit Pay

Two areas previously largely neglected in public personnel administration are now being given much attention—performance appraisal and merit pay. Since financial stringencies in government limit creation of new positions and costs must be kept down, greater effort is being devoted to obtaining increased productivity from employees. For this endeavor to succeed, as accurate as possible assessment of the work performance of employees is required, and salary and other recognition of employees proportionate to their contributions to the organization should be provided. Merit pay has been very rare in the public service. Usually salary increases have been limited to one-step increments within the salary grade annually, although some jurisdictions have also provided for "extra-meritorious" increases for outstanding performance, but these additional increases have been sparingly granted and been limited to one additional step raise per year. Since salary increments within the grade usually are small, the extra amount does not increase the pay very much. Unfortunately, it has been true that outstanding, good, and fair employees have usually been treated alike as far as salary raises are concerned.

This chapter consists of two parts, the first dealing with performance appraisal, and the second with merit pay. As stated in Chapter 9, merit pay is so closely related to performance appraisal that it is appropriate to discuss the two subjects together.

■ PERFORMANCE APPRAISAL

In the late 1950s, Felix Nigro referred to service ratings as a dark area in public personnel administration because the results with the systems in use had been so dismal.[1] Generally, there was much skepticism and even a feeling of futility—shared by both employees and supervisors—that it ever would be possible to develop effective evaluation plans.

Various kinds of plans were being used, the most common type being trait rating, often employing a graphic rating scale. The immediate supervisor (the rater) marked at designated spaces on the scale (a continuum) the degree to which a particular factor described the employee (the ratee). Most of the factors represented personality traits, such as initiative, courtesy, cooperation, and enthusiasm; some did relate to work performance, such as quantity and quality of work.

The degree to which the factor described the employee was often indicated by modifiers, such as *fairly* dependable, *very* dependable, and *unusually* dependable. Brief explanations were given on the rating form as to what each factor meant, but usually these explanations lacked precision. For example, for cooperation the form might instruct the rater, "consider manner of handling interpersonal relations." The highest rating for this factor might be, "goes out of the way to cooperate," the lowest, "shows very poor cooperation."[2] This created two difficulties for the rater: first, the factor definitions were not clear and, second, no specific guidance was given as to how to measure the degree to which a factor represented the ratee.

Using the graphic rating scale, supervisors can rate employees rapidly, placing check marks at the spaces indicated on the form. Ease of administration is desirable, and it is largely for this reason that trait rating was widely adopted. Generally speaking, the more refined the evaluation plan, the more time-consuming its use becomes. However, if ease of administration produces worthless results, as so often has been true with trait rating, then it is a poor method to use.

The subjective element cannot be eliminated completely from any rating plan because the rating official is asked to make judgments about the services of the employee. The plan should be so designed as to help the rater make as objective judgments as pos-

---

[1]Felix A. Nigro, *Public Personnel Administration* (New York: Holt, Rinehart, and Winston, 1959).

[2]See Elaine F. Gruenfeld, *Performance Appraisal: Promise and Peril* (Ithaca, N.Y.: School of Industrial and Labor Relations, Cornell University, 1981).

sible, but, further, supervisors should themselves want to make honest evaluations of the employee's performance. Since the employee's rating usually has a bearing on whether or not he or she receives a salary increase or other favorable treatment, many supervisors give better ratings than the ones they believe the ratee really deserves. The problem raters face is that if other supervisors rate leniently, then by comparison they seem unfair to the workers under their supervision.

There is no easy solution to this problem and it may never be solved completely, but our purpose in this brief historical review is to emphasize that generally no sustained attention was given to improving service ratings. Very minor resources in funds and staff time were devoted to employee evaluations. Training programs for rating officials were nonexistent or of very limited duration, perhaps several hours, and supervisors put off completing the evaluation forms until right before the due dates. The night before, supervisors often were seen leaving the office loaded down with briefcases containing the numerous rating forms.

As public personnel programs broadened and techniques became more sophisticated, service evaluation remained in the same neglected state, through the post-World War II period and thereafter until the late 1970s. This is a statement of the general picture but it by no means was a universal one. Some state and local jurisdictions substantially improved their evaluation systems, and after World War II, at all levels of government, there was a period of interest in developing *performance* rating plans, that is, evaluation of the facts of the employee's performance rather than vague personality characteristics. However, as it became clear that plans based on job standards against which to measure employee performance require much expenditure of funds and staff time, this interest tended to wane. Sometimes the rating plan was supposed to be based on performance, but supervisors continued to rate according to impressions of the personality and of service of the employee.

The Example of the Federal Service

The preceding picture was true in the federal service although the Civil Service Commission's guidelines to the agencies stated that the rating should be based on performance. This is documented in a 1978 report of the General Accounting Office, entitled "Federal Employee Performance Rating Systems Need Fundamental Changes."[3]

At the time of the study, legal requirements for ratings were those in the Performance Rating Act of 1950. Although this statute required that performance requirements be made known to the employees and that they be currently apprised of their supervisors' rating of their performance, the GAO found that during a recent annual rating period, "about every third employee at five of six agencies indicated insufficient job knowledge and feedback on their performance." A review of action taken during fiscal 1976 by ratings appeal boards in three Civil Service Commission regions revealed that in almost half the cases decided the boards "cited the lack of performance requirements or outdated position descriptions." A Civil Service Commission regional director stated, "Supervisors are often unable to furnish statements on what is actually required on the job, beyond performing the duties listed in the position description. This leads us to believe that performance requirements appear only when they are needed to document an outstanding or unsatisfactory rating."

Of 190 supervisors personally contacted by GAO, 88 percent stated they had not formally or informally established performance requirements and discussed them with their employees. Their explanation was that "the process was unnecessary, not required, or too difficult." In general the GAO found that supervisors had unreviewed discretion to decide whether and how to implement statutory requirements and agency directives dealing with ratings. For example, although each of the agency systems reviewed required frequent or ongoing supervisor-employee discussions about the employees' performance, 8 of the 10 agencies left the interpretation of this requirement to the supervisor. In 6 of the 10 agencies, from 25 to 57 percent of the employees contacted during the survey said such informal discussions with the supervisor *never* took place. In 4 of 6 of the agencies, about half the supervisors said they never had received training in the major elements of performance evaluation, and some who had received such training did not think it "very helpful." The GAO concluded that the "lim-

---

[3]*Report to the Congress by the Comptroller General of the United States, Federal Employee Performance Rating Systems Need Fundamental Changes* (Washington, D.C.: March 1978).

ited descriptive nature of the performance factors provided insufficient information about employee work expectations and accomplishments." Although some forms had comment sections, comments made were limited to justifying outstanding, unsatisfactory, or marginal ratings.

To some extent, this general failure of performance appraisal as it actually took place in federal agencies was due to certain poorly conceived provisions in the Performance Rating Act of 1950. This legislation required summary adjective ratings of the employee's performance as a whole: Outstanding, Satisfactory, and Unsatisfactory, with an optional fourth category that in practice was rarely used. For several reasons, the statutory three-level rating system became a one-step system.

For one thing, the law provided that outstanding ratings could be given "only when *all* aspects of performance not only exceed normal requirements, but are outstanding and deserve special commendation." (Italics ours) This is a very difficult, some would say, virtually impossible standard to meet. Second, although the statute also provided that a rating of unsatisfactory was a basis for "removal from the position in which the performance was unsatisfactory," in 1960 a court of claims ruled that the Lloyd-LaFollette Act of 1912 and the Veterans Preference Act of 1944 took precedence over the 1950 legislation, and, consequently, dismissal could not be automatic when the employee received an unsatisfactory rating. This court ruling was interpreted possibly to grant two statutory appeals rights—the first after receipt of the notice of unsatisfactory performance and the second after the management's initiation of dismissal action. Since this dual process was costly and very time-consuming, federal officials "preferred to initiate adverse action proceedings immediately and dispense with the unsatisfactory performance rating altogether." The GAO found that as a result almost all employees were receiving ratings of satisfactory— since 1954 more than 99 percent. When it proposed the Civil Service Reform Act of 1978, the Carter administration put this figure at about 95 percent for all agencies.

The Federal Salary Reform Act of 1962 contained a provision intended to improve the rating process that made it worse. The provision was that granting of within-grade increases would no longer be tied to receiving satisfactory or better ratings, as previously provided by law. Instead, the basis for granting the increases would be an independent determination by the agency head that the employee had met an "acceptable level of competence." The rationale was that supervisors were not critically rating employee performance because they did not want to deprive them of within-grade increases and otherwise damage their status. With very few exceptions, agency heads routinely gave certifications of acceptable performance, so no basic change took place.

There is a school of thought, reflected in the reports of both Hoover commissions for reorganization of the federal executive branch, that ratings should not be tied in with personnel actions such as salary increases, promotions, and dismissals. Both Hoover Commissions recommended that this tie-in be eliminated, that summary adjective ratings be abolished, and that supervisors have confidential chats with employees to discuss strengths and weaknesses in their performance and work out a concrete program for correcting deficiencies and speeding the employee's future development. Supervisors would report periodically to management on their subordinates' progress, identifying those with promise for advancement, those not deserving within-grade increases, and those recommended for transfer because they were not properly placed in their present assignments.[4]

However, under the plan recommended by the Hoover Commission supervisory evaluations *would* determine the employee's future status. The method for making this determination would be different: no summary ratings and confidential instead of "public ratings." This procedural change, it was believed, would encourage supervisors to make honest appraisals, and employees would no longer be making invidious comparisons of their adjective ratings. Management would also have the flexibility to consider various evidences of the employee's value to the organization, rather than being required to give a prescribed weight to an immediate supervisor's rating made under a system of "public rewards and penalties."

These recommendations were not accepted in the federal government, but a few state and local jurisdictions did separate ratings from personnel actions.

---

[4]Commission on Organization of the Executive Branch of the Government, *Personnel Management* (Washington, D.C.: Government Printing Office, 1949), p. 33, p. 40, and Commission on Organization of the Executive Branch of the Government, *Personnel and Civil Service* (Washington, D.C.: Government Printing Office, 1955), pp. 63–65.

The Civil Service Reform Act of 1978 and Thereafter

If one reviews the contents of the personnel journals since 1978, one finds a very noticeable increase in the number of articles on performance appraisal. Suddenly, a subject largely ignored is given a great deal of attention.

The Civil Service Reform Act of 1978 (CSRA) has been a great stimulus for this new interest because its passage was the culmination of intensifying sentiment in the country for improving the productivity of public employees and obtaining more and better service for the taxpayer's dollar. To improve employee productivity, it is widely believed, a sound system of evaluating the work results achieved by the individual employees is needed, as well as a compensation plan that provides pay in proportion to work achievement. Since government's biggest expense is for employee salaries and benefits, removing the unproductive worker and providing appropriate rewards for the very productive ones should become firmly established public policy. It must be emphasized, however, that while passage of the CSRA did spur many state and local governments to take action to improve their performance appraisal and pay incentive systems, some had already made considerable progress in these areas.

Provisions of the CSRA on performance appraisal

The CSRA contains two sections on performance appraisal systems: one for the Senior Executive Service and the other for most other employees in the executive branch.

Discussing first the system that applies to most employees, it *requires* each agency to develop one or more systems for the periodic appraisal of employee performance. Each system must provide in accordance with OPM regulations for establishment of performance standards that to the maximum extent feasible permit evaluation of job performance on the basis of objective criteria. Agencies must encourage employee participation in the development of the performance standards, and the employee ratings are to serve as a basis for training, rewarding, reassigning, promoting, reducing in grade, retaining, and removing employees. Employees are to be assisted in improving unacceptable performance, and no one is to be reassigned, reduced in grade, or removed for unacceptable performance without the opportunity to demonstrate acceptable performance.

Agencies are no longer required to give summary adjective ratings although they may do so. Appraisals must be based on the job to be performed, not on general characteristics such as courtesy and adaptability, and performance standard is defined as "the statement of the quality, quantity, etc., required of the performance of a component of an employee's job." Standards are to be prepared for every aspect of an employee's job, whether or not a critical element of the job. "Critical element" is any requirement of the job that is so important that inadequate performance of it outweighs acceptable or better performance in other aspects of the job. (The legislation defines unacceptable performance as "performance of an employee which fails to meet established performance standards in one or more critical elements of each employee's position.")

Under the Performance Rating Act of 1950, agencies were required to provide "one impartial review" of a rating if requested by the employee; those rated unsatisfactory could also appeal to an agency board of review and, if not satisfied with that board's decision, appeal further to an independent statutory appeal board. Under the reform act, the employee has the option of appealing his or her rating through the negotiated grievance procedure or the agency grievance procedure.

An employee whose performance is rated unacceptable and whom management proposes to reduce in grade or remove is entitled to: 30 days' advance notice that identifies the specific instances of unacceptable performance on which the proposed action is based, as well as the critical elements of the employee's position involved in each instance of unacceptable performance; to be represented by an attorney or other representative; and a reasonable time to answer orally or in writing. The decision to retain, reduce in grade, or remove the employee must be made within 30 days after expiration of the notice period. The employee may appeal a reduction in grade or removal for unacceptable performance through the negotiated grievance procedure if that procedure covers such matters or appeal to the Merit Systems Protection Board.

In considering such an appeal both arbitrators under the negotiated grievance procedure and the MSPB must be guided by the standard that the agency must show substantial evidence for its action. The previous standard for adverse actions for alleged incompetence had been preponderance of evidence. (The legislation retains the preponderance of evidence standard for those removed for misconduct.)

During the consideration of the reform act, the unions, concerned about the possibility of employees' receiving unsatisfactory ratings for politically inspired or other nonmerit related reasons, opposed original provisions in the administration bill that would have put the burden of proof on the employee to show that he or she should not be dismissed. The provisions described above were a compromise about which the unions and many employees have many reservations. Shortly after enactment of the legislation, the unions, in a submission to the Federal Labor Relations Authority, maintained that the language of the act meant that performance standards were subject to negotiation, a contention flatly rejected by OPM and the Carter and Reagan administrations. The FLRA has ruled that performance standards are *not* negotiable, but that *how* the standards are developed and the manner in which employees participate in the establishment of the standards are negotiable. The FLRA also ruled that the standards must be "fair and equitable," and that unions convinced that they were not could take the issue to arbitration. The Reform Act established a deadline of October 1, 1981, for the agencies to complete the task of identifying critical elements of positions and of establishing performance standards and communicating them to the employees.

As to the Senior Civil Service, the CSRA provides that each agency shall, in accordance with standards established by OPM, develop for its Senior Executive Service officials one or more performance appraisal systems based on "criteria which are related to the position and which specify the critical elements of the position." The appraisals are to be based on both individual and organizational performance, taking into account such factors as: (1) improvements in efficiency, productivity, and quality of work or service, (2) cost efficiency; (3) timeliness of performance; (4) other indications of the effectiveness, productivity, and quality of the performance of the employees for whom the senior executive is responsible; and (5) meeting affirmative action goals and equal employment opportunity requirements.

Each such performance appraisal system must provide for annual summary ratings of levels of performance as follows: (1) one or more successful levels; (2) a minimally satisfactory level, and (3) an unsatisfactory level. The supervising official of the senior executive makes an initial evaluation of the executive's performance. In accordance with OPM regulations, each agency establishes one or more performance review boards that review these initial evaluations, conduct such further review as is deemed necessary, and then make recommendations to the agency head on senior executives' ratings.

Any career executive receiving a rating at any of the fully successful levels may be given the cash bonus referred to in Chapter 4. As stated in Chapter 4, a senior executive receiving an unsatisfactory rating must be reassigned or transferred within the SES or removed from SES, but any executive who receives two unsatisfactory ratings in any period of five consecutive years must be removed from SES. An executive who twice in any period of three consecutive years receives less than fully successful ratings must also be removed from SES. Senior executives may challenge their appraisals before a final decision is made, but, since removal from SES for performance is not an adverse action, they have no appeal rights. However, if an SES executive believes a personnel action is discriminatory, he or she may appeal to the Equal Employment Opportunity Commission, and, if an executive believes a personnel action has been taken for political reasons or in retaliation for whistleblowing, the executive may bring the matter before the special counsel of MSPB.

The experience with appraisals under the CSRA

For the most part, federal agencies met the deadline dates in the CSRA for the implementation of new performance appraisal plans. Under the legislation, the GAO is required to review the effectiveness of these plans, and it has released several reports on the subject. OPM, MSPB, and independent researchers have also made studies of the post-CSRA experience with performance appraisal.

In its reports, GAO early pointed out that the deadlines for implementation were much too short. GAO stresses that most federal agencies had little or no experience with performance-based appraisal systems, and that private sector experts believe several years of pretesting of pay-for-performance plans are a prerequisite for successful results. The CSRA deadlines were so short that very little pretesting took place, and it is not surprising that the GAO has found inadequacies in the functioning of the post-CSRA appraisal systems. At the same time, it has found positive benefits, and the gist of its reports is that the CSRA's provisions on appraisals are sound although certain improvements in their administration are needed.

In September of 1983, the GAO released a report analyzing the implementation in nine federal agencies of performance appraisal systems for employees not covered by the SES or the merit pay system.[5] On the positive side, it reported that "the major benefit appears to be better communication between employees and supervisors. Employees who helped prepare their performance standards have gained a better understanding of their responsibilities and of their supervisors' expectations. Supervisors, in turn, have had to define job requirements more clearly and explicitly." Among the shortcomings the GAO found were:

> Many employees did not actively participate in the development of the performance standards for their jobs.
>
> Not all employees were advised of the performance standards at the beginning of the appraisal period.
>
> Performance standards often were not clearly stated in measurable terms, failed to distinguish levels of accomplishment, and did not clearly identify unacceptable performance.
>
> Higher officials' review of ratings was often perfunctory.
>
> Agencies' procedures for tying-in appraisal ratings with personnel decisions were often vague, and employees did not perceive a direct relationship between the appraisals and such decisions.
>
> Agency and OPM evaluations of appraisal systems to identify problems and recommend improvements had been limited.

While these findings indicate that there is much need for improvement, they also point to inherent difficulties in designing and administering any appraisal plan. Particularly difficult is the formulation of job standards since in government for most positions output cannot be measured by counting units of production as in a factory. Amount of work completed is important, but so is the quality of that work and evaluations of quality are matters of opinion. However, the GAO cites examples of performance standards that fall far short of specificity, such as "work review will be thor-

---

[5]*Report to the Director, Office of Personnel Management, New Performance Appraisals Beneficial But Refinements Needed* (Washington, D.C.: General Accounting Office, September 15, 1983).

ough, accurate, etc." Failure to tie in the appraisals with decisions about the status of the employee is lamentable since clearly establishing such a relationship was a major purpose of the CSRA.

In May of 1984, the GAO issued a report on SES performance appraisal systems in 10 agencies employing about 34 percent of those holding SES positions in the government.[6] In this report, the GAO stresses that prior to CSRA there was no "government-wide executive performance system . . . for setting performance goals and objectives and gauging performance against them, and taking steps to reinforce excellent performance and to stimulate improvement in or eliminate mediocre performance." The SES and the provisions in CSRA for evaluating the performance of SES members were intended to remedy this deficiency.

The GAO found that for the most part the agencies had met the requirement to put into effect SES performance plans, albeit hastily because of the deadline of less than one year after the effective date of the legislation. It also found that executives in the 10 agencies included in a questionnaire survey generally were satisfied with their own performance plans and appraisals. (The performance plan is a written statement of the executive's responsibilities and of the job standards against which his or her performance is to be measured.) However, 57 percent of these same executives thought their agency's SES appraisal system had minimal effect on performance; no impact on, or had even worsened, communications with superiors or subordinates; and was not worth its cost.

The inadequacies in administration of the appraisal plans included: (1) Performance plans seldom expressed CSRA appraisal criteria, contained standards stated only in general terms, were not prepared for all executives, and were not prepared on time or revised as job responsibilities changed; (2) officials in 7 of the 10 agencies said they did not emphasize measuring the contribution of an individual executive in the attainment of organization goals, a process they found too difficult, particularly in the absence of data on organization accomplishments; (3) performance review board members indicated that performance measurement data were not used in the appraisal and award process, and that "award decisions were based on such factors as job difficulty, the importance of the position, or the board member's personal knowledge

[6]*Report to the Congress, An Assessment of SES Performance Appraisal Systems* (Washington, D.C.: General Accounting Office, May 16, 1984).

of the executive's performance." (Award refers to the bonuses and honorary ranks SES members may receive.)

The GAO notes that the negative opinions of SES executives about their agency's appraisal system could well have been influenced by their dissatisfaction with the reduction in the number of executives eligible for bonuses. (See Chapter 4) While the inadequacies in the administration of the appraisal plans are hardly minor, again some of the failures can be attributed to the basic difficulties in developing performance standards, in this case for managerial jobs where sometimes the position itself is hard to define. The authors of the CSRA put great emphasis on rewards for an individual executive's contribution to organization goals but may have been much too optimistic about the agencies' being able to measure organization results and an individual's contribution to those results.

Other studies have been made of the experience with post-CSRA performance appraisal plans; we will describe one we believe to be particularly relevant.[7] The federal installations studied are four Navy Department laboratories where thoroughgoing appraisal systems to meet CSRA criteria were developed. The evaluation process at these laboratories consists of performance planning, interim reviews, and a final appraisal.

In the planning stage, the supervisor and the employee decide on work objectives for the employee, based on the important elements in his or her job and on agency policy directives. At this time, standards are established for measuring the degree to which the employee attains the work objectives. During the interim reviews, the supervisor and the employee go over the employee's accomplishments and make any needed changes in the work objectives. At the final appraisal meeting, the supervisor reviews the employee's performance in meeting the objectives and decides the employee's performance rating (it ranges from outstanding to below standard/needs improvement).

Questionnaire surveys were made of the perceptions the personnel in these four laboratories had of the appraisal systems in use during 1979, 1981, and 1982, thus affording a comparison between the pre- and post-CSRA periods. The 1982 questionnaire responses showed "growing confidence in the accuracy and job-

---

[7]John J. DeMarco and Lloyd G. Nigro, "Implementing Performance Appraisal Reform in the United States Civil Service," *Public Administration* 61, no. 1 (Spring 1983).

relatedness of evaluations," but it was also "evident that the laboratories had not managed to eliminate the high levels of cynicism and uncertainty" about the appraisals found in 1979. DeMarco and L. G. Nigro state, "It seems that many laboratory staff remain unconvinced that their evaluations will really affect their pay, chances for promotion, and job opportunities. It should be noted that the laboratories are not unique; a 1980 survey of federal managers (GS 13–15 and Senior Executive Service) revealed an increase over 1979 in the percentage who doubted there was a connection between performance appraisals and other personnel actions."

Besides the questionnaire surveys, scientific, technical, and administrative personnel in 12 work units were interviewed. In each of these work units, the "unit supervisor, his or her supervisor at the next level in the organization, and ten to twenty unit members were interviewed." These interviews demonstrated a significant change in the "psychology of evaluations, compared with the previous system of trait rating. More attention was being given to the objectives-setting" process because supervisors and employees realized that it would produce the "criteria used to make later judgments about actual work performance. Many of those interviewed felt that the process forced them to think more carefully about their performance objectives and ways of accomplishing them."

Significantly, a majority of the supervisors interviewed expressed frustration over the demands on their time made by the new appraisal system with its requirements for careful definitions of work objectives and objective measurements of performance. It was reported that in several work units supervisors "were resorting to very broadly defined objectives and standards in order to avoid conflicts with subordinates and lighten their own workloads."

This tendency to "generalize objectives" and to "blur performance criteria" obviously reduces the objectivity of the appraisals, and as DeMarco and L. G. Nigro warn, "If supervisors are unwilling or unable to devote the time and other resources needed to make them work, the laboratory appraisal systems will almost certainly face severe difficulties." They note that throughout the federal government supervisors were also "complaining about the costs and technical difficulties" of implementing "CSRA-type performance appraisal methods," and that OPM had responded by telling "managers to avoid overly specific objectives and standards in favor of more broadly defined and judgmental criteria. . . . One interpretation of OPM's revisions is that it is encouraging a return to the more subjective, trait-oriented patterns of pre-CSRA evaluations because the Congress and the Reagan administration are unwilling to expend the considerable resources necessary to fully implement the CSRA as it was envisioned by its authors."

Recent experiences with performance appraisal in state and local governments

Quite a few state and local governments have recently adopted new appraisal systems intended to base ratings on objective facts of performance. We will describe two such new systems—one introduced in the state government of Iowa and the other in New York City pursuant to provisions of a new City charter adopted in 1975. Discussion of these two examples will bring out again the soundness of trying to make the evaluations more objective but also the difficulties of doing so.

In 1977, Iowa inaugurated a state government-wide appraisal-by-objectives system. This action followed early introduction of the management-by-objectives (MBO) concept in some of the larger state agencies. MBO focuses on defining and attaining carefully-defined work targets; appraisal-by-objectives is an application of the MBO approach to evaluation of employee performance.

Our description of the appraisal-by-objectives system in Iowa is based on an article by Dennis Daley describing the results of research by the Iowa Merit Employment Department.[8] There are three basic components to the Iowa plan: first, at the beginning of the annual evaluation period, preparation by the supervisor and the employee of a job description in the form of a statement of *Responsibilities and Standards/Results Expected;* second, after discussion with the employee, preparation by the supervisor of a *Performance Review/Rating* at the end of the evaluation period; and third, at this same time, an essay evaluation by the supervisor, entitled *Summary of Total Job Performance and Future Performance Plans,* in which the supervisor "lists the employee's areas of strength and those areas needing improvement."

The employee is notified in advance of the meeting with the

---

[8]Dennis Daley, "Monitoring the Use of Appraisal-by-Objectives in Iowa: Research Note," *Review of Public Personnel Administration* 3, no. 3 (Summer 1983).

supervisor held to prepare the statement of *Responsibilities and Standards/Results Expected,* and is provided with "copies of previous evaluations for use as guides." At this meeting, they select four or five major responsibilities of the employee (sometimes a larger number) and describe them in writing, using a "results-oriented format with specific standards against which the achievement of these results are measured." Each responsibility is weighted according to its importance, and the final rating of the employee is the weighted average of his or her ratings on all the responsibilities selected.

In observing the employee's performance during the evaluation period, supervisors are encouraged to use what is known as the "critical incident" approach. This means that the supervisor notes and records examples of how the employee performs in situations that test his or her effectiveness in carrying out significant tasks. If negative incidents are noted, the supervisor must explain to the employee what is being done wrong, indicate how the employee can correct the deficiency, and keep a record of corrective action.

When supervisor and employee meet at the end of the evaluation period, they discuss the employee's performance in meeting the responsibilities mutually agreed upon at the beginning of the period. Worksheets are used at this meeting, and the supervisor prepares the final evaluation of the employee sometime after the meeting. While employees may write their comments on the final evaluation form, very few do so. *In the Summary of Total Job Performance and Future Performance Plans,* supervisors record the training and development plans they recommend for improving the employee's performance.

When the new appraisal-by-objectives plan was introduced, a series of training sessions was held, but training for new supervisors and refresher courses "appear to have been given a low priority in Iowa, as is generally the case in public sector personnel systems."

Research by the Iowa Merit Employment Department showed that the experience with the new appraisal system indicated "notable successes" but also "numerous faults." On the positive side, somewhat more than half the responsibility statements sampled were prepared with the desired results-oriented format. That format requires definition of a "specific, actual job outcome rather than a general category or class of activities." Only 11 percent of the responsibility statements evidenced "no effort at compliance."

However, more than half the standards for measuring performance sampled were found to be "unmeasurable." As Daley writes, "This is a serious problem for it attacks the heart of the performance appraisal system, posing a threat to its validity." He concludes that while the research showed that "appraisal-by-objective is possible . . . and numerous individuals can master its details and procedures, just as clearly, it is evident that this is not a simple task." Much of the difficulty, he believes, is attributable to "inadequate or nonexistent training in performance appraisal techniques for persons coming into supervisory or managerial roles."

Turning to New York City, the new charter approved in 1975 requires the method of evaluating performance to be valid and job-related.[9] Ratings must be based upon objective and precise rating factors developed through a thorough job analysis; the rating official is the immediate supervisor; and he or she must consistently observe the performance of the ratees. Trait rating is rejected as insufficiently job-related.

A tasks and standards approach is employed, whereby the major tasks performed by the employee are defined and standards are established for measuring performance on each task. The standards can be expressed in terms of a product or service to be produced, the results to be achieved or other consequences to be brought about, or the specific behaviors to be displayed. If personal characteristics have an important bearing on performance, they can be expressed as performance standards in the form of statements which explain how the characteristics are to be displayed. For example, in the case of a stenographer or typist: "Accepts reasonable assignments without excessive discussion, argument, or explanation."

The supervisor initially proposes the task definitions and standards, with input from the employee, and a *Tasks and Standards Sheet* is completed and signed by both supervisor and employee. (The rating period is usually one year.) The employee receives a separate rating for each task as well as an overall rating, the latter derived by the supervisor from the general tendency indicated by the individual task ratings, and taking into account the importance of each task.

There are five levels of overall ratings, as follows:

---

[9]See Peter Allan and Stephen Rosenberg, "The Development of a Task-Oriented Approach to Performance Evaluation in the City of New York," *Public Personnel Management* 7, no. 6 (January–February 1978).

Unsatisfactory. Performance did not meet one of the most critical standards, and it was consistently at this level despite sufficient and adequate attempts by the superior to correct performance.

Conditional. Performance did not meet one or more of the attainable standards. However, this level of performance is not of long duration, and it is considered possible that plans to assist the employee will enable him or her to perform satisfactorily in the future.

Satisfactory. The employee, because of his or her efforts, basically attained all of the standards; or failure to attain the standards was primarily due to external conditions beyond the employee's control.

Superior. Employee significantly exceeded the standards; or the employee merely attained the standards but the circumstances under which the tasks were carried out were so difficult as to require superior effort and/or knowledge, skills, and abilities simply to attain the standards.

Outstanding. The employee far exceeded the standards; or the circumstances in which the employee carried out the tasks were so extraordinarily difficult as to make attainment of the normal standards an outstanding achievement.

It can be said that both the Iowa and New York City performance appraisal systems are thorough efforts to base the evaluations on actual performance, rather than general impressions of the employee. At the same time, it is clear that it is very difficult to develop measurable standards of performance and otherwise to control the element of subjectivity in the evaluation process. Training for the supervisors in rating objectives and methods is helpful, indeed a prerequisite for developing a successful plan, yet, as stated previously in this chapter, output in government usually cannot be quantified as in a factory.

Performance results are often intangible and may depend on attributes of personality, but when, as in the New York City example, the standards are expressed in terms of behavior, imprecise words such as "reasonable" and "excessive" must be used. Obviously, supervisors will disagree, sometimes vehemently, over what a "reasonable" assignment is, and whether the employee accepted an assignment without "excessive" discussion or argument. And what is meant by "argument"? Anyone can make criticisms of this type of performance standards since it is hard to state the standard precisely. Our purpose here is simply to point to the difficulties encountered even in thoroughly-conceived plans for basing the evaluations on the facts of performance. Of course, the answer is not to return to simple trait rating systems. Fortunately, the current emphasis on improving evaluations in government is so great that it appears unlikely that the efforts to develop true *performance* rating systems will lapse as they did after World War II.

The Element of Trust and Appraisals

No matter how technically and administratively sound the appraisal system, it will not succeed if employees lack confidence in "the integrity and good intentions of an organization's top leadership" and supervisors. "The higher the levels of trust on all levels, the more likely employees will be to take the risks associated with changing established ways of doing things. If a climate of distrust exists, workers may opt for the *stat s quo* and try to sabotage the innovation because they see it as an attempt to threaten or punish them." Further, if employees lack commitment to the organization and its goals, they will have no deep interest in new policies and systems adopted by the management.

In their surveys of employee attitudes, both the OPM and the researchers who studied the four naval laboratories previously referred to found that "trust in the *organization* is relatively low."[10] Forty-two percent of the respondents to the OPM survey, and 44 percent of those queried at the naval laboratories, agreed with the statement, "Employees here feel that you can't trust this organization." Thirty-six percent of the respondents in the OPM survey and 38 percent at the laboratories agreed that "When changes are made in this organization, the employees usually lose out in the end." Confidence in the immediate supervisor was much higher. Sixty-one percent of the respondents in the OPM survey and 62 percent at the naval laboratories agreed that "My supervisor deals

---

[10]See Lloyd G. Nigro, "Attitudes of Federal Employees Toward Performance Appraisal and Merit Pay: Implications for CSRA Implementation," *Public Administration Review* 41, no. 1 (January/February 1981).

with subordinates well." Furthermore, "over 90 percent of those sampled in both surveys *cared* about what happened to their organizations."

There are many reasons why this high percentage of federal employees distrusts the management of their agencies. In the final chapter in this book, we explain this distrust in some detail. The negative perceptions of employees are based largely on what they believe to be the *attitudes towards them* of the general public, the press and television, and chief executives, legislators, and others in society. Actually, the favorable opinion found of the immediate supervisor is very important because it is the supervisors who do the rating. Thus, if dissatisfaction with government policies and top agency managements is ameliorated, prospects for employee acceptance of the appraisal system would improve.

Must Performance Appraisal in Government Fail?

We pose this question because initial disappointments with the new performance-based appraisal systems have caused pessimism that *any* evaluation system can succeed in government. Often it is stated that favoritism for partisan political reasons inevitably will influence the evaluations of individual employees, particularly those of career executives by the political policy-making officials at the top of the agency.

Yet the GAO found that 71 percent of SES executives sampled believed that their performance appraisal accurately reflected the quality of their performance and the performance of their unit or program.[11] One of the findings of a July, 1983, questionnaire survey by the Merit Systems Protection Board of 7,861 executive branch employees was that 61 percent of the respondents believed their ratings in the preceding year "gave a fair and accurate picture of their actual performance."[12] Undoubtedly, there are instances when biased appraisals are given, from partisan political motivation and probably much more often for reasons of personal politics and favoritism, but no appraisal plan, despite the appeals mechanisms provided, can eradicate all such abuses.

Much of the pessimism about performance appraisal stems from

[11]*Report to the Congress, An Assessment of SES Performance Appraisal Systems,* p. 13.

[12]*Report on the Significant Actions of the Office of Personnel Management During 1982* (Washington, D.C.: Merit Systems Protection Board, December 1983).

misgivings about those who do the evaluating of employee performance—the immediate supervisors. At the beginning of this chapter we noted the reluctance of many supervisors to make frank appraisals of the performance of their subordinates. As rater, the supervisor is in a difficult position because at least some employees do not want to hear any negative comments about their work. Nor will some make serious efforts to follow the work improvement suggestions of the supervisor because they reject the criticisms in the first place. The supervisor also is in the uncomfortable position of judge (determining the rating) and of helper (assisting the employee to improve work performance.) These roles are not inherently incompatible but carrying out both of them is inherently difficult.

What a supervisor is stimulated to do depends greatly on the administrative climate in the agency. If top management does not strongly support the appraisal plan, supervisors lack the backing they need to make frank judgments about employees. A management not fully committed to the appraisal program will not authorize the training programs needed to develop supervisory evaluation skills. Developing and implementing a performance appraisal system makes many demands upon the time of employees, supervisors, the personnel office, and of higher level executives. If top management gives evidence of not wanting to see so much time and effort devoted to the appraisals, supervisors will be guided accordingly. Allan and Rosenberg describe how in New York City one appraisal plan for managers failed because it was not supported by agency managements or the mayor, and how a substitute plan was accepted because it had the backing of top management and the mayor.[13]

The evidence to date does not establish that performance appraisal systems must fail. The findings referred to in this chapter mostly indicate that developing and administering such systems is difficult, that a major effort is underway in the federal and many state and local governments to implement true *performance* evaluation plans, and that some progress is being made towards that goal. Perhaps these latest efforts were initiated with too much optimism about obtaining quick good results, but perhaps also this optimism was needed to revive appraisal efforts from dormancy

---

[13]Peter Allan and Stephen Rosenberg, "Getting a Managerial Performance Appraisal Plan Under Way: New York City's Experience," *Public Administration Review* 40, no. 3 (July–August 1980).

and despair. If there is no formal appraisal system, agencies will continue to make evaluations of employees, rewarding some and not rewarding others. A formal system can greatly reduce the subjectiveness of these judgments about the individual employee.

■ MERIT PAY

The Civil Service Reform Act provides for a merit pay system for supervisors and management officials in General Schedule grades 13 through 15. This system, which became effective throughout the federal government in October of 1981, included more than 100,000 supervisors and managers. The intention of the framers of the CSRA was to make this the first step, to be followed by extension of merit pay to all federal executive branch employees if the experience with GS 13–15 supervisors and managers proved successful.

A distinctive characteristic of the first experiment with merit pay in the federal service is that the GS 13–15 supervisors and managers were guaranteed only half the annual comparability increases other GS employees receive. The remaining half of the comparability increase, together with the within-grade increases they would have received under the old system, were placed in funds for particular organization groups of employees called "merit pay pools." Based on their performance ratings, the employees within each pool competed with one another for merit pay increases paid out of the pool. Budgetary considerations explain this arrangement: the objective was to have merit pay but not to exceed the amounts that would have been expended under the former pay system.

In an intensive study of the implementation of merit pay in the departments of Agriculture, Housing and Urban Development, and Navy during fiscal years 1981 and 1982, the General Accounting Office reported that "less than 10 percent of the respondents in each Department wanted to retain the merit pay system as currently implemented, and even among the top performers who responded, less than 15 percent favored retaining the system" without change. "Between 31 and 39 percent of both years' respondents in each Department favored retaining merit pay but wanted the system revised. . . . Approximately half of all survey employees wanted to return to the General Schedule for pay increases."

The GAO also found that in both years studied "between 78 and

86 percent of the respondents in the three agencies believed that merit pay had not motivated them to perform better." About 20 percent responded that money helped motivate them to a great or very great extent, 60 percent that it motivated them to some extent or a little, and 20 percent that it did not motivate them at all.[14]

Researchers Jone L. Pearce and James L. Perry analyzed employee attitudes towards merit pay in five federal agencies over an 18-month period and found that the employees were no "more highly motivated under merit pay than under the previous time-in-grade compensation policies." Pearce and Perry wrote, "It is not that federal managers do not value pay as a reward. . . . Where the present merit pay program fails as a motivational program is in the methods used to measure performance. These managers report that effort is *less* likely to lead to a good performance rating, and therefore these managers believe that merit pay does not encourage them to perform their jobs well or contribute to their agencies' effectiveness."

Why did a program intended to motivate better performance fail so badly? First, the appraisal systems were put into effect with a very short deadline and without pretesting. Many of the respondents did not consider that the performance standards for their positions were correct and/or that the ratings they received were accurate. Emphasis on statistical measurements of performance led to "gaming," as in the following example:

> Most of SSA's [Social Security Administration] performance statistics can be "manipulated" with no direct harm (or benefit) to a claimant. For example, for the processing-time statistics, one can simply fill out an application but not let the claimant sign it until the earnings records and proofs are received. Therefore, the two weeks it takes someone to obtain a birth or marriage certificate are not counted in processing time statistics, and the claimant experiences no delay in payment, but the manager receives a better performance rating.

Second, the requirement that no more money be spent on merit pay than that expended under the previous system set a restrictive upper limit on the "potential salary gain associated with outstanding performance." Competition among those in a merit pay pool seems fair enough, but a "fixed rather than a variable, merit pay

---

[14]Report to the Chairwoman, Subcommittee on Compensation and Employee Benefits, Committee on Post Office and Civil Service, House of Representatives, *A 2-Year Appraisal of Merit Pay in Three Agencies* (Washington, D.C.: General Accounting Office, March 26, 1984).

budget heightens the significance of allocational errors (for example, unnecessarily large payments to poorer performers)—because one employee's gain is another employee's loss—it becomes more difficult to create expectations that rewards will be contingent on performance. In a nutshell, if all managers and supervisors receive relatively uniform performance appraisals, the reward differentials among managers will be trivial and merit pay will have negative motivational effects."

Third, pool managers modified appraisal ratings to conform to their views on "merit pay goals," but this produced "managed ratings" and raises the question, "If the ratings are accurate, why should they be manipulated?" Fourth, there are many aspects of the government environment that make it difficult for employees to form positive attitudes towards merit pay than in the private sector. Budgetary restraints, and inflexibilities such as the pay cap referred to in Chapter 9, are good examples. It is no surprise, then, that Pearce and Perry conclude that the "merit pay experiment at grades 13–15" does not warrant extending coverage to "employees in grades 1–12."[15]

In late 1984, Congress passed and President Reagan approved new legislation replacing the merit pay pool system with a new one providing for performance-based raises and bonuses. Under this new system, to begin in 1985, GS 13 through 15 supervisors and managers who receive performance appraisals of "fully successful" receive the full annual comparability increase and a 1 percent merit increase as well. Those rated "exceeds fully successful" receive the comparability increase and a 1.5 percent merit raise, and may also receive a performance award of at least 2 percent and no more than 10 percent of salary. Those rated "outstanding" receive the comparability increase, a 3 percent merit raise, and a 2 to 10 percent performance award. Finally, those rated "minimally successful" get an increase equal to one-half of the comparability increase, and those evaluated as "unsatisfactory" get no raise at all. The new legislation provides that SES performance awards will no longer be limited to 50 percent of the SES members in the agency. Passage of the new legislation represents affirmation by Congress and the President of the merit pay principle, but only experience will tell how successful the new system is.

---

[15]Jone L. Pearce and James L. Perry, "Federal Merit Pay: A Longitudinal Analysis," *Public Administration Review* 43, no. 4 (July–August 1983).

In the summer of 1985, OPM regulations extending merit pay to all GS employees and increasing the weight given to performance ratings in layoffs went into effect after being delayed by Congress. As this is written, new efforts are being made by unions and others opposed to this change to prevent the application of these regulations.

One of the assumptions of the CSRA is that merit pay has proved a success in the private sector. While that sector is free of many of the difficult factors that exist in the government environment, the literature on merit pay in business reports failures as well as successes. For example, in some companies budgetary restrictions limit merit increases to amounts too small to serve as motivators.[16]

In an article entitled "There Is No Merit in Merit Pay," one business school faculty member reported that merit pay, far from increasing productivity often causes managers to "reward their employees with resignations, bitterness, or poorer work performance." He found that middle managers employed under merit pay systems thought that merit pay punished more than it rewarded; generated undesirable competition among colleagues and inhibited cooperation among them; created much stress because the evaluation standards were subjective and imprecise; and at best had a neutral effect on productivity and at worst, a negative one.

The failures in the federal service have not proved that merit pay must fail, but rather that an effective system had not been found. Since merit pay is so new, much more time is needed in the efforts to develop an effective plan. According to the GAO, "Compensation experts have stated that it may take 5 to 10 years for a merit pay system to operate as intended."[17] The experience to date with the federal experiment certainly makes clear that budgetary retrenchment and merit pay are exceedingly difficult to accommodate.

Other versions of merit pay exist in state and local governments, such as: basing salary increases on degree of success in meeting performance goals developed cooperatively by managers and their subordinates; granting managers "authority to recommend employees for any size increase consistent with budget restraints";

---

[16]Gruenfeld, *Performance Appraisal: Promise and Peril*, p. 24.

[17]A. Mikalachki, "There Is No Merit in Merit Pay," *Business Quarterly*, Spring 1976, published by School of Business Administration, University of Western Ontario, London, Ontario, Canada. See also Albert Shanker, "Supervisors Sabotage Merit Pay," *New York Times*, May 6, 1984, editorial section.

granting early step increases, perhaps up to the mid-point of the salary range, on the basis of length of service but basing subsequent ones on "documented high performance on the job"; and varying the size of the step increase depending on the quality of performance.[18] In work activities where quantifiable measures of performance are available, such as water meter reading and trash collection, in some jurisdictions bonuses are paid for individual and group performance.[19] As performance evaluation standards improve, the prospects for success with these new plans increase.

BIBLIOGRAPHY

Allan, Peter, and Rosenberg, Stephen. "Getting a Managerial Performance Appraisal Plan Under Way: New York City's Experience." *Public Administration Review* 40, no. 4 (July–August 1980).

_____. "The Development of a Task-Oriented Approach to Performance Evaluation in the City of New York." *Public Personnel Management* 7, no. 6 (January–February 1978).

Buck, Lawrence S. "Executive Evaluation: Assessing the Probability for Success in the Job." *Review of Public Personnel Administration* 3, no. 3 (Summer 1983).

DeMarco, John J., and Nigro, Lloyd G. "Implementing Performance Appraisal Reform in the United States Civil Service." *Public Administration* 61, no. 1 (Spring 1983).

Gruenfeld, Elaine F. *Performance Appraisal: Promise and Peril.* Ithaca, N.Y.: School of Industrial and Labor Relations, Cornell University, 1981.

Kikoski, John F., and Litterer, Joseph A. "Effective Communications in the Performance Appraisal Interview." *Public Personnel Management* 12, no. 1 (Spring 1983).

Lopez, Felix, Jr. *Evaluating Employee Performance.* Washington, D.C.: International Personnel Management Association, 1968.

Nalbandian, John. "Performance Appraisal: If Only People Were Not Involved." *Public Administration Review* 41, no. 3 (May–June 1981).

---

[18]Bureau of Intergovernmental Personnel Programs, U.S. Civil Service Commission, *Conference Report on Public Personnel Management Reform*, January 23, 1978, pp. 60–62.

[19]See John M. Greiner, Roger E. Dahl, Harry P. Hatrie, and Annie P. Millar, *Monetary Incentives and Work Standards: Impacts and Implications for Management and Labor* (Washington, D.C.: Urban Institute, 1977).

Nigro, Lloyd G. "Attitudes of Federal Employees Toward Performance Appraisal and Merit Pay: Implications for CSRA Implementation." *Public Administration Review* 41, no. 1 (January–February 1981).

———. "CSRA Performance Appraisals and Merit Pay: Growing Uncertainty in the Federal Work Force." *Public Administration Review* 42, no. 4 (July–August 1982).

Pearce, Jone, and Perry, James L. "Federal Merit Pay: A Longitudinal Analysis." *Public Administration Review* 43, no. 4 (July–August 1983).

Stewart, Debra W., and Garson, G. David. *Organizational Behavior and Public Management*. New York: Dekker, 1983. Part II—Management Applications.

12 Promotions and Other Status Changes

This chapter will deal with these aspects of the in-service personnel program: promotions; transfers and mobility; reductions-in-force; and dismissals. Promotions are, of course, indispensable for career service, and promotion policy has a great bearing on the state of employee morale. An organization's personnel constitute the human resource pool that it has devoted considerable effort to recruiting and upon whose will to perform at high levels of effectiveness it depends. Personnel administrators devote much of their time to promotional problems, and many of the grievances filed under collective bargaining agreements are appeals of promotional decisions. Transfers often present difficult problems in reconciling management and individual employee needs, and greater mobility of employees is considered desirable for training and other purposes. Cycles of expansion and contraction and controversies over layoff policies have long been a part of the government scene, and the budgetary cutbacks of recent years have intensified these controversies. Civil service laws were passed to protect workers from discharge for partisan political reasons, but concern soon developed that dismissals for unsatisfactory service were far too few. As we saw in Chapter 11, new approaches for evaluating job performance and removing unsatisfactory workers are now being tried.

■ PROMOTIONS

Promotions are subject to the same legal requirements for validation of selection methods as original appointments. Since supervisory appraisals often play a significant part in evaluating candidates for promotion, the discussion of appraisals in Chapter 11 is very relevant. For appraisals to be valid in selections for promotion, the evaluation should be of ability to perform the duties of the promotional position, rather than of performance in the job currently held. For that reason, a separate appraisal form is often used in evaluations for promotion.

Basic Policy Issues in Promotion

The basic policy issues in promotions are designation of the area of competition and determination of the criteria and methods for ranking candidates. If only employees of the organizational subdivision in which the vacancy occurs can be considered, this could unduly narrow the selection base, particularly if the number of employees encompassed is small. In filling promotional jobs, the objective should be to obtain a sufficient number of well-qualified candidates from among whom to make a selection.

If such number can be found within the organizational subdivision (e.g., section, division, branch), then there usually is no need to consider persons from the outside. In government, the area of consideration has often been much too restricted, but this picture is improving. In some state and local governments, competition has been widened by permitting all employees in the city or state government who meet the minimum qualifications for the job to take promotional examinations. In the federal service, OPM instructions to the agencies state that "areas of consideration must be sufficiently broad to ensure the availability of high-quality candidates, taking into account the nature and level of the positions covered."[1] For higher-level positions in some federal agencies the area of competition is often nationwide.

Employee morale suffers when management appoints persons from outside the organization who are not as well-qualified as those employed within it. Appointing officers frequently suffer from the illusion so typical of all humans that the grass on the other side of the street is greener. Close to their own subordinates, they know their faults intimately, and the candidate from the outside may glitter by comparison. However, there may be a serious problem

---

[1] OPM Federal Personnel Manual Letter 335-12, December 29, 1978.

of inbreeding, so to obtain fresh viewpoints it may be justifiable to appoint some persons from the outside who are at least as well-qualified as the best candidates within the organization. It has often been said that there should be a balance between promotion-from-within and promotion-from-without, but there is much disagreement as to when such a balance has been reached.

Unions justifiably press for promotion-from-within, but sometimes they seek contract clauses restricting competition to such point that management will not have a sufficient number of well-qualified candidates to consider for promotion. In the federal service, unions have tried to negotiate restriction of promotional competitions to those within the bargaining unit. This means that employees elsewhere in the agency may not be considered, no matter what the situation as to the availability of persons well-qualified for the promotion within the bargaining unit.

There are strong differences of opinion between employees and the unions on the one hand and management on the other as to what "well-qualified" means. Thus the question of evaluation of qualifications to which we now turn is intimately related to that of determination of the area of competition.

Evaluation of candidates for promotion

In state and local government merit systems, methods of evaluating candidates for promotion are generally the same as those used in competitions for original entrance. Minimum qualifications for the job are determined; applications from those not meeting these qualifications are rejected; the capacities of those passing this first hurdle are measured through the written tests and other measurement devices described in Chapter 10; names of those who receive passing scores on the total examination are placed on a promotional register; and names are certified from this register to fill openings in accordance with the same rules for certification as in original appointments. Additional points are sometimes given for length of service but usually not very many, and sometimes the candidate's last performance appraisal is given some weight.

The rationale for using much the same procedures for promotional as for original entrance competitions has been to avoid promotions based on political or other nonmerit considerations. Unfortunately, in the process excessive rigidity has often been built into the promotion system. Those who are critical of original entrance selection procedures are even more so of using essentially the same procedures for promotional selections. Use of written tests for promotion is challenged by those who believe that an "employee's work history is a more reasonable indicator of probable success in a higher job." One authority maintains that written tests should not be used to "determine suitability for promotion . . . unless the nature of the test is such that it can clearly demonstrate that some workers would be a danger to either themselves or those around them or that they would be definitely incapable of performing the job to which they might be promoted."[2]

Traditionally, police departments have relied almost exclusively on written tests in promotional competitions for the higher ranks. Recently, the Police Executive Research Forum, a national organization of police chiefs and sheriffs, announced a new model promotional policy that emphasizes the need for other evaluation methods besides written tests, specifically promotional potential ratings and oral interviews for sergeants and lieutenants, and assessment centers and promotional potential ratings for captains. In this model policy, the function of the written test is to evaluate the candidates' knowledge of social ethics, management of human and fiscal resources, guidelines of supervision, leadership, and administration, agency policies and procedures, criminal law and procedures, community relations, and techniques of employee development.

Scores on these written tests constitute only one factor in promotional decisions. Ratings by the candidate's supervisor, oral interviews, and review of the individual's entire service record are also important parts of the promotional examination. The oral interviews, conducted by a panel of trained senior officers, focus on candidates' communication skills, problem solving abilities, and management styles. To minimize bias on the part of senior officers of the agency, it is recommended that senior officers from other law enforcement agencies and civilians serve as members of the interview panel. Furthermore, the model policy emphasizes that the promotional procedures employed should measure only the knowledges, skills, and abilities required for the particular rank.

In the federal service, as provided in OPM instructions, the agencies develop merit promotion plans that must meet three basic

---

[2]William H. Enneis, "Statement before the House Post Office and Civil Service Subcommittee," in *Personnel Testing and Equal Employment Opportunity* (Washington, D.C.: Government Printing Office, 1971), pp. 16–20.

requirements besides that for sufficiently broad areas of competition:

1. The procedures for promoting employees must be based on merit and made available in writing to candidates. All actions relating to promotion—"whether identification, qualification, evaluation, or selection of candidates—shall be made without regard to political, religious, or labor organization affiliation or nonaffiliation, marital status, race, color, sex, national origin, nondisqualifying physical handicap, or age, and shall be based solely on job-related criteria."

2. "To be eligible for promotion or placement [in a particular promotional job], candidates must meet the minimum qualification standards prescribed" by OPM for the job.

3. "Selection procedures will provide for management's right to select or not select from among a group of best qualified candidates. They will also provide for management's right to select from other appropriate sources, such as unemployment priority lists, reinstatement, transfer, handicapped or Veterans Readjustment eligibles or those within reach on an appropriate OPM certificate [register]. In deciding which source or sources to use, agencies have an obligation to determine which is most likely to meet best the agency mission objectives, contribute fresh ideas and new viewpoints, and meet the agency's affirmative action goals."[3]

The third requirement does not prevent agencies from agreeing to promotion-from-within clauses in union contracts, but it makes clear that management has the option to fill higher jobs by other means than promotion-from-within.

Promotion procedures in the federal service differ from those in state and local government merit systems in two respects. First, while written tests are sometimes used in the federal service, they most often are not. In state and local merit systems, more use is made of promotional written tests.

Second, in the federal service, the responsibility for ranking candidates for promotion is usually that of a promotion panel in the particular agency. These panels determine which candidates meet OPM's minimum qualifications for the position and of these which should be placed in the best qualified group. OPM instructions

---

[3]Federal Personnel Manual Letter 335-12, December 29, 1978.

read, "a reasonable number of the best qualified candidates are referred for selection."[4] In state and local merit systems, the selecting officer is limited to the number of names certified by the central personnel agency, and, as explained in Chapter 10, that number often is three.

Promotion panels in the federal service usually consist of three to seven agency program officials and personnel office representatives. Some of the program officials on the panel usually are representatives of the organization subdivision in which the opening is being filled.[5] As one example only, the Internal Revenue Service requires that "panels must consist of at least three voting members, including at least one member who has direct working knowledge of the position to be filled. A representative of the Personnel Office should also sit in as a nonvoting member, so that control and documentation of panel actions meet validity and job-relatedness requirements." The IRS policy also states that "wherever feasible, women and/or minorities should be included as panel members."[6]

In a comprehensive analysis of federal agency collective bargaining agreements with the unions, George Sulzner found that, although there was language in many of the agreements restricting promotional competitions in some manner that would benefit employees within the particular bargaining unit, management and union officials he contacted thought that these clauses had a "negligible impact on operations." The reason was that agencies already had similar provisions in their regulations or functioned on that basis and believed "it was good policy to promote from within the rank and file." Several of the union representatives Sulzner interviewed stated that the contract language on promotions encouraged management to "select from the entire unit, not just a department, and this incentive helped cut down preselection and improved the promotion prospects of their constitutuents."[7] The latter finding illustrates the pragmatic approach of unions: The best area of consideration is the one that most improves the promotion prospects of members of the union.

Preselection takes place when the evaluation process is so ma-

---

[4]Federal Personnel Manual Letter 335-13, "Guidelines for Evaluation of Employees for Promotion and Internal Placement," December 31, 1979.
[5]Ibid.
[6]Internal Revenue Service Manual, Employment, 0335.264, 4-2-81.
[7]George T. Sulzner, *The Impact of Labor Management Relations upon Selected Federal Personnel Policies and Practices* (Washington, D.C.: Government Printing Office, Office of Personnel Management Document, 1979), pp. 83–85.

nipulated that the person the selecting official wants to get the promotion does get it. Since much discretion in promotion matters is delegated to the agencies and to selecting officials, some observers believe preselection is virtually impossible to eradicate in the federal service. This is why unions concentrate on negotiating contract provisions they believe will prevent preselection and on monitoring compliance with these provisions. They try to "reduce the subjective judgment of management in making promotions by lowering the weight given performance evaluations, by defining rating criteria in the negotiated agreement, by maximizing union participation in the rating process, and by restricting management freedom to select from among qualifying employees."[8]

The weight given seniority. There has been—and remains—much concern that unions will obtain such strong seniority clauses that the merit principle of ranking according to relative ability to do the job will have been abandoned. The International Personnel Management Association states, "If the jurisdiction has one or more strong unions (and a strong labor relations law), seniority is almost certain to be demanded as an important consideration in promotion."[9] Employee pressures for the seniority principle existed long before the spread of collective bargaining in government, and these pressures have had substantial impact on civil service systems, such as the narrowing of areas of competition and increasing of the weight for length of service in promotions. The question, then, is whether collective bargaining has led to even greater emphasis upon seniority in promotions.

In the federal service, "provisions making seniority a factor in promotions are not negotiable."[10] Seven of the 20 agreements studied by Sulzner contained seniority tie-breaking clauses, but, since candidates are rarely equal in all other respects, these clauses had very little impact. In state and local governments, many contracts provide for promotion of the most senior employee meeting the minimum qualifications for the position.[11] Stanley and Cooper rea-

---

[8]Ibid., p. 82.

[9]International Personnel Management Association, *Guidelines for Drafting a Public Personnel Administration Law* (Washington, D.C.), p. 35.

[10]B. Virginia Comella, "Labor Relations and the Federal Personnel Specialist," *Public Personnel Management* 9, no. 2 (March–April 1980): 104.

[11]Bureau of Labor Statistics, *Collective Bargaining Agreements for State and County Government Employees* (Washington, D.C.: Government Printing Office, 1976), pp. 21–22.

son that promoting on this basis to jobs like truck loader does no real damage to the merit principle and also benefits morale, but doing so in the case of supervisory positions would "seriously weaken the fabric of urban government."[12] The late Jerry Wurf, president of the American Federation of State, County, and Municipal Employees, AFL-CIO, defined merit as meeting the "criteria" for the job and maintained that the senior employee among those who qualify should be awarded the promotion. Although stating that for professional positions "seniority alone is not always enough for distinguishing between jobs," Wurf believed it was "an important consideration."[13] AFSCME's position on this matter has not changed.

However, public employee leaders and unions do not have a unanimous view on the weight to be given to seniority. In a Brookings Institution study, Jack Steiber and two assistants conducted approximately 300 interviews in 53 cities and 23 states and found that "some police and fire fighter leaders prefer merit to seniority as a criterion for promotion because it would advance the course of professionalization."[14] There is no comprehensive nationwide research that compares the emphasis given to seniority in promotions before and after the spread of collective bargaining. Most unions have given greater priority to other matters, but there clearly is enough support by some unions for basing promotions on length of service to justify the belief in management and other quarters that this represents a real threat to the merit principle.

Arbitration and Promotions

In the federal service, decisions as to *who* should be promoted are nonnegotiable: this is a management right that cannot be bargained away. However, Title VII of the Civil Service Reform Act of 1978 provides that management must make the promotion selection from "among properly ranked and certified candidates for promotion." Properly ranked and certified means in accordance with provisions of law, OPM and other applicable government regula-

---

[12]David T. Stanley, with Carole L. Cooper, *Managing Local Government under Union Pressure* (Washington, D.C.: Brookings, 1972), pp. 44–45.

[13]Senate Subcommittee on Labor, *National Public Employment Relations Act, 1974*, 93rd Congress, 2d Session (Washington, D.C.: Government Printing Office, 1974), pp. 172–182.

[14]Jack Steiber, *Public Employee Unionism: Structure, Growth, Policy* (Washington, D.C.: Brookings, 1973), p. 122.

tions, and the procedures called for in the collective agreement. In arbitration cases, if a promotion action does not violate the law, OPM or other applicable government regulations, or the contract's promotion procedures, the arbitrators will deny any grievance by one of the candidates who was not selected for the promotion. If the promotion action was in error, the arbitrator does not have the power to order retroactive promotion with back pay for a candidate unless that person would have "positively and certainly" received the promotion but for the error. The arbitrator usually orders "rerunning the action and/or giving the wronged employee priority consideration for future vacancies."[15]

In state and local governments, arbitrators will not overturn promotion decisions unless they believe that management failed to apply properly the promotional criteria and procedures called for in the contract. For example, an arbitrator concluded that the employer did not fully comply with a contract clause that provided that vacancies were to be filled on the basis of experience, competence, qualifications, length of service, and other relevant factors. The selecting official had chosen someone for the promotion on the basis of personal knowledge of that candidate's personality but had failed to make an adequate investigation of the personality characteristics of a second applicant who, in the arbitrator's judgment, was clearly superior to the person selected in terms of the available objective measurements of all the applicants.

The arbitrator wrote, "In a case such as the instant one, where the judgment turns on subjectively determined personality traits, and where those making the judgment have substantial personal knowledge of one applicant and little or none of a second applicant who ranks higher in most objective factors, fairness requires that a vigorous effect be made, utilizing all available means, to inquire into the personality traits of the second applicant. The record indicates that this was not done here." He did not order that the promotion be awarded to the second applicant. Rather he ruled that the relative merits of both persons should be reconsidered by the employer in a "manner in keeping with the attached opinion."[16]

[15]Comella, "Labor Relations and the Federal Personnel Specialist," 104. See also Office of Labor-Management Relations, U.S. Civil Service Commission, *Grievance Arbitration in the Federal Service* (Washington, D.C., July 1977); and Frank D. Ferris, "Remedies in Federal Sector Promotion Grievances," *Arbitration Journal* 34 (June 1979): 34–37, 43.

[16]Estelle Tracy (ed.), *Arbitration Cases in Public Employment* (New York: American Arbitration Association, 1969), pp. 84–90.

Just like prudent arbitrators who decide federal government promotion grievances, he would not usurp management's role and make the promotion selection himself. If it is clear that a promotion would have been awarded to the grievant except for a contract violation, arbitrators in state and local government cases will, as in the federal government, order that the grievant be given the promotion.

■ TRANSFERS AND MOBILITY

Transfer may refer only to horizontal movements—that is, movement between positions in job classes neither higher nor lower in the salary plan—or it may include promotions as well. We will be concerned here with all movements of administrative, professional, and technical (APT) personnel to achieve the advantages of *mobility,* a concept much emphasized in career management. Transfers also can be permanent or temporary, which contributes to administrative flexibility.

There has been concern for some time that in the American public service, movement of APT personnel has been much too restricted—between agencies in the same jurisdiction, between jurisdictions, and between the public and private sectors. In the federal service, most openings in executive positions have been filled from within the agency, and employees generally have remained with the same agency after rising to middle-level executive posts. This same lack of mobility is characteristic of state and local governments where movement has generally been restricted to positions within a single agency. In the past, there has also been little interchange between the federal government and state and local jurisdictions, although this picture improved somewhat with passage of the Intergovernmental Personnel Act of 1970. This legislation contains provisions, still in force and funded, to facilitate intergovernmental transfers. While many government workers have a background of some private employment, little planned interchange of executives between the public and private sectors has taken place, although this situation has also improved.

The Rationale for Mobility

The rationale for mobility is that it broadens the experience of the person, deepens his or her insights, and generally makes for a more valuable employee. From management's standpoint, it also makes possible deploying employees to those jobs within the agency where their services are most needed at a particular time. Too, if there is substantial movement of personnel between agencies, this means that the jurisdiction has a cadre of APT personnel familiar with a wide range of governmental programs and operating problems. In the case of intergovernmental transfers because so many important functions of government are now shared by all levels of government, interchange makes for better understanding of the points of view of counterpart personnel, as in welfare, public health, agricultural, and law enforcement programs.

The obstacles to employee mobility have been numerous, and inevitably some will always remain since for personal reasons employees may not be in a position to accept transfers. Of course, in a scheme like the federal government's Senior Executive Service, members will be expected to make themselves available for intraagency transfer, but the intention is to consider the employee's reaction to a proposed transfer, and involuntary interagency transfers are prohibited by law. Conditions in the economy sometimes create formidable obstacles to transfers: At present, housing costs in Washington, D.C., and on the West Coast are so very high that for management to insist on moving an employee to these locations could inflict a real hardship upon the employee. The challenge for management is to do everything possible to remove those obstacles to mobility that deter even the most enterprising employees and at the same time to remove the fears of those who are overcautious about taking new assignments.

Interchange of Personnel Under the IPA

Until passage of the Intergovernmental Personnel Act (IPA) in 1970, with very few exceptions employees could not transfer between the federal government and state or local jurisdictions without losing retirement, leave, and other fringe benefit rights, not to mention the salary loss often involved if the move was from the generally higher paying federal agencies to a state or local government. Title IV of the IPA provides for temporary assignments (up to two years) of federal employees to state and local governments (including institutions of higher education), and vice versa, to perform "work of mutual concern" to the participating agencies.

The transferees are either detailed from their home agencies or given leave without pay.

In the case of federal employees, their salary, annual and sick leave, life insurance, health benefit, and unemployment compensation rights remain the same as if they had continued in their usual assignments with their agencies. The federal, state, or local agencies concerned negotiate arrangements for payment of salary and travel and transportation expenses to or from the place of assignment; one of the participating agencies can pay all salary and travel costs, or these costs can be shared. When state or local government employees are assigned to federal agencies, the latter may reimburse the state or local entity for all or part of the transferees' salaries; the same applies to travel expenses. The federal agencies can pay employer contributions for retirement, life insurance, and health benefits if the state or local government fails to continue these contributions. This legislation is administered by the OPM, and in negotiations over payment of salary or travel expenses, the principle is that the jurisdiction benefiting the most from the transfer should generally pay the larger share.

Transfers Between Government and the Private Sector

An executive interchange program between the federal government and the private sector has been functioning since 1970, based upon an executive order issued by President Lyndon Johnson. The purpose is to promote better understanding between the sectors and to permit each to learn from the other. Assignments are for one-year periods, and the participants are men and women in mid-career (Grades 13, 14, and 15). The program has been small, but several hundred executives from the federal government, private industry, and institutions of higher education have taken part. The Reagan administration has expanded the number of participants in the program because it fully supports the rationale that "businessmen and bureaucrats can indeed learn from one another."[17]

Nominations of federal employees to participate in the interchange program must be personally approved by the head of the sponsoring agency. By now, almost every federal agency has participated in this program. Private organizations participating have

---

[17]Barbara Gamarekian, "A Capital Sabbatical: Reagan Revives a Program in Which Executives and Bureaucrats Change Jobs," *New York Times*, October 25, 1981.

included International Paper Company, Deere and Company, General Electric, AT&T, General Motors, IBM, Xerox, and Texaco. The program is administered by the President's Commission on Personnel Interchange.

One problem in the interchange program is that some federal agencies have had more difficulty than the private companies in holding open jobs for the executive's return to the agency. A difficulty for the private company executive is that he or she may suffer a substantial loss in salary in accepting the tour of duty with the government, but some companies make up the difference in salary.

Employee organization views on transfers

As revealed during congressional consideration of the Civil Service Reform Act of 1978, employee organizations do not contest the need for mobility, but they want to be sure that employees' rights are fully protected. Although they offered amendments to certain provisions during the legislative history of the IPA, employee organization leaders supported the principles of the legislation, including the desirability of intergovernmental transfers.[18]

The framework of reference in most collective bargaining agreements on transfers is the entire workforce, and the concern is with protection of employees' rights in voluntary and involuntary transfers. Some contracts simply state that management will establish a system whereby employees may indicate their preferences for transfers to appropriate vacancies, and others provide that in filling vacancies by transfer seniority shall govern. Unions are concerned that employees on temporary detail to work in higher classifications should receive the pay of the higher class or a percentage increase above the pay for the job held prior to the detail. They are also concerned that time limits be placed on temporary assignments to higher level jobs and that the job be declared a permanent one and filled on that basis after expiration of the time limit, but not necessarily by the person who was detailed to it. Agreements sometimes provide for a more senior or more qualified employee to bid on the job if it is made a permanent one.[19]

---

[18]Senate Subcommittee on Intergovernmental Relations, *Intergovernmental Personnel Act of 1967, Intergovernmental Manpower Act of 1967* (Washington, D.C.: Government Printing Office, 1967), pp.231–243.

[19]Bureau of Labor Statistics, *Collective Bargaining Agreements for State and County Government Employees*, pp. 22–23.

As to involuntary transfers, the contract may require management to give notice in advance and to explain to the employee the reasons for the action. It may also specify that employees with the least seniority are to be transferred first. In some school teacher contracts, all involuntary transfers to a different school are prohibited. Some contracts also prohibit transfers for disciplinary reasons. Management rights clauses usually include the right to transfer personnel; while this means that transfers are not a mandatory subject for negotiation, management may, in its discretion, negotiate aspects of transfer policy and procedures to the extent legally possible.

■ REDUCTIONS-IN-FORCE

Management policies and actions are severely tested when reductions-in-force are necessary because of budgetary cuts, program changes, or reorganization. Programs may peak and then decline or even be phased out; such instability is characteristic of government. While reductions-in-force occur with greater frequency and impact in the federal government, they also constitute a serious problem in state and local governments where they are accentuated by the financial pinch resulting from limited, inflexible revenue sources. Currently, reductions-in-force are a major problem in public personnel administration.

The basic policy questions are: Who should be laid off, in what order, and according to what criteria? Should order of layoff be based on seniority or some plan that considers both seniority and merit? What weight should be given to veterans' preference? What consideration, if any, should be given to the agency's future needs for certain kinds of workers? What should the role of employee organizations be in the formulation and implementation of reduction-in-force policies? What responsibility should the jurisdiction have for reemploying laid-off employees?

In August 1981 the International Personnel Management Association reported the results of a questionnaire survey it made of layoff procedures in randomly selected public jurisdictions. Fifty-four percent of the respondents stated that the order of layoff in their jurisdiction was governed by seniority while 46 percent said that it was determined by both seniority and performance appraisal ratings. Seventy-nine percent of the respondents maintain reemployment rosters of laid-off employees for positions for which they can qualify. Forty-three percent maintain these rosters for at least one year, 14 percent for two years, and 11 percent for three or four years. Seventy-four percent actively help laid-off workers obtain another position in the jurisdiction. Forty-two percent give employees two weeks' advance notice before the layoff begins, 14 percent one month's notice, and 7 percent more than one month's notice. Thirteen percent use a flexible notification period, depending on the situation.

Effects on affirmative action policies were both positive and negative. "The positive effect included the retraining of women for non-traditional jobs and the development of a provision in collective bargaining contracts for maintaining minorities over senior non-minority employees at a maximum rate of 5 percent. The negative effects included a reduction in minority employment from 21.9 percent to 19.6 percent, placing recently rehired minorities on reduction in force lists, and reducing the number of positions filled through affirmative action."[20]

In the federal service, as provided in OPM regulations, the agencies decide which jobs to eliminate; this is a management decision which is not reviewable by the OPM or the Merit Systems Protection Board. The agencies fix the competitive area, which usually is a single office or installation in the field service or a bureau or similar organization at headquarters, and then group positions by competitive level, that is, by the type and grade of work. In each competitive area, employees with similar jobs compete for retention—GS-3 stenographers with GS-3 stenographers, GS-11 accountants with GS-11 accountants. Retention registers are prepared for each competitive level.

Ranking within retention registers is on the basis of a formula which combines four factors: type of appointment (tenure); veterans preference; length of service; and performance rating. Specifically, three tenure categories are established: Group I, consisting of career employees not serving probation; Group II, career employees still serving probation and career-conditional employees who have not completed a three-year service requirement; and Group III, indefinite employees, employees serving under temporary appointments pending establishment of registers, and those serving under nonstatus nontemporary appointments. Employees with temporary appointments and those with unsatisfactory

---

[20]"IPMA Layoff Survey Results," *IPMA News,* August 1981.

performance ratings are not placed in any of these categories. They do not compete for retention and must be released from the level before any person in Groups I, II, or III is released.

Within each tenure category, employees are divided into three subgroups: AD for veterans with a compensable service-connected disability of 30 percent or more; A for all other veterans; and B for nonveterans. (The AD subgroup was added as the result of provisions in the Civil Service Reform Act of 1978.) Within each subgroup, ranking is by service dates which reflect total federal service, both civilian and military. Prior to passage of the reform act, performance was recognized by adding four additional years of service for those receiving performance ratings of outstanding and two additional years for those receiving ratings between satisfactory and outstanding. Since less than 1 percent of employees received outstanding ratings and since very few agencies had levels of rating between satisfactory and outstanding, the credit for performance was almost nonexistent.

Selection of those to be released from the competitive level starts with the lowest tenure category and with the employee in subgroup B who has the latest service date, which means that nonveterans are released before veterans. Those in subgroup AD who have not been rated unsatisfactory are retained ahead of other veterans. Employees in Group III can be separated because they have no right to another job; employees in Groups II or I must be offered reassignments in another competitive level if the agency has suitable positions from which the incumbents can be bumped. Suitable position is one in the same or a lower grade for which the individual is fully qualified and which is occupied by someone in a lower subgroup. The bumped person is entitled to displace someone in a lower subgroup. Thus many individuals may be bumped simply to lay off one employee. Names of those laid off are placed on reemployment priority lists for two years in the case of those in Group I and for one year for those in Group II. During this time, the agency must consider those on these lists for any vacancies in the commuting area for which they can qualify. In addition, those in Groups I and II can apply through their agencies for placement assistance under the OPM's Displaced Employee Program.

Employees may appeal to MSPB if they believe that provisions of law and OPM regulations have not been applied correctly to them in reductions-in-force. Those in bargaining units with negotiated grievance procedures that cover reductions-in-force must use the negotiated procedure and may not appeal to MSPB.

This system gives great weight to veterans preference because in each subgroup nonveterans with long years of service are displaced before veterans with *any* service. Consequently, some nonveterans have been wary of federal employment. Besides the dislocations, bumping creates much paperwork, the cost of which often has been thousands of dollars. In truth, federal government layoff policies have had a devastating effect, as described in an article by Harry C. Dennis, Jr. He reports the following:

> Since nonproductive employees often have greater seniority, when their jobs are abolished they "simply bump someone else." That "someone else" often is a productive employee.
>
> Because of veterans preference, in 40 federal agencies women administrators were laid off at 2.2 times the average rate for all employees. The "last hired, first fired" policy discriminates against both women and minorities; minority administrators were laid off at 3.5 times the rate for all employees.
>
> Those longest at a grade or salary—those promoted the least often—are safest in a reduction-in-force because they tend to have more service. Those promoted quickly are more vulnerable because they have less service.
>
> Employees displaced but not separated by RIFS often are sadly under-utilized, such as doctors bumped to file clerk positions.
>
> Training funds are also cut although retraining may be the only way to replace skills lost because of RIFS.
>
> The effect on morale is terrific. Employees are alienated because veterans preference and seniority are more important than quality of performance.[21]

The new OPM regulations referred to in Chapter 11 provide that employees would continue to be ranked by tenure groups, within these groups by veterans preference and then by seniority, but service credit for each of the last three performance ratings at the "fully successful" and higher levels would be increased as follows: 10 years for an "outstanding" rating; 7 years for an "exceeds

---

[21]Harry C. Dennis, Jr., "Reductions-in-Force: The Federal Experience," *Public Personnel Management* 12, no. 1 (Spring 1983).

fully successful" rating; and 5 years for a "fully successful" rating. Bumping could be to no more than two grades below the position from which the employee is released. The GAO has recommended mandatory rehiring for future openings of qualified RIF-separated employees over nonfederal government applicants.

The employee organization role in reductions

In the federal government, union contracts may provide policies and procedures that supplement but do not conflict with law and OPM regulations. The agreements often provide for advance notice to the union of impending layoffs and of the reasons for such action, and the union is given the opportunity to present its views on the implementation of the reductions. In some contracts the employer agrees to make the competitive area as broad as possible and commits itself to filling existing vacancies as far as possible with employees who otherwise would be separated. In turn, the union may agree to help explain to the employees the reasons for the reductions. Management is required by law and rulings of the Federal Labor Relations Authority to consult with the bargaining agent before announcing a reduction-in-force and the bargaining agent has the right to negotiate concerning th impact of the reduction-in-force on working conditions.

Collective agreements in state and local governments also prescribe detailed advance notice and other procedures. A Bureau of Labor Statistics study reported:

> Layoff provisions included a wide variety of related actions including attempts to avoid or minimize layoffs, the actual layoff procedure, and the order of recall. . . . Before the actual layoff of regular employees occurred, management might choose to reduce hours of all employees, or . . . might decide first to lay off nonregular employees or to transfer employees to vacancies not affected by the reduction. . . . The unit of layoff and the order of layoff might be set forth, applying either straight seniority or seniority in combination with skill and ability. Bumping rules could be stipulated . . . and the retention of seniority during layoff and the order of recall, which is not necessarily the same as the order of layoff.[22]

At all levels of government, unions exert political pressures to prevent layoffs, and they have many successes in this respect.

---

[22]Bureau of Labor Statistics, *Collective Bargaining Agreements for State and County Government Employees*, pp. 26–27.

There are some cases of no-layoff clauses in state and local governments, but generally "arbitrators have upheld the right of the employer to abolish jobs or reduce the work force for economic reasons."[23]

■ DISCIPLINE

Our brief discussion of discipline in this chapter will omit the grievance procedure, appeals, and employees' constitutional rights. These are the topics of Chapter 14 and 15.

Much has been written about how discipline should be viewed positively as a means of correcting and stimulating employee performance rather than as a punitive weapon. The Los Angeles County Civil Service Commission stresses that there should be a clear-cut written statement of disciplinary policy "which is known to all employees and is uniformly and impartially carried out. Such a policy statement may include the agency's definition of 'discipline,' under what conditions corrective actions will be taken, what they consist of, and the agency's position regarding fairness, consistency, and adequate investigation and review." It should also specify the responsibilities of all concerned with disciplinary matters—supervisors, agency heads, personnel officers, the central personnel agency, employee organizations, and employees themselves. All legal requirements, contract provisions, and procedural steps should be set forth unambiguously in the administrative manuals and instructions. The responsibilities and authority of first-line supervisors should be given particular attention, since skillful supervision removes the causes of many grievances and, when formal disciplinary action is necessary, permits dealing effectively with the problem rather than exacerbating it.[24]

In their survey of 132 U.S. and Canadian state, provincial, and local governments, Saso and Tanis found that 106 had written disciplinary policies and the remainder had at least well-known informal rules and traditional practices. Only 15 of the respondents had penalty schedules showing the penalty for each kind of infraction of the rules. Many personnel experts believe these sched-

---

[23]June Weisberger, *Job Security and Public Employees* (Ithaca, N.Y.: Institute of Public Employment, New York State School of Industrial and Labor Relations, Cornell University, March 1973), p. 54.

[24]Carmen D. Saso and Earl Tanis, *Disciplinary Policies and Practices*, Public Employee Relations Library, no. 40 (Chicago: International Personnel Management Association, 1973), pp. 5–6.

ules are too inflexible and do not take into account the circumstances of particular cases and the employee's previous record. In the jurisdictions studied, disciplinary policy guidelines were formulated by the central personnel agency or by the personnel director, pursuant to legal requirements. In the majority of cases, the union role was limited to representing employees in grievance proceedings and formal hearings. However, this study was published in 1973, and later Bureau of Labor Statistics reports have established that in many state and local government agreements disciplinary procedures have been "arrived at through negotiations" rather than being prescribed by rules and regulations of the governments involved.[25] At all levels of government, the union role in disciplinary policies and procedures is now substantial. To many unions, disciplinary policy is as important as economic benefits.

In the federal service, law and OPM regulations govern disciplinary policies and procedures, as they do in discharges for unacceptable performance, previously discussed in this chapter. Union contract provisions further define disciplinary policies and procedures and secure protections for employees beyond those stipulated by law and OPM regulations. Following are only two examples of many that could be given:

> Interstation transfers shall not be used as a form of discipline. Involuntary transfers shall not be made when there are employees in the commuting area from which the transfer is to be made who are willing to transfer and who meet position requirements.
> The employer agrees that no personnel shall be assigned to perform the work of a collection agency for debts allegedly due by an employee to a private individual or firm. It is recognized that all employees are expected to pay promptly all just financial obligations.[26]

Collective agreements in state and local governments often spell out the kinds of disciplinary action that management may impose, for example, limiting them to oral reprimand, written reprimand, suspension, or discharge. They also may list the possible causes for disciplinary action, such as insubordination, dishonesty, absence without official permission, drunkenness on duty, although

---

[25]Bureau of Labor Statistics, *Collective Bargaining Agreements for State and County Government Employees*, p. 24.

[26]See Felix A. Nigro, "Personnel Administration by Handshake," *Civil Service Journal* 12, no. 4 (April–June 1972): 28–30.

the contract may also state that discipline shall be for just cause. Some contracts specify graduated penalties to be imposed for repetition of prohibited conduct, such as first a verbal warning, then a written warning, then suspension without pay for a number of days, and, finally, dismissal.

It is often required that the employer provide both the employee and the union with a detailed written statement of the charges including "dates, times, and places." The right of the employee to discuss the disciplinary action with the union steward or other authorized representative of the union is also frequently stated. Some contracts provide that "if the employer has reason to reprimand an employee, it shall be in a manner that will not embarrass the employee before other employees or the public." Another procedural protection often negotiated is the right of employees to see and respond in writing to negative reports on their performance and conduct entered into their personnel records. As one special example, police collective bargaining contracts sometimes specify procedures for considering grievances filed by a member of the public against a police officer.[27] To summarize, as in other aspects of personnel administration, disciplinary provisions in collective agreements represent efforts, often quite successful, by management and the union to develop and apply sound policies and practices to their mutual benefit.

BIBLIOGRAPHY

Caubler, George H., Jr. "Alternative to a Reduction in Force." *Public Personnel Management* 11, no. 1 (Spring 1982).

Comella, Virginia. "Labor Relations and the Federal Personnel Specialist." *Public Personnel Management* 9, no. 2 (March–April 1980).

Dennis, Harry C., Jr. "Reductions-in-Force: The Federal Experience." *Public Personnel Management* 12, no. 1 (Spring 1983).

Johnson, Arthur. "Equity in the Public Workplace: Retrenchment, Employment Security, and Alternative Placement." *Public Personnel Management* 12, no. 2 (Summer 1983).

McKelvey, Jean T. "Discipline and Discharge." In *Arbitration in*

---

[27]See Bureau of Labor Statistics, *Collective Bargaining Agreements for State and County Government Employees*, pp. 24–25, and Bureau of Labor Statistics, U.S. Department of Labor, *Collective Bargaining Agreements for Police and Fire Fighters* (Washington, D.C.: Government Printing Office, 1976), pp. 83–87.

Practice, edited by Arnold Zack. Ithaca, N.Y.: New York State School of Industrial and Labor Relations, Cornell University, 1984.

Merit Systems Protection Board. *Reduction-in-Force in the Federal Government, 1981: What Happened and Opportunities for Improvement.* Washington, D.C.: Government Printing Office, June 1983.

Saso, Carmen D., and Tanis, Earl. *Disciplinary Policies and Practices.* Public Employee Relations Library, no. 40. Washington, D.C.: International Personnel Management Association, 1973.

Smith, Russ. "Promotion and Other Changes in Standing." In *Handbook on Public Personnel Administration and Labor Relations,* edited by Jack Rabin, Thomas Vocino, W. Bartley Hildreth, and Gerald J. Miller. New York: Dekker, 1983.

Sulzner, George T. *The Impact of Labor-Management Relations upon Selected Federal Personnel Policies and Practices.* Office of Personnel Management Document. Washington, D.C.: Government Printing Office, 1979.

13 Training

Training is extremely important in an organization's internal extraction process because its purpose is to help employees improve their capacities to contribute to organizational effectiveness. (See Chapter 3.) A well-conceived training program not only helps employees improve their skills but also inculcates them with the organization's mission and values. The key role of training is aptly described in the following statement:

> The new concept that is floating in the air, stimulated no doubt by the impetus of systems theory, defines a social system (world, nation, community, organization, home) as *a system of learning resources*. When we start thinking this way, we have to redefine the nature and purpose of the HRD [human relations development] operation. Its task now becomes that of identifying *all* of the resources for learning in an environment and finding the most effective ways of linking these resources to the developmental needs of the occupants of the environment.[1]

Unfortunately, training programs on any substantial scale were started very late in government, and even now training is not a highly developed function in many public jurisdictions. However, most public employers now accept responsibility for providing at least some training, whereas formerly many did not. It has been many years now since training programs in government were a rarity, and the renewed emphasis in American society since the 1950s on the value of education and learning to meet changed needs has led to greater recognition of the importance of training.

However, the budget stringencies of recent years have caused a reduction and even elimination of some training activities in

---

[1]Malcolm Knowles, "Some Thoughts about Environment and Learning," *Training and Development Journal* 34, no. 1 (February 1980): 43.

many jurisdictions. In truth, training has always been a fragile activity in government, because "many public organizations see human resource development as a frill—to be enjoyed in good times when money is more readily available but to be cut when money supplies dwindle."[2] Yet financial stringency makes training even more important because "public administrators and their organizations will continue to be expected to provide services across a broad front of governmental responsibilities. Unfair as it may seem, they will also be pushed to achieve high levels of performance while their budgets become increasingly tight and uncertain."[3]

Even during periods when funds are available, it is often difficult to build support within the organization for making a bigger investment in the training function. Much of training is future-oriented—to improve the capacity of the employees to meet the future requirements of the organization, as well as their own individual developmental needs at different stages in their careers. Many line managers tend to be very much present-oriented, to concentrate on achievement of work goals of the current budget year and to be distrustful of expenditures for staff time that may or may not bring results at some future date. Frank B. Sherwood, first director of the Federal Executive Institute, writes, "It is against this natural inclination that the public manager must guard. . . . The transitory, political leadership inevitably will deal in terms of shortened time frames that emphasize task accomplishments and individual payoffs."[4]

In Chapter 1, we discussed how certain characteristics of traditional civil service systems hinder the ability of managers to manage. W. D. Heisel, a leading figure in public personnel administration and one who could be considered a pioneer in the field, gives examples of how "the typical bureaucracy found in government impedes the development of future managers."

To begin with, line management is not given the key role in

---

[2]Lue Rachelle Brim-Donohoe, "A Case for Human Resources Development," *Public Personnel Management* 10, no. 4 (Winter 1981): 365.

[3]Lloyd C. Nigro, "Developing Human Resources for the Public Sector: The New Challenge to Public Management," in William B. Eddy (ed.), *Handbook of Organization Management* (New York: Dekker, 1983), p. 279.

[4]Frank P. Sherwood, "The Education and Training of Public Managers," in William B. Eddy (ed.), *Handbook of Organization Management* (New York: Dekker, 1983), p. 44.

executive development. Rather that role is given to the personnel office or training department, and consequently line managers are relieved of "any feeling of responsibility for the development of subordinates." This split between executive development training programs and the managers themselves is worsened because the training director "over-emphasizes off-the-job educational experiences rather than on the job experiences. The training director needs to develop a record of activity (inputs) to justify his existence. This record too often takes the form of counting how many employee hours are spent in the classroom, forgetting that each hour in a classroom is the loss of an hour of productive working time." Like other personnel authorities critical of traditional personnel systems, Heisel believes that line management, rather than the personnel office, should be entrusted with the responsibility for planning and carrying out executive development programs, with the "training director . . . best cast in a support role—the expert who is on tap, not on top."

Heisel lists as other bureaucratic impediments to executive development: rigid position classification plans that make it difficult to "detail employees to unrelated work for the purpose of broadening experience"; reward systems that do not "encourage managers to train subordinates . . . if they are rewarded at all for accomplishment, it is for accomplishment in terms of productivity today, not a better organization for tomorrow"; promotion systems that reduce the "incentive for the prospective manager to learn on the job," as when scores on tests are the basis for promotion, quoting a police chief who said, "Most of us were good police officers who became chiefs because we were able to perform well on a three-hour, paper-and-pen test one Saturday morning"; an "over-concern with the technical qualifications of managers rather than their managerial qualifications [that] may impede the progress of the highly capable generalist"; and pension systems that lock employees in their present jobs and prevent transfer to "positions in other departments which would lead to potential further advancement."[5] These examples cited by Heisel bring out clearly the interdependency between success in training programs and elimination of mistaken practices in other aspects of the personnel program.

---

[5] W. D. Heisel, "A Non-Bureaucratic View of Management Development," *Public Personnel Management* 9, no. 2 (March–April 1980): 94–98.

■ THE ORGANIZATIONAL FUNCTIONS OF TRAINING

Formal organizations are held together by a "glue" of formal and informal rules defining how members should think and behave. Jobs are performed according to accepted procedures, and relationships between employees and work units are controlled by a web of laws, policies, traditions, and group norms. Complex organizations are characterized by numerous detailed regulations covering the technical aspects of the work. Such processes as formulating a budget, designing a bridge, or programming a computer are controlled by complicated decision rules that must be followed. There is virtually no aspect of organizational life that escapes the influence of rules. Many of these rules are fairly straightforward, such as everybody shall report for work at a designated hour of the day. Others which concern interpersonal behavior and authority relations are much more subtle and more difficult, particularly for new employees, to ascertain.

It is important to recognize that training plays an essential part in making organizations manageable. Without a membership that is for the most part "programmed" to make organizationally appropriate (rational) decisions, organizations would have to control employees much more closely. Herbert A. Simon has written that

> . . . training influences decisions "from the inside out." That is, training prepares the organization member to reach satisfactory decisions himself [herself], without the need for the constant exercise of authority or advice. In this sense, training procedures are alternatives to the exercise of authority or advice as means of control over the subordinate's decisions.[6]

Training is a key variable in the design of administrative systems. Highly trained personnel mean savings in supervisory costs and time.[7] In contrast, an untrained or undertrained workforce forces management to limit opportunities for employee discretion and to control behavior directly through very close supervision of all phases of the work. Any initial savings in salary expense or training budgets are quickly lost in increased managerial costs.

Insofar as it effectively supplies employees with the facts, frames of reference, and values involved in making acceptable decisions, training is an invaluable resource. It is critically important in con-

---

[6]Herbert A. Simon, *Administrative Behavior: A Study of Decision-making Processes in Administrative Organization*, 2d ed. (New York: Free Press, 1957), p. 15.
[7]Ibid., pp. 15–16.

temporary organizations, which achieve control through instilling habits of coordination and cooperation rather than through the exercise of command or the imposition of hierarchical authority.[8] Where technical or professional specialization is involved, administrators do not have the expertise to tell subordinates how to carry out their tasks. Under these conditions, controls must be internalized so that employees are self-controlling. The role of training, therefore, is not just to help build and maintain a technically competent staff. It also must function as a central process through which influence can be exerted throughout the organization and as a powerful source of control over individuals' behavior.[9]

The mutuality of training as a benefit to both the organization and the individual is a dominant theme of modern views of training which see it as a process aimed at changing behavior. The desired "new" behavior must be considered valuable both to the organization and the individual.[10] This was the opinion of the "founder" of scientific management, Frederick W. Taylor. Although he is very much identified with such developments as standardizing work and training workers to conform to organizational demands, he also stressed development of the individual worker:

> After we have studied the workman, so that we know his possibilities, we then proceed, as one friend to another, to try to develop every workman in our employ, so as to bring out his best facilities and to train him to do a higher, more interesting and more profitable class of work than he has done in the past.[11]

Contemporary training concepts and techniques concurrently emphasize employee self-development and organizational requirements as Bertram Gross has noted.[12] This self-development value has historically been associated with training in the United States. The organization focuses on the intellectual, social, and psychological growth of the individual with the rationale that mature, creative, innovative employees will contribute greatly to organizational effectiveness over the long run.

---

[8] See Harlan Cleveland, *The Future Organization: A Guide for Tomorrow's Managers* (New York: Harper & Row, 1972), pp. 65–68.

[9] Simon, *Administrative Behavior*, p. 227.

[10] William C. Scott, *Organization Theory: A Behavioral Analysis for Management* (Homewood, Ill.: Irwin, 1967), p. 326.

[11] Frederick W. Taylor, "The Principles of Scientific Management," in Harwood F. Merrill (ed.), *Classics in Management* (New York: American Management Association, 1960), p. 93.

[12] Bertram Gross, *The Managing of Organizations* (New York: Free Press, 1964), p. 789.

Contemporary organizations rely on successful role performance in many different, very specialized functional areas. Because of the complexity of their programs, most public agencies try to recruit persons who already possess the necessary intellectual, social, and other skills; in other words, they look for *pretrained* candidates for employment. However, complete control over the talents and values of entering employees is seldom, if ever, achieved. Further, the existing skills and knowledges of even the best prepared personnel must be added to as the agency is called on to cope with new situations.

Respecting managers in government, Sherwood emphasizes that most of their training in executive skills must take place *"after entry into"* the service. This is because most are recruited into particular occupations, based on professional competence rather than administrative experience and ability. Sherwood writes, "Bear in mind that nearly three-fourths of the scientists in the federal executive corps were attracted by a particular assignment or occupational opportunity; similarly, nearly half the non-scientists were so attracted. Rather clearly, this means that the managerial leadership resources of the government cannot be taken for granted. They must be identified and developed."[13]

■ THE PSYCHOLOGY OF TRAINING

There are psychological dimensions to training that must be understood and taken into account for training programs to succeed, no matter how well-planned and executed they may be from a technical standpoint. A training program can be a significant change experience for the participants, who may perceive it as threatening, especially if it poses a challenge to beliefs they hold deeply or questions the way they have been doing their jobs. Those who plan training programs should anticipate these psychological reactions and give careful attention to the following factors in the design of the training activities: (1) motivation, (2) perceived relevance, (3) psychological climate, and (4) feedback.

Motivation

Trainees learn best when they are positively motivated to participate and feel the need for training on a personal level. Change is

---

[13]Sherwood, "The Education and Training of Public Managers," p. 46.

far easier to accomplish when trainees are psychologically "ready" for training and believe that it will help them perform better. Douglas McGregor maintained that many employers follow a "manufacturing model" of training that is entirely organization-centered: "The requirements of the organization are paramount. Individuals are selected, oriented, appraised, rotated, promoted, sent to school—all within an administrative framework which leaves them relatively little voice in their own career development."[14] This "manufacturing model" is avoided when, as for some time now in many public agencies, individual employee development plans are worked out on a partnership basis between superior and subordinate.

From a psychological standpoint, voluntary training is probably the most likely to be accepted and profited from, and training methods should be geared to individual differences in readiness and motivation.

Perceived Relevance

A major problem encountered by trainers is resistance by trainees who do not believe that what they are undergoing is relevant to *their* work. Organizational psychologist Harold J. Leavitt states that "learning cannot be exclusive of the needs of the learner. And what is learned best is what is relevant to the current needs of the learner, not what may be revelant to his future needs."[15]

Unfortunately, administrators and trainers too often decide on training needs without bothering to consult with employees. Management assumes that what it believes is logical and relevant will be so perceived by the trainees. A sound approach is to study carefully the perceptions of the employees and to involve them in the process of planning and executing the training experience. Accordingly, when the City of Phoenix, Arizona, decided to emphasize training, its Organization Development Administrator and its Training Administrator conducted interviews on training needs not only with a substantial number of departmental executives and middle managers and with representatives of five unions, but also

---

[14]Douglas McGregor, *The Human Side of Enterprise* (New York: McGraw-Hill, 1960), p. 19.

[15]Harold J. Leavitt, *Managerial Psychology*, 2d ed. (Chicago: University of Chicago Press, 1964), p. 307.

sampled employee opinion through an attitude survey to which more than one half of the employees responded.[16]

Supportive Climate

Training is most likely to succeed when it is conducted in an atmosphere of trust and support. Since the supervisor frequently functions as trainer, giving on-the-job instructions to subordinates, a supervisor who behaves in a threatening or otherwise unsympathetic manner can severely hamper the learning process. Subordinates are very much aware that the supervisor will later make evaluations of how they are performing on the job. They are hesitant to risk errors during the learning process and may not report their own training needs because they believe it would "look bad" on their records.

Rensis Likert observed a general "unwillingness of subordinates to bring their problems to the man who has the major control over their destiny in the organization. His influence upon their promotions and their future in the company is so great that they cannot afford to let him see their weaknesses."[17] Likert pointed to research findings to the effect that when the training and performance evaluation roles are separated, the employee is more willing to report problems and to solicit help from the supervisor-trainer. It is apparent that supportive managerial and group settings reduce psychological tensions and create conditions under which employees find it easier to accept the challenge of trying to learn new skills and improve their ability to perform their work.[18] It has been commented often in the literature on training that top management often expresses interest in and supports training activities but is unwilling to let employees practice on the job what they learned during the training sessions. The management climate is professedly but not actually supportive of training.

Unfortunately, supervisors who otherwise might be enthusiastic about training activities are not so because they have become disenchanted with the training programs in their agencies. Quoting Sherwood again, "Many training programs are just plain bad, for

---

[16]See Leland G. Verheyen and Louis Olivas, "Attitude Survey Supports Training Needs," *Public Personnel Management* 9, no. 1 (January–February 1960).

[17]Rensis Likert, *New Patterns of Management* (New York: McGraw-Hill, 1961), pp. 53–54.

[18]Ibid., pp. 166–169.

a variety of reasons. Although many of the failures can be accounted for on grounds of philosophical and design inadequacy, a high level of amateurism must also be recognized as a major contributor."[19]

Feedback

Quick, specific feedback about performance helps trainees learn with a minimum of wasted time and effort. They should not have to wait any longer than necessary to find out how well they are doing. Accurate feedback given at the proper time provides the information they need to guide their efforts at improvement.

James N. Mosel sees the training process as consisting of three phases: input, output, and feedback. *Input* is the content or substance of the training exercise, such as learning how to prepare a budget statement; *output* is the behavior produced, in this case the trainees' efforts to apply what they have learned about preparing such statements; and *feedback* is the information given them about how well they are preparing the statements. "*As knowledge of performance increases, learning increases both in rate and level.*"

Mosel stresses that feedback is most effective when (1) it adds meaningfully to the receivers' knowledge about their output, (2) it tells them "what to do as well as what not to do," (3) it informs them when they are performing correctly, and (4) it is specific rather than general.[20] Similarly, Likert stressed the value of short feedback cycles:

> Short feedback cycles can give each individual continuous information about his successes and failures. He can then concentrate on correcting his weaknesses and need not waste time learning what he already knows. This is a much more efficient training process than companywide programs which assume that all individuals need the same training.[21]

Professional trainers anticipate and are prepared to deal with blockages in the feedback loop. It is always possible that those undergoing training will reject or misinterpret feedback informa-

---

[19]Sherwood, "The Education and Training of Public Managers," p. 60.

[20]James N. Mosel, "How to Feed Back Performance Results to Trainees," in Robert T. Golembiewski and Michael Cohen (eds.), *People in Public Service* (Itasca, Ill.: Peacock, 1970), pp. 388–389, 391–393.

[21]Likert, *New Patterns of Management*, pp. 204–205.

tion for emotional reasons or because they do not understand it. Special care should be taken to see that feedback is presented in clear, unambiguous terms and whenever possible in ways that do not threaten the trainee's self-concept.

The four dimensions of training psychology discussed above hardly exhaust the subject. Public personnel administrators should be aware of the contributions learning theory and psychology can make to improving the efficacy of public service training.

Now that performance evaluation is being approached in a much more thorough way in the public service than previously, the periodic appraisal review between supervisor and subordinate can become an effective method of training. Previously its value in training was very limited.

■ DETERMINING TRAINING NEEDS

A useful approach to analyzing fundamental training needs is in terms of goals and cause-effect relations. Assuming that inadequacies in worker performance are found to exist, what can the training be expected to accomplish? What will its operational goals be? Opinions on these matters run from virtual unanimity to almost complete disagreement.

Inadequate performance by lathe operators would suggest such highly specific training objectives as satisfactory output and acceptable quality. However, the objectives are less easily specified in a situation where groups of workers or several organizational units are failing to cooperate or coordinate. Several objectives can be suggested: (1) improved interpersonal relationships, (2) increased administrative capability in coordination and control, or (3) better understanding of the technical and social dimensions of the other group or unit's functions. The root causes of the problem must be fully understood before training goals can be chosen.

Without some form of agreement on these goals, it is impossible to move to the next step: selecting the most effective training methods. Here again, certainty may run from very high to very low. Even with relative certainty about *what* should be accomplished, there usually are questions to be answered about *how* to attain the desired ends. These are problems in cause-effect relations. There are no universal remedies for any and all organizational problems, although at one time or another many executives and trainers have acted as if certain kinds of training programs or methods were the answers to all difficulties. Program objectives and training methods should be integrated in a training plan that top management is willing to support and promote.

Depending on the degree of certainty about goals and cause-effect relations (means), certain strategies will have to be utilized. In one situation there is high certainty about goals and means, so the logical behavior is to implement the indicated training program. In a second situation, there is agreement on means but not on goals. The likely reason for this is a tendency to have "faith" in a training technique if it has worked once before. The appropriate strategy is to challenge this assumption and to ask that a rationale for a particular training method be given before it is implemented. In a third situation, agreement on both goals and means is low, which obviously suggests the need to initiate a diagnostic process and search for agreement on both goals and means. In a fourth situation, goals are specific and agreed on, so a controlled search for methods should begin.

Trainers who make this kind of analysis are contextual strategists who are guiding a process of change and development in the direction of the highest possible certainty along both dimensions—goals and cause-effect relations. This process may not seem to be directly related to the organization's immediate problems, but it represents a conscious effort to create conditions under which it will be possible to attack and eliminate these problems at the lowest cost to the organization.[22]

■ INTERNAL AND EXTERNAL TRAINING

Internal training is provided by the agency itself, utilizing its own premises and resources. *External training* takes place at facilities outside the agency, either elsewhere within government or outside it, such as institutions of learning, foundations, and industrial or commercial organizations. Examples of external training *within* government are the Office of Personnel Mangement's training centers for middle-level managers and its Federal Executive Institute for top-level executives.

Although internal training can be closely controlled by the agency management, it has several drawbacks. For one thing,

[22]Felix A. Nigro and Lloyd G. Nigro, "The Trainer as a Strategist," *Public Personnel Management* 3, no. 3 (May–June 1974): 193–198.

many agencies are unable to support an in-house training staff of the size, diversity, and specialized nature required to meet all training needs that might arise. Besides staffing costs, it is expensive to buy and maintain the equipment, libraries, and other facilities needed for a comprehensive intraorganizational training program. Internal training tends also to be parochial, frequently serving as a vehicle for teaching standard procedures and inculcating organizational viewpoints and values. In such case, it is largely limited to functioning as a mechanism for organizational maintenance.

Change-oriented or "broadening" training for employees is difficult to execute successfully within the constraining atmosphere of long-established agency attitudes. Testing new ideas or experimenting with alternative behavioral patterns usually produces best results in a challenging as well as supportive social-psychological environment. Edgar H. Schein describes the limitations of internal training as follows:

> The essential elements to unfreezing are the removal of supports for the old attitudes, the saturation of the environment with the new attitudes to be acquired, a minimizing of threat, and a maximizing of support for any change in the right direction . . . it becomes immediately apparent that training programs or other activities which are conducted in the organization at the place of work for a certain number of hours per day or week are far less likely to unfreeze and subsequently influence the participant than those programs which remove him for varying lengths of time from his regular work situation and normal social relationships.[23]

Although external training takes employees away from their normal work environment, it too presents problems. One is the difficulty, previously mentioned, that trainees may experience when they return to their agencies and try to use what they have learned. It cannot be assumed that the knowledges, skills, and viewpoints acquired will fit easily into established organizational routines. If agency management fails to encourage use on the job of what has been learned, some trainees will be frustrated when they attempt to do so, and others will not even try to apply the new methods and ideas. Best results are achieved when management actively participates in the planning phase of external training

---

[23]Edgar H. Schein, "Management Development as a Process of Influence," in David R. Hampton (ed.), *Behavioral Concepts in Management* (Belmont, Calif.: Dickensen, 1968), pp. 114–115.

and is prepared to make organization changes to accommodate the expected impact of the training; also when there is a clear understanding throughout the agency of the relationships between the training and the needs of the organization, and management should provide psychological support for trainees when they return; otherwise, the consequences for both the trainees and the organization could be highly dysfunctional.

■ TRAINING METHODS

Successful training depends on the appropriateness of the instructional methods chosen and the skill with which they are employed. The relative effectiveness of the available techniques depends on many factors, such as the substance of what is being imparted or taught and the age, experience, and other characteristics of the participants. Training specialists sometimes become overenthusiastic in extolling the virtues of one method over all others. In practice, several different training devices are usually employed in any one program because no one method is invariably the most effective. Some of the instructional methods commonly used are discussed below.

On-the-Job Training

In on-the-job training, workers are instructed while they carry out their regularly assigned duties and responsibilities. An example is apprenticeship training given beginners by journeymen in the skilled trades. Journeymen carpenters or plumbers, for example, assign tasks to an apprentice, explain how the work should be performed, demonstrating the use of tools, and then monitor the apprentice's performance. During the training process both journeymen and apprentices are carrying out daily work routines and are expected to meet production schedules. The apprentices may not turn out much work, but they do produce something while *learning* the job.

As another example, the "rookie" FBI agent may be assigned to accompany an experienced investigator who is responsible both for carrying out his or her regular work and for training the recruit. The senior agent may have to question suspected lawbreakers or witnesses to crimes; the junior officer notes the methods used, participating very little in the actual work, but is there to help if needed and is constantly absorbing important details.

As the above illustrations indicate, "coaching" is an integral aspect of on-the-job training. Note this description:

> In coaching, the supervisor does more than merely help a subordinate perform his job with ever-increasing competence. The coach's aim is to help someone else exploit his [her] potentialities as a self-developing individual. He [she] gives his [her] subordinate increasing opportunities to perform difficult tasks that are not far enough beyond the subordinate's capacity to break him [her] down. It also involves enough counselling to help the subordinate keep afloat but not enough to save him [her] the painful effort of self-propulsion and self-instruction.[24]

Coaching also is exemplified by apprenticeship systems for managerial personnel, in which the training takes place within the context of a one-to-one relationship between the trainee and an experienced executive. In the assistantship model, trainees are assigned to executives as aides or deputies and are given a series of developmental assignments to familiarize them with the activities and problems of the particular work activity. The administrator-coach not only provides information and guidance but also serves as a role model for trainees. As trainees note how the coach perceives problems, copes with different situations, and deals with superiors and subordinates, they learn and internalize organizationally appropriate behaviors. The coach must be prepared to devote the necessary time and energy to working closely with the trainee, carefully selecting problems to be dealt with, and providing feedback at the most telling points in the learning process. The coach cannot regard the trainee as a competitor or simply a convenient handler of menial tasks. A trusting relationship must be developed in which the trainee feels able to rely on the executive's judgment and feedback.

Most on-the-job training is carried out by supervisors, and coaching—formal or informal—is basically a supervisory responsibility. A training-conscious organization is one in which supervisors are trained in coaching skills and evaluated on how well they perform in this respect. Ultimately, an organization's on-the-job training capacity will depend on the coaching skills of all levels of supervision.

---

[24]Gross, *Managing of Organizations*, p. 884.

Rotation

In job rotation schemes, employees' work assignments are varied on a planned basis in order to expose them to a succession of valuable learning experiences. Trainees may be rotated from one aspect of an activity to another until they have obtained experience in all aspects, as when personnel interns are assigned in turn to each division of the personnel office. Rotation may be between organization units in the same kind of work, the purpose being to provide the stimulus of a new work environment, or it may be between different functions, such as from line to staff activities. The transfers may be for limited periods of time or on an indefinite basis, but the purpose is the same: to help the employee develop his or her potential.

Individualized planning and coaching are integral elements of sophisticated rotation systems. Job transfers are geared to each employee's needs and capabilities, so that the employee is kept on each job long enough to be able to profit from it. Excessive rotation is a real danger, particularly if the assumption is that the change in and of itself will benefit the employee. Without attention from management, rotation can become a formalistic and largely purposeless ritual. If this happens, the "rotated employee is in danger of learning superficially, like a tourist in a foreign land."[25]

Lectures

The lecture is an economical method of delivering factual knowledge to large groups of people, but, as many teachers and students know, there is no guarantee that learning will take place. A major problem is the passivity of the targets. In the lecture format, communication flows in only one direction—from the lecturer to the listeners. Trainees do not have much opportunity to practice what they have "learned" and receive comparatively little feedback.

Since the lecture technique is geared to groups, not individuals, everybody gets the same treatment at the same pace, and individual abilities, interests, and motives are not recognized. Also, when the purpose is to present ideas and problems, as in management training, many people believe discussion usually is more effective than straight lecture. They say that the lecturer tends to be dogmatic and to teach principles or rules of conduct which the

---

[25]Leavitt, *Managerial Psychology*, p. 306.

listener is expected to accept without questioning. There is little evidence that lectures significantly change attitudes or behavior.[26]

Discussions

Guided by a leader who is competent in group dynamics, problem-centered discussion groups can be an effective learning device. The discussion method permits free communication between the discussion leader and the members of the group on the one hand, as well as between members of the group on the other. In this "permissive" atmosphere, each participant is encouraged to clarify his or her thinking and to ponder carefully the statements of others.

In effectively conducted discussions, the participants are trained to think for themselves; they are not presented with ready-made solutions or statements of principles and, it is believed, are more likely to apply on the job what they have absorbed from the group interaction. Good discussion leaders do not steer the discussion along the lines of their own thinking. However, they see to it that the group establishes a purpose or goal and that the discussion does not drift from the subject or become a forum for the expression of individual opinions.

The Case Method

Both in internal training in government and in classes and seminars at outside institutions of learning, the case method often is used. In fact, many of the advantages which are claimed for discussion as a training technique are based largely on the successful use of cases.

The "case" is a description, usually in written but sometimes in filmed form, of a real-life situation that has occurred in some phase of administration. In human relations training, cases are selected that illustrate problems arising in the relationships among people within a particular organization, not only at the same level but also at different levels, as well as situations involving relationships with people outside the organization. The facts in the case are presented in detail; sometimes the solution which was reached to the particular problem is also included. Another technique is to include

---

[26]United Nations, *Handbook of Training in the Public Service* (New York: Department of Economic and Social Affairs, Public Administration Branch, 1966), pp. 235–241.

everything but the solution and then let those participating in the discussion suggest one. Cases may be lengthy or relatively brief. There is no set format which is used in preparing them; different ways of presenting the material are used.

The advantage of the case method is that the participants deal with concrete situations and exchange opinions as to how to best deal with the problems contained in the case being discussed. Thus, there is sharing of experience, exposure to the questions and critical comments of the other discussants, and the opportunity to develop "habits of mind that are particularly relevant to real-life tasks and action."[27]

Role-Playing

Role-playing is a form of practice experience based on case situations. In the procedure usually followed, a conference leader prepares the case beforehand in writing and, as the session opens, distributes copies to each person present. In human relations training, the case typically presents a problem involving two or more persons, such as an employee's having done something for which he or she should be disciplined. One person in the group plays the role of the supervisor, and another acts out the part of the subordinate. On the basis of the facts presented in the case, the supervisor calls in the subordinate and administers discipline just as would take place in real life. The other members of the group, constituting the audience, critically watch the performance of each principal in the act. Once the act is concluded, the conference leader takes over and asks them to give their comments.

Frequently, the criticisms they make are helpful and illuminating to those who have played the roles. In real life, the supervisor may be unaware of such subtleties as the tone or inflection of his or her voice. Perhaps the supervisor's whole approach in trying to correct the subordinate's conduct is wrong. All this may come to light during the discussions that follow, but everyone is exposed to the same scrutiny and criticism. Sometimes the act is repeated until everyone present has played one or both of the roles.

---

[27]John Desmond Glover, Ralph M. Hower, and Renato Tagiuri, *The Administrator: Cases on Human Aspects of Management,* 5th ed. (Homewood, Ill.: Irwin, 1973), p. xiv.

On occasion, role-playing is the spontaneous culmination of an animated discussion during a supervisory training conference. The discussion leader has not prepared any case beforehand, but someone describes a problem in supervision. At this point, another participant advances his or her opinion as to how such a problem should be handled and volunteers to act out the part of the supervisor or is asked to do so by the conference leader. The other parts are assigned, and so the discussion suddenly becomes a role-playing session. This is one of the advantages of this training technique—it can be used flexibly without the need for extended advance preparation. All that is necessary is an imaginative disposition on the part of the conference participants and their willingness to be guinea pigs.

Role-playing is an inexpensive training method which deeply involves the role-players and usually maintains high interest on the part of the observers. Human relations skills are practiced under conditions permitting a wide margin of experimental trial and error, and, since the mistakes made are fictional only, they do not cost the enterprise anything.

Simulation and Management Games

Simulations have been used widely in training for technical and physical skills and are now popular in management training as well. In a simulation, trainees are placed in carefully contrived situations and asked to carry out certain assignments or to accomplish specified objectives. Participants are assigned roles, and each is provided with a "data" package with information on the situation, roles, and rules of the game. Trainees face a series of tasks relating to managing relationships, organizing to accomplish objectives, and designing and acting out problem-solving strategies. During the simulation, individual participants and groups are asked to make decisions and solve problems as they arise. Actions taken at one stage affect the course of the simulation as it moves through succeeding phases. Some of the more sophisticated simulations use computers to generate information and feedback on decision outcomes.

Because feedback on all of these activities is given rapidly at appropriate points in the simulation, the participants can apply this feedback within the context of the simulation and learn more effective behaviors as they proceed. After the simulation is finished, a debriefing or group critique of what transpired takes place in which the entire sequence of events is examined in the light of relevant concepts and practices.

The primary value of simulations and games is their capacity to motivate and involve trainees actively in bridging the gap between theory and practice. Situational thinking is required, and real-world issues must be dealt with under conditions of uncertainty and risk. Participants get a feel for the importance of teamwork and communication. A well-designed simulation can be generalized and related to similar processes and problems in many different organizations. If this goal is achieved, the simulation is far more than an entertaining game; it is a powerful learning experience.[28]

Obviously, as Schacter writes, "It is extraordinarily difficult to develop scenarios that test how people react in extreme or provocative situations." She points out, for example, that "police recruits cannot be placed in an atmosphere where their lives are endangered to see how they handle themselves under fire." Referring to collective bargaining simulations, she notes that the players lack the "vested interest" in victory that grips management and union negotiators in a real-life situation. Yet, she suggests, this can be counteracted by basing a student's grade on "team achievement at the bargaining table."[29] Presumably, team achievement would be judged not only by ability and persistence in presenting and maintaining a bargaining stance but also by flexibility in making trade-offs with the other team and reaching a settlement.

■ ORGANIZATION DEVELOPMENT

Organization Development (OD) has been defined as a "long-range effort to introduce consciously planned change into an organization in ways that involve its members, both in diagnosis of problems and perceptions of change."[30] Specifically, it "involves the application of behavioral science knowledge to facilitate change, to build

[28]See Gilbert B. Siegel, "Gaming Simulation in the Teaching of Public Personnel Administration," *Public Personnel Management* 6, no. 4 (July–August 1977).

[29]Hindy Lauer Schacter, "Simulations for Training and Assessment: The Problem of Relevance to the Real World," *Public Personnel Management* 9, no. 3 (1980): 226.

[30]Robert T. Golembiewski (ed.), "Symposium on Public Sector OD," *Southern Review of Public Administration* 1, no. 4 (March 1978): 408.

skills in people, and to resolve problems; and these problems can be at the personal, extrapersonal, small group, intergroup, or organizational levels."[31] OD trainers, whether in-house or outside consultants, jointly with the personnel of an organization seek to diagnose accurately the cause of problems that interfere with organizational effectiveness and to agree upon the interventions (change processes) deemed most likely to improve the organization's functioning. In the process of making this diagnosis, the organization structure as well as interpersonal relationships are explored since structure and human relations are closely related.

OD is based on the assumption that in "most organizations, the level of interpersonal support, trust, and cooperation is much lower than is desirable and necessary."[32] Often conflict between different individuals and groups within the organization takes place on a destructive "win-lose" basis, rather than being resolved through "win-win" strategies whereby both sides to the struggle develop a more constructive relationship.

In the action research model of OD, information is collected about the organization and its individuals and groups; that information is used for "organizational and problem diagnosis"; the agreed-upon interventions (changes) are implemented; and based on feedback on the results obtained, new strategies are developed and tested. Numerous different OD interventions are employed, depending on the diagnosis of the organization's difficulties; team-building, modifications in organization structure, changes in supervisory methods, individual counseling of employees are some examples. Also sometimes employed is sensitivity training in which the participants meet with the trainer to explore the impact of their behavior on themselves and others.[33] Sensitivity training has been much criticized for alleged destructive impact on the participants, and because of the psychological approaches used in OD in general it is obvious that much depends upon the competence of the OD trainer. After several decades of use in the public service, OD generally is regarded as an established and potentially effective way of changing behavior in organizations.

---

[31]R. Wayne Boss, "Organization Development: A Vehicle for Improving the Quality of Work Life," in William B. Eddy (ed.), *Handbook of Organization Management* (New York: Dekker, 1983), p. 257.

[32]Ibid., p. 259.

[33]Ibid., pp. 260–265.

■ INTERNSHIPS

Internships merit special consideration in any discussion of training activities because they provide a bridge between theoretical preparation and "live" or practical work. Our reference here is to internships for college students as part of their academic programs or after they receive their degrees. As the term "internship" is now used, it may also refer to persons who have work experience but have entered training programs for a new kind of work or career. For them, the internship experience is a bridge to that new work or career. The elements of internship programs are basically the same whether or not the interns in government have had other work experience.

College student interns spend a specified period (usually from six months to a year) working in an administrative agency or the legislature as an integral part of their educational program and professional training. Although practices vary from school to school, interns often take classes concurrently. They are sometimes paid by the agency, with summer internships a convenient arrangement.

The college student may be preparing for a career in some subject matter area such as forestry, agriculture, or social work, or for a career as an administrator. Our remarks will be centered on administrative internships for college students, but many of our comments will apply also to internships in other kinds of work.

The fundamental purpose of the internship experience is to place students in an environment where they can begin to form *personal comprehension* of the administrative process.[34] The internship brings students face-to-face with the fact that administration involves real people, real choices, and real consequences. Working in a public agency allows interns to test the concepts and techniques they have learned in the classroom and to see how they are applied in practice. Perhaps even more important, they can acquire and internalize a "feel" for administrative problems and managerial styles. Active participation and observation are the keys. As Mary Parker Follett, one of the founders of modern organizational psychology, put it: "Concepts can never be presented

---

[34]Michael Polanyi, *The Study of Man* (Chicago: University of Chicago Press, 1959), pp. 11–39.

to me merely, they must be knitted into the structure of my being, and this can be done only through my own activity."[35]

The internship also serves the function of introducing the intern to "role models and acceptable standard of practice" in the line of work. As James Wolf writes, "The internship is a powerful socializer vis-à-vis the values and norms of the profession." Internships also "help students learn how to establish career linkages with practitioners in their field of interest(s). . . . Students can use internship contacts as counselors, mentors, and/or tipsters to career information and job possibilities. Also, just as the internship gives the employer the opportunity to size up students for possible full-time employment with the agency, it also helps students assess their competencies for possible future career choices. By testing the knowledge and skills which they develop in the classroom, students can ascertain the likelihood of career success in given roles."[36]

An effective internship program is built on continuing cooperative arrangements between public agencies and educational institutions. Bilateral planning and execution are needed. Both sides must be clear as to the roles interns will play, the commitments and responsibilities of all parties, and the overall rationale of the internship in work practice as well as in educational terms. So that all concerned know their responsibilities and roles, joint committees of administrators, teachers, and students are valuable in the planning and evaluation of internship programs. Someone in the agency, perhaps the personnel director or an aide, should supervise and monitor the on-the-job performance of interns, and a representative of the school should be formally designated as responsible for the academic phase of the program.[37] Many internship programs have produced poor results because the institution does not free enough time of the academic coordinator to permit following closely the progress of the interns and/or the failure of agency representatives to provide meaningful work experiences for the interns.

The interns should not be isolated from their academic home

---

[35]Mary Parker Follett, *Creative Experience* (Gloucester, Mass.: Peter Smith, 1951), p. 151.

[36]James Wolf, "The Student Responsibility Model of Public Service Internships," *Southern Review of Public Administration* 3, no. 2 (September 1979). See also Sherwood, "The Education and Training of Public Managers," pp. 53–56.

[37]United Nations, *Handbook of Training in the Public Service*, pp. 255–258.

bases. Too often, the internship experience is compartmentalized, and little effort is made to integrate it into the mainstream of the students' education in public administration. This is unfortunate because the basic purpose of an internship is to help the student integrate concepts and experiences into a meaningful whole. Guidance and feedback from faculty and other students should be readily available, perhaps through seminar meetings in which students, faculty, and practicing administrators can meet on a regular basis to discuss and analyze each intern's experiences and perceptions.

Interns contribute skills and viewpoints that can be profitably tapped if the organization's personnel makes the effort to do so. Obviously, the first step is to place interns where they are most likely to help. While interns may properly be placed in administrative units that are understaffed, their indiscriminate use as "labor" destroys the purpose of the internship. Work that is relevant to each intern's interests and career goals is far more likely to stimulate a meaningful contribution. It is essential that agency personnel make interns feel welcome and valued, rather than treating them as a burden that must be tolerated. This tends to become a self-fulfilling prophecy, in that neglect by the host agency leads to apathy and disinterest on the part of the intern. Concern and support for the intern, in contrast, provide fertile ground for the stimulation and growth of motivation and commitment.

■ EVALUATION OF TRAINING PROGRAMS

For the expenditure of public funds on any program or activity to be justified, there should, of course, be clear evidence that the desired results are being obtained. For various reasons, it usually is very difficult to demonstrate that training programs are effective in improving the capacities and performance of the participants. This makes training programs particularly vulnerable to budget reductions and even elimination in times of financial stringency and taxpayer resentment over the costs of government. In most cases, the results of training programs are much less visible to legislators, taxpayers, and others than work-load data for other phases of the personnel program such as recruitment and examinations. While numbers of recruits and examinations do not tell anything about the quality of either the persons hired or the tests, it is recognized that some recruitment must take place and that candidates must be examined. Training tends to be regarded as a dubious activity no matter what its potentiality that can safely be cut back or terminated.

For some kinds of work in government, those where performance can be measured by units of work produced, evaluation of training programs is relatively easy. The output of such workers as machine operators can be physically examined to determine whether or not it is satisfactory, and their production can be measured before and after training. In some kinds of training for non-production workers, such as reading improvement, physical counts of performance can also be made before and after the instruction given (in this case number of comprehended words per minute), but there are only a few such programs.

For most government employees, quantitative measurements of performance are unavailable or, where available, are unreliable because they do not indicate how well the employee is doing the job. The services of researchers cannot be evaluated on the basis of how many reports they write or how many requests for data they answer, any more than a medical doctor's worth can be measured by the number of patients served. In a great many government jobs, such as those of executives, the personal qualities required are intangible, and agreement may even be lacking as to what the critical duties and responsibilities of the position are.

In a succinct analysis, Enid Beaumont, executive director of the National Institute of Public Affairs, explains why evaluation of training programs is so very difficult. For evaluation studies to be sound methodologically, comparisons should be made between the job performance of the trainees after receiving the training with that of control group(s) of persons who did not participate in the training program. The problem is in finding persons to include in control groups who can be considered the equivalents of those who participated in the training. There are many individual differences in employees, and these differences may provide better explanations of quality of job performance than whether or not a person participated in a particular training program. As Beaumont writes, "The clear isolation of the variable of formal training out of the myriad of forces upon individuals and organizations is somewhat like the blind describing an elephant." Evaluation studies should also be longitudinal, that is, study changes in the later job performance of the trainees over a number of years, but, because of the limited financial resources devoted to training in government and other difficulties, such studies are very rare.

Because of the problems, few evaluation studies have been made of governmental training activities that meet the methodological standards of "pure research social scientists."[38] Too often, the only evaluation that takes place is to ascertain the opinions of the trainees as to what they learned from the training sessions. The method usually used for this purpose is to have them fill out unsigned questionnaires at the end of the sessions. Much cynicism is expressed about this method because often the trainees have been guests of the sponsoring organization, even being housed at its facilities, and consequently are reluctant to criticize the host. There also is a tendency to complete the questionnaires hastily in order to make airline reservations or otherwise return to work. The procedure is not valueless because it can produce significant feedback from the trainees concerning their reactions to the training. However, since the purpose of the training is to improve job performance and capacities *after* the training, simply getting the trainees' reactions cannot be considered adequate evaluation of the training program. The same point can be made about measurements of what the trainees learned by administering tests to them during or at the end of the training. Unless it can be demonstrated that these test scores correlate positively with the quality of trainees' later job performance, this also does not constitute adequate evaluation of the training.

In the case of executives, it is not only difficult to get agreement on the critical elements in the job, but also on the measurements of effectiveness in the job. If the measurements of executive performance are in error, obviously the evaluation results of executive development programs are flawed.

As Beaumont emphasizes, while these formidable difficulties in training evaluation do exist, evaluation efforts should continue, and she indicates five major areas in which these efforts should take place:

1. Review of the opportunities provided employees of all kinds for developmental activities and of the method used in determining training objectives. Relevant questions are: Are training programs changed in accordance with changes in the organization's objectives? Are line officials "closely involved"

---

[38]Enid Beaumont, "Training Evaluation: Opportunities and Constraints," in Chester A. Newland (ed.), "Symposium: Public Sector Training—Diversity, Diversion, Discipline," *Southern Review of Public Administration* 2, no. 4 (March 1979): 498.

in the decisions reached as to training needs and objectives? They are in a very good position to determine "performance deficiencies."

2. Are the career development plans prepared for individual employees "supportive" of and "compatible" with organizational goals?

3. Are training officials included in agency workforce planning at all levels of the agency?

4. Are studies made of the "impact of formal training on organizational performance even if not specifically meeting the research obligations of social science"?

5. Are reviews made of the "level of staff professionalism" of the "training team"?[39]

Some research of this nature is taking place, so there is reason to be hopeful about the future of training evaluation.

■ TRAINING: AN INVESTMENT IN PERSONAL AND ORGANIZATIONAL RENEWAL

Before closing this chapter, we want to reemphasize that training can be a vehicle for organizational and personal development. The rapid pace of social and technological change has made adaptation a virtual necessity for both organizations and individuals. The days when high school or college graduates could reasonably assume that they were prepared for a lifelong career or vocation are gone. People now face the prospect of a relatively continuous educational and training process throughout their lifetimes. The same is true of organizations—their survival and effectiveness depend upon willingness of management to invest in the career development of their employees.

The concept of training as a lifetime process is one many persons in the public service are reluctant to accept. As Clark Kerr states:

> There is a case for some degree of generality in the educational system because of the rapidity of change and growth of knowledge during the course of a career. A technically trained work force needs to be able to follow and adapt to changes in its specialties and to learn to shift to new fields. Generality is also required for those coordinating and leading the specialists.[40]

---

[39]Ibid., 506–507.
[40]Clark Kerr et al., *Industrialism and Industrial Man* (New York: Oxford University Press, 1964), p. 20.

To say, as some do, that training is a luxury or something that cannot be afforded is to say that we are willing to accept the gradual erosion of our human and organizational capabilities. The question to be asked of managers, personnel administrators, and the public is: Can we afford not to educate and train our public employees?

BIBLIOGRAPHY

Beckhard, Richard. *Organization Development: Strategies and Models*. Reading, Mass.: Addison-Wesley, 1969.

Boss, R. Wayne. "Organization Development: A Vehicle for Improving the Quality of Work Life." In *Handbook of Organization Management*, edited by William B. Eddy. New York: Dekker, 1983.

Byers, Kenneth T., ed. *Employee Training and Development in the Public Sector*. Washington, D.C.: International Personnel Management Association, 1970.

Garson, G. David. "Personnel Training and Development." In *Handbook on Public Personnel Administration and Labor Relations*, edited by Jack Rabin, Thomas Vocino, W. Bartley Hildreth, and Gerald J. Miller. New York: Dekker, 1983.

Schein, Edgar H., and Bennis, Warren A. *Personal and Organizational Change Through Group Methods*. New York: Wiley, 1965.

Sherwood, Frank P. "The Education and Training of Public Managers." In *Handbook of Organization Management*, edited by William B. Eddy. New York: Dekker, 1983.

Tickner, Fred J. *Modern Staff Training*. London: University of London Press, 1952.

United Nations. *Handbook of Training in the Public Service*. New York: Department of Economics and Social Affairs, Public Administration Branch, United Nations, 1966.

14 Grievances and Appeals

Until the introduction of collective bargaining in government on an extensive basis, formal grievance procedures were not a very important part of public personnel administration. Indeed, in many jurisdictions they were not even required. As we use the term "grievance" here, it refers to employee complaints about any work-related matter and thus is not limited to appeals of dismissals and other actions taken by management against the employee (adverse actions).

The early civil service commissions were much concerned with protecting the employee from removal for political partisan reasons. As the concept of personnel administration expanded in the 1930s and thereafter, attention was given to trying to understand *all* causes of employee dissatisfaction, including those with their source in poor supervisory practices, and formal procedures were developed for hearing grievances. In large jurisdictions, the individual agencies were required to establish such formal procedures in conformance with civil service commission guidelines. The appeals jurisdiction of the commission often was limited to adverse actions with all other complaints channeled through the agency grievance procedures.

One sign of an effective grievance procedure is that it is invoked by more than just a few employees, but this often was not the case because employees lacked confidence in the procedure or feared retaliation for invoking it. Because the agency procedures were management-adopted, often without real consultation with employees and their representatives, workers tended to distrust them. Furthermore, in the administration of the procedure, management often was hostile to or unenthusiastic about representation of the grievant by representatives of employee organizations. For example, President Kennedy's Task Force on Employee-Management

Relations in the Federal Service found that "for many Government agencies, complaints and dissatisfactions are considered to be purely personal problems which have no bearing on group or collective relationships," whereas ordinarily a private company "will look upon its grievance system as part of an overall industrial relations structure."[1]

Collective bargaining has altered this situation by creating a bilateral structure for determining conditions of work in which negotiated grievance procedures play much the same role as in the private sector. In collective bargaining programs at all levels of government, the great majority of agreements, just as in the private sector, now contain a grievance procedure and also provide for final-step resolution of grievances by binding arbitration. Since the union negotiates the procedure with management and an independent arbitrator makes the final ruling on a grievance, employees trust the procedure and do not fear retaliation for using it because they know that such punitive action by management constitutes an unfair labor practice under the agreement. The continuous monitoring by unions referred to in Chapter 6 takes place largely in the course of administration of the grievance procedure. The new importance of grievance resolution is evidenced by the fact that, whereas previously consideration of this topic was scant in the literature of public personnel administration, it is now abundant and constantly growing.

In jurisdictions without collective bargaining, management-adopted grievance procedures continue, but management now often is more tolerant of union representation of the grievant. Where collective bargaining programs function, negotiated grievance procedures often do not completely replace the management-adopted ones.

For one thing, collective agreements may not have been negotiated in some work units and, even where they have been, supervisors often are excluded from the bargaining unit and, in the absence of a management-adopted or agency procedure, as it is often called, would have no procedure under which they could file complaints. Also, although in the bargaining unit, an employee may prefer to grieve under an agency procedure and is usually

---

[1]President's Task Force on Employee-Management Relations in the Federal Service, A Policy for Employee-Management Cooperation in the Federal Service (Washington, D.C.: Government Printing Office, 1961), p. 22.

given the option of using the contract or the agency procedure for the same kind of complaint. However, he or she may not utilize both procedures (just one bite of the apple is permitted). Sometimes the scope of the negotiated procedure is narrow, and the employee utilizes the agency system because many kinds of complaints can be filed under it. Furthermore, the win-loss ratio may be better for the grievants under the agency than under the negotiated procedure.

In this chapter, we will describe both management-adopted and negotiated procedures, the latter at greater length because of the spread of collective bargaining, and binding grievance arbitration will be discussed in detail.

■ MANAGEMENT-ADOPTED PROCEDURES

In a study published some years ago, William G. Scott documents how in many kinds of organizations—private businesses, unions, the Roman Catholic Church, the military, and federal, state, and local government agencies—management has acted unilaterally to establish internal appeals procedures that are in effect systems of justice for the employees. Scott believes that the "formal organization is as much a legal system as it is an economic, social, or information system." He examines various explanations of why management in violation of the scalar principle (determinate hierarchy and unity of command) accepts the restraints on its discretion imposed by appeals systems. He concludes that the best explanation is that creation of appeal systems is in fact consistent with classic organization theory, particularly with the "coordinative principle," best expressed as "unity of action for obtaining goals." In his opinion, in classical theory there is a hierarchical ranking of principles, and some principles like chain of command may be "suspended in whole or in part if coordination is improved by so doing."[2] Coordination is improved by appeals systems because these systems facilitate cooperative relationships within the organization. Another explanation of management-adopted appeals mechanisms is that they are inspired by considerations of industrial humanism and of respect for the democratic principle. We have

---

[2]William C. Scott, *The Management of Conflict: Appeals Systems in Organizations* (Homewood, Ill.: Dorsey, 1965), p. v.

presented this theory of management-adopted procedures because there also is a theoretical basis for the negotiated procedures—namely, that they are the only really fair ones because they are jointly formulated and operated by management and the union.

It is difficult to generalize about the detailed features of management-adopted grievance systems, but some observations can be made. Much emphasis is placed on the responsibility of supervisors to try as promptly as possible to resolve grievances informally so that they do not fester and deepen the grievant's discontent. Accordingly, it is often provided that employees should initially present their grievances to their immediate superiors orally, rather than in writing. The informality of this process, it is believed, creates an atmosphere in which it is easier for employee and supervisor to reach a solution. If the grievance cannot be resolved in this way, the employee then submits it in writing to the immediate supervisor. If the supervisor denies the grievance, the employee can then appeal to higher levels, up to the agency head. Since there has been an unfortunate history of providing so many levels of appeal that much delay ensues before the final decision on a grievance is made, efforts are made to keep these levels to a minimum.

At a certain step in the procedure, the grievant often can request a hearing and submit written documentation of his or her side of the case and give oral testimony. In state and local governments, the hearing takes place before a "hearing examiner, an appeals board, a merit council or civil service commission . . . whose decision may or may not be final."[3] Sometimes several hearings are provided, which draws out the total process. In the federal service, the grievant may appeal from the agency to the Merit Systems Protection Board (MSPB) which provides a hearing and whose decision is final.[4]

■ NEGOTIATED PROCEDURES

To understand the full range of matters that can be grieved under a negotiated grievance procedure, the contract must be read in its

---

[3]Robert N. White, "State Grievance and Appeals Systems: A Survey," *Public Personnel Management* 10, no. 3 (Fall 1981): 313.

[4]See *Survey of Appeal and Grievance Systems Available to Federal Employees*, General Accounting Office, Washington, D.C., October 20, 1983.

entirety. Agreements vary greatly in the scope of the rights and benefits granted the employees, as well as in the mutual responsibilities assumed by management and the union. If the grievance definition is limited to disputes arising over the interpretation and application of the terms of the contract, and the contract scope is very restricted, then grievances filed under the agreement will be far fewer than when both contract scope and the grievance definition are broad. As Phillips L. Garman writes, an example of a very broad grievance definition is "any problem" of the employee or any "difference between the union and the employer."[5] Usually the definition is not that comprehensive; however, often it extends beyond the contract provisions to any complaint over application to the employee of any existing laws, rules, procedures, regulations, administrative orders, or even work rules of the employer. Such a grievance definition makes many matters grievable even if the contract covers very few matters.

Many management officials object to the broad grievance definitions because they believe that when the agreements also provide for binding arbitration the "vast majority of management decisions on personnel matters" will be subject to "potential reversal" by arbitrators. The quoted words appear in a report by the National League of Cities and the Police Executive Research Forum on police collective bargaining agreements. The report continues:

> Other public employers adopt a different rationale, based on the belief that many or all employee or union complaints should be grievable. They believe that such a liberal policy will diminish employee dissatisfaction and thereby improve police officer morale and productivity. This line of reasoning may explain why a broad definition of grievance was included in a significant minority of the contracts studied.[6]

Grievances may be filed by individual employees or on their behalf by the majority union, or by a group of employees having the same grievance, or on behalf of such group by the union. Under some agreements, the union can file a grievance against the

---

[5]Phillips L. Garman, "Grievance Procedures in Health Care Establishments," *Journal of Health and Human Resources Administration* 2, no. 1 (August 1979): 76.

[6]Steven A. Rynecki, Douglas A. Cairns, and Donald J. Cairns, *Police Collective Bargaining Agreements: A National Management Survey* (Washington, D.C.: National League of Cities and Police Executive Research Forum, 1978), p. 16.

employer (e.g., failure to maintain the safety conditions required in the contract) or by the employer against the union (e.g., failure to fulfill the contractual obligation to counsel union members on compliance with safety regulations). Group grievances save considerable time both for the employer and the union in investigating complaints and in preparing for meetings to attempt to resolve the grievances. As the example of safety procedures shows, provisions for the employer and the union to grieve against the other permits going directly to the believed source of the difficulty.

The number of steps or levels of review varies, but often there are three or four steps. Often the grievance is not submitted in writing at the first (informal) step, "which is in many ways one of mutual investigation."[7] Rather the grievance is presented in writing at the second step on a form mutually agreed to by the parties with space provided for management's response and its reasons for accepting or denying the grievance.

Respecting discharge and other disciplinary action, some agreements provide for submitting the grievance at a specified intermediate, rather than the initial step, because the authority of lower echelon management personnel in such matters is limited and because it is desired that final disciplinary decisions not be delayed excessively.

In those agreements that permit filing of grievances by the union against management and vice versa, some require the grievance to follow the same route as that of an individual employee. Others specify two separate procedures—one for employee grievances, the other for union or employer grievances. If a single procedure is required for all grievances, it is sometimes provided that union or employer grievances skip the informal step and be initiated at the first formal step, which means in writing.

In some agreements, as the final step before arbitration or in lieu of arbitration, grievance committees or panels are employed to obtain and analyze the facts relating to the agreement or to try to mediate the grievance. In some cases, there is experimentation with a combination of mediation and arbitration. Sometimes, the factfinding is by a hearing examiner, rather than by a committee.

Since a number of employees may have the same grievance

---

[7]Garman, "Grievance Procedures in Health Care Establishments," 78. See also Kurt H. Decker, "Public-Sector Grievance Arbitration Procedures," in Jack Rabin, Thomas Vocino, W. Bartley Hildreth, and Gerald J. Miller (eds.), *Handbook on Public Personnel Administration and Labor Relations* (New York: Dekker, 1983).

about a working condition, provision may be made for consolidation of these complaints into a group grievance.

Time limits are usually provided for submission of the grievance and for its processing at each step in the procedure. These time limits include deadlines that management must meet in giving its reply. Typically, the deadline for initial submission specifies a certain number of days after the occurrence that caused the grievance or after the employee could reasonably be expected to have learned of the incident. This illustrates the arbitrator's discretion because he or she may be confronted with conflicting testimony as to when the employee could possibly have learned of the incident (e.g., promotion or other favored treatment of another employee). Without time limits on initial submission, "individual employees may file grievances many months after alleged violations have occurred, when witnesses might not remember the incident and documents may have been mislaid or destroyed."[8]

As to the steps after initial submission, the deadline for appealing a grievance that has been denied to the next step in the procedure varies. For some steps (e.g., appeal to arbitration), the deadline often is longer than that for the other steps. If the union does not appeal within the time limits, the grievance usually is considered terminated. On the other hand, if management fails to make a decision within the time limits for giving the response, the grievance automatically moves to the next step. Without these step-to-step deadlines, grievances would pile up and delays would be excessive.

From the management standpoint, Decker writes, "This minimizes the union's opportunity for backlogging grievances between the grievance procedure's last step and arbitration. Unions attempt this for two reasons. First, it enables them to establish a 'trading situation' with the public employer because of the number of grievances scheduled for arbitration. Second, it is hoped that many of these grievances will be heard by the same arbitrator, maximizing the chances for 'split' decisions, that is, it places subconscious pressure on the arbitrator not to decide all grievances in favor of one party."[9] It should be noted that many arbitrators deny that they pursue a strategy of "split decisions," and it is clear that many do not. On occasion, in organizations with hostile relations between

---

[8]Rynecki, Cairns, and Cairns, *Police Collective Bargaining Agreements*, p. 17.
[9]Decker, "Public-Sector Grievance Arbitration Procedures," pp. 439–440.

management and the union, the union will flood the procedure with many grievances, and unions sometimes support grievances they do not expect to win because this provides an opportunity to express their general dissatisfactions with management.

While the sign of an effective grievance procedure is that it is made use of by employees, effectiveness is also measured by the degree to which grievances are resolved at the informal level of consultation between the employee and the immediate supervisor. Accordingly, forward-looking management and unions give much attention to identifying the basic causes of grievances and to training of supervisors and union stewards respectively.

The union steward (he or she represents the union in dealings with management in a given part of the organization) has a very important responsibility from the union side in investigating the facts about employee grievances. Below is pertinent material extracted from one union's *Steward's Manual:*

> A steward should address problems before they arise, determine how changes in conditions of work will affect employees and communicate with them on a continuous basis.
>
> It is the steward's responsibility to investigate and determine the validity of all complaints in his/her area of stewardship responsibility.
>
> The resolution of a complaint involves four basic steps: *investigating the complaint, determining the validity* of the complaint, *taking action* on the complaint, and finally *checking the results*.
>
> The investigation of a complaint starts when the complaint is received—that is, when the steward is contacted by an individual about a problem. At this point, the steward starts to assemble a file of facts concerning the case. The file should include any documentation that reflects facts pertinent to the problem, statements (signed if possible) from witnesses, and any notes taken during the interviews.
>
> For a legitimate complaint, analysis and evaluation of the facts must reveal an injustice with sufficient support to take action. A complaint should not be considered legitimate, although it may appear so, if there is insufficient support for an action.
>
> If the complaint is a legitimate grievance, the steward should then prepare and present the grievance in accordance with the proper procedure.
>
> Be timely; file the grievance as soon as possible after it arises.
>
> Arrange meeting(s) with the supervisor or other appropriate management official.
>
> Keep the employee informed about the progress of his/her complaint action.

If you are not able to resolve the grievance at your level of responsibility, carry it forward to the appropriate steward in your local's chain-of-command.

The end of the complaint action is the follow-up on the adjustment (corrective action). The follow-up is very important. At this time it can be determined if the complaint has been successfully resolved and if the complainant is satisfied.[10]

Similarly, management provides training for supervisors in how to manage relationships with subordinates so as to remove causes for grievances and in how to resolve grievances informally. Supervisors are instructed to listen carefully to the grievant and the steward, investigate the facts relating to a grievance, be thoroughly familiar with the negotiated grievance procedure, obtain information on previous settlements of similar grievances, resolve doubts as to how to respond to a grievance by checking with higher levels of supervision and with the labor relations officer, and make a complete record of the grievance, management's response, and the final disposition of the case. Decker stresses the need for a positive program to inform employees about new policies and programs affecting them. . . . Fewer grievances will result if employees are told about the conduct and performance that is expected and the penalties imposed for any violation of policy or poor performance."[11]

Contracts usually allow the steward or other union representative a certain amount of time during working hours to investigate grievances. The number of hours per week permitted may be specified or else a "reasonable" amount of time is allowed. Commonly, the union representative is required to obtain permission of his immediate supervisor before leaving the work site in order to investigate a grievance, as well as to clear with the supervisor of the grievant before visiting him or her at work. When the contract allows "reasonable time," management sometimes believes that union representatives are away from work too often investigating grievances, or the union that management is unduly restricting the time given union representatives to investigate grievances. If such disagreement leads to filing of a grievance against the other party and the grievance goes to arbitration, the arbitrator decides what

---

[10]*NFFE Steward's Manual*, Education and Training, National Federation of Federal Employees (Washington, D.C.: 1979): pp. 11–17.

[11]Decker, "Public-Sector Grievance Arbitration Procedures," p. 438.

is "reasonable time" based on past practices in the organization and the other facts in the case.

■ ARBITRATION

The objective of any dispute settlement procedure is to provide "finality"—a final step at which the conflict is resolved. Before binding grievance arbitration took firm hold in industry, unresolved grievances led to many strikes. Strikes are generally illegal in the public service, but they do occur, sometimes over grievances in the absence of arbitration. The argument for binding grievance arbitration is basically the same for both industry and government: the fairness of settling the dispute by submitting it to a neutral who studies the facts and evaluates arguments on both sides.

In the early stages of the rapid growth of collective bargaining in government, many public employers opposed binding grievance arbitration as an illegal delegation of legislative powers. There were judicial precedents to support this point of view, but courts now generally reject the illegal delegation of power argument and are according binding grievance arbitration in government the same status as in the private sector. In that sector, based on United States Supreme Court decisions, the courts will not accept initial jurisdiction over grievance cases and will review arbitral awards "only according to a very narrowly prescribed standard, thus discouraging both refusals to arbitrate and appeals from arbitration awards."[12] The principal grounds for judicial review are that the arbitrator exceeded his or her powers under the contract (which is to interpret the contract, not to add to or subtract from it); incorrectly decided a question of federal or state law; was "guilty of fraud, corruption, conflict-of-interest or some other breach of his [her] obligation to decide the case . . . with scrupulous fairness."[13]

As Garman contends, unions and management are not "enamoured of the arbitration process or arbitrators' decisions, but rather . . . they find arbitration better than the alternatives." As he further notes, both management and the union "sometimes find

---

[12]Russell A. Smith, Harry T. Edwards, and Theodore Clark, Jr., *Labor Relations in the Public Sector: Cases and Materials* (Indianapolis, Ind.: Bobbs-Merrill, 1974), p. 892.

[13]Tim Bornstein, *Arbitration: Last Step on the Grievance Route* (Washington, D.C.: Labor Management Relations Service, United States Conference of Mayors, 1978), pp. 9–10.

it difficult to overrule their subordinates, particularly on the union side since the leaders are elected by the members." Since the arbitrator makes the final decision, he or she is blamed, not top management or the union leaders. Of course, since the parties share the costs of arbitration (the arbitrator's per diem fee and expenses), indiscriminate resort to arbitration can be expensive. Actually, "with experience, the parties learn not to take questionable cases to arbitration. They think of the costs, financial as well as psychological, and also of the danger of getting a 'bad' precedent established as part of the contract."[14]

Contracts providing for binding arbitration sometimes exclude from arbitration certain provisions of the agreement. The explanation is that management would not agree to making the matters involved subject to arbitration or, as often has been the case in government, that provisions of law require other means of settling disputes over these questions, such as a separate appeals system for discharges and suspensions.

The Arbitrators

Grievance arbitration may be by one person or by a board of three or more. Recently the trend has been to use a single arbitrator. State public worker collective bargaining statutes usually provide for the agency administering the legislation to establish panels of qualified persons to serve as arbitrators, mediators, or factfinders. The parties may avail themselves of that service or themselves select an arbitrator from another source, perhaps the American Arbitration Association. In the federal service, the parties usually request the Federal Mediation and Conciliation Service (FMCS) to supply the names of arbitrators from its list. The FMCS list is sometimes also used by the parties in state and local governments. Where names are provided from lists, procedures for selection of the arbitrator vary. Sometimes several names are provided, perhaps five or seven and, if the parties cannot agree on the arbitrator, each party in turn strikes one name from the list until only one remains and that person becomes the arbitrator. The toss of a coin may determine which party starts the process of striking off names.

In some jurisdictions, a permanent umpire is employed in the interests of consistency in awards and because he or she will de-

---

[14]Garman, "Grievance Procedures in Health Care Establishments," 80–81.

velop intimate knowledge of the kinds of grievances that recur. The ad hoc approach—picking different arbitrators on a case-by-case basis—is more widespread, largely because the volume of cases is small and the parties do not want to be "locked in" by one person whom they believe might decide too many cases against them.[15]

Arbitrators are predominantly attorneys or university professors, the majority being attorneys. A legal background is not necessary for arbitration, and there is some criticism that attorneys overjudicialize the process. Since the process is quasi-judicial and evidence must be carefully weighed, a legal background is valuable, and the legal profession has shown great interest in arbitration. Although organizations like the American Arbitration Association (AAA) stress that there is a shortage of arbitrators, it is estimated that about 10 percent of the present supply of arbitrators gets about 90 percent of the cases.[16] The explanation is that the parties are very reluctant to try new arbitrators—as they have been to select female arbitrators.

When assigned to a case, the arbitrator arranges with the parties for the time and place of the hearing. At the hearing, the parties present evidence and offer testimony by witnesses to support their side of the case. As Frank Zeidler, permanent umpire for Milwaukee County, states, the "proceedings should be neither too formal nor too informal"; strict rules of evidence like those in court proceedings are not followed which puts the burden on the arbitrator to exercise good judgment in allowing testimony and admitting documents for the record.[17] As explained by the AAA, the customary order of the proceedings is:

> (1) opening statement by the initiating party, followed by similar statement by the other side; (2) presentation of witnesses by the initiating party, with cross-examination by the responding party; (3) presentation of witnesses by the responding party, with cross-examination by the initiating party; and (4) summation by both parties, usually following the same order as in the opening statements.[18]

---

[15]Frank P. Zeidler, *Grievance Arbitration in the Public Sector*, Public Employee Relations Library, no. 38 (Washington, D.C.: International Personnel Management Association, 1972), pp. 6–7.

[16]Donald Austin Woolf, "Arbitration in the Federal Service: A Primer," *Public Personnel Management* 7, no. 5 (September–October 1978): 300.

[17]Zeidler, *Grievance Arbitration in the Public Sector*, p. 14.

[18]Robert Coulson, *Labor Arbitration: What You Need to Know* (New York: American Arbitration Association, 1978), p. 61.

In disciplinary cases, the employer usually goes first.

In arbitration hearings, the care with which each party presents its case is very important. While the arbitrator has the authority to request more information and to subpoena witnesses, as a neutral he or she cannot seem to be helping a party to develop the case. Ordinarily, the arbitrators base their decisions on the pres- entations of the parties and will ask for additional information only when they believe it essential for understanding and deciding the case. Poor presentations by the union or management often are responsible for their losing a case. Accordingly, the parties develop manuals and other instructional material to prepare their representatives for arbitration hearings.

Where testimony is contradictory, as it frequently is, the arbitrator must decide whom and what to believe. After reciting the checklist of 11 criteria from the *California Evidence Code* for determining the credibility of witnesses, a participant at an annual meeting of the National Academy of Arbitrators commented:

> Anyone driven by the necessity of a decision to fret about credibility, who has listened over a number of years to sworn testimony, knows that as much truth must have been uttered by shifty-eyed, perspiring, lip-licking, nail-biting, guilty-looking, ill at ease, fidgety witnesses as have lies issued from calm, collected, imperturbable, urbane, straight-in-the-eye perjurers.[19]

The parties sometimes arrange for a full verbatim record of the hearings to be taken and transcribed. They may also file posthearing briefs in lieu of or in addition to closing statements. Because of the costs and delays that transcripts and posthearing briefs entail, their use is discouraged by the AAA and other organizations and persons concerned about the many weeks it has taken before final issuance of many arbitral awards. If there is no transcript, arbitrators rely on their notes and/or tape recording of the proceedings and the documentation submitted at the hearing.

Arbitrators' Decisions

A small percentage of arbitrators' decisions or summaries of them are published by Commerce Clearing House, the Bureau of National Affairs, and other organizations. Arbitrators are not bound

---

[19]Office of Labor Relations, Office of Personnel Management, *The Federal Labor-Management Consultant,* May 26, 1972.

by previous precedents unless they involve the same parties and contracts, but they occasionally consult and cite them in their decisions. They weigh the evidence and interpret the contract *as a whole*.

Sometimes one of the parties tries to persuade the arbitrator to interpret the contract language in such a way as to gain an advantage it could not obtain during the contract negotiations. If the interpretation sought would, in the arbitrator's opinion, constitute giving a meaning not reasonably to be drawn from the history of the negotiations or the contract language, he or she will deny the request. However, because they could not agree on a certain matter, the parties sometimes agree upon ambiguous contract language. Then if an important grievance is referred to arbitration, it is up to the arbitrator to decide its meaning.

The only thorough way of finding out how arbitrators decide cases is to read a good sample of their decisions. In the appendix to this chapter at the end of this book, as only one example, the entire text of an arbitrator's decision is reproduced in *City of Portland, Oregon, Bureau of Police, and Portland Police Association*. We have selected this case because the arbitrator's decision is a very lucid presentation of how arbitrators decide cases. The decision's format is that usually followed by arbitrators: Statement of Issue, Statement of Facts, Position of the Parties, Decision, and Award, although the terminology for these headings varies.

It should be noted how carefully the arbitrator cites the contract provisions and refers to the record of consideration of the grievance prior to arbitration. The fact that the hearing took eight days to complete and "consumed some 1650 pages of transcript" is unusual, since in a disciplinary case the hearing often lasts a day or less and, when transcripts are made, they run far fewer pages. It should be stressed that the arbitrator's report is a brief summary only of the written evidence and of the oral testimony. The reader does not get the full picture nor would he or she get it by listening to a complete tape recording of the proceedings. The recording reproduces all the words said, but it does not show the demeanor of the witnesses and one hears references only to the documents submitted in evidence, not the complete texts.

The arbitrator in this, the "opposum case," applies the usual criteria followed by arbitrators. Did management make a thorough investigation before it took disciplinary action against the grievants? Did it respect the due process rights of the grievants before it imposed the discipline? Was the principle of progressive discipline followed? Was the discipline meted out to the grievants consistent with that received in the past by employees for similar infractions? Was the disciplinary penalty proportionate to the offense? Were there mitigating circumstances that justify reducing the penalty, and, if so, what is the appropriate penalty? Were the past records and performance of the grievants fairly considered in determining the severity of the penalty? Which side's definition of just cause—management's or the union's—is the correct one? And, in this case, what weight should be given to public opinion, and have statements by management about public reaction to the grievants' conduct been proved to be true? Arbitration is no easy task, as the appendix certainly demonstrates.

BIBLIOGRAPHY

Decker, Kurt H. "Public-Sector Grievance Arbitration Procedures." In *Handbook on Public Personnel Administration and Labor Relations*, edited by Jack Rabin, Thomas Vocino, W. Bartley Hildreth, and Gerald J. Miller. New York: Dekker, 1983.

Elkouri, Frank, and Elkouri, Edna Asper. *How Arbitration Works*. 3d ed. Washington, D.C.: Bureau of National Affairs, 1976.

Grodin, Joseph R. "Judicial Response to Public Sector Arbitration." In *Public Sector Bargaining*, edited by Benjamin Aaron, Joseph R. Grodin, and James L. Stern. Washington, D.C.: Bureau of National Affairs, 1979.

Holden, Lawrence T., Jr. "Grievance Arbitration." In *Portrait of a Process: Collective Negotiations in Public Employment*, by Public Employment Relations Service. Fort Washington, Pa.: Labor Relations Press, 1979.

Landis, Brooks I. *Value Judgments in Arbitration: A Case Study of Saul Wallen*. Ithaca, N.Y.: New York State School of Industrial and Labor Relations, 1977.

Peterson, Donald J.; Rezier, Julius; Reed, Keith A. *Arbitration in Health Care*. Rockville, Md.: Aspen, 1981.

Rynecki, Steven B., and Hill, Marvin, Jr. *Preparing and Presenting a Public Sector Grievance Arbitration Case*. Washington, D.C.: International Personnel Management Association, 1972.

Scott, William G. *The Management of Conflict: Appeals Systems in Organizations*. Homewood, Ill.: Dorsey, 1965.

Zack, Arnold, ed. *Arbitration in Practice*. New York: American Arbitration Association, 1984.

————. *Understanding Grievance Arbitration in the Public Sector*. Report prepared for Division of Public Employee Labor Relations, U.S. Department of Labor. Washington, D.C.: Government Printing Office, 1974.

Zeidler, Frank *Grievance Arbitration in the Public Sector*. Washington, D.C.: International Personnel Management Association, 1972.

15 Constitutional Rights and the Public Employee

This chapter consists of two parts: first, a presentation of the constitutional *rights* of the public employee, and, second, a discussion of the public employee's *obligation* to respect the constitutional rights of members of the public. The first part will be longer because there are many court decisions to summarize. The second part, while shorter, deals with the important question of the personal liability of public employees for infringement of constitutional rights of private parties who sue for monetary damages and other relief in the courts. In recent years, the liability of governments and of its agents for monetary damages has grown appreciably because of new U.S. Supreme Court rulings, so that any book on public personnel administration should address this topic.

■ RIGHTS

A major reason for the emergence of the new public personnel administration is the judiciary's changed conception of the constitutional rights of the public employee. The employment relationship in government in the mid-1950s, as described by Arch Dotson, was lopsided.[1] The public employer imposed many conditions on public employees which they had to accept to keep their jobs, and the only responsibilities of the government were those stated in statutes and thus subject to revocation by the legislature. The employee did not have any rights in the job based on the Constitution; in fixing the terms of employment, the government

---

[1]Arch Dotson, "The Emerging Doctrine of Privilege in Public Employment," *Public Administration Review* 15, no. 2 (Spring 1955): 77–88.

could and did deny the employee civil and political rights enjoyed by workers in the private sector.

The due process clause of the Fifth and Fourteenth amendments to the federal Constitution was held not to apply to public employees because, as stated in *Bailey* v. *Richardson* (1951), government employment could not be considered property, it could not be "perceived" to be liberty, and it "certainly" was not life. "Due process of law is not applicable unless one is being deprived of something to which he has a right."[2] Accordingly, public employees were not entitled to substantive or procedural due process; they could, for example, be barred from partisan political activity (substantive) and denied the right to a hearing in loyalty cases (procedural). In 1892 Justice Holmes had stated that "The petitioner may have a constitutional right to talk politics, but he has no constitutional right to be a policeman."[3] As Dotson observed, "from the assertion that there exists no constitutional right *to* public employment, it is also inferred that there can be no constitutional right *in* public employment. The progression is that, since there are no fundamental claims in employment, employment is maintained by the state as a privilege."[4]

The scope of judicial review of personnel actions in government was very limited, and "for the most part . . . the basic factual merits of controversies between employees and managers, and the range of discipline warranted were left to the discretion of managers."[5]

Since the 1950s, the courts have rejected the view of government employment as privilege and substituted the doctrine that "whenever there is a substantial interest, other than employment by the state, involved in the discharge of a public employee, he can be removed neither on arbitrary grounds nor without a procedure calculated to determine whether legitimate grounds exist."[6] They have been examining the facts in discharge and other cases involving the employment relationship and nullifying the public

---

[2]341 U.S. 918 (1951).

[3]*McAuliffe* v. *Mayor of New Bedford*, 155 Mass. 216, 29 N. E. 517 (1892).

[4]Dotson, "Emerging Doctrine of Privilege," 87.

[5]Anthony L. Mondello, "Contemporary Issues. . . .," *Civil Service Journal* 13 no. 3 (January–March 1973): 43.

[6]David H. Rosenbloom, "Some Political Implications of the Drift Toward a Liberation of Federal Employees," *Public Administration Review* 31, no. 4 (July–August 1971): 421. See also Deborah D. Goldman, "Due Process and Public Personnel Management," *Review of Public Personnel Administration* 2, no. 1 (Fall 1981).

employer's actions if they are not believed to be supported by substantial evidence or where there is evidence of abuse of discretion or of arbitrary or capricious action. While it is true that in some decisions the U.S. Supreme Court under Chief Justice Warren E. Burger has subjected public employer personnel actions to less rigorous scrutiny than the Court applied in the 1960s and the 1970s, the privilege doctrine has not been reestablished in its original form. Indeed, some of the Court's recent decisions, as well as those of lower federal courts, have extended constitutional rights of public employees. In this chapter, we will cover some of the principal areas in which public employees now are protected by the Constitution.

The Property and Liberty Interest in Public Employment

U.S. Supreme Court decisions in the 1970s established that public employees can have property and liberty interests in their jobs that warrant protection of the due process clause of the Fifth and Fourteenth Amendments to the federal Constitution.

Board of Regents v. Roth

As defined by the Court, property interests are not limited to money, real estate, and physical things but include whatever affects the livelihood of an individual (e.g., welfare benefits, eligibility for occupational licenses). In *Board of Regents* v. *Roth* (1972), the Court identified the attributes of property interests protected by procedural due process. The individual must have more than an abstract need or desire for the benefit in question; he must have a "legitimate claim of entitlement to it," not simply a "unilateral expectation of it." "It is a purpose of the ancient institution of property to protect those claims upon which people rely in their daily lives, reliance that must not be arbitrarily undermined."

Roth, a university teacher who had been hired for the fixed term of one academic year, was given no reason when he was told that he would not be rehired. Under Wisconsin law, the decision whether or not to hire a nontenured teacher was left to the "unfettered discretion of University officials," and under board of regents rules no reason had to be given nor was a review or appeal provided. Roth brought court action in which he charged that the university's failure to give any reason for his nonretention and to grant him a hearing deprived him of procedural due process. Hearing the case on appeal, the Supreme Court majority first established that the *"nature* of the interest at stake" had to be determined; specifically, was Roth's interest within the Fourteenth Amendment's protection of liberty and property?

The Court decided that although there might be situations in which denial of reemployment would affect liberty this was not true in Roth's case. The state had not made any charges against him which might reflect upon his good name, reputation, honor, or integrity; it had done nothing to prevent his finding other employment. "It stretches the concept too far to suggest that a person is deprived of 'liberty' when he simply is not rehired in one job but remains as free as before to seek another." The Court made clear that had it found Roth to have a liberty interest he would have been entitled to notice and an opportunity to be heard although he did not have tenure. As to a property interest, Roth did not have one because the terms of his appointment "secured absolutely no interest in reemployment for the next year." He did have an abstract concern in reemployment but not a *"property* interest sufficient to require the University authorities to give him a hearing. . . ."[7]

Perry v. Sinderman

In *Perry* v. *Sinderman* (1972), the Court ruled that even though an educational institution (Odessa State College in Texas) stated in its faculty guide that it had no tenure system, there could be an unwritten "common law" that certain employees had the equivalent of tenure (de facto tenure). If it was proved in court that there was a mutual expectation of continued employment on the teacher's part and that of the institution, then continued employment could not be terminated except for cause. This would entitle the teacher to an evidentiary hearing, although not necessarily to reinstatement. The important consideration was that the teacher would be able to challenge the sufficiency of the reasons for nonretention and argue his or her case for reinstatement. In this decision, the Court did not state that the hearing was required before dismissal; it made no mention of when the hearing need be held.[8]

---

[7]408 U.S. 564, 92 S. Ct. 2701, 33 L. Ed 548 (1972).
[8]408 U.S. 593, 92 S. Ct. 2694, 33 L. Ed 2d 570 (1972).

Arnett v. Kennedy

In *Arnett* v. *Kennedy* (1974), both property interest and free speech rights were involved. Kennedy, a nonprobationary employee in the competitive civil service, had been dismissed from his position as a field representative in the Chicago regional office of the Office of Economic Opportunity for allegedly making recklessly false and defamatory statements about other OEO employees. When he received the notification of proposed adverse action, Kennedy was advised of his right under Civil Service Commission and OEO regulations to reply to the charges both in writing and orally, but he elected not to do so. Instead he argued that the charges were unlawful because the "standards and procedures established by and under the Lloyd-LaFollette Act for the removal of nonprobationary employees from the federal service unwarrantedly interfere with those employees' freedom of expression and deny them procedural due process of law." (We are now concerned with Kennedy's property and liberty interest in his job; later in this chapter the constitutionality of Lloyd-LaFollette with respect to freedom of expression will be discussed.)

Kennedy maintained that since he had a property interest in his job he was entitled to a pretermination evidentiary proceeding before an impartial hearing officer. The Lloyd-LaFollette Act states that "examination of witnesses, trial, or hearing is not required but may be provided in the discretion of the individual directing" the dismissal; Civil Service Commission regulations provided that the employee was entitled to an evidentiary hearing either before or after the decision to take the action. In OEO the only trial-type hearing available typically was held after dismissal.

The district court ruled that Kennedy was entitled to the evidentiary pretermination hearing. When the case was heard by the Supreme Court on appeal, four separate opinions were filed. Six of the justices concurred that a trial-type pretermination hearing was not required; the remaining three thought it was. *Six justices agreed that Kennedy had a property interest in his employment.*

Justices William H. Rehnquist, Warren E. Burger, and Potter Stewart accepted that Kennedy "did have a statutory expectancy that he not be removed other than for 'such cause as will promote the efficiency of the service.' " However, this right was qualified by the statute itself which does not require hearings. Hence they held Kennedy was not entitled to any hearing and surely not a pretermination hearing. Kennedy's procedural rights depended on the statute, not the Constitution, a view rejected by Justices Lewis F. Powell and Harry A. Blackmun in their opinion. They could not agree that the "constitutional guarantee of procedural due process accords to appellee no procedural protections against arbitrary or erroneous discharge other than those expressly provided in the statute," and that the "statute governing federal employment determines not only the nature of appellee's property interest, but also the extent of the procedural protections to which he may lay claim." If so, no matter what the nature of the person's property interest, he could be deprived of it without notice or hearing at any time.

Notwithstanding, Powell and Blackmun did not believe Kennedy was entitled to a pretermination evidentiary hearing. Whether or not to grant such a hearing depended upon a "balancing process in which the Government's interest in expeditious removal of an unsatisfactory employee is weighed against the interest of the affected employee in continued public employment." The government's and the public's interest was to maintain "employee efficiency and discipline"; besides there was the additional expense of a prior trial-type hearing. Kennedy's interest was in avoiding loss of income as he waited for a posttermination hearing, a delay which could be considerable. But, reasoned Powell and Blackmun, he might have "independent resources to overcome any temporary hardship," he might be able to find a job in private enterprise, and, failing all else, he would be eligible for welfare benefits.

In a separate opinion, Justice Byron White agreed with Powell and Blackmun that Kennedy's due process procedural rights originated in the Constitution, and he also agreed that a trial-type pretermination hearing was not required, but he believed a "minipretermination hearing" of notice and opportunity to respond was required. White's interpretation was that Kennedy had been denied his constitutional rights because the OEO would have had him respond to the notification of dismissal by appearing before the very person who had ordered him fired—the regional director. White's reasoning was the same as Powell's and Blackmun's on Kennedy's economic problems; he could find employment in the private sector or if necessary "draw on the welfare system."

Justices Thurgood Marshall, William J. Brennan, and William O. Douglas considered previous Supreme Court decisions to be conclusive that Kennedy's property and liberty interests were so great that an evidentiary trial-type pretermination hearing was required. The stigma of dismissal from government employment implicated "liberty interests"; since in posttermination hearings as many as a fourth of all agency dismissals were found to be illegal and there was considerable delay between discharge and the holding of the hearing, the employee's loss of income was substantial. The argument that the employee could go on welfare exhibited "gross insensitivity to the plight of these employees," since welfare applicants "must be all but stripped of their worldly goods" to be eligible for benefits.

The majority decision in *Arnett* v. *Kennedy* created much unfavorable reaction among public employees, not only because of the denial of the pretermination hearing, but also because, except for Marshall, Brennan, and Douglas, the Court held that the Lloyd-LaFollette Act provision authorizing removal "for such cause as will promote the efficiency of the service" was not unconstitutionally vague and overbroad when applied to speech. The determinations with respect to property and liberty rights did solidify previous Supreme Court rulings and make clear that they cover both nonteachers and teachers.[9] Considering the decision in *Arnett* v. *Kennedy* as a whole, constitutional authority David H. Rosenbloom believed it "represents a limitation on the degree of due process which must be afforded employees prior to termination," and further that "three justices endorsed a line of reasoning which would deconstitutionalize such dismissals almost entirely, and three others construed the constitutional requirements to be minimal."[10]

Bishop v. Wood

While not abrogating its dictum that tenured public employees are entitled to due process hearings in discharge cases, the Court in *Bishop* v. *Wood* (1976) showed that it was "less likely to find the existence of tenure" than previously.[11] The city of Marion, North

---

[9]416 U.S. 134 (1974).

[10]David H. Rosenbloom, "The Employee in Court: Implications for Urban Government," in Charles H. Levine, *Managing Human Resources: A Challenge to Urban Governments* (Beverly Hills, Calif.: Sage, 1977), p. 67. See also Philip L. Martin, "The Improper Discharge of a Federal Employee by a Constitutionally Permissible Process: The OEO Case," *Administrative Law Review* 28, no. 1 (Winter 1976).

[11]Carl F. Goodman, "Changing Direction of Public Employment Law," *PA News*

Carolina, had discharged a policeman without giving him a hearing despite the fact that he was a permanent employee of the city. The policeman brought suit in district court, charging that as a permanent employee he had a property interest in his job and a constitutional right to a pretermination hearing. The city ordinance dealing with dismissals of permanent employees required that the employee be given written notice of the action and of the reasons for it, but it did not provide for a hearing.

The district court interpreted the ordinance as granting no right to continued employment but merely conditioning the employee's removal on compliance with the procedures stated in the ordinance. Hearing the case on appeal, the U.S. Supreme Court majority upheld the district court judge, accepting his interpretation of what the ordinance meant under North Carolina state law. Thus, "*Bishop* appears to say that if the state courts (or lower federal courts) interpret state law or city ordinance in such a way as not to grant tenure, the Supreme Court will not interfere."[12] The dissenting U.S. Supreme Court justices maintained that the policeman was deprived of a clear property right in his job without due process of law and that the majority, by holding that the states have unfettered discretion in defining "property" for purposes of the due process clause of the federal Constitution, had adopted an interpretation rejected by a majority of the Court in *Arnett* v. *Kennedy*. Goldman concludes that the "Court was calling a halt to the *expansion* of judicial involvement in the procedural aspects of public personnel management." (Italics ours)[13]

Freedom of Expression

The leading U.S. Supreme Court decision on free speech rights of public employees is *Pickering* v. *Board of Education* (1968). Pickering, a high school teacher in Illinois, was dismissed by the board of education for writing a letter to a local newspaper criticizing the board. Several efforts by the board to raise funds by bond issues had been defeated by the voters. In his letter, Pickering alleged that the superintendent of schools had stated that teachers oppos-

---

and *Views* 26, no. 10, October 1976, Washington, D.C.: American Society for Public Administration, p. 7.

[12]Ibid. See 426 U.S. 341 (1976).

[13]Goldman, "Due Process and Public Personnel Management," 24.

ing a bond referendum "should be prepared for the consequences" and claimed that the board was allocating a disproportionate amount of school funds to athletic activities. The Illinois courts upheld the dismissal, rejecting claims of First and Fourteenth Amendment protections on the ground that as a teacher Pickering should refrain from making public statements about the school's operation "which in the absence of such position he would have an undoubted right to engage in."

Rejecting the proposition that public employment could be subjected to any conditions no matter how unreasonable, the Court ruled for Pickering, finding that his First Amendment rights had been violated. However, while teachers could not constitutionally be compelled to relinquish a right "they would otherwise enjoy as citizens to comment on matters of public interest with the operation of the public schools in which they work," the state did have interests as an "employer in regulating the speech of its employees that differ significantly from those it possesses in connection with regulation of the speech of the citizenry in general." What should be balanced in each case was the interests of the teachers as citizens to comment on matters of public concern and those of the public employer in providing efficient services to the public.

Applying this balancing test, the Court noted that Pickering's statements were not directed to persons with whom he would normally have contact in his daily work as a teacher, so there was "no question of maintaining either discipline by immediate superiors or harmony among co-workers." Furthermore, Pickering did not have such close working relationships with the board or the superintendent as to make personal loyalty and confidence necessary. The Court rejected any inference from the board's position that Pickering could be dismissed for substantially correct statements because "sufficiently critical in tone." While Pickering had stated that the board was spending $50,000 annually for transportation of athletes when the true figure was $10,000, the board could easily have rebutted him by publishing the correct figures. Pickering had done nothing to bring into question his fitness as a teacher; in the circumstances of the case, his statements on school policies enjoyed the same protection as those by any citizen. The Court referred to its decision in *New York Times* v. *Sullivan* (1964), in which it ruled that under the First or Fourteenth Amendments public officials are prohibited from recovering damages for defamatory falsehoods relating to their official conduct unless they prove that the statements were made with "knowledge of their falsity or with reckless disregard for their truth or falsity."[14]

Returning to *Arnett* v. *Kennedy*, Kennedy had maintained that the standard in the Lloyd-LaFollette Act, dismissal for "such cause as will promote the efficiency of the service," was too vague; employees had no way of knowing what behavior or speech could cost them their jobs.

Justice Rehnquist, ruling on this issue for six justices, disagreed, quoting a previous decision of the Court to the effect that the "root of the vagueness doctrine is a rough idea of fairness." Congress could not be expected to spell out in detail the prohibited conduct because of the practical difficulties in framing a statute "both general enough to take into account a variety of human conduct and sufficiently specific to provide fair warning that certain kinds of conduct are prohibited." These justices believed the act did not authorize discharge for "constitutionally protected speech," proscribing only "public speech which improperly damages and impairs the reputation and efficiency of the employing agency." In this opinion, Rehnquist was joined by Burger, Powell, Stewart, Blackmun, and White.

Justices Marshall, Brennan, and Douglas disagreed. Noting that the majority had cited the statement in *Pickering* v. *Board of Education* that the government had significantly different interests in regulating the speech of its own employees as compared with the general citizenry, they stressed that *Pickering* also established that teachers may not constitutionally be denied their rights as citizens to comment on matters of public concern and to criticize their superiors. They pointed out that Senator Robert LaFollette, in illustrating the abuses to be "cured by the bill," cited the instance of a postal employee's being dismissed for publicizing insanitary conditions in the Chicago Post Office building, conditions condemned by Chicago public health officers. In their opinion, the majority had evaded the issue by stating that Lloyd-LaFollette could not deny constitutionally protected speech. Since no statute can "reach and punish constitutionally protected speech," the majority had "merely repeated the obvious."

When the decision in *Arnett* v. *Kennedy* was announced, some writers and union leaders interpreted it as a new Court doctrine

---

[14]391 U.S. 563, 88 S. Ct. 1731, 20 L. Ed 2d 811 (1968).

that public employees could make no criticisms of their superiors and were being gagged. As the preceding analysis shows, the Court did not upset *Pickering* v. *Board of Education;* the balancing test still applies. That test, however, has long been unacceptable to those who believe it leaves too much room for the government arbitrarily to suppress employees' free speech rights. A decision that the Lloyd-LaFollette Act was unconstitutionally overbroad would not have been inconsistent with the balancing test; many people feel the Court should have so ruled.

More Recent Decisions

More recent U.S. Supreme Court decisions have increased concern that the Court is narrowing the protections established in *Pickering.* One such case is *Connick* v. *Myers,* decided by a five-to-four vote in April of 1983. Connick, U.S. district attorney in New Orleans, wanted to transfer Myers, an assistant district attorney in his office, to a different section of the criminal court, but Myers strongly objected to the transfer. Shortly thereafter she prepared, and distributed to other assistant district attorneys in the office, a questionnaire concerning transfer policy, the need for a grievance committee, the level of confidence in supervisors, and whether employees felt pressured to work in political campaigns. Connick then told her that she was being terminated for refusing to accept the transfer and that her distribution of the questionnaire represented insubordination.

Myers brought action in U.S. district court which ordered her reinstated. The district court believed that the real reason for the dismissal was her distribution of the questionnaire, not her objection to the transfer. Interpreting *Pickering,* the judge decided that the questions in the questionnaire dealt with matters of public concern and that its distribution did not disrupt the work of the district attorney's office or injure working relationships of the personnel in the office. The circuit court of appeals affirmed the district court's ruling, but the Supreme Court majority, in an opinion written by Justice White, upheld the dismissal, maintaining that the district and circuit courts had misapplied *Pickering.*

Basically, the Court majority determined that the questionnaire did not deal with matters of public concern, except for the question about coerced political activity. Being disciplined for asking that question did infringe upon Myers' free speech rights, but in the total context of the facts in the case, this infringement was outweighed by the potential damage to working relationships in the district attorney's office and the undermining of his authority. White wrote, "Indeed the questionnaire, if released to the public, would convey no information at all other than the fact that a single employee is upset with the status quo." The Court majority found it significant that Myers, in its estimation, did not seek to inform the public that Connick's office was failing to discharge its responsibilities in the investigation and prosecution of criminal cases.

In the minority opinion, Justice Brennan stated that the questionnaire did address matters of public concern because it discussed subjects that could reasonably be expected to be of interest to the public in judging how the district attorney was discharging his responsibilities. The information sought in the questionnaire was of public concern because personnel decisions that adversely affect morale can ultimately impair governmental efficiency.

Brennan wrote: "Such extreme deference to the employer's judgment is not appropriate when public employees voice critical views concerning the operations of the agency for which they work. . . . The Court's decision today inevitably will deter public employees from making critical statements about the manner in which government agencies are operated for fear that doing so will provoke their dismissal." The minority Justices found no evidence that the questionnaire substantially impeded the functioning of the district attorney's office, and they disagreed with the statement in the majority opinion that *Pickering* did not require the employer to wait until destruction of working relationships occurred before taking disciplinary action.[15]

William C. Bush v. *William R. Lucas*, decided by a unanimous vote in June of 1983, dealt with the judicial remedies the Court should provide for a public employee whose constitutional rights have been violated. In 1974, Bush, an aerospace engineer with the National Aeronautics and Space Administration at its George C. Marshall Space Flight Center, was twice reassigned to new positions while the facility was being reorganized. He objected to both reassignments and sought review by the U.S. Civil Service Commission.

In May and June of 1975, while his appeals to the Commission

---

[15]103 *Supreme Court Reporter,* 1684–1702.

were still pending, Bush made public statements, some in two television interviews, that were highly critical of the facility. The media quoted him as saying that his job was a travesty and that the taxpayers' money was being spent fraudulently and wastefully at the Center.

In August of 1975 the Center initiated action to remove him for maliciously making misleading and often false statements that adversely affected public confidence in government services. Bush was given the opportunity to file a written response to the charges and to make an oral presentation before agency officials. The Center then decided that, although Bush's conduct did justify removal, since it was a first offense a lesser penalty of reduction in grade from GS-14 to GS-12, amounting to a salary loss of about $9,716, was appropriate.

The Federal Employee Appeals Authority upheld this demotion, but the Civil Service Commission's Appeals Review Board, applying the balancing test in *Pickering*, decided that the demotion violated Bush's constitutional rights. Its finding was that while Bush's statements were somewhat exaggerated, they were not wholly without truth, they did stimulate public debate, and the extent of proven disruption of the agency's operations did not justify abrogation of the exercise of free speech. The Board ordered that the demotion be cancelled and that Bush receive $30,000 in back pay. NASA accepted this decision; however, while his appeal was still pending, Bush had filed action in an Alabama state court against Lucas, the Center Director, seeking monetary damages for violation of his constitutional rights. This action was removed to federal district court which ruled Bush had no course of action for damages in view of the available remedies under Civil Service Commission regulations.

Hearing this case on appeal, the Supreme Court, with Justice Stevens writing the unanimous decision, said that the Court assumed Bush's constitutional rights had been violated and also that the Civil Service Commission remedies did not fully compensate him for the harm he had suffered. The Court also acknowledged that in the absence of statutory remedies provided by act of Congress, it had the power to order damages for violations of constitutional rights. However, in this particular case it was not appropriate to do so because Bush's claims arose out of an employment relationship governed by comprehensive procedural and substantive provisions giving meaningful remedies against the government. Congress, the Court stated, would be in a better position to create a new judicial remedy for the issue involved.[16]

Bush v. *Lucas* has lesser significance than *Connick* v. *Myers* because the Supreme Court was not ruling on whether or not a public employee's constitutional rights had been violated. Yet *Bush* v. *Lucas* does not reflect the activist approach to providing redress for the employee that critics of the Court believe *Pickering* and other previous decisions require.

Loyalty Oaths

Before 1960, the U.S. Supreme Court upheld loyalty oaths within a "relatively confined area"[17] as reasonable regulations for government employment, provided there was no adverse effect on those who during their period of affiliation with a proscribed organization were innocent of its purposes. In *Weiman* v. *Updegraff* (1952), the Court voided an Oklahoma loyalty oath requiring all state employees to swear that they were not, and during the preceding five years had not been, members of any organization listed by the U.S. Attorney General as "communist front" or "subversive." The Oklahoma Supreme Court had construed this oath as excluding persons from state employment solely on the basis of membership, regardless of their knowledge of the purposes and activities of the organizations concerned. The U.S. Supreme Court ruled that the due process clause does not permit a state, in attempting to bar disloyal persons from its employment, to classify innocent with knowing association.[18]

In *Cramp* v. *Board of Public Instruction* (1961), the Florida Supreme Court held constitutional a state statute requiring all employees of the state and its subdivisions to swear in writing that they had never lent "aid, support, advice, counsel, or influence to the Communist Party." The U.S. Supreme Court ruled that the meaning of the oath was so vague and uncertain that the state could not within the due process clause of the Fourteenth Amendment force an employee to take it at the risk of subsequent prosecution for perjury or immediate dismissal.[19]

---

[16]Ibid., 2404–2418.

[17]Thomas L. Emerson, *The System of Freedom of Expression* (New York: Random House, 1970), p. 225.

[18]344 U.S. 183 (1952).

[19]368 U.S. 278 (1961).

A later loyalty case before the U.S. Supreme Court, *Elfbrandt* v. *Russell* (1966), concerned an oath drafted by the Arizona legislature which was intended to eliminate vagueness. Employees were subject to perjury and discharge if they knowingly became members of the Communist Party or any other organization advocating the overthrow of the government. The Court declared the oath unconstitutional, arguing that (1) political groups may embrace legal and illegal aims and one may join such groups without embracing the latter; (2) those who join an organization without sharing its unlawful purposes and without participating in its unlawful activities pose no threat to constitutional government; and (3) to presume conclusively that those who join a "subversive" organization share its unlawful aims is forbidden by the principle that a state may not compel citizens to prove that they were not engaged in criminal advocacy. The Arizona act unnecessarily infringed on the freedom of political association because it was not "narrowly drawn to define and punish specific conduct as constituting a clear and present danger."[20]

Emerson concludes that the impact of these and other U.S. Supreme Court decisions is that the "disclaimer oath is beset with constitutional requirements almost impossible to meet."[21] To be proscribed, the advocacy must not only be of the action type but also create a probable danger, and the association must be knowing rather than innocent and active rather than passive with definite intent to further the illegal objectives of the organization. Since these questions can "really be ascertained only on a case-by-case, rather than a blanket, basis," it is "virtually impossible for either the Federal or a State government to impose a meaningful loyalty oath upon its employees."[22]

Private Life and Morals

With court sanction, public agencies for many years barred from employment and discharged persons for immoral conduct which was defined to include extramarital relations and homosexualism, but court decisions in this area have changed significantly. The courts began this shift by requiring the public employer to describe clearly the individual's conduct which constitutes "immoral con-

---

[20]384 U.S. 11, 86 S. Ct. 1238, 16 L. Ed. 2d 321 (1966).
[21]Emerson, *The System of Freedom of Expresion,* p. 241.
[22]Ibid., p. 240.

duct" as in homosexuality. They then began to reverse disciplinary actions where their review of the facts showed no connection between the employee's behavior and the efficiency of the service. This precedent, established in *Norton* v. *Macy* (1969) by the court of appeals for the District of Columbia, is the one now applied.

Norton, an employee of NASA, was arrested by District of Columbia police after he had been observed during the early morning hours picking up another male in his car. Notified that Norton was in custody, the NASA security chief sat in on part of the police interrogation. Norton was given a traffic summons after he denied making homosexual advances to the male he had picked up. The security chief invited Norton to NASA offices where he questioned him until 6:00 A.M., and during this interrogation Norton admitted to homosexual tendencies and mutual masturbation with males in high school and college. Although he denied being a homosexual, NASA concluded he was and fired him for "immoral, indecent, and disgraceful conduct."

The court voided the dismissal, noting that the agency had said Norton was a good worker and that there were no security risks involved, only the danger of public scandal. Since there was no showing that Norton's conduct had "some ascertainable deleterious effect on the efficiency of the service," the dismissal was arbitrary, particularly since the appellant had not flaunted his conduct.[23]

In *Singer* v. *U.S. Civil Service Commission* (1976), the commission had ordered the Equal Employment Opportunity Commission to discharge the plaintiff because the commission had determined that he had made known both his employment by EEOC and his homosexual conduct with frequent resultant media publicity. In the commission's judgment, this had caused a loss of public confidence in the government and was detrimental to the efficiency of the service. The court upheld the commission, ruling that there was a nexus between the plaintiff's conduct and the efficiency of the service and that the open and notorious flaunting of his conduct was sufficient to sustain "a rational connection between the facts relied upon and the conclusions reached."[24]

The courts are also requiring a "rational nexus" between private conduct and performance on the job in cases involving heterosexual activity. In *Mindel* v. *Civil Service Commission* (1970), a postal

---

[23]417 F. 2d 1161, D.C. Cir. (1969).
[24]9th Cir. No. 74–2073 (January 14, 1976).

clerk was removed for living with a young woman "without benefit of marriage." Relying on *Norton,* the court deemed the dismissal a violation of due process and the right to privacy. The plaintiff held a nonsensitive position, his conduct was discreet and not illegal under California law, no notoriety or scandal were involved, and there was no connection with his job performance.[25] In *Major* v. *Hampton* (1976), the plaintiff, an employee of the Internal Revenue Service, was dismissed for behavior that "tends to discredit himself or the service" because he and three other men rented an apartment for the purpose of engaging in sexual relations with consenting women during off-duty hours. The court held that the dismissal was arbitrary and had no relationship to a valid governmental objective. It refused to consider the plaintiff's morality or integrity and limited its review of the facts in the case to whether his behavior had discredited him or the IRS. In the absence of any evidence introduced indicating that the plaintiff's "actions were calculated to arouse, or did in fact arouse, odium for the employee or the IRS," the court concluded that the removal was based on a mere moral judgment without rational basis.[26]

Patronage Dismissals and Hiring

A very new area in which the U.S. Supreme Court has established constitutional rights is patronage dismissals.

Dismissals

In *Elrod* v. *Burns* (1976), a Court majority ruled that removals of nonpolicymaking employees solely for reasons of their affiliation with a particular political party violate their First Amendment rights. This decision is particularly interesting because in effect the justices constituting the majority (Brennan, White, Marshall, Stewart, and Blackmun) engaged in a debate with the three dissenting justices (Powell, Burger, and Rehnquist) about the role of and consequences of patronage hiring and dismissal practices in the American democratic system of government.

The suit originated with an action filed in district court by several employees, all Republicans, employed by the Cook County

---

[25]312 F. Supp. 485, N. D. Cal. (1970).
[26]E. D. La., No. 75–1634 (c) (February 23, 1976).

Sheriff's Office. The sheriff, a Republican, had been replaced in December 1970 by Richard Elrod, a Democrat. In Cook County, it long had been the practice for an incoming sheriff of a different political party to replace noncivil service employees with members of his own party if the holdover employees lacked or failed to obtain requisite support from the incoming party or to affiliate with it. Accordingly, the respondents were dismissed solely because they neither supported nor were members of the Democratic Party and had failed to obtain the sponsorship of one of its leaders.

Delivering an opinion in which White and Marshall joined, Brennan wrote, "The cost of patronage is the restraint it places on freedoms of belief and association. In order to maintain their jobs, respondents were required to pledge their political allegiance to the Democratic Party, work for the election of other candidates of the Democratic Party, contribute a portion of their wages to the Party, or obtain the sponsorship of a member of the Party, usually at the price of one of the first three alternatives." Not only did the political patronage system coerce belief and association, but by "conditioning public employment on partisan support," it also deterred existing employees and those seeking jobs to support "competing public interests."

Since previous decisions of the Court had clearly established that a "significant impairment of First Amendment rights must survive exacting scrutiny," the benefits gained by "conditioning the retention of public employment on the employee's support of the in-party" would have to "outweigh the loss of constitutionally protected rights." Saying this, Brennan then proceeded to examine, one by one, the principal arguments advanced in favor of patronage.

One such argument was that holdover employees of different "political persuasions" than those of the in-party would "not have the incentive to work effectively" and may even "be motivated to subvert the incumbent administration's efforts to govern effectively." This reasoning is not persuasive for several reasons. For one thing, the wholesale removals and replacements that take place with each change of administration result in inefficiency, not efficiency. Further, the replacements are not necessarily more qualified than the persons dismissed because "appointment often occurs in exchange for the delivery of votes, or other party service, not job capability." It is also doubtful that "mere difference of political persuasion motivates poor performance"; the Court had "consistently recognized that mere political association is an inadequate basis for inputing disposition to ill-willed conduct."

Still, continued Brennan, it may be argued that, under the patronage system, employees of the in-party are motivated to perform well in order to keep the party in power and ensure retaining their jobs and that the replacements will be "highly accountable to the public." But there is a "means less intrusive than patronage" for achieving employee accountability, namely the "ability of officials more directly accountable to the electorate to discharge employees for cause and the availability of merit systems."

Brennan then turns to a second claim—that patronage is necessary to ensure the political loyalty of employees and to prevent them from "obstructing the implementation of policies of the new administration." While there is some justification for this contention, it cannot "validate patronage wholesale" because patronage dismissals can be limited to policy-making positions. The line between policy and nonpolicy-making positions is difficult to draw; it is the government's responsibility to demonstrate that the position is a policy-making one.

The petitioners (Elrod et al.) also had argued that patronage dismissals were essential for maintenance of the democratic process, maintaining that "we have contrived no system for the support of party that does not place considerable reliance on patronage." Brennan refutes by pointing out that "political parties existed in the absence of active patronage practices prior to the administration of Andrew Jackson" and "have survived substantial reduction in their patronage power through the establishment of merit systems." Without patronage, the democratic process functions "as well . . . perhaps even better, for patronage dismissals also retard that process . . . and can result in the entrenchment of one or a few parties to the exclusion of others." Any gain to representative government provided by patronage was "insufficient to justify its sacrifice of First Amendment rights."

Stewart and Blackmun concurred in upholding the plaintiff, but they thought the single substantive question in the case was "whether a nonpolicymaking, nonconfidential employee can be discharged from a job that he is satisfactorily performing upon the sole ground of his political beliefs," and their judgment was in the negative. Their view was that they were not required to consider the constitutional validity of "confining the hiring of some governmental employees to those of a particular political party," and they would "intimate no views whatever on that question."

In a dissenting opinion in which Burger and Rehnquist joined, Powell began by pointing out that partisan considerations influenced appointments as early as George Washington's administration and that patronage hiring was widely practiced in some states before Andrew Jackson's presidency. Powell cites historian Carl Russell Fish's belief that the patronage system played a significant part in democratizing American politics because it ended the domination of political affairs by an "aristocratic class" and "broadened the base of political participation." Agreed, in many cases the patronage system "also entailed costs to government efficiency," but the principal motivation for civil service reform was not "perceived impingement on employees' political beliefs," but rather the conviction that patronage induced corruption and inefficiency in the civil service and gave power to the "professional politicians" who relied on having patronage to dispense.

Powell points out that the respondents willingly accepted patronage jobs and were "fully familiar with the 'tenure' practices long prevailing in the sheriff's office." He believes they benefited from, rather than were penalized for, their political beliefs and activities, and he agrees with a decision of the supreme court of Pennsylvania "that the beneficiaries of a patronage system may not be heard to challenge it when it comes their time to be replaced."

In Powell's judgment, patronage hiring practices have stimulated political activity and strengthened political parties, "thereby helping to make government accountable." Referring to Brennan's statement that elimination of patronage politics would not cause the "demise of political parties," Powell observes that "one cannot avoid the impression, however, that even a threatened demise of parties would not trouble the plurality." He stresses that there are numerous routine, obscure elective offices in local governments and that the media generally shows little interest in elections for these offices "with consequent disinterest and absence of intelligent participation on the part of the public." If candidates for these offices did not have patronage to dispense, they were unlikely to "attract donations of time or money from voluntary groups."

To Powell, it was naive to think that political activities at local levels were motivated by "some academic interest in 'democracy' or other public service impulse." He states, "For the most part, as every politician knows, the hope of some reward generates a major portion of the local political activity supporting parties." Powell concludes, "History and long prevailing practice across the country support the view that patronage hiring practices make a sufficiently substantial contribution to the practical functioning of our democratic system to support their relatively modest intrusion on First Amendment rights."[27]

In a six-to-three decision rendered on March 31, 1980, in *Branti* v. *Finkel,* the Court broadened the ruling in *Elrod* v. *Burns.* In *Branti* v. *Finkel,* the plaintiffs were assistant public defenders in Rockland County, New York, who had been appointed by a Republican public defender. In 1978, the newly appointed public defender, a Democrat, announced that he planned to dismiss Republican holdover public defenders and replace them with Democrats. A federal district court blocked the removals, relying on *Elrod* v. *Burns.* The district court's ruling was approved by the circuit court of appeals, and the public defender then appealed to the Supreme Court.

The Supreme Court denied the appeal, finding nothing in the duties of an assistant public defender that justifies conditioning employment on political affiliation. The court agreed with the district court's finding that assistant public defenders had "very limited, if any responsibility" for implementing policy decisions in the public defender's office. However, it went beyond *Elrod* v. *Burns* by stating, "The ultimate inquiry is not whether the label 'policymaker' or 'confidential' fits a particular position, rather the question is whether the hiring authority can demonstrate that party affiliation is an appropriate requirement for the effective performance of the public office involved."

Writing for the majority, Justice Stevens stated, "Under some circumstances a position may be appropriately considered political even though it is neither confidential nor policy-making in character." On the other hand, it was "equally clear that party affiliation is not necessarily relevant to every policy-making or confidential position." The three dissenting justices objected that the majority decision was overly broad and vague and "cast serious doubt on the propriety of dismissing United States Attorneys." Only future decisions of the Court can clarify the ruling in *Branti* v. *Finkel.* Certainly the decision clearly indicates that elective and politically

---

[27]427 U.S. 347, 96 S. Ct., 2673 (1976).

appointed officials should be prepared to prove in court that a political removal meets Justice Stevens's test.[28]

Hiring

In September 1979, a federal district judge ruled that the patronage hiring system for city and county jobs in Cook County was unconstitutional. The suit was filed by an attorney who had run as an independent in an election for delegates to the 1970 Illinois Constitutional Convention and by a voter who supported his candidacy. They argued that through the use of governmental power and indirectly of public funds the Democratic machine in Cook County coerced the political behavior of patronage employees and thus violated the rights of independent candidates to fair and equal participation in the electoral process. In accepting this contention, the judge concurred that political hiring served to aid Democratic candidates and thus discriminated against independents. While this decision has altered the patronage system in Cook County and Chicago, it "has fallen far short of eliminating it" since various strategies are used to circumvent civil service requirements.[29]

Veterans Preference

In *Personnel Administrator* v. *Feeney* (1979), the U.S. Supreme Court ruled that a Massachusetts statute granting veterans absolute preference in civil service appointments did not constitute sex discrimination and was not a violation of the equal protection clause of the Fourteenth Amendment. The statute in question provides for employment of a veteran who passes a test before *any* nonveteran who passes it, regardless of relative test scores. The constitutionality of the law was challenged by Helen B. Feeney, a former state civil service employee, who lost out for promotion several times to veterans with lower test scores.

Writing for the Court majority, Justice Stewart noted that the statute did overwhelmingly benefit men but this was attributable

---

[28]Linda Greenhouse, "Supreme Court Rules Party Affiliation No Basis to Dismiss Public Employees," *New York Times*, April 1, 1980.

[29]Nathanial Sheppard, Jr., "Chicago's Administration Held in Contempt in Dispute on Patronage," *New York Times*, November 9, 1980. See also James D. Nowlan (ed.), *Inside State Government* (Urbana, Ill.: Institute of Government and Public Affairs, U. of Illinois, 1982), pp. 56–62.

largely to federal laws and policies restricting enlistment of women in the armed forces and to the "simple fact that women have never been subjected to a military draft." When the litigation began, over 98 percent of the veterans in Massachusetts were male and only 1.8 percent female. Feeney maintained that although the statute made no distinction between men and women it was gender-based because it favored a "status reserved under federal military policy primarily to men" and because its adverse impact on the employment of women was "too inevitable to have been unintended." Stewart disagreed, finding no intention on the part of the Massachusetts legislature to "incorporate in its public employment policies the panoply of sex-based and assertedly discriminatory federal laws that have prevented all but a handful of women from becoming veterans." Absolute preference for veterans may be unwise policy, but the Fourteenth Amendment "cannot be made a refuge from ill-advised laws."

The two dissenting justices—Marshall and Brennan—were convinced that the statute *did* evince "purposeful gender-based discrimination." Although neutral in form, it was "anything but neutral in application," since it inescapably reserved a disproportionate share of public employment to men, and since its legislative history indicated that the legislators knew it would have a very negative impact on women. The statute reflected and perpetuated "precisely the kind of archaic assumptions about women's roles" that the Court had previously held invalid.[30]

Dress and Personal Appearance

Recent court rulings have put the burden of proof on the employer to "show that any restrictive dress regulation is not arbitrary, but necessary to prevent disruption."[31] In *Lucia* v. *Duggan* (1969), the plaintiff was clean-shaven until he grew a short, neat, and well-trimmed beard over the Christmas holidays. He returned to school and taught for two weeks without disruption, but the school superintendent told him there was an unwritten policy against

---

[30]"Excerpts from Opinions in Court's Ruling Upholding Veterans' Job Preference," *New York Times*, June 6, 1979.

[31]June Weisberger, *Job Security and Public Employees* (Ithaca, N.Y.: Institute of Public Employment, New York State School of Industrial and Labor Relations, Cornell University, 1973), p. 29.

beards. The board sent him a letter requesting him to shave it off; when he did not do so, it voted to suspend him for seven days, the plaintiff receiving no notice that the board was considering such action. The board later suspended him for two more days for still wearing the beard and voted to meet again to consider dismissing him.

The plaintiff was not notified of the proposed meeting, but it was publicized locally. He asked that the meeting be postponed so he could obtain legal counsel, but this was not done. At the meeting, he met with the board in executive session and again requested postponement, but it was denied. He was fired, and no mention was made in the minutes of the reason for the action. The court ruled that the plaintiff had been denied due process because he had not been told what the charges were. Furthermore, the absence of a predismissal written or announced policy that male school teachers should not wear beards in the classroom amounted to an indiscriminate merging of a legislative-type function (determining whether wearing of a beard should be grounds for dismissal) and a judicial-type function (deciding whether the teacher was wearing the beard without reasonable explanation and whether the dismissal was suitable).[32]

In *Garrett* v. *City of Troy* (1972), a municipal employee was dismissed for failure to trim or remove his moustache and sideburns. The court held that the removal was not a violation of due process since the city acted upon the basis of substantial evidence that the employee's appearance caused unfavorable comments by the general public and other city employees and interfered with the proper functioning of the city. What constitutes substantial evidence to one court may not, of course, do so to another.[33]

Being a nudist was the issue in *Bruns* v. *Pomerleau* (1970). The plaintiff, a practicing nudist, claimed that refusal to accept his application as a probationary patrolman violated the First, Fifth, and Fourteenth Amendments. The police chief defended the plaintiff's rejection, arguing the need to maintain discipline and morals and to have a good public image. The court upheld the plaintiff, noting (1) there was nothing unusual about his background except for being a nudist; (2) no proof had been supplied that his being a nudist would interfere with performance of police duties; and (3)

---

[32]303 F. Supp. 112, D. Mass. (1969).
[33]341 F. Supp. 633, E. D. Mich. (1972).

other police officers and federal employees were members of the same nudist organization.[34]

Political Activities

It has been a long-standing practice for the political activities of millions of public employees to be greatly restricted. Historically, the purpose of federal and state legislation providing such restriction was to prevent coercion of public employees in elections and other partisan political activities, assure their political neutrality, and protect the merit system and the efficiency of the service. The Hatch Act of 1939 applies to all employees in the federal executive branch except for the President, the Vice President, heads and assistant heads of executive departments, members of the White House staff, and officials who determine national policy and are appointed by the President with Senate confirmation. On the basis of a 1940 amendment, its coverage was extended to state or local government employees "whose principal employment is in connection with any activity which is financed in whole or in part by loans or grants made by the United States."[35] However, a later amendment contained in the Federal Campaign Act of 1974 permits such state and local government employees to participate in certain partisan political activities, to be explained later in this chapter.

Specifically, the Hatch Act prohibits the "use of official authority or influence for the purpose of interfering with an election or affecting the result thereof" and, in the case of federal employees, taking "any active part in political management or in political campaigns." Since the first prohibition deals with action, not thought, it poses no problem for First Amendment rights; the need for the government to protect against such interference is generally not disputed. The second is sweeping, affects thought, and has in the opinion of many made the covered employees political eunuchs.[36] The act is enforced by the Office of Personnel Management, except that for federal employees not in the competitive civil service the enforcement responsibility rests with the employing department. For federal employees the most severe penalty for violation is re-

---

[34]319 F. Supp. 58, D. Md. (1970).
[35]Ch. 410, 53 Stat. 1147, ch. 640, 54 Stat. 767.
[36]"Collective Bargaining and Politics in Public Employment," *UCLA Law Review* 19, no. 6 (August 1972): 968–969.

moval and the minimum penalty suspension without pay for 30 days. In the case of state and local employees, if the OPM finds that a violation has occurred, it decides whether removal is warranted. If it recommends removal but the state or local government employer does not comply, the federal funding agency must withhold from the grant or loan an amount equal to two years' pay of the employee.

Federal employees are prohibited from the following: campaigning for partisan candidates or political parties; working to register voters for one party only; making campaign speeches or engaging in other activity to elect a partisan candidate; being a candidate or working in a campaign if any candidate represents a national or state political party; soliciting or collecting contributions or selling tickets to political fund-raising functions; distributing campaign material in a partisan election; organizing or managing political rallies or meetings; holding office in a political club or party; and circulating nominating petitions and campaigning for or against a candidate or slate of candidates in a partisan election.

Subject to departmental regulations, the following activities are permitted: registering and voting according to one's choice; assisting in voter registration drives; expressing opinions about candidates and issues publicly or privately; participating in campaigns where none of the candidates represents a political party; contributing money to a political organization or attending a political fund-raising function; wearing or displaying political badges, buttons, or stickers, but this may be restricted by agency regulations while the employee is carrying out official duties; attending political rallies and joining political clubs, but they cannot take active part in the conduct of a rally or in the management of a partisan political club; signing nominating petitions; and campaigning for and against referendum questions, constitutional amendments, municipal ordinances, and so on.

To varying degrees, most state and local government restrict their employees' political activities. Some have laws more restrictive than the Hatch Act, for example, prohibiting voluntary contributions and permitting employees "only to express their opinions privately," but most states have laws which are more lenient.[37]

---

[37]See Commission on Political Activity of Government Personnel, *A Commission Report, Vol. 2, Research* (Washington, D.C.: Government Printing Office, 1968), pp. 91–157; *UCLA Law Review* 19, no. 6 (August 1972): 970–983; and Melvin Hill,

The issue of constitutionality

In 1947, in *United Public Workers* v. *Mitchell,* the U.S. Supreme Court by a four-to-three decision upheld the Hatch Act prohibition on "taking an active part in political management or in political campaigns," ruling that it did not violate the First, Fifth, Ninth, and Tenth Amendments. Stating that the "fundamental human rights" concerned were not absolute, the majority defined the Court's task as that of balancing the "extent of the guarantees of freedom against a congressional enactment to protect a democratic society against the supposed evil of political partisanship by classified employees of government." The standard it applied was that the conduct regulated be "reasonably deemed by Congress to interfere with the efficiency of the public service." Since Congress and the President were responsible for efficient public service, if in their judgment efficiency was "best obtained by prohibiting active participation by classified employees in politics as party officers or workers," it saw "no constitutional objection."[38]

In a companion case, *Oklahoma* v. *United States Civil Service Commission,* the Court sustained the provision in the Hatch Act prohibiting state and local government employees in federally aided programs from being active in political management or in political campaigns. While under the Tenth Amendment the federal government could not directly regulate political activities of state officials and local employees, it could do so indirectly by fixing "the terms upon which its money allotments to States shall be disbursed."[39]

In July 1972, after a long period of rising public employee discontent with the Hatch Act, a three-judge federal district court by a two-to-one decision declared unconstitutional the Hatch Act prohibition of political activity by federal employees. The majority did not question the government's interest in so restricting federal employees; its concern was that the prohibition lacked precision and that the act was "capable of sweeping and uneven application." It referred to a provision in the act adopting by reference all rulings and decisions on prohibited political activities made by the commission prior to 1940; to understand the law, the employee had to be familiar with some 3,000 decisions made by the commission

Jr., "The 'Littler Hatch Acts': State Laws Regulating Political Activities of Local Government Employees," *State Government* 52, no. 4 (Autumn 1979).
[38]330 U.S. 75, 67 S. Ct. 556, 91 L. Ed. 754 (1947).
[39]330 U.S. 127 (1947).

between 1907 and 1939. While generally praising the commission for its enforcement of the act, it concluded that

> any conscientious public servant concerned for the security of his job and conscious of the latent power in his supervisor to discipine him . . . must feel continuously in doubt as to what he can do or say politically. The result is unacceptable when measured by the need to eliminate vagueness and overbreadth in the sensitive area of free expression.[40]

In 1973, in a six-to-three decision in *United States Civil Service Commission* v. *National Association of Letter Carriers, AFL-CIO,* the Supreme Court reaffirmed its decision in *United Public Workers* v. *Mitchell.* It found that there was nothing "fatally overbroad about the statute" and that the commission's regulations were "set out in terms that the ordinary person exercising ordinary common sense can sufficiently understand and observe, without sacrifice to the public interest," and were not impermissibly vague. The restrictions on endorsements in advertisements, broadcasts, and literature and on speaking at political party meetings in support of partisan candidates for public or party office, the major areas of difficulty, were "clearly stated, they are political acts normally performed only in the context of partisan campaigns by one taking an active role in them, and they are sustainable for the same reasons that the other acts of political campaigning are constitutionally proscribable."[41]

In a case decided on the same day, *Broadrick* v. *Oklahoma,* the Court also upheld the section of Oklahoma's merit system law containing Hatch Act-type political activity restrictions. The Court majority ruled that the statute contained explicit standards, the prohibitions were confined to clearly partisan political activity, and the activities in which the particular plaintiffs were engaged were not constitutionally protected.[42]

In 1976, Congress passed a bill to permit federal employees to take part in political campaigns and to seek nomination or election to any office, but President Ford vetoed the measure. Since then efforts in Congress to pass a similar bill have failed. The issue is

---

[40]*National Association of Letter Carriers, AFL-CIO, et al.* v. *United States,* D. D. C., July 31, 1972.

[41]*United States Civil Service Commission* v. *National Association of Letter Carriers,* 93 S. Ct. 2880, 37 L. Ed. 2d 796 (1973).

[42]93 S. Ct. 2908, 37 L. Ed. 2d 830, 41 L. W. 5111 (1973).

not dead because many people believe that to protect them from political coercion federal employees have been stripped of their political rights—too high a price to pay.

The amendment to the Hatch Act passed in 1974 referred to earlier allows state and local government employees to: serve as officers of political parties, attend meetings, vote on candidates and issues, and take an active part in the management of a political party, club, or other organization, solicit votes in partisan elections, organize and reorganize political groups, promote and participate in fund-raising activities of partisan candidates and political parties, act as challengers or poll watchers during partisan elections, drive voters to the polls in such elections, initiate or circulate partisan nominating petitions, and be candidates for or serve as delegates, alternates, or proxies to political party conventions. The only remaining prohibitions are being a candidate for elective office, soliciting contributions while on the job, and using official authority to influence nominations or elections. However, where more restrictive state laws governing political activities of public employees exist, the state laws remain in effect.

The Right to Organize and Strike

Although since 1935 when Congress passed the Wagner Act private sector workers have had a legal right to collective bargaining, there is no similar federal legislation for state and local government employees. Title VII of the Civil Service Reform Act of 1978 enacts into law collective bargaining rights for federal employees provided by executive order since 1962.

Historically, employee unions were resisted in the federal service, particularly the Post Office Department, until passage in 1912 of the Lloyd-LaFollette Act. This act prohibits the removal or reduction in rank or compensation of any postal employee for joining any organization not affiliated with an outside body which imposes an obligation to engage in, or support, a strike against the United States. Although postal workers alone were specified, in later years this statute was interpreted by extension to apply to all federal employees. For most federal employees, collective bargaining rights were not granted until President John F. Kennedy's Executive Order 10988 (see Chapter 1). Employee unions were also generally resisted in state and local governments, and it was not until 1959 that the first state passed legislation authorizing collective bargaining for employees under its jurisdiction. There has been a long battle to obtain recognition of unions and collective bargaining rights, and in many state and local governments it continues.

The rights to organize and to collective bargaining

The right to organize has been established by the courts as a constitutional right of association under the First and Fourteenth Amendments since *McLaughlin* v. *Tilendis* (1968). The plaintiffs, two probationary teachers in the Cook County, Illinois, school system, charged they had been terminated for union activity, and a district court upheld the school authorities, stating that the plaintiffs had no right to join or form a labor union. In reversing the district court, the court of appeals pointed out, "Just this month the Supreme Court held that an Illinois teacher was protected by the First Amendment from discharge even though he wrote a partially false letter to a local newspaper in which he criticized the school board's policy" *(Pickering)*. There was no showing that the plaintiffs' activities had interfered with the "proper performance" of their classroom duties. "If teachers can engage in scathing and partially inaccurate public criticism of their school board, surely they can form and take part in associations to further what they consider to be their well-being."

As to the trial judge's concern that the union might engage in strikes and other action affecting the "very ability of the governmental entity to function," the court of appeals, citing the Supreme Court's ruling in *Elfbrandt* v. *Russell,* said that even if the record had showed that the union had been "connected with unlawful activity" they could not be charged with "their organization's misdeeds" simply because of their membership.[43] In 1969, *McLaughlin* v. *Tilendis* was cited by the court of appeals in a ruling that the city of North Platte, Nebraska, had violated the constitutional right of association of two employees in the street department who had been discharged for joining a union *(American Federation of State, County, and Municipal Employees, AFL-CIO* v. *Woodward).*[44]

---

[43]398 F. 2d 287 (1968).
[44]406 F. 2d 137 (1969).

In *Atkins* v. *City of Charlotte* (1969), both the right to organize and the right to bargain collectively were at issue. One North Carolina statute prohibited state and local government employees from becoming or remaining members of labor organizations which were, or became, affiliated with any national or international union that had collective bargaining as one of its purposes. A second statute declared illegal any agreement or contract concerning public employees between any state or local agency and a labor organization. The plaintiffs, members of the Charlotte Fire Department, complained that these statutes were overbroad and violated the First Amendment and the due process and equal protection clauses of the Fourteenth Amendment. They wanted to become members of a local which would become affiliated with the International Association of Fire Fighters.

The district court hearing the case found the statute denying organization rights "void on its face as an abridgment of freedom of association protected by the First and Fourteenth Amendments. . . . The flaw in it is an intolerable 'overbreadth' unnecessary to the protection of valid state interests." Expressing a social policy view, the court said, "It is beyond argument that a single individual cannot negotiate on an equal basis with an employer who hires hundreds of people. Recognition of this fact of life is the basis of labor-management relations in this country." The city of Charlotte itself had admitted in its brief that organization rights of pubic employees were being increasingly recognized and that collective bargaining might be beneficial in many situations for municipal fire fighters, but it feared that national affiliation could lead to strikes and "fires raging out of control." The court did not "question the power of the State to deal with such a contingency," but the statute made association with any labor union illegal, even unions opposed to strikes.

Concerning collective bargaining, the court's view was that this right "so firmly entrenched in American labor-management relations rests upon national legislation and not upon the Federal Constitution." There is nothing in that Constitution which "entitles one to have a contract with another who does not want it," so it was "but a step further to hold that the State may lawfully forbid such contracts with its instrumentalities."[45]

---

[45]296 F. Supp. 1068 (1969).

The right to strike

In 1971, in *United Federation of Postal Clerks* v. *Blount,* a U.S. district court ruled there was no constitutional right of public employees to strike. The United Federation of Postal Clerks sought invalidation of several federal statutes that denied federal employment to those participating in any strike against the U.S. government or asserting a right to such strikes. The plaintiff contended that the absolute prohibition of strike activity contained in these provisions violated employees' rights of association and free speech and denied them equal protection of the law. It also argued that the language "to strike" and "participate in a strike" was vague and overbroad and violated both the First Amendment and the due process clause of the Fifth Amendment.

The court pointed out that under the common law neither public nor private workers had a constitutional right to strike, and collective action on their part often was considered conspiracy. When the right of private employees to strike was granted, it was by statute (in the National Labor Relations Act); since public workers "stand on no stronger footing in this regard," in the absence of a statute they do not have the strike right. Since there is no constitutional right to strike, it is not "irrational or arbitrary for the government to condition employment on a promise not to withhold labor collectively."

As to the plaintiff's argument that the provisions were constitutionally overbroad in applying to all employees "regardless of the type or importance of the work they do," it made no difference whether their jobs were essential or nonessential or whether similar jobs were performed by private workers who can strike. Where fundamental rights are not involved, a particular classification does not violate the equal protection clause if "any state of facts reasonably may be conceived to justify it." Therefore, "there is latitude for distinctions rooted in reason and practice, especially where the difficulty of drafting a no-strike statute which distinguishes among types and classes of employees is obvious."

Concerning the contention that the word "strike" and the phrase "participate in a strike" were vague, the court did not agree. The definition of strike in the Taft-Hartley Act—"any concerted stoppage of work by employees . . . and any concerted slowdown or other concerted interruption of operations by employees"—was evidence that the meaning of the word was clear. As to "participation," the government during the oral argument had represented that this meant striking, that is, action in concert with others to withhold services, and the court said:

> We adopt this construction of the phrase, which will exclude the First Amendment problems raised by the plaintiff in that it removes from the strict reach of these statutes and other provisions such conduct as speech, union memberships, fund-raising, organization, distribution of literature and informational picketing, even though those activities may take place in concert during a strike by others.[46]

The district court's decision was later affirmed by the U.S. Supreme Court in a one-line judgment.

While several state governments have passed laws granting public employees in these states a limited right to strike, there is little present likelihood that Congress will pass such legislation for federal employees.

■ OBLIGATIONS

In deciding public policy with respect to obligations of public employees to respect constitutional rights of private individuals, two considerations must be weighed. They are: (1) the need of the government to function effectively and of its employees to be able to take action without fear of being penalized for doing their jobs faithfully; and (2) the need to protect individuals from unjustified injurious action by government and its agents.

Key questions in determining the liability of public employees are: Should government workers be granted *absolute* immunity from suit for monetary damages for acts they take within the scope of their official duties? If not, should any public officials be given absolute immunity, and, if so, which ones? Should employees be granted *qualified* rather than absolute immunity, based on the "good faith and reasonableness" of their conduct, and, if so, which ones should enjoy this qualified immunity and how should good faith and reasonableness be determined?

The concept of immunity of public officials is derived from the principle of sovereign immunity of governments, which stems from the English common law doctrine that the king can do no wrong. For many decades now, the federal and the state governments have waived much of this sovereign immunity and permit private parties

---

[46]325 F. Supp. 879 (D.D.C.). Aff'd 404 U.S. 802 (1971).

to sue them in the courts for damages, as in the case of contract claims. The ability to govern, it was realized, did not require the state to be absolutist and deny any redress to individuals with legitimate claims against the government. However, it has only been in recent years that the U.S. Supreme Court has ruled that private individuals can obtain monetary damages in suits against federal, state, and local governments and their agents for violations of constitutional rights, and with very few exceptions public officials now have qualified, rather than absolute, immunity from such damages.

Immunities of public officials are based on the common law, statutory law, and the federal and the state constitutions. These are the sources the courts consult in making decisions on the immunities of given officials, and in making these rulings the judges not only consider previous court decisions but also make their own judgments as to what is best for public policy.

Before the 1970s, the U.S. Supreme Court protected administrative officials against civil damage suits, the leading case being *Spalding* v. *Vilas* (1896).[47] Spalding, who represented postmasters seeking a salary increase, sued Postmaster General Vilas for distributing a notice to the postmasters that allegedly depicted Spalding as a common swindler who should not be paid by his clients. Spalding sought monetary damages for the injury to his reputation and business. The Court ruled that Vilas had absolute immunity, "however improper his motives may have been." The essential consideration, it said, was that "the head of an Executive Department, keeping within the limits of his authority, should not be under any apprehension that the motives that control his official conduct may, at any time, become the subject of inquiry in a civil suit for damages. It would seriously cripple the proper and effective administration of public affairs as entrusted to the executive branch of government, if he were subjected to any such constraint."

In effect, the Court placed department heads in the same category as judges, for under the common law, even if members of the judiciary show malicious intent in their decisions they have absolute immunity from damage suits. The justification for this absolute immunity is that it is necessary to protect the independence of the judiciary even if it shelters some judges with the wrong motives. The Court saw compelling reasons for granting Vilas the same degree of immunity, and in later years it also granted ab-

---

[47]161 U.S. 483 (1896).

solute immunity to the Acting Director of the federal Office of Rent Stabilization and to many other public administrators, "including a deputy U.S. marshall, a district director and collection officer of the IRS, a claims representative of HEW, and a secret service agent."[48]

In *Bivens* v. *Six Unknown Named Agents of Federal Bureau of Narcotics* (1971),[49] the Court moved in a completely different direction, authorizing damage suits against federal officials for constitutional violations and reopening the whole question of what immunities these officials should have. Bivens brought suit in federal district court against the Bureau agents who he complained in November of 1965 entered his apartment without a search warrant, manacled him in front of his wife and children, searched the apartment from "stem to stern," arrested him, and even threatened to arrest his whole family. Specifically, Bivens sought $15,000 in damages from each of the agents for causing him "great humiliation, embarrassment, and mental suffering because of their unlawful conduct."

The district court dismissed the complaint, on the ground that the suit should be heard in state court because the rights of privacy asserted were creations of state, not federal, law. The district court also ruled that in any event the defendants were immune from liability by virtue of their official position. The court of appeals affirmed the district court's ruling that the suit should be heard in state court but did not pass upon the question of liability.

The Supreme Court majority emphatically stated that the federal courts *did* have jurisdiction. Essentially, its decision was that the Fourth Amendment to the federal Constitution's prohibition of unreasonable searches and seizures could not be enforced if the agents' action in entering Bevins's apartment without a warrant had to be judged in accordance with the provisions of state law against trespass. The Fourth Amendment, Justice Brennan wrote for the majority, "operates as a limitation upon the exercise of federal power regardless of whether the State in whose jurisdiction that power is exercised would prohibit or penalize the identical act if engaged in by a private citizen." Although the Fourth Amendment did not specifically provide for the remedy of damage suits, the

---

[48]David H. Rosenbloom, "Public Administrators' Official Immunity and the Supreme Court: Developments During the 1970s," *Public Administration Review* 40, no. 2 (March-April 1980).

[49]403 U.S. (1971).

Supreme Court had the power to authorize such suits even in the absence of a federal statute so providing.

Since the appeals court had not ruled upon the question of the agents' immunity from damages, the Supreme Court remanded the case to the appeals court for a determination on this question. The appeals court ruled that the agents did not have an absolute immunity because to have it would mean that in exercising their discretionary powers they could enter a dwelling without a warrant or probable cause and make an arrest. However, as Rosenbloom writes, "So entrenched was the notion of immunity that the appeals court left the door open for the agents to develop a good-faith defense based on the reasonability of the officials' actions at the time they occurred."[50] Nonetheless, *Bivens* was a very significant decision, because it established the right to sue in federal court for monetary damages, a right which would be meaningless if no damages could be assessed under any circumstances.

The Civil Rights Act of 1871 and Damage Suits

The U.S. Supreme Court decisions on liabilities of public employees for unconstitutional acts discussed up to this point have dealt with federal, not state and local government employees. Turning to the state and local government levels, our discussion logically must begin with a provision of the Civil Rights Act of 1871 (42 U.S. Code 1983) that reads:

> Every person who, under color of any statute, ordinance, regulation, custom or usage of any state or territory, subjects or causes to be subjected any citizen of the United States or other person within the jurisdiction thereof to the deprivation of any rights, privileges, or immunities procured by the Constitution and laws shall be liable to the party injured in any action at law, suit in equity, or other proper proceeding for redress.

Congress passed this legislation in the post-Civil war reconstruction period to protect the former slaves from discrimination, but decisions of the Supreme Court deferring to the police powers of the state in voting rights and other civil rights cases caused this 1871 Act to become "largely dormant."[51]

---

[50]David H. Rosenbloom, *Public Administration Law: Bench v. Bureau in the United States* (New York: Dekker, 1983), p. 194.
[51]Ibid., p. 189.

In *Scheur* v. *Rhodes* (1974),[52] the petitioners, representatives of the estates of students killed on the Kent University University campus, brought damage actions under 42 U.S. Code 1983 against the governor, the Adjutant General of the Ohio National Guard, various other Guard officers and enlisted members, and the University president. They charged that these officials, acting under color of state law, "intentionally, recklessly, willfully and wantonly" caused an unnecessary Guard deployment on the campus and ordered the Guard members to perform illegal acts resulting in the students' deaths. The U.S. district court in which the suit was brought dismissed the complaints for lack of jurisdiction; the appeals court affirmed on that ground but also on the alternative ground that the common-law doctrine of executive immunity was absolute and barred action against the state officials.

In its decision, the Supreme Court first ruled that the federal courts did have jurisdiction. Turning then to the appeal court's determination that the state officials possessed absolute immunity, the Court declared, "It can hardly be argued, at this late date, that under no circumstances can the officers of state government be subject to liability under this statute [42 U.S.C. 1983]." The very purpose of the statute was to protect against abuses of authority by state officials, so it could not be considered that Congress intended for these officials to have absolute immunity. The Court pointed out that, as one example, it had never granted absolute immunity to police officers, and that police had only a qualified immunity from damage suits depending on whether or not an arrest was made in good faith and with probable cause.

Similarly, the Court continued, officials of the executive branch have a qualified, not an absolute, immunity. Since higher officials have more discretion than lesser ones, their range of discretion must be broad. The Court concluded, "These considerations suggest that, in varying scope, a qualified immunity is available to officers of the executive branch of government, the variation being dependent upon the scope of discretion and responsibilities of the office and all the circumstances as they reasonably appeared at the time of the action on which liability is sought to be based. It is the existence of reasonable grounds for the belief formed at the time and in light of all circumstances, coupled with good-faith be-

---

[52]416 U.S. (1974).

lief, that affords a basis for qualified immunity of executive officers for acts performed in the course of official conduct."

The Court did not rule on whether the defendants had acted reasonably and with good faith because it considered that the evidence before the district and appeals courts was not sufficient for any finding as to good faith properly to be made. Accordingly, the Court remanded the case to the lower courts for further proceedings to determine the liability of the defendants, but the case was later settled out of court.

In *Wood et al.* v. *Strickland et al.* (1975),[53] the U.S. Supreme Court set forth a standard for determining whether a state or local government official is entitled to qualified immunity. This suit was brought under statute 42 U.S.C. 1983 by Peggy Strickland and Virginia Crain, students in an Arkansas high school, against members of the school board, two school administrators, and the Special School District of Mena, Arkansas. Strickland and Crain had been expelled from the Mena Public High School on grounds that they had violated a school regulation prohibiting the use or possession of intoxicating beverages at school or school activities. Complaining that their constitutional due process rights were violated because they were not given a full-fledged hearing before being expelled, they sought compensatory and punitive damages.

The district court ruled in favor of the school officials and the school district on the basis that they were immune from damages because there was no proof that they acted with "malice in the sense of ill will" towards the two students. The appeals court decided that the students' substantive due process rights had been violated and remanded the case to the district court for a new trial on the question of damages. It disagreed with the district court that specific intent to harm wrongfully was a requirement for recovery of damages. All that needed to "be established was that the defendants did not, in the light of all circumstances, act in good faith. . . . The test is an objective, rather than a subjective one."

Hearing this case on appeal, a U.S. Supreme Court majority held that the school board members did not have the absolute immunity from damages they claimed. They did have a qualified immunity, but it was true that the lower federal courts had not defined this immunity "with a single voice. There is general agreement on the existence of a 'good faith' immunity, but the courts

---

[53]420 U.S. (1975).

have either emphasized different factors as elements of good faith or have not given specific content to the good faith standard."

Noting the disagreement between the district and appeals court over whether the test of good faith should be objective or subjective, the Court majority held that "the appropriate standard necessarily contains elements of both. The official himself must be acting sincerely and with a belief that he is doing right, but an act violating a student's constitutional rights can be no more justified by ignorance or disregard of settled, indisputable law on the part of one entrusted with supervision of students' daily lives than by the presence of actual malice." The school board member was not immune from damages "if he knew or reasonably should have known that the action he took within his sphere of official responsibility would violate the constitutional rights of the student affected, or if he took the action with the malicious intention to cause a deprivation of constitutional rights or other injury to the student." In other words, even if officials act without malicious intent, they lose immunity if their conduct reveals lack of knowledge of constitutional rights of individuals of which in their official capacities they should be fully aware. However, "a compensatory award will be appropriate only if the school board member has acted with such impermissable motivation or with such disregard of the students' clearly established constitutional rights that his action cannot reasonably be characterized as being in good faith."

The Court majority believed this standard was clear, would not discourage officials from taking necessary actions, would impel them to be familiar with relevant court decisions, and at the same time would deter them from acting unconstitutionally. In its dissenting opinion, the Court minority flatly disagreed. The test was far from clear because constitutional scholars themselves disagreed about what was "settled, indisputable law" and "unquestioned constitutional rights." It was so harsh that it left "little substance to the doctrine of qualified immunity." Further, "ignorance of the law is explicitly equated with actual malice." The minority justices also expressed strong doubt that "qualified persons will continue in the desired numbers to volunteer for service in public education" since the majority decision so significantly increased the "possibility of personal liability."

Since the prohibitions of 42 U.S.C. 1983 apply to state and local governments and not to the federal government, until 1978 *Bivens* remained as the U.S. Supreme Court's leading decision on immunities of federal employees. It will be recalled that *Bivens* authorized damage suits against federal officials but did not spell out the Court's position on the test to be applied in granting employees immunity. In *Butz* v. *Economou* (1978),[54] the Court ruled that *"federal* officials should enjoy no greater zone of protection when they violate *federal* constitutional rules than do *state* officers." (Italics ours.)

This suit originated after an unsuccessful effort by the Department of Agriculture to revoke or suspend the registration of Economou's commodity futures commission company. Economou maintained that the Department had taken the action against him because he had been an outspoken critic of the agency, that his constitutional right of free speech was thereby infringed, and that the Department had also violated his due process rights by issuing complaints against him without the notice or warning required by law. Accordingly, he sought damages from the Secretary and Assistant Secretary of Agriculture and other Department officials.

The U.S. government requested the district court to dismiss the complaint because the individual defendants had official immunity. The district court held that the defendants would be entitled to immunity if they could show that "their alleged unconstitutional acts were within the outer perimeter of their authority and discretion," and it dismissed the suit because it concluded that the "alleged unconstitutional acts were both within the scope of their authority and discretionary." The appeals court reversed this decision, on grounds that the Supreme Court in decisions since *Bivens* had elucidated the principles governing the immunity of executive branch officials. In these decisions, the Supreme Court had established that officials exercising discretionary functions "did not need the protection of an absolute immunity from suit, but only a qualified immunity based on good faith and reasonable grounds." The appeals court noted that other circuit courts had "concluded that the Supreme Court's development of official immunity doctrine in 42 U.S.C. 1983 suits against state officials applies with equal force to federal officers sued on a cause of action derived directly from the Constitution, since both types of suits serve the same function of protecting citizens against violations of their constitutional rights by government officials."

The Supreme Court fully concurred with the appeals court,

---

[54] 438 U.S. (1978).

pointing out that in *Spalding* the Postmaster General had not been guilty of disregard of "obvious statutory or constitutional limitations on his powers." The Court stated that as a general rule executive branch officials charged with constitutional violations had qualified immunity from damages only, but there were some officials whose special functions required a full exemption from liability, specifically hearing examiners and administrative judges in agency adjudications, and agency officials performing functions analagous to those of a prosecutor. The case was remanded to the lower courts for decision in accordance with these principles.

The Liability of State and Local Governments

A successful suit for monetary damages against a state or local government employee for violation of one's constitutional rights does not guarantee that the damages will be paid because the employee may lack the financial resources. From another standpoint, since often the employee is acting in accordance with official policy and directives, it is not fair for him or her to have to make payment while the public employer escapes responsibility.

In *Monroe* v. *Pape* (1961), the U.S. Supreme Court ruled that local governments were wholly immune from suit under 42 U.S.C. 1983 because in its opinion the legislative history did not indicate that Congress meant the word "person" to include municipal governments. In *Monell et al.* v. *Department of Social Services of New York et al.* (1978), the Court disagreed and reversed this decision.[55]

Monell et al. were female employees of New York City's Department of Social Services and of the Board of Education who brought a class action suit under 42 U.S.C. 1983 against the Department and its commissioner, and the Board of Education and its Chancellor, and the Mayor. They claimed that their constitutional rights had been violated because official policy required them as pregnant employees to take unpaid leaves of absence before such leaves were needed for medical reasons, and they sought back pay for this unlawful forced leave.

The U.S. district court found that the acts complained of were unconstitutional but held that back pay damages could not be assessed against the City because under *Monroe* v. *Pape* municipal-

---

[55]436 U.S. (1978).

ities were immune. The appeals court concurred that the City could not be sued for damages, but the Supreme Court majority, in a detailed review of the legislative history of 42 U.S.C. 1983, concluded that Congress *did* intend the word "person" to include municipalities. Accordingly, the Court majority ruled that local governing bodies and local officials can be sued directly for monetary relief where the alleged action is unconstitutional implementation or execution of a policy statement, ordinance, regulation, or decision officially promulgated by those whose edicts or acts may fairly be said to represent official policy.

Since a municipality's financial resources, although not unlimited, are greater than those of an employee, the decision in *Monell* meant that the person whose constitutional rights had been violated was in a better position to obtain monetary damages. However, if the municipality can claim the same good faith defense that its employees can assert, since judges and juries often accept that the act complained of was taken in good faith, the person still would find it difficult to obtain damages.

In *Owen* v. *City of Independence* (1980),[56] the U.S. Supreme Court held that municipalities are *not* entitled to the same good faith defense as an employee. This suit was brought under 42 U.S.C. 1983 by Owen, the city's Chief of Police, who had been discharged after an investigation of the police department. He was given no reason for the dismissal, simply a written advice stating that the action was being taken pursuant to a provision in the city charter. Owens sued the city, the city manager, and the members of the City Council for violation of his substantive and procedural due process rights. The appeals court ruled that, although the city had violated Owen's constitutional rights, all the defendants, including the city were entitled to qualified immunity based on the good faith of the city.

The Supreme Court majority warned that, since the purpose of 42 U.S.C. 1983 is to protect persons wronged by abuse of government authority and to deter future constitutional violations, municipalities do not have qualified immunity for good-faith constitutional violations. If they did, in view of the qualified immunity possessed by most government officials, many victims of municipal malfeasance would have no remedy if the city could assert a good faith defense.

---

[56]445 U.S. (1980).

Knowledge that a municipality will be liable for all of its injurious conduct, whether or not committed in good faith, should create an incentive for officials to err on the side of protecting constitutional rights. "Furthermore, the threat that damages might be levied against the city may encourage those in a policymaking position to institute internal rules and programs designed to minimize the likelihood of unintentional infringements on constitutional rights." Also, with the threat of personal liability removed, employees would not be inhibited in discharging their responsibilities.

In *Maine* v. *Thiboutot* (1980),[57] the U.S. Supreme Court ruled that the language "and laws" in 42 U.S.C. 1983 encompassed claims based on purely statutory violations of federal law, as well as abridgements of the Constitution. In this case, the Court majority found that in withholding welfare payments to Thiboutot, Maine had violated the federal Social Security Act and in so doing, 42 U.S.C. 1983.

The majority based this ruling on earlier decisions of the Court that it believed implicitly suggested that 42 U.S.C. 1983 remedies encompassed violations of statutory as well as constitutional law. Since the states administer many programs based on federal legislation, *Thiboutot* is a far-reaching decision.

It should be remembered that *Owen* and *Thiboutot* do not apply to federal employees because 42 U.S.C. 1983 is a prohibition on those acting under state, not federal, law. This means that if the federal government, not the employee, is to be responsible for damages in civil suits, Congress must so legislate. Bills are now being considered in Congress to make the U.S. government liable for all constitutional violations and for it to be the exclusive defendant in suits against federal employees acting within the scope of their duties. We will refer to these bills in our summary analysis at the end of this chapter.

The President and Personal Liability

Whether or not the President of the United States has absolute immunity from civil damages liability was the issue in *Nixon* v. *Fitzgerald* (1982).[58] Fitzgerald had testified before congressional committees about cost overruns on the C-5 A transport plane and

---

[57]448 U.S. (1980).
[58]*Federal Reports*, No. 79–1738, June 1982.

been dismissed from his position as a management analyst with the Department of the Air Force. At one point, President Nixon in a public statement said that he had ordered the discharge, a statement the White House later retracted. Fitzgerald sued Air Force officials, certain White House aides, and Nixon himself for violation of his constitutional free speech rights.

The Court majority ruled that Nixon did have absolute immunity because of the importance of the presidential office and the need to maintain the constitutional principle of separation of powers. Since there were other means of holding the President accountable such as impeachment, absolute immunity for the chief executive would not leave the nation unprotected.

Nixon v. *Fitzgerald* is also an important decision because in their opinion written by Justice Powell, the Court majority further elaborated its position on the whole question of liability of government officials performing discretionary functions. These officials, Powell wrote, "generally are shielded from liability for civil damages insofar as their conduct does not violate clearly established statutory or constitutional rights of which a reasonable person would have known."

In *Wood* v. *Strickland,* it will be recalled, the Court majority held that the standard to be applied in judging an official's conduct contained elements of both subjectivity (his or her intent) and of objectivity (did the official disregard "settled, indisputable law"?). The decision in *Nixon* v. *Fitzgerald* eliminates the subjective test of whether or not the defendant had acted with malicious intent.

Summary Analysis

The preceding discussion summarizes what the U.S. Supreme Court has ruled to date on personal liability of public employees for damages in civil suits alleging constitutional violations. For the public employee, knowledge of these rulings is vital, particularly because of the Court's reliance on the single "objective" standard of knowledge of the law. Just what the law is often is in doubt, but in *Wood* v. *Strickland* the Court majority did say that the official could not be expected to predict the "future course of constitutionality."[59]

Some legal commentators believe that the elimination of the sub-

---

[59]420 U.S. (1975).

jective test (intent) will make it easier for employees to defend themselves. In jury trials, they say, defendants have difficulty convincing jurors that they acted in good faith whereas they are more successful in satisfying them that the law was unclear or inconclusive. As to 42 U.S.C. 1983 suits, other authorities state that the record clearly shows that recovery of damages is unlikely. Frequently, the complainant is a person with a poor social background charged with committing a crime, and the jury tends to sympathize with the police officer. If the suit is against a high level state official, judges stress the scope of the official's discretion and the latitude she or he should have in taking actions. Too, it is also difficult to measure in monetary terms the damage suffered by the complainant.[60]

Still, most public employees have qualified immunity only, and in contemporary litigious society, many public employees are being sued for damages which may be awarded. The ideal situation would be one in which the individual has maximum protection from unconstitutional acts by the state and its agents; government officials are very careful not to be guilty of such acts; and the public employer is not harassed by frivolous suits.

Currently, hundreds of suits are pending against federal employees, the majority against middle managers for taking certain personnel actions. That most of these suits are ill-founded is revealed by the fact that very few result in collectable judgments. Supporters of the bills now in Congress to make the government the sole defendant in such suits and to make it responsible for any damage judgments stress the beneficial effect passage would have on the morale of the many employees who are being or might be sued.

Like so many other problems in government today, the employee liability one is multifaceted. Governments and their agents may act maliciously, arbitrarily, or simply erroneously, with consequently serious injury to private individuals. Yet governments must act and obstacles should not be placed in the way of effective enforcement of the laws and of official policy. If constitutional violation results from an employee's faithful implementation of official policy, the public employer should be liable because it is the

---

[60]See Joseph Katten, "Knocking on Wood: Some Thoughts on the Immunities of State Officials to Civil Rights Damage Action," *Vanderbilt Law Review* 30, no. 5 (October 1979), and "Developments in the Law Section 1983 and Federalism," *Harvard Law Review* 90, pt. 2 (1977).

directing party and the employee simply an agent. The U.S. Supreme Court has established certain guidelines for governments and employees to follow, but governments and their agents must decide what is the correct action to take in a particular situation.

BIBLIOGRAPHY

Aronin, Louis. "Due Process Rights and Restrictions on Employees." In *Portrait of a Process: Collective Negotiations in Public Employment*, by Public Employment Relations Service. Fort Washington, Pa.: Labor Relations Press, 1979.

Cooper, Phillip. *Public Law and Public Administration*. Palo Alto, Calif.: Mayfield Press, 1983.

Goldman, Deborah. "Due Process and Public Personnel Management." *Review of Public Personnel Administration* 2, no. 1 (Fall 1981).

Hildreth, W. Bartley, Miller, Gerald J., and Rabin, Jack. "The Liability of Public Executives: Implications for Practice in Personnel Administration." *Review of Public Personnel Administration* 1, no. 1 (Fall 1980).

McFeeley, Neil D. "Patronage: The Public Service and the Courts." *Public Personnel Management* 10, no. 3 (Fall 1981).

Meier, Kenneth J. "Ode to Patronage: A Critical Analysis of Two Recent Supreme Court Decisions." *Public Administration Review* 41, no. 5 (September/October 1981).

Rabin, Robert J. "The Protection of Individuals and Their Rights." In *Portrait of a Process: Collective Negotiations in Public Employment*, by Public Employment Relations Service. Fort Washington, Pa.: Labor Relations Press, 1979.

Rosenbloom, David H. *Public Law and Public Administration: Bench and Bureau in the United States*. New York: Dekker, 1983.

16 The Future of Public Personnel Administration

For some years now there has been widespread disillusionment with government, symbolized in the complaint that "government doesn't work." Many elective officials and much of the public place the blame for the failures of public programs principally upon the "bureaucrats" and on the personnel system in government. Against this background, public personnel agencies currently must deal with the painful effects of budgetary reductions that have necessitated layoffs and created fears in employees and their dependents that there will be many other reductions-in-force. At the same time, merit system administrators see their own budgets substantially reduced although many more demands are made on public personnel administration, such as meeting test validity requirements, prolonged negotiations with the unions, and public pressures to make government more productive.

Without any intention of excusing inadequacies of public personnel systems, three realities are often overlooked:

(1) As already stated in this book, the government environment is a peculiar one, and personnel policies and practices of the private sector often cannot be emulated successfully.

(2) The state of the art in many technical aspects of personnel administration is still not very advanced, and simple, quick solutions to some of the technical problems are not available.

(3) There are such profound, often irreconcilable, differences of opinion over what values should govern public personnel policy that it is impossible to foresee a public personnel administration that does not displease many people.

■ PECULIARITIES OF THE GOVERNMENT ENVIRONMENT

The peculiarity of government that should be mentioned first is that, because they work for the people, public employees experience a morale problem not found in private establishments. Even in countries like Britain with its history of a prestigious higher civil service, government workers are now much criticized, but in the United States public service has *never* been held in high esteem. Popularly, despite the many evidences to the contrary, it is believed that those with talent and drive choose private employment and that the mediocrities opt for the security of public employment (which, of course, in many cases does not exist).

Because of this lack of prestige, employees working even in urgently-needed government programs cannot expect the public to value their services but can expect to read disparaging remarks about themselves in the newspapers and to hear the same on radio and television. People do not work for pay or security alone. Indeed, many able persons are attracted to government service because of the challenge of programs vital for the well-being of society. Certainly there are many poor performers in government, but there is no evidence that the same proportion is not found in private organizations. The difference is that the private sector worker is not exposed to the same constant scrutiny, criticism, and unfounded attacks as is the government employee.

Under these conditions, high morale is difficult to achieve and maintain in government, and this situation has deteriorated greatly in recent years because during their electoral campaigns leading political figures, including the Presidents, seem to run against the bureaucracy as much as anything else. Furthermore, incumbent Presidents have made statements implying or openly stating that the real "problem" in government is the bureaucracy. Obviously, there are bureaucratic failures, but to put the major blame on the public employee is only to conceal from the public the reality that it is not easy in the complex society we have today for political leaders, legislators, and administrators to conceive and carry out effective programs. Although they have not been the only chief executives to put public employees in a poor light, both Jimmy Carter and Ronald Reagan have spoken of the "bureaucracy" in unfavorable terms. It does not help when administrations seek to "clarify" their position saying that it is not the government worker who is at fault but the "bureaucratic system" since public employees know that they are a large part of the system.

There are various explanations of why the Civil Service Reform Act of 1978 has failed as yet to achieve the hoped-for results, but the National Academy of Public Administration stresses that the sources of the threats to civil service reform are "mostly external to the Act itself,"[1] and the actions and attitudes of the Presidents, the Congress, the press, and the general public that contribute to the poor employee morale constitute a critical external factor.

To be a public employee generally is to expect not to receive the same percentage cost-of-living pay adjustments that private sector workers receive. Further, the public employee is made the sacrificial goat when chief executives and legislators hold down their pay as an "example" of inflation control to the private sector. Government executives do not expect to earn the same level salaries as in industry, but, as discussed in Chapter 9, they never foresaw a paycap that prevented them from getting *any* salary increases for years.

These are special problems of government, and it is true that these underpaid executives of their own free will chose government employment. To dismiss the problem in this way ignores that many executives have left government or plan early retirement, and that the morale of those who remain hardly is stimulated by this adverse environment.

Turning to governmental personnel systems, there are rigidities that make it extremely difficult to borrow private sector practices. Merit pay, discussed in Chapter 11, is a good example. Government pay scales are narrow, so merit raises tend to be small, and also as recounted in Chapter 11, legislation may reduce the size of any bonuses, or the merit pay plan may seek to economize by reducing cost-of-living raises for those receiving merit pay increases. Obviously, if merit raises and bonuses are to motivate the employee, they must be in substantial amounts. Of course, these pay rigidities could be eliminated but, again because this is government, many of them likely will not be.

The political time frame is a short one. As the experience with the Civil Service Reform Act of 1978 demonstrates, political leaders set unrealistically short deadlines for achieving results, new administrations with different philosophies and priorities come in, and legislators change their minds because of what they believe to

---

[1]*Civil Service Reform Act 1978–81: A Progress Report* (Washington, D.C.: National Academy of Public Administration, October 1981), p. 32.

be abuses with new programs like bonuses. The public employee works in an unstable political environment, not the secure one popular myth projects.

■ THE STATE OF THE ART

Often it is assumed that, once personnel problems are identified and there is public support for solving these problems, the solutions will not be difficult to find within a relatively short time despite strained budgets. Test validity, discussed in Chapter 10, is a good example. As the case of PACE shows, it may take years and expense far greater than anticipated to develop a valid examination. Often, technical expertise to make validity studies is lacking, as in many small local governments, yet EEO goals and timetables are supposed to be met.

Performance evaluation is another illustration. On the face of it, why should it be difficult to evaluate employee performance? Yet, as indicated in Chapter 11, several very difficult requirements must be met. Everybody with responsibility in the administration of the appraisal plan should understand what each performance standard means and what the evidences are in employee performance of reaching or failing to reach that standard; supervisors should be effective in counseling employees on their performance; and nothing in the plan and its use in making personnel decisions should cause the supervisor not to want to make an honest evaluation of the employee's performance. It is because the judgments to be made are so subjective that it is very difficult to meet these requirements, simple as they sound.

Unquestionably, in some areas deficiencies in the state of the art are the fault of personnel policymakers and of personnel technicians and can be remedied if there is a will to use new approaches and methods. Job evaluation and pay-setting are examples. In the discussion of comparable worth in Chapter 9, it was noted that job evaluation experts themselves state that there are many arbitrary judgments made in developing plans whether of the position classification or factor point rating type. They also do not dispute that in some cases tasks performed in jobs held mostly by males are overvalued by comparison with those in jobs held mostly by women. Careful review of existing job evaluation plans—many of which have been in use for years without serious scrutiny—would make it possible to correct the undervaluing of "female" tasks, with consequent pay adjustments upward.

Substantial steps can be taken towards providing more equitable pay for women without completely ignoring market rates. Neuse cites Colorado Springs where the city personnel director's analysis convinced him that sex discrimination explained to some extent why pay for women was less than that for male employees. He could not determine how much of the differential was caused by discrimination against women but he estimated that 80 percent was attributable to sex bias. His decision, accepted both by the city and the employees, was to reduce the "differences in salaries between comparable female and male dominated classes" by "80 per cent over four years."[2]

Policymakers in government should reflect that often the only effective weapon available for those in underpaid occupations has been to withhold their services. Much of the substantial improvement in pay since the 1960s for nurses, school teachers, and other occupations employing many women was attributable largely to union organization, collective bargaining, and employee militancy. Initiative in government to reform job evaluation and pay plans is a sound way of removing legitimate causes of employee unhappiness over pay.

Civil service systems are still burdened with hoary practices that can easily be discarded, such as unrealistically high educational qualifications for positions that do not require that much schooling. Arbitrary requirements, like the rule of three in certifying names for appointment, still remain although selection experts themselves know that small differences in test scores have no predictive validity. Administrative convenience, not sound practice, still dictates many personnel procedures, even those whose deficiencies have long been recognized. A federal judge who ruled that a physical test used in New York City for selecting fire fighters discriminated against women, ordered the requirements ended that the candidate be able to carry a 120-pound dummy on one shoulder up and down a flight of stairs, to scale an eight-foot wall, and to run a mile. The judge said, "Firefighting takes its toll, not as the result of maximum strength or speed, even at critical moments,

---

[2]Stephen M. Neuse, "A Critical Perspective on the Comparable Worth Debate," *Review of Public Personnel Administration* 3, no. 1 (Fall 1982): 6, 17–18.

but rather through the physical demands extending over long periods of time which necessitate paced performance at less-than-maximum levels."[3]

■ THE VALUE CLASHES OVER POLICIES

Generally, the greatest dissatisfactions with public personnel administration are over the basic policies followed. Since what are involved are disagreements over the values to be reflected in these policies, much controversy exists between opposed groups in the community.

There are many examples of these policy clashes. As discussed in Chapter 7, there has been a long, heated public debate over the use of remedial hiring ratios. Other examples are veterans preference and political activities of public employees, discussed in Chapter 15. Comparable worth is now much debated, and there is intense pressure group activity pro and con. The role of the unions is another emotionally-charged issue. Still other examples could be given, but suffice it to say that what is considered right in public personnel policies depends upon the views and interests of the individual and the particular group. Thus, it is impossible to develop personnel policies that please everyone, but unfortunately for public personnel administration *it* is blamed by those who disagree with the policies followed.

Notwithstanding, public personnel workers find much challenge in their jobs, as do many other public employees in theirs. The obstacles and limiting realities are understood and faced, and in general it can be expected that public personnel administration will continue to improve, as it has over the years since merit systems were first adopted. The present period of budgetary retrenchment is a particularly difficult one but so it is for government and the society in general.

BIBLIOGRAPHY

House Subcommittee on Civil Service, *Civil Service Oversight*. 98th Congress, 1st Session. Washington, D.C.: Government Printing Office, 1983.

---

[3]Joseph P. Fried, "Women Win Ruling on Fire Department Test," *New York Times*, March 6, 1982.

Nigro, Felix A. "Public Personnel Administration: From Theodore Roosevelt to Ronald Reagan." *International Journal of Public Administration* 6, no. 1 (1984).

Parker, John D. "Public Personnel Administration in the Year 2000 A. D.." In *Human Resource Management in Public Organizations: A Systems Approach,* edited by Gilbert Siegel. Los Angeles: University Publishers, 1972.

CHAPTER 6 APPENDIX
Excerpts from Public Employe Relations Act of State of Pennsylvania

■ ARTICLE I

Public Policy

Section 101. The General Assembly of the Commonwealth of Pennsylvania declares that it is the public policy of this Commonwealth and the purpose of this act to promote orderly and constructive relationships between all public employers and their employes subject, however, to the paramount right of the citizens of this Commonwealth to keep inviolate the guarantees for their health, safety and welfare. Unresolved disputes between the public employer and its employes are injurious to the public and the General Assembly is therefore aware that adequate means must be established for minimizing them and providing for their resolution. Within the limitations imposed upon the governmental processes by these rights of the public at large and recognizing that harmonious relationships are required between the public employer and its employes, the General Assembly has determined that the overall policy may best be accomplished by (1) granting to public employes the right to organize and choose freely their representatives; (2) requiring public employers to negotiate and bargain with employe organizations representing public employes and to enter into written agreements evidencing the result of such bargaining; and (3) establishing procedures to provide for the protection of the rights of the public employe, the public employer and the public at large . . .

Sections of the Public Employee Relations Act of the State of Pennsylvania have been deleted.

■ ARTICLE III

Definitions

Section 301. As used in this act:

(1) "Public employer" means the Commonwealth of Pennsylvania, its political subdivisions including school districts and any officer, board, commission, agency, authority, or other instrumentality thereof and any nonprofit organization or institution and any charitable, religious, scientific, literary, recreational, health, educational or welfare institution receiving grants or appropriations from local, State or Federal governments but shall not include employers covered or presently subject to coverage under the act of June 1, 1937 (P.L.1168), as amended, known as the "Pennsylvania Labor Relations Act," the act of July 5, 1935, Public Law 198, 74th Congress, as amended, known as the "National Labor Relations Act."

(2) "Public employe" or "employe" means any individual employed by a public employer but shall not include elected officials, appointees of the Governor with the advice and consent of the Senate as required by law, management level employes, confidential employes, clergymen or other persons in a religious profession, employes or personnel at church offices or facilities when utilized primarily for religious purposes and those employes covered under the act of June 24, 1968 (Act No. 111), entitled "An act specifically authorizing collective bargaining between policemen and firemen and their public employers; providing for arbitration in order to settle disputes, and requiring compliance with collective bargaining agreements and findings of arbitrators."

(3) "Employe organization" means an organization of any kind, or any agency or employe representation committee or plan in which membership includes public employes, and which exists for the purpose, in whole or in part, of dealing with employers concerning grievances, employe-employer disputes, wages, rates of pay, hours of employment, or conditions of work but shall not include any organization which practices discrimination in membership because of race, color, creed, national origin or political affiliation.

(4) "Representative" means any individuals acting for public employers or employes and shall include employe organizations.

(5) "Board" means the Pennsylvania Labor Relations Board.

(6) "Supervisor" means any individual having authority in the

interests of the employer to hire, transfer, suspend, layoff, recall, promote, discharge, assign, reward or discipline other employes or responsibly to direct them or adjust their grievances; or to a substantial degree effectively recommend such action, if in connection with the foregoing, the exercise of such authority is not merely routine or clerical in nature but calls for the use of independent judgment.

(7) "Professional employe" means any employe whose work: (i) is predominantly intellectual and varied in character; (ii) requires consistent exercise of discretion and judgment; (iii) requires knowledge of an advanced nature in the field of science or learning customarily acquired by specialized study in an institution of higher learning or its equivalent; and (iv) is of such character that the output or result accomplished cannot be standardized in relation to a given period of time.

(8) "Unfair practice" means any practice prohibited by Article XII of this act.

(9) "Strike" means concerted action in failing to report for duty, the wilful absence from one's position, the stoppage of work, slowdown, or the abstinence in whole or in part from the full, faithful and proper performance of the duties of employment for the purpose of inducing, influencing or coercing a change in the conditions or compensation or the rights, privileges, or obligations of employment.

(10) "Person" includes an individual, public employer, public employe, authority, commission, legal representative, labor organization, employe organization, profit or nonprofit corporation, trustee, board or association.

(11) "Membership dues deduction" means the practice of a public employer to deduct from the wages of a public employe, with his written consent, an amount for the payment of his membership dues in an employe organization, which deduction is transmitted by the public employer to the employe organization.

(12) "Budget submission date" means the date by which under the law or practice a public employer's proposed budget, or budget containing proposed expenditures applicable to such public employer is submitted to the Legislature or other similar body for final action. For the purposes of this act, the budget submission date for the Commonwealth shall be February 1 of each year and for a nonprofit organization or institution, the last day of its fiscal year.

(13) "Confidential employe" shall mean any employe who works: (i) in the personnel offices of a public employer and has access to information subject to use by the public employer in collective bargaining; or (ii) in a close continuing relationship with public officers or representatives associated with collective bargaining on behalf of the employer.

(14) "Wages" means hourly rates of pay, salaries or other forms of compensation for services rendered.

(15) "Commonwealth employe" means a public employe employed by the Commonwealth or any board, commission, agency, authority, or any other instrumentality thereof.

(16) "Management level employe" means any individual who is involved directly in the determination of policy or who responsibly directs the implementation thereof and shall include all employes above the first level of supervision.

(17) "Meet and discuss" means the obligation of a public employer upon request to meet at reasonable times and discuss recommendations submitted by representatives of public employes: Provided, That any decisions or determinations on matters so discussed shall remain with the public employer and be deemed final on any issue or issues raised.

(18) "Maintenance of membership" means that all employes who have joined an employe organization or who join the employe organization in the future must remain members for the duration of a collective bargaining agreement so providing with the proviso that any such employe or employes may resign from such employe organization during a period of fifteen days prior to the expiration of any such agreement.

(19) "First level of supervision" and "first level supervisor" means the lowest level at which an employe functions as a supervisor.

■ ARTICLE IV

Employe Rights

Section 401. It shall be lawful for public employes to organize, form, join or assist in employe organizations or to engage in lawful concerted activities for the purpose of collective bargaining or other mutual aid and protection or to bargain collectively through representatives of their own free choice and such employes shall also have the right to refrain from any or all such activities except as may be required pursuant to a maintenance of membership provision in a collective bargaining agreement.

■ ARTICLE V

Pennsylvania Labor Relations Board

Section 501.   The board shall exercise those powers and perform those duties which are specifically provided for in this act. These powers and duties shall be in addition to and exercised completely independent of any powers and duties specifically granted to it by other statutory enactments.

Section 502.   The board shall have authority from time to time to make, amend and rescind such rules and regulations as may be necessary to carry out the provisions of this act. Such rules and regulations shall be effective upon publication in the manner which the board shall prescribe.

Section 503.   The board shall establish after consulting representatives of employe organizations and of public employers, panels of qualified persons broadly representative of the public to be available to serve as members of fact-finding boards.

■ ARTICLE VI

Representation

Section 601.   Public employers may select representatives to act in their interest in any collective bargaining with representatives of public employes.

Section 602. (a) A public employer may recognize employe representatives for collective bargaining purposes, provided the parties jointly request certification by the board which shall issue such certification if it finds the unit appropriate . . .

Section 603.   (a) A public employe, a group of public employes or an employe organization may notify the public employer that thirty per cent or more of the public employes in an appropriate unit desire to be exclusively represented for collective bargaining purposes by a designated representative and request the public employer to consent to an election.

(b)   If the public employer consents, the public employe, group of public employes or employe organization whichever applicable may submit in a form and manner established by the board an election request. Such request shall include a description of the unit deemed to be appropriate, the basis upon which it was determined that thirty per cent or more of the employes desired to be represented and a joinder by the public employer. The board may on the basis of the submissions order an election to be held or it may at its discretion investigate or conduct hearings to determine the validity of the matters contained in such submissions before determining whether or not an order should issue.

(c) If a public employer refuses to consent to an election, the party making the request may file a petition with the board alleging that thirty per cent or more of the public employes in an appropriate unit wish to be exclusively represented for collective bargaining purposes by a designated representative. The board shall send a copy of the petition to the public employer and provide for an appropriate hearing upon due notice. If it deems the allegations in the petition to be valid and the unit to be appropriate it shall order an election. If it finds to the contrary it may dismiss the petition or permit its amendment in accordance with procedures established by the board. . .

Section 604. The board shall determine the appropriateness of a unit which shall be the public employer unit or a subdivision thereof. In determining the appropriateness of the unit, the board shall:

(1) Take into consideration but shall not be limited to the following: (i) public employes must have an identifiable community of interest, and (ii) the effects of over-fragmentization.

(2) Not decide that any unit is appropriate if such unit includes both professional and nonprofessional employes, unless a majority of such professional employes vote for inclusion in such unit.

(3) Not permit guards at prisons and mental hospitals, employes directly involved with and necessary to the functioning of the courts of this Commonwealth, or any individual employed as a guard to enforce against employes and other persons, rules to protect property of the employer or to protect the safety of persons on the employer's premises to be included in any unit with other public employes, each may form separate homogenous employe organizations with the proviso that organizations of the latter designated employe group may not be affiliated with any other organization representing or including as members, persons outside of the organization's classification.

(4) Take into consideration that when the Commonwealth is the employer, it will be bargaining on a Statewide basis unless

issues involve working conditions peculiar to a given governmental employment locale. This section, however, shall not be deemed to prohibit multi-unit bargaining.

(5)   Not permit employes at the first level of supervision to be included with any other units of public employes but shall permit them to form their own separate homogenous units. In determining supervisory status the board may take into consideration the extent to which supervisory and nonsupervisory functions are performed.

Section 605.   Representation elections shall be conducted by secret ballot at such times and places selected by the board subject to the following:

(1)   The board shall give no less than ten days notice of the time and place of such election.

(2)   The board shall establish rules and regulations concerning the conduct of any election including but not limited to regulations which would guarantee the secrecy of the ballot.

(3)   A representative may not be certified unless it receives a majority of the valid ballots cast.

(4)   The board shall include on the ballot a choice of "no representative."

(5)   In an election where none of the choices on the ballot receives a majority, a run-off election shall be conducted, the ballot providing for a selection between the two choices or parties receiving the highest and the second highest number of ballots cast in the election.

(6)   The board shall certify the results of said election within five working days after the final tally of votes if no charge is filed by any person alleging that an "unfair practice" existed in connection with said election. If the board has reason to believe that such allegations are valid, it shall set a time for hearing on the matter after due notice. Any such hearing shall be conducted within two weeks of the date of receipt of such charge. If the board determines that the outcome of the election was affected by the "unfair practice" charged or for any other "unfair practice" it may deem existed, it shall require corrective action and order a new election. If the board determines that no unfair practice existed or if it existed, did not affect the outcome of the election, it shall immediately certify the election results.

(7)   (i) No election shall be conducted pursuant to this section in any appropriate bargaining unit within which in the preceding twelve-month period an election shall have been held nor during

the term of any lawful collective bargaining agreement between a public employer and an employe representative. This restriction shall not apply to that period of time covered by any collective bargaining agreement which exceeds three years. For the purposes of this section, extensions of agreements shall not affect the expiration date of the original agreement.

(ii) Petitions for elections may be filed with the board not sooner than ninety days nor later than sixty days before the expiration date of any collective bargaining agreement or after the expiration date until such time as a new written agreement has been entered into. For the purposes of this section, extensions of agreements shall not affect the expiration date of the original agreement.

Section 606. Representatives selected by public employes in a unit appropriate for collective bargaining purposes shall be the exclusive representative of all the employes in such unit to bargain on wages, hours, terms and conditions of employment: Provided, That any individual employe or a group of employes shall have the right at any time to present grievances to their employer and to have them adjusted without the intervention of the bargaining representative as long as the adjustment is not inconsistent with the terms of a collective bargaining contract then in effect: And, provided further, That the bargaining representative has been given an opportunity to be present at such adjustment.

Section 607. If there is a duly certified representative: (i) a public employe or a group of public employes may file a petition for decertification provided it is supported by a thirty per cent showing of interest, or (ii) a public employer alleging a good faith doubt of the majority status of said representative may file a petition in accordance with the rules and regulations established by the board, subject to the provisions of clause (7) of section 605.

■ ARTICLE VII

Scope of Bargaining

Section 701. Collective bargaining is the performance of the mutual obligation of the public employer and the representative of the public employes to meet at reasonable times and confer in good faith with respect to wages, hours and other terms and conditions of employment, or the negotiation of an agreement or any question arising thereunder and the execution of a written contract incorporating any agreement reached but such obligation does not compel either party to agree to a proposal or require the making of a concession.

Section 702.   Public employers shall not be required to bargain over matters of inherent managerial policy, which shall include but shall not be limited to such areas of discretion or policy as the functions and programs of the public employer, standards of services, its overall budget, utilization of technology, the organizational structure and selection and direction of personnel. Public employers, however, shall be required to meet and discuss on policy matters affecting wages, hours and terms and conditions of employment as well as the impact thereon upon request by public employe representatives.

Section 703.   The parties to the collective bargaining process shall not effect or implement a provision in a collective bargaining agreement if the implementation of that provision would be in violation of, or inconsistent with, or in conflict with any statute or statutes enacted by the General Assembly of the Commonwealth of Pennsylvania or the provisions of municipal home rule charters.

Section 704.   Public employers shall not be required to bargain with units of first level supervisors or their representatives but shall be required to meet and discuss with first level supervisors or their representatives, on matters deemed to be bargainable for other public employes covered by this act.

Section 705.   Membership dues deductions and maintenance of membership are proper subjects of bargaining with the proviso that as to the latter, the payment of dues and assessments while members, may be the only requisite employment condition.

Section 706.   Nothing contained in this act shall impair the employer's right to hire employes or to discharge employes for just cause consistent with existing legislation.

■ ARTICLE VIII

Collective Bargaining Impasse

Section 801.   If after a reasonable period of negotiation, a dispute or impasse exists between the representatives of the public employer and the public employes, the parties may voluntarily submit to mediation but if no agreement is reached between the parties within twenty-one days after negotiations have commenced, but in no event later than one hundred fifty days prior to the "budget submission date," and mediation has not been utilized by the parties, both parties shall immediately, in writing, call in the service of the Pennsylvania Bureau of Mediation.

Section 802. Once mediation has commenced, it shall continue for so long as the parties have not reached an agreement. If, however, an agreement has not been reached within twenty days after mediation has commenced or in no event later than one hundred thirty days prior to the "budget submission date," the Bureau of Mediation shall notify the board of this fact. Upon receiving such notice the board may in its discretion appoint a fact-finding panel which panel may consist of either one or three members. If a panel is so designated or selected it shall hold hearings and take oral or written testimony and shall have subpoena power. If during this time the parties have not reached an agreement, the panel shall make findings of fact and recommendations:

(1) The findings of fact and recommendations shall be sent by registered mail to the board and to both parties not more than forty days after the Bureau of Mediation has notified the board as provided in the preceding paragraph.

(2) Not more than ten days after the findings and recommendations shall have been sent, the parties shall notify the board and each other whether or not they accept the recommendations of the fact-finding panel and if they do not, the panel shall publicize its findings of fact and recommendations.

(3) Not less than five days nor more than ten days after the publication of the findings of fact and recommendations, the parties shall again inform the board and each other whether or not they will accept the recommendations of the fact-finding panel.

(4) The Commonwealth shall pay one-half the cost of the fact-finding panel; the remaining one-half of the cost shall be divided equally between the parties. The board shall establish rules and regulations under which panels shall operate, including, but not limited to, compensation for panel members.

Section 803. If the representatives of either or both the public employes and the public employer refuse to submit to the procedures set forth in sections 801 and 802 of this article, such refusal shall be deemed a refusal to bargain in good faith and unfair practice charges may be filed by the submitting party or the board may on its own, issue an unfair practice complaint and conduct such hearings and issue such orders as provided for in Article XIII.

Section 804.   Nothing in this article shall prevent the parties from submitting impasses to voluntary binding arbitration with the proviso the decisions of the arbitrator which would require legislative enactment to be effective shall be considered advisory only.

Section 805.   Notwithstanding any other provisions of this act where representatives of units of guards at prisons or mental hospitals or units of employes directly involved with and necessary to the functioning of the courts of this Commonwealth have reached an impasse in collective bargaining and mediation as required in section 801 of this article has not resolved the dispute, the impasse shall be submitted to a panel of arbitrators whose decision shall be final and binding upon both parties with the proviso that the decisions of the arbitrators which would require legislative enactment to be effective shall be considered advisory only.

Section 806.   Panels of arbitrators for bargaining units referred to in section 805 of this article shall be selected in the following manner:

(1)   Each party shall select one member of the panel, the two so selected shall choose the third member.

(2)   If the members so selected are unable to agree upon the third member within ten days from the date of their selection, the board shall submit the names of seven persons, each party shall alternately strike one name until one shall remain. The public employer shall strike the first name. The person so remaining shall be the third member and chairman.

Section 807.   The costs of the arbitrators selected under the provisions of section 806 shall be paid by the Commonwealth under rules and regulations established by the board.

■ ARTICLE IX

Collective Bargaining Agreement

Section 901.   Once an agreement is reached between the representatives of the public employes and the public employer, the agreement shall be reduced to writing and signed by the parties.

Any provisions of the contract requiring legislative action will only be effective if such legislation is enacted.

Section 902. If the provisions of the constitution or bylaws of an employe organization requires ratification of a collective bargaining agreement by its membership, only those members who belong to the bargaining unit involved shall be entitled to vote on such ratification notwithstanding such provisions.

Section 903. Arbitration of disputes or grievances arising out of the interpretation of the provisions of a collective bargaining agreement is mandatory. The procedure to be adopted is a proper subject of bargaining with the proviso that the final step shall provide for a binding decision by an arbitrator or a tri-partite board of arbitrators as the parties may agree. Any decisions of the arbitrator or arbitrators requiring legislation will only be effective if such legislation is enacted:

(1) If the parties cannot voluntarily agree upon the selection of an arbitrator, the parties shall notify the Bureau of Mediation of their inability to do so. The Bureau of Mediation shall then submit to the parties the names of seven arbitrators. Each party shall alternately strike a name until one name remains. The public employer shall strike the first name. The person remaining shall be the arbitrator.

(2) The costs of arbitration shall be shared equally by the parties. Fees paid to arbitrators shall be based on a schedule established by the Bureau of Mediation. . .

■ ARTICLE X

Strikes

Section 1001. Strikes by guards at prisons or mental hospitals, or employes directly involved with and necessary to the functioning of the courts of this Commonwealth are prohibited at any time. If a strike occurs the public employer shall forthwith initiate in the court of common pleas of the jurisdiction where the strike occurs, an action for appropriate equitable relief including but not limited to injunctions. If the strike involves Commonwealth employes, the chief legal officer of the public employer or the Attorney General where required by law shall institute an action for equitable relief, either in the court of common pleas of the jurisdiction where the strike has occurred or the Commonwealth Court.

Section 1002.   Strikes by public employes during the pendency of collective bargaining procedures set forth in sections 801 and 802 of Article VIII are prohibited. In the event of a strike during this period the public employer shall forthwith initiate an action for the same relief and utilizing the same procedures required for prohibited strikes under section 1001.

Section 1003.   If a strike by public employes occurs after the collective bargaining processes set forth in sections 801 and 802 of Article VIII of this act have been completely utilized and exhausted, it shall not be prohibited unless or until such a strike creates a clear and present danger or threat to the health, safety or welfare of the public. In such cases the public employer shall initiate, in the court of common pleas of the jurisdiction where such strike occurs, an action for equitable relief including but not limited to appropriate injunctions and shall be entitled to such relief if the court finds that the strike creates a clear and present danger or threat to the health, safety or welfare of the public. If the strike involves Commonwealth employes, the chief legal officer of the public employer or the Attorney General where required by law shall institute an action for equitable relief in the court of common pleas of the jurisdiction where the strike has occurred or the Commonwealth Court. Prior to the filing of any complaint in equity under the provisions of this section the moving party shall serve upon the defendant a copy of said complaint as provided for in the Pennsylvania Rules of Civil Procedure applicable to such actions. Hearings shall be required before relief is granted under this section and notices of the same shall be served in the manner required for the original process with a duty imposed upon the court to hold such hearings forthwith.

Section 1004.   An unfair practice by a public employer shall not be a defense to a prohibited strike. Unfair practices by the employer during the collective bargaining processes shall receive priority by the board as set forth in Article XIV.

Section 1005.   If a public employe refuses to comply with a lawful order of a court of competent jurisdiction issued for a violation of any of the provisions of this article the public employer shall initiate an action for contempt and if the public employe is adjudged guilty of such contempt, he shall be subject to suspension, demotion or discharge at the discretion of the public employer, provided the public employer has not exercised that discretion in violation of clauses (1), (2), (3) and (4) of subsection (a) of section 1201, Article XII.

Section 1006. No public employe shall be entitled to pay or compensation from the public employer for the period engaged in any strike.

Section 1007. In the event any public employe refuses to obey an order issued by a court of competent jurisdiction for a violation of the provisions of this article, the punishment for such contempt may be by fine or by imprisonment in the prison of the county where the court is sitting or both in the discretion of the court.

Section 1008. Where an employe organization wilfully disobeys a lawful order of a court of competent jurisdiction issued for a violation of the provisions of this article, the punishment for each day that such contempt persists may be by a fine fixed in the discretion of the court.

Section 1009. In fixing the amount of the fine or imprisonment for contempt, the court shall consider all the facts and circumstances directly related to the contempt including but not limited to: (i) any unfair practices committed by the public employer during the collective bargaining processes; (ii) the extent of the wilful defiance or resistance to the court's order; (iii) the impact of the strike on the health, safety or welfare of the public, and (iv) the ability of the employe organization or the employe to pay the fine imposed.

Section 1010. Nothing in this article shall prevent the parties from voluntarily requesting the court for a diminution or suspension of any fines or penalties imposed. Any requests by employe representatives for such participation by the public employer shall be subject to the requirements of "meet and discuss."

■ ARTICLE XI

Picketing

Section 1101. Public employes, other than those engaged in a nonprohibited strike, who refuse to cross a picket line shall be deemed to be engaged in a prohibited strike and shall be subject to the terms and conditions of Article X pertaining to prohibited strikes.

■ ARTICLE XII

Unfair Practices

Section 1201. (a) Public employers, their agents or representatives are prohibited from:

(1) Interfering, restraining or coercing employes in the exercise of the rights guaranteed in Article IV of this act.

(2) Dominating or interfering with the formation, existence or administration of any employe organization.

(3) Discriminating in regard to hire or tenure of employment or any term or condition of employment to encourage or discourage membership in any employe organization.

(4) Discharging or otherwise discriminating against an employe because he has signed or filed an affidavit, petition or complaint or given any information or testimony under this act.

(5) Refusing to bargain collectively in good faith with an employe representative which is the exclusive representative of employes in an appropriate unit, including but not limited to the discussing of grievances with the exclusive representative.

(6) Refusing to reduce a collective bargaining agreement to writing and sign such agreement.

(7) Violating any of the rules and regulations established by the board regulating the conduct of representation elections.

(8) Refusing to comply with the provisions of an arbitration award deemed binding under section 903 of Article IX.

(9) Refusing to comply with the requirements of "meet and discuss."

(b) Employe organizations, their agents, or representatives, or public employes are prohibited from:

(1) Restraining or coercing employes in the exercise of the rights guaranteed in Article IV of this act.

(2) Restraining or coercing a public employer in the selection of his representative for the purposes of collective bargaining or the adjustment of grievances.

(3) Refusing to bargain collectively in good faith with a public employer, if they have been designated in accordance with the provisions of this act as the exclusive representative of employes in an appropriate unit.

(4) Violating any of the rules and regulations established by the board regulating the conduct of representation elections.

(5) Refusing to reduce a collective bargaining agreement to writing and sign such agreement.

(6) Calling, instituting, maintaining or conducting a strike or boycott against any public employer or picketing any place of business of a public employer on account of any jurisdictional controversy.

(7) Engaging in, or inducing or encouraging any individual employed by any person to engage in a strike or refusal to handle goods or perform services; or threatening, coercing or restraining any person where an object thereof is to (i) force or require any public employer to cease dealing or doing business with any other person or (ii) force or require a public employer to recognize for representation purposes an employe organization not certified by the board.

(8) Refusing to comply with the provisions of an arbitration award deemed binding under section 903 of Article IX.

(9) Refusing to comply with the requirements of "meet and discuss."

■ ARTICLE XIII

Prevention of Unfair Practices

Section 1301. The board is empowered, as hereinafter provided, to prevent any person from engaging in any unfair practice listed in Article XII of this act. This power shall be exclusive and shall not be affected by any other means of adjustment or prevention that have been or may be established by agreement, law, or otherwise.

Section 1302. Whenever it is charged by any interested party that any person has engaged in or is engaging in any such unfair practice, the board, or any member or designated agent thereof, shall have authority to issue and cause to be served upon such person a complaint, stating the charges in that respect, and containing a notice of hearing before the board, or any member or designated agent thereof, at a place therein fixed, not less than five days after the serving of said complaint. Any such complaint may be amended by the board, member or agent conducting the hearing at any time prior to the issuance of an order based thereon. The person so complained of shall have the right to file an answer to the original or amended complaint and to appear in person, or otherwise, to give testimony at the place and time set in the complaint. In the discretion of a member or agent conducting the hearing or of the board, any other person may be allowed to intervene in the said proceeding and to present testimony. In any such proceeding, the rules of evidence prevailing in courts of law or equity shall be followed but shall not be controlling.

Section 1303. Testimony shall be taken at the hearing and filed with the board. The board upon notice may take further testimony or hear argument. If, upon all the testimony taken, the board shall determine that any person named in the complaint has engaged in or is engaging in any such unfair practice, the board shall state its findings of fact, and issue and cause to be served on such person an order requiring such person to cease and desist from such unfair practice, and to take such reasonable affirmative action, including reinstatement of employes, discharged in violation of Article XII of this act, with or without back pay, as will effectuate the policies of this act. Such order may further require such person to make reasonable reports, from time to time, showing the extent to which the order has been complied with. If, upon all the testimony, the board shall be of the opinion that the person or persons named in the complaint has not engaged in or is not engaging in any such unfair practice, then the board shall make its findings of fact and shall issue an order dismissing the complaint. A copy of such findings of fact, conclusions of law, and order shall be mailed to all parties to the proceedings. . .

■ ARTICLE XIV

Unfair Practices During Article VIII Procedures

Section 1401. Notwithstanding any of the provisions of Article XIII, the board upon the filing of a charge alleging the commission of an unfair labor practice committed during, or arising out of the collective bargaining procedures set forth in sections 801 and 802 of Article VIII of this act, shall be empowered to petition the court of competent jurisdiction for appropriate relief or restraining order.

Upon the filing of any such petition the board shall cause notice thereof to be served upon such person and thereupon the court shall have jurisdiction to grant to the board such temporary relief or restraining order as it deems just and proper.

■ ARTICLE XV

Judicial Review

Section 1501.   The board shall except where an employe of the Commonwealth is involved have power to petition the court of common pleas of any county wherein the unfair practice in question occurred, or wherein any person charged with the commission of any unfair practice resides or transacts business, for the enforcement of such order and for appropriate temporary relief or restraining order, and shall certify and file in the court a transcript of the entire record in the proceeding, including the pleadings and testimony upon which such order was entered and the findings and order of the board. In the instance of the exception involving the said Commonwealth employes, the board shall file its petition in the Commonwealth Court. Upon such filing, the court shall cause notice thereof to be served upon such person, and thereupon shall have jurisdiction of the proceeding and of the question determined therein, and shall have power to grant such temporary relief, restraining or mandamus order as it deems just and proper or requisite to effectuate the policies of this act and to make and enter upon the pleadings. testimony, and proceedings set forth in such transcript a decree enfc 'cing, modifying and enforcing as so modified, or setting aside, in v nole or in part, the order of the board. The parties before the court shall be the board, the person charged with the commission of any unfair labor practice, and may include the charging party. No objection that has not been urged before the board, its members or agents shall be considered by the court unless the failure or neglect to urge such objection shall be excused because of extraordinary circumstances. The findings of the board as to the facts, if supported by substantial and legally credible evidence, shall be conclusive. . . . The jurisdiction of the court of common pleas, or the Commonwealth Court, as the case may be, shall be exclusive within the limits of its jurisdiction, and its judgment and decree shall be final, except that the same shall be subject to review by the Supreme Court on appeal by the board or any party in interest, irrespective of the nature of the decree or judgment of the amount involved. . . .

Section 1502.   Any person aggrieved by a final order of the board granting or denying, in whole or in part, the relief sought in any unfair practice case, or by an order certifying or refusing to certify a collective bargaining agent of employes in any representation case, may obtain a review of such order in the court of common pleas of any county where the unfair practice in question was alleged to have been engaged in, or wherein such person or employer in a representation case resides or transacts business, or in the instance of Commonwealth employes in the Commonwealth Court, as the case may be, by filing in such court, within thirty days after the final order has been issued by the board, a written petition praying that the order of the board be modified or set aside. A copy of such petition shall be forthwith served upon the board, and the board shall file in the court a transcript of the entire record in the proceeding certified by the board, including the pleadings and testimony and order of the board. Upon such filing, the court shall proceed in the same manner as in the case of an application by the board under section 1501, and shall have the same exclusive jurisdiction to grant to the board such temporary relief, restraining or mandamus order as it deems just and proper or requisite to effectuate the policies of this act, and in like manner to make and enter a decree enforcing, modifying, and enforcing as so modified, or setting aside, in whole or in part, the order of the board, and findings of the board as to the facts, if supported by substantial and legally credible evidence, shall in like manner be conclusive. The parties before the court shall be any person aggrieved by an order of the board, as aforesaid, and the board and any other party to the board proceeding. The jurisdiction of the court of common pleas, or the Commonwealth Court, as the case may be, shall be exclusive within the limits of its jurisdiction, and its judgment and decree shall be final, except that the same shall be subject to review of the Supreme Court on appeal by the person aggrieved, or the board, irrespective of the nature of the decree or judgment or the amount involved. . .

■ ARTICLE XVII

Employe Organizations

Section 1701.   No employe organization shall make any contribution out of the funds of the employe organization either directly or indirectly to any political party or organization or in support of any political candidate for public office.

The board shall establish such rules and regulations as it may find necessary to prevent the circumvention or evasion of the provisions of this section.

If an employe organization has made contributions in violation of this section it shall file with the board a report or affidavit evidencing such contributions within ninety days of the end of its fiscal year. Such report or affidavit shall be signed by its president and treasurer or corresponding principals.

Any employe organization which violates the provisions of this section or fails to file any required report or affidavit or files a false report or affidavit shall be subject to a fine of not more than two thousand dollars ($2,000).

Any person who wilfully violates this section, or who makes a false statement knowing it to be false, or who knowingly fails to disclose a material fact shall be fined not more than one thousand dollars ($1,000) or imprisoned for not more than thirty days or both. Each individual required to sign affidavits or reports under this section shall be personally responsible for filing such report or affidavit and for any statement contained therein he knows to be false.

Nothing herein shall be deemed to prohibit voluntary contributions by individuals to political parties or candidates . . . .

■ ARTICLE XXIII

Effective Date

Section 2301. This act shall take effect in ninety days, except that the provisions of Article V and the amnesty provisions of the repealer shall take effect immediately.

APPROVED—The 23rd day of July, A. D. 1970.

RAYMOND P. SHAFER

The foregoing is a true and correct copy of Act of the General Assembly No. 195.

Secretary of the Commonwealth.

CHAPTER 7 APPENDIX
Affirmative Action Plan Components

Specific requirements for developing and implementing written affirmative action programs are spelled out in Revised Orders No. 4 and 14 issued by the Office of Federal Contract Compliance Programs (OFCCP) of the U.S. Department of Labor. The following "affirmative action checklist" identifies the major components of an affirmative action program as derived from Revised Orders No. 4 and 14.

1. Issue a written equal employment opportunity policy and affirmative action commitment;
2. Publicize the policy and commitment, both internally and externally;
3. Appoint a top official to direct and implement the program;
4. Survey the present work force to identify underutilization of female and minority employees by department and by major occupational classification;
5. Develop and implement specific action plans to achieve equal employment opportunity;
6. Establish a monitoring system to audit and evaluate progress for each aspect of the plan;
7. Develop supportive organizational and community programs; and
8. Develop goals and timetables to increase the utilization of protected class members where underutilization has been identified.

A brief explanation of these major components is provided below.

Issue a written equal employment opportunity policy and affirmative action commitment

An official policy should be developed and issued by your organization's policymaking body or chief executive to indicate the organization's commitment to equal employment opportunity.

From *Equal Employment Opportunity and Affirmative Action* by Karen Ann Olsen. Used with permission of the Labor-Management Relations Service of the U.S. Conference of Mayors.

Publicize the policy and commitment both internally and externally

Internally, the policy should be publicized and specific information about the program made available through meetings, bulletin board announcements, new employee orientation sessions, union-management meetings and training programs. The policy statement should be included in personnel manuals and employee handbooks, and copies should be printed and distributed. Externally, the organization should publicize its equal employment opportunity policy and affirmative action commitment to citizens of the community, job applicants, recruitment sources, and business organizations. Advertisements, correspondence, and purchase orders should include statements such as "An Equal Opportunity Employer." Recruitment sources currently used for seeking job applicants should be notified, and special efforts should be made to contact new sources which could be helpful in the recruitment of members of protected classes. Printed materials, advertisements, and job postings should indicate the organization's policy, should provide sufficient notice of job openings to facilitate broadening of recruitment efforts, and should not include stereotyped or sexist language.

Appoint a top official to direct and implement the program

Appointment of an official with sufficient authority and resources to direct the program will demonstrate the priority status which the organization places on the program and will provide the means for implementing it. The individual appointed should be accountable for program results to the organization's chief administrator. Specific responsibilities and accountabilities should also be assigned to all managers and supervisors, including the manager of the affirmative action program.

Survey the present work force to identify underutilization of female and minority employees by department and major occupational classification

A work force analysis is the first step; it will show the number and percentage of employees by sex and racial group (Caucasian, black, Hispanic, American Indian or Alaskan native, and Asian or

Pacific islander) in each location, department, and major occupational category (for example: officials and managers, professionals, clerical workers, protective service workers, etc.). In
conducting the work force analysis, make sure the occupational
categories used are specific enough to reveal levels of pay and
responsibility. This analysis will indicate patterns of concentration
and underutilization of protected class members.

Next determine the estimated availability of qualified protected
class members for each of the major occupational categories.
Obtain labor market statistics from the areas (local, regional, or
national for different kinds of jobs) in which the organization can
reasonably expect to recruit available protected class members
with required job skills. There are a number of sources for such
statistics including: the U.S. Bureau of Labor Statistics, the U.S.
Census Bureau, the U.S. Office of Education, and your state
employment service. Also, the availability of promotable, trainable and transferable protected class members within the organization should be ascertained.

A comparison of the percentage of available, qualified protected
class members by major occupational category with those currently employed by the organization in each category will determine
the extent of underutilization. This analysis will be the basis for
establishing affirmative action goals and timetables.

Develop and implement specific action plans to achieve equal employment opportunity

The organization's personnel policies, practices and programs, all
privileges, terms and conditions of employment, and labor-
management contracts should be audited and evaluated to ensure
that they are consistent with the organization's policy of equal
employment opportunity. Where problem areas are identified,
action should be taken as soon as possible to make changes
necessary for compliance with equal employment opportunity
policy. If provisions of labor-management contracts are found to be
inconsistent with the policy, the union representative should be
contacted and requested to renegotiate such provisions. It should
be pointed out to the union representative that where terms and
conditions of employment established by bilateral agreement are
illegal under federal or state laws both the employer and the union
are vulnerable as defendants in a law suit.

Audit requirements

When auditing current employment practices and terms and conditions of employment, the following areas should be carefully scrutinized:

1. Recruitment;
2. Minimal job qualifications;
3. All aspects of the selection process, including
   Application forms,
   Ratings of education and experience,
   Examinations,
   Interviews,
   Previous employer or background checks,
   Promotion policies and methods, and
   Certification and appointment procedures;
4. Performance evaluations;
5. Wages and benefits;
6. Layoff and recall;
7. Demotions, disciplinary action, and discharge;
8. Training and career development programs;
9. Seniority and transfer provisions;
10. Social and recreational programs and other employment conditions.

When employment practices result in an adverse impact on and underutilization of protected class members and when they cannot be justified based on job relevancy, undue hardship, other factors of business necessity, or lack of suitable alternatives with less adverse impact, it will be necessary for the employer to change such employment practices. Inequities in terms and conditions of employment which adversely affect protected class members and which cannot be justified on the basis of factors other than race, color, creed, sex, age, religion, national origin, or disability should be remedied.

Below, major types of employment practices and terms and conditions of employment which should be included in an audit are briefly reviewed and pertinent questions are raised under each area of inquiry.

1. Recruitment
   a. Has an applicant flow record been established so that persons can be identified as protected class members? (This is necessary so that the organization's recruitment procedures can be evaluated as to their effectiveness in attracting members of protected classes as job applicants.)
   b. Is recruitment conducted primarily by "walk-in" or "word-of-

mouth?" (This could result in a small number of protected class job applicants, depending on the organization's location and the make-up of the current work force.)

c. Is an affirmative action file maintained to include protected class applicants who have not been hired but are qualified candidates for future openings?

d. Are protected class members utilized in the recruitment process?

e. Have community resource organizations and citizen action groups which may serve as recruitment sources for protected class members been informed of the employer's policy and job openings?

f. Do advertisements of job openings indicate the employer's policy of equal employment opportunity?

g. Are media resources with a high percentage of readership or audience composition of protected classes used for advertising job openings?

2. Minimal job qualifications

a. Are qualifications job-relevant and based on up-to-date job descriptions?

b. Has the "minimal" level of qualifications been established based on a careful job analysis?

c. Have job qualifications been analyzed to determine whether they have an adverse impact on members of protected classes?

d. Have the job qualifications of current employees been surveyed by job classification to identify whether current qualifications, particularly those for education and previous experience, are realistic?

3. Selection procedures

a. Do application forms require information regarding protected class status (race, color, creed, religion, sex, national origin, or age) or other areas of inquiry which could be used to discriminate illegally against applicants? (If such information is collected on the application form, an employer may be required in case of charges of discrimination to prove that such information had not been used to discriminate illegally against the applicant—a difficult case to prove.)

b. Are protected class members utilized to screen applications and interview applicants?

c. Where previous job-relevant experience and education of applicants are rated, have specific written standards been established for such evaluations?

d. Are all examinations, including written, oral, and performance tests, job-relevant?

e. Are examinations scheduled and conducted consistent with principles of equal opportunity and open competition?

f. What is the strategy for determining passing scores?

g. What are the criteria for selection of oral examination panels?

h. Does the oral examination panel receive training to increase the objectivity and reliability of evaluations and to understand the organization's commitment to examination procedures consistent with principles of equal employment opportunity?

    i. Do all examinees receive equal treatment?

    j. Have examination results been analyzed to determine whether there is an adverse impact on members of protected classes?

    k. Do performance tests, if used, include measurement of job-relevant skills based on a careful job analysis?

    l. Are preemployment interview questions relevant to job performance?

    m. Have areas of interview inquiry been reviewed and questions eliminated which could be used to discriminate illegally against applicants based on race, color, creed, sex, religion, national origin, or age? (For example, questions which relate to child care plans asked of women but not of men are considered to be discriminatory on the basis of sex.)

    n. Do previous employer reference checks include personal information which is not relevant to job performance?

    o. Are applicants informed that previous employers will be contacted to obtain job-relevant information which may have an effect on their opportunities for employment with the organization?

    p. Have employees and supervisors been informed that protected class employees are eligible for promotion to any job for which they qualify, regardless of whether such jobs have in the past been filled by members of protected classes?

    q. Are supervisors required to submit a written justification for passing over qualified protected class employees for promotions?

    r. What is the employer's policy regarding promotion from within versus appointment from outside the organization? Does this policy have an adverse impact on protected class members?

    s. What procedures have been established to identify employees interested in and qualified for promotion?

    t. Is selection for promotion based on job-relevant criteria?

    u. Does the certification and appointment procedure ensure the consideration of best qualified candidates?

    v. Does the system provide job-relevant criteria for consideration by the appointing authority in selecting the best qualified candidates for appointment?

    w. What policy is applicable to those certified candidates who are repeatedly passed over?

    x. Do appointing officials receive training in interviewing and selection consistent with equal employment opportunity principles?

    y. Are appointing officials required to interview all candidates certified to them; if not, are they encouraged to do so?

4. Performance evaluations

    a. Have specific performance standards been developed for evaluation? ("Global" or "overall" ratings are particularly vulnerable to bias based on factors other than performance—which may include race, sex, national origin, etc.)

    b. Have performance standards been communicated adequately to employees and supervisors?

    c. Does the performance evaluation procedure provide for an interview between supervisor and employee in which the employee's performance evaluation is reviewed and in which the employee is given an opportunity to add written comments?

d. Are written performance evaluations considered in making training and job assignments, transfers, and promotions?

5. Wages and benefits
   a. Where there is a salary range for hiring or promotion, are females and/or minorities offered lower starting pay than males?
   b. Have similar jobs been compared with respect to skill, effort, responsibility, and working conditions to determine whether there is equal pay for equal work?
   c. If pay differentials do exist for jobs that are substantially equal given skill, effort, responsibility, and working conditions, what is the basis for such pay differentials? (Pay differentials may legally exist based on bona fide seniority, merit, or incentive programs or on piecework systems but are illegal if based on sex, race, etc. of job incumbents.)
   d. Have all supervisory and managerial personnel who participate in compensation decisions been briefed on the requirements of the Equal Pay Act?
   e. Have jobs in the same "family" (for example, clerical jobs) been compared to determine if they are properly graded? (For example, if women in lower salary grades perform duties of jobs classified into higher salary grades, this may constitute a violation of the Equal Pay Act.)
   f. What factors are salary increases based on—performance, seniority, automatic step increase, "cost-of-living" adjustments, or collective bargaining provisions? Are these factors equitably applied in granting individual salary increases?
   g. Are some benefits available only to "principal wage earner" or "head of household?" (Such a practice is discriminatory against female employees.)
   h. Are benefits provided for wives and families of male employees also available to husbands and families of female employees?
   i. Are benefits provided for wives of male employees also available to female employees?
   j. Are pregnancy, miscarriage, childbirth, and recovery dealt with on the same basis as other temporary disabilities?
   k. Are males and females eligible for retirement on the same basis including equal retirement age and equal benefits?

6. Layoff and recall
   a. Have affirmative action records been established to monitor layoff and recall and to see if current practices have a disparate effect on protected class members?
   b. Are layoff and recall conducted on an organization-wide seniority basis in cases where protected class members previously could not enter certain job classifications and therefore acquire job or departmental seniority?

7. Demotions, disciplinary action, and discharge
   a. Have affirmative action records been established to monitor demo-

tions, disciplinary action, and discharge in order to see if current practices have a disparate effect on protected class members?

b. Does a personnel or equal employment opportunity officer formally monitor disciplinary actions so that discrimination can be identified and promptly rectified?

c. As a matter of good personnel policy and to provide a defense against discrimination charges are written records maintained on disciplinary action and rule infractions (even when no disciplinary action was taken)? Does the organization maintain job performance records that document poor performance when it occurs?

d. Are supervisors and managers provided with training in progressive discipline for just cause and consistent application of discipline?

e. Are supervisors and managers provided with written discipline standards that provide specific, objective guidelines for administering disciplinary action?

f. Are appeal procedures equally available to all employees?

g. Have termination records been reviewed to determine whether any of the following forbidden criteria were the basis for terminations: termination of female for marrying or becoming pregnant (sex discrimination); termination after employee was placed in job where failure was inevitable; termination for complaining about discrimination or filing charges of discrimination against the employer; and termination based on an employee's failure to get along with co-workers who practice discriminatory harassment?

8. Training and career development

a. Are affirmative action records maintained regarding the participation of women and minorities in training programs and career development opportunities?

b. Have these records been analyzed to determine whether women and minorities are underrepresented in relation to their percentage of the work force, in training programs, and career development opportunities?

c. What are the criteria for selecting employees for training? (Such selection decisions should not be based on race, color, age, sex, national origin, or religion.)

d. Are all employees informed of training and educational opportunities (tuition refund, for example) made available by the organization?

e. Among the persons who administer the training and career development programs, are there any minorities and women?

f. Have training programs been developed to provide supervisors and managers with information on equal employment opportunity and the organization's affirmative action commitment?

9. Seniority and transfer provisions

a. Are seniority lists segregated by race, color, religion, sex, or national origin? (Segregated seniority lists on the bases of these factors are illegal under Title VII.)

b. Are seniority lists segregated for "heavy" and "light" job classifications? (It is unlawful discrimination based on sex if there are dual seniority lists for "heavy" jobs held by men and "light" jobs held by women.)

c. Does the current seniority system penalize minorities and women as a result of past discrimination? (For example, a departmental seniority system that makes it difficult for minorities and females to transfer out of lower-paying departments into which they've been locked by previous discrimination may be illegal unless it can meet the "bona fide" seniority system exception.)

d. If layoffs are pending, has every practical possibility been explored for avoiding a disparate impact on minorities and females who may have less seniority due to past discrimination than white males?

10. Social and recreational programs and other employment conditions

a. If social and recreational programs are provided for workers, are they made equally available to all employees?

b. Is the working environment monitored periodically to ensure that it is free of intimidation and other types of harassment based on race, color, creed, age, disability, sex, religion, or national origin?

c. Are supervisors and managers aware of their responsibilities to take action, including discipline as necessary, to stop such harassment if it occurs?

d. Have work rules been reviewed to determine that they are not discriminatory? (Examples of discriminatory rules: longer rest periods for women than for men; prohibiting employees from speaking foreign languages on the premises; and "protective" rules such as prohibiting women from lifting objects in excess of a certain weight limit.)

e. Have work rules been consistently enforced?

f. Are work assignments made on a nondiscriminatory basis?

Establish a monitoring system for each aspect of the program and evaluate progress

Effective implementation and achievement of any program is dependent on periodic monitoring, evaluation of progress, and remedial action when necessary. The employer should develop a system for keeping records by sex and race of: applicant flow, hiring, wages and benefits, promotion, transfer, demotion, layoff and recall, disciplinary action and discharge, and training and career development programs. Such records will permit analysis to determine whether there is an unjustifiable adverse impact of current employment policies and practices on women and minorities, resulting in barriers to the achievement of equal employment opportunity and affirmative action goals. Periodic monitoring and reporting to all levels of management can result in appropriate and timely remedial action.

Develop supportive organizational and community programs

Internal support services designed to facilitate the achievement of equal opportunity and affirmative action may include, for example, training programs on equal employment opportunity and affirmative action for supervisors and managers; career counseling for employees; work programs on a part-time, temporary, job-sharing, or work-study basis; referral to appropriate community resources for assistance with transportation or day care; and communication with employee unions. The participation of key members of the organization in community action groups and programs to promote improvements in employment, education, and training should be encouraged. The organization may find participation in community activities such as job fairs helpful in affirmative action recruiting efforts.

Develop goals and timetables to improve utilization of women and minorities where underutilization has been identified

The establishment of both short-range and long-range numerical employment goals is required to increase the employment of women and minorities in each area where underutilization has been identified. Goals are not to be confused with quotas. The distinction is an important one since failure of the employer to understand the difference can result in illegal discrimination in hiring, promotion, and transfer.

■ GOALS VERSUS QUOTAS

A *goal* is a numerical objective which is realistically set, given consideration of the number of expected job openings and the availability of qualified women and minorities in the relevant labor market recruitment areas. In making employment decisions, employers are not required by law to: give preference to women and minorities; hire a less qualified person in preference to a better qualified one; or hire a person who does not have the necessary job-relevant qualifications. Goals are management objectives to increase the utilization of women and minorities. Therefore, they represent a commitment to affirmative action which is not inconsistent with the principle of merit hiring. The goal setting process recognizes that individuals will be compared with each other on the basis of individual qualifications—including knowledge, skill, interests, aptitudes, etc.—necessary to job performance.

A *quota* may be defined as court-ordered hiring and/or promotion of specified numbers or ratios of minorities and women in positions from which the court has found they have been excluded due to unlawful discrimination. In implementing a quota system, employers establish separate eligibility lists for white males and for women and/or minorities. Candidates are then selected from these separate eligibility lists in the ratio ordered by the court for a given period of time or until a given representation of women and/or minorities is achieved in the job classifications covered by the court order. Until the Supreme Court clarifies whether quotas are valid for public employers, such employers should not undertake them without court approval.

In accordance with Revised Orders No. 4 and 14 developed by the Office of Federal Contract Compliance (OFCCP), goals and timetables are to be included in affirmative action programs to increase employment of women and minorities in each area where underutilization has been identified. While the Vocational Rehabilitation Act and the Vietnam Era Veterans' Readjustment Assistance Act require employers covered by the act to take affirmative action in employment of the handicapped and Vietnam veterans, employers are not required to develop goals and timetables for these protected classes.

Where there is a serious deficiency in the number of minorities and women employed, compared with the available supply of qualified members of these groups, an overall long-range employment goal (for example, five years) can be established. Such a goal would project in percentage the future composition of the work force, taking into account affirmative action efforts by the employer in the interim. Normally set for a year's duration, short-range goals establish a plan for increasing the utilization of women and minorities so that the organization's overall long-range goal will be met. In setting both short- and long-range goals, it is essential that the employer consider relevant information regarding the availability of qualified women and minorities and results that could be reasonably expected from implementing affirmative action steps identified in the program. Such careful consideration should result in the development of realistic and attainable goals and timetables.

The first step in short-range goal setting is to estimate the number of job openings which will occur in each occupational category during the coming year. Anticipated expansion, cutbacks, and estimates of turnover based on past experience should be considered in arriving at this estimate. Then, based on the availability of qualified women and minorities in the appropriate recruitment area and in the current work force, taking into account training and promotion opportunities, numerical goals should be established *separately* for women and minorities. A single goal for all minorities is generally acceptable, unless the work force analysis has identified the significant underutilization of one or more minority groups, in which case it may be desirable to set separate goals for each minority group.

The organization's progress in attaining short-range goals should be monitored periodically, evaluated, and reported to all levels of management annually. This evaluation will be helpful in identifying those action steps which have proven to be successful or unsuccessful and will also indicate problem areas where renewed efforts and new approaches are required. Based on progress made in attaining short-range goals, adjustments may be made in overall long-range goals. Included in the annual evaluation report should be a description of affirmative action steps taken to increase the utilization of women and minorities and an explanation where goals have not been attained. It is important to document good faith affirmative action efforts made to achieve realistic goals so that this information is available to interested citizen groups and enforcement agencies.

CHAPTER 14 APPENDIX
Arbitration Decision
City of Portland

Decision of Arbitrator

In re CITY OF PORTLAND, BUREAU OF POLICE and PORTLAND POLICE ASSOCIATION, August 7, 1981

Arbitrator: Gary L. Axon

■ DISCHARGE

—Misconduct—Adverse publicity—Police officers-propriety of penalty ➤ 118.03 ➤ 118.640 ➤ 100.55 ➤ 118.6481

Penalty of discharge was excessive for police officers who deposited carcasses of dead animals on public sidewalk known to officers as trouble spot, despite adverse publicity given episode in news media which was given great weight in decision to discharge. Extent of publicity generated is no accurate measure of harm inflicted on bureau; failure of employer to speak directly with grievants or their immediate supervisors constitutes serious flaw in investigation; evidence establishes that grievants would be able to return to work as effective police officers; grievants had outstanding work records which were completely unblemished prior to incident; grievants deeply regretted incident; employer's legitimate interest in discouraging this type of behavior and maintaining its credibility will be served by lesser penalty which will put other police officers on notice that grievants' conduct will not be tolerated.

—Misconduct—Reduction of penalty ➤ 100.55 ➤ 118.03 ➤ 118.640

Appropriate penalty for police officers who were discharged for depositing dead animals on public sidewalk known to be trouble spot is 30-day suspension without pay, notwithstanding contention that city charter precludes suspension of more than 30 days and only legal option that employer had for discipline beyond 30 days was termination and, therefore, when faced with two alternatives, 30-day suspension is far too lenient.

Appearances: For the employer — David W. Morthland (Miller, Nash, Yerke, Wiener and Hager), attorney.

For the union—Will Aitchison, attorney.

■ ADVERSE PUBLICITY

I. Statement of Issue

AXON, Arbitrator:—Did the City have just cause to terminate G__ and W__ under the terms of the labor agreement? If not, what should the remedy be?

II. Relevant Contractual Provisions

Article 2

"2. *MANAGEMENT RIGHTS.* The City shall retain the exclusive right to exercise the customary functions of management including, but not limited to, directing the activities of the Bureau, determining the levels of service and methods of operation including subcontracting and the introduction of new equipment; the right to hire, lay off, transfer and promote; to discipline or discharge for cause, to determine work schedules and assign work and any other such rights not specifically referred to in this Contract. Management rights, except where abridged by specific provisions of this Contract or general law, are not subject to the Grievance Procedure."

Article 22

"22. *DISCHARGE AND DEMOTION.* Discharge or demotion shall be for just cause, and in such case, an officer in permanent status may choose between two avenues of appeal: (1) He may exercise his right of appeal by Civil Service Rules of the City of Portland, or (2) the Association may, in lieu of those provisions established pursuant to the City Charter, be allowed to take up the matter at Step II of the Grievance Procedure. These two avenues of appeal do not apply to an officer who: (1) Is separated as a result of failing to complete the current educational requirements or the eighteen (18) months' entry level probationary period, or (2) fails to successfully complete the twelve (12) months' probationary period in a promotional position and is reverted to his former classification."

Bureau of Police, General Order, *310.10 Conduct, Standard of*

"Every member of the Bureau of Police will constantly strive to attain the highest professional standard of conduct. Employees, whether on duty or off duty, shall be governed by the ordinary and reasonable rules of good conduct and behavior, and shall not commit any act tending to bring reproach or discredit upon the Bureau or the City of Portland. Members shall obey and execute promptly the orders of their superior officers. They will conduct themselves in the discharge of their duties and their relations with the public and other members of the Bureau in a diplomatic and professional manner and in accordance with the laws of United States, the State of Oregon, ordinances of the City of Portland and the Manual of Rules and Procedures of the Bureau, to most effectively achieve the mission of the Bureau."

III. Statement of Facts

The grievants in this case were employed by the City of Portland as police officers. Officer G__ had been a police officer for the City for approximately 7 years. Officer W__ had been a police officer for the City for approximately 5 years. Both of the grievants are college graduates with degrees in law enforcement. The grievants have been evaluated as superior officers during their careers with the City. The City did not deny that both grievants were good police officers. The grievants up until this incident had never been the subject of disciplinary action.

On March 12, 1981, the grievants were assigned to patrol district 582 in the North Precinct of Portland. The grievants were checking alleys which burglars had been using to gain access to residences. Officer W__, who was driving the car, spotted an opossum in front of the car. He sped up and ran over the opossum with his car, killing the opossum. Subsequently, Officer W__ used the police car to run over and kill a second opossum. Later, the two officers clubbed three other opossums to death with their police batons. They placed the dead animals on the floor in the back seat of the patrol car.

The grievants were uncertain of what to do with the dead animals. Officer W__ testified he considered using the pelts of the animals but rejected the idea after closer examination revealed the pelts were not useable. It should be noted here that Officer W__ maintains a trap line during the nine winter months of the year, and it is on the basis of his trapping experience that he made the determination of pelt quality. The grievants testified they then decided to put the dead opossums in the back of a sergeant's car at North Precinct. The idea was abandoned after they learned that this particular sergeant was not on duty. Officer G__ suggested that they place the dead opossums in the parking lot between the Burger Barn Restaurant and Weimer's Hardware Store on Union Avenue, near Shaver Street.

At about 10:20 p.m. the grievants called for a "meet" with other officers at the parking lot. Eight other Officers responded to the call for this "meet." The grievants removed the carcasses of the dead animals from the car and showed them to their fellow officers. The testimony indicated that there was little conversation at the scene. One officer testified he heard Officer G__ state that he and Officer W__ intended to make a presentation or a gift. The grievants each picked up two dead opossums and carried them across the parking lot and threw the dead opossums onto a public sidewalk on Union Avenue in front of the Burger Barn Restaurant.

The grievants returned quickly to their car and left the scene. The other police cars left the parking lot immediately after the grievants left the scene. Police radio records indicated that from the time Officer G__ called for a "meet" and the last car cleared the parking lot a total of approximately four minutes time had elapsed.

The son of the owner of the Burger Barn called Channel 2 news to inform them what had happened. The incident was reported in the local news media the following day. Officer W__ told his sergeant on March 14, 1981, that he and G__ were involved in the opossum incident of March 12, 1981. The Bureau initiated an Internal Affairs Division (IAD) investigation of March 16, 1981. The IAD report confirmed that the grievants were involved in the March 12 incident. Charges were then brought against the grievants on March 23, 1981, alleging a violation of Section 310.10 of the Bureau's rules and regulations. The rule provides in part as follows:

"Every member of the Bureau of Police will constantly strive to attain the highest professional standard of *conduct. Employees, whether on duty or off duty, shall be governed by the ordinary and reasonable rules of good conduct and behavior, and shall not commit any act tending to bring reproach or discredit upon the Bureau or the City of Portland.* Members shall obey and execute promptly the orders of their superior officers. They will conduct themselves in the discharge of their duties and their relations with the public and other members of the Bureau in a diplomatic and professional manner and in accordance with the laws of United States, the State of Oregon, ordinances of the City of Portland and the Manual of Rules and Procedures of the Bureau, to most effectively acheive the mission of the Bureau."

The specification of charges was stated:

"*Specification*
On March 12, 1981, you obtained four (4) opossums and placed them on the sidewalk in front of the Burger Barn restaurant, 3962 NE Union, thereby bringing discredit upon the Bureau of Police."

A disciplinary hearing was held on March 26, 1981 to examine the charges. The grievants were represented by Stan Peters, President of the Portland Police Association. The hearing was taped, transcribed and made a part of the record of this arbitration. The grievants admitted they had placed the opossums in front of the Burger Barn restaurant on March 12. At the close of the hearing, Chief Baker informed the grievants he felt he would be able to inform the grievants of the results of the hearing and of the attendant disciplinary action by the afternoon of March 26.

The Chief went immediately to the office of Charles Jordan, Police Commissioner, to discuss what action should be taken as a result of the opossum incident. Chief Baker relayed to Jordan the testimony given at the disciplinary hearing. Further, the Chief provided Jordan with a review of the grievants' work record. He also reviewed the responses the grievants had given to questions at the disciplinary hearing. At the conclusion of the meeting, Commissioner Jordan indicated that the grievants should be terminated. Chief Baker concurred and further stated he would have made the same recommendation.

A notice of termination was prepared which stated in part:

"Your termination has been ordered as a result of your conduct on March 12, 1981, which was in violation of Section 310.10 *Conduct, Standard of,* of the official Manual of Rules and Procedures of the Bureau of Police. On that date, you obtained four (4) opossums and placed them on the sidewalk in front of the Burger Barn restaurant, 3962 NE Union, thereby bringing discredit upon the Bureau of Police."

The notice was dated March 30, 1981 and signed by Commissioner Jordan. The officers filed grievances which stated as follows:

"My discharge was not for just cause and the penalty imposed was inappropriate under the circumstances."

The grievance were denied by Commissioner Jordan.

The Association elected to take the matter to arbitration pursuant to Section 22 of the labor agreement. The submission agreement provided that all procedural steps prior to arbitration had been complied with. The submission agreement granted the Arbitrator authority to formulate a statement of the issue in the absence of agreement by the parties. The hearing was transcribed by a court reporter and post-hearing briefs were timely filed. The parties stipulated that the Arbitrator had 30 days from the date of receipt of the briefs to render an award.

IV. Position of the Parties

A. *The City:* The City contends it had just cause to terminate the grievants. According to the City, "the focal point of this case is that a police officer is a public servant in a position of great power and public trust." The City alleges that the wrongful conduct of the grievants brought great discredit and reproach to the Portland Police Bureau. Further, the City reasons that extremely high standards of discipline and accountability are essential for efficient and effective police work. The City maintains that public trust and confidence are fundamental to a properly functioning police agency. Thus, the City concludes that just cause in this case requires the considerations of public trust and confidence.

Accordingly, the City contends that the Arbitrator does not have the unqualified authority to substitute the Bureau's determination of what constitutes just cause with his own determination. The City points to the combined experience and expertise of Commissioner Jordan and Chief Baker in police operations as a basis for arbitral restraint. Therefore, the City submits that unless the Arbitrator finds that Commissioner Jordan and Chief Baker's decision to terminate the grievants was arbitrary, capricious or manifestly unreasonable, its decision should be sustained.

The City asserts there are no mitigating circumstances which justify the grievants' actions. Further, the City dismisses the grievants' stated reason for their actions in placing the opossums at the Burger Barn was to solve morale problems among their fellow officers on the shift; that the sole purpose was to make their fellow officers laugh. The grievants chose the Burger Barn area because it was a "trouble spot" known to all officers. The City completely rejected the stated reasons as an excuse for the grievants' conduct. In the City's view, the grievants' intention was to harass citizens in a way to make their fellow officers laugh.

Further, the City maintains the grievants, as experienced street officers, knew their conduct was wrong and that they should have known better. Hence, because of their experience, the grievants should have known that their acts would have an adverse impact on the Bureau. The City concludes that in light of the deliberate violation of the public trust it had no choice but to discharge the officers.

In addition, the City denies that discharge of the grievants under the circumstances of this case was too severe. The City alleges that progressive discipline is not appropriate where intentional and deliberate acts of wrongdoing are involved. The City believes that progressive discipline will not heal the wounds caused by the grievants. According to the City, "if anything, progressive discipline might infect that wound and retard its healing." For these reasons, the City submits that Commissioner Jordan and Chief Baker did not error when they resolved that progressive discipline should not be used in this case.

The City denies the claim by the Association that the discharging of the grievants in this case was inconsistent with discipline administered by the Bureau in other disciplinary cases. The City maintains that because of the public trust issue, this case cannot be compared to previous discipline imposed by the Bureau. The City urged that the "arbitrator simply must recognize the substantial difference in this case from prior cases of misconduct on the basis of the lack of notoriety of other cases." Finally, the City terms the assertion that identical discipline must be given in each case as "totally unrealistic."

Further, the City maintains that the discharge was not precipitous or preconceived but made only after Chief Baker and Commissioner Jordan had carefully considered all of the facts. The City denies that any procedural defect exists because Commissioner Jordan refused to meet with the grievants. The City argues that Jordan and Baker made a full and complete investigation before reaching the decision to terminate the grievants.

Lastly, the City contends that even if the Arbitrator determines that the discharge was too severe, the grievants should not be reinstated. According to the City, the public supports the discharges as evidenced by the number of letters written to the City supporting the discharges. The City argues that grievants cannot return to work and be effective because citizens will not cooperate with them. In addition, the City alleges that reinstatement is inappropriate because serious violations of law have occurred. For these and other reasons stated in its brief, the City concludes that reinstatement is inappropriate even if the Arbitrator determines that the discharges were too severe a punishment.

B. *The Association:* The Association does not claim that the grievants should go unpunished for their conduct on March 12, 1981. The Association takes the position that discharge was too severe under the circumstances of this case. The Association submitted twelve reasons why the discharges must be viewed as inappropriate. Hence, the Association concludes that the discharges of Officers W__ and G__ were not for just cause.

The Association maintains that the burden of proving just cause lies with the City. According to the Association, the contract provides only for the just cause standard and not the "arbitrary and capricious" standard asserted by the City. Further, the Association maintains that where the alleged misconduct carries the stigma of social disapproval, the City has the burden of proving by clear and convincing evidence that its actions were proper.

The Association contends that the discipline imposed in this case was not in keeping with discipline meted out by the City for similar offenses in the past. The Association maintains once disparate treatment is demonstrated, a finding that the level of discipline imposed was not for just cause is required. The Association alleges that the evidence of past discipline demonstrated that the Bureau has been "so inconsistent that it may be safely stated *that there are no* standards for the imposition of discipline within the Bureau."

The Association maintains that the discharges were not for just cause because the City failed to adequately investigate the incident before imposing discipline. Specifically, the Association charges that Commissioner Jordan, the individual who made the decision, did not have all the relevant facts as of March 26, the day the decision was made to terminate the grievants. The Association pointed to the fact that Commissioner Jordan refused to speak with the grievants, the other eight officers at the scene on March 12, or any of the grievants' immediate supervisors. Finally, the Association alleges that neither Commissioner Jordan nor Chief Baker made even a "perfunctory examination of the history of discipline within the Bureau."

The Association asserts that the Bureau failed to consider three mitigating circumstances which in the Association's view would have led to the imposition of suspensions. They were as follows:

"(1) The fact that the actions of Officers W__ and G__ were motivated not by an intention to injure or harass any individuals, but rather were motivated by an attempt to solve an extremely serious problem on North Precinct's afternoon relief; (2) the fact that the decision of Officers W__ and G__ to proceed to Union and Shaver was not a deliberately and extensively plotted one, but rather was a spur-of-the-moment decision; and (3) the fact that Officers W__ and G__ are sincerely apologetic about the March 12 incident, and have publicly apologized to all affected persons."

Thus, the Association concludes that because these factors were not considered by the City, the discharges imposed cannot be for just cause.

Further, the Association contends that the discharges cannot stand because the incident was brought about by a lack of supervision. According to the Association, the supervisors at North Precinct allowed a serious dispute between officers to grow unabated so as to be a significant factor in the March 12 incident. Also, the Association alleges that because the supervisors failed to communicate their concepts of discipline to rank and file police officers, this failure to communicate serves as a cause of the March 12 incident. Hence, the Association concludes that the "spur-of-the-moment decision by Officer G__ to use the opossums as a device of humor to try and bring the avenue officers together again" was in part a response to lack of adequate supervision in the precinct.

The Association maintains that failure of an employer to properly train an employee prevents the employer from relying on a disciplinary decision which is attributable to the lack of training. In the view of the Association, the failure of the City to provide some sort of racial sensitivity or cultural awareness training was a contributing factor to the March 12 incident. Therefore, the Association concludes a less severe sanction than discharge is appropriate.

The Association relied heavily on the principle that the degree of discipline must be reasonably related both to the seriousness of the employees' offense and the employees' work record. The Association points out that the City concedes that the grievants were good police officers. The Association argued that the evidence demonstrated that both officers were dedicated, innovative, courageous and competent police officers. The Association cited in detail examples of commendations, situations where the officers risked their own lives, and the high esteem in which both grievants were held by their fellow officers to support their claim. Further, the Association cited the officers work on the "Alberta Park Detail" and the "bicycle patrol" as illustrations of their innovative approach to their jobs. The Association concluded that "their work records would demand not just that they be given another chance, but also that they not be discharged for their first mistake they have made in a combined twelve years on the Bureau."

The Association contends that the discharges were not for just cause because the principles of progressive discipline were not followed. According to the Association, Officers W__ and G__ are the type of employees whose work records establish that they and the City will benefit from progressive discipline. From the Association's perspective, the grievants are the type of employees who would have responded to a suspension and would continue to provide valuable service to the City in the future.

The Association alleges that the City has subsequent to its decision to discharge the grievants changed and expanded the reasons for the discharge. The Association argues that the discharge "must stand or fall on the reasons given at the time of discharge." The Association points to what it termed as post-hoc justifications for the discharges raised by the City. The Association identified the new reasons given by the City after the discharges as the fact a crime had been committed, calling eight other officers off their details, the fact that officers had killed opossums, and the fact the Bureau believed the officers intended to harass somebody during the March 12 incident. The Association claims that the attempt to rely on post-hoc reasons for the discharges are evidence that Commissioner Jordan failed to have the facts and mitigating circumstances before him on March 26. The Association reasons that the City is forced to resort to justifications which never entered the mind of Commissioner Jordan. These additions, according to the Association, are not permitted under arbitral law.

Further, the Association contends that the discharges of W__ and G__ were politically motivated. For proof here the Association relies on the circumstantial evidence that the decision maker acted in an inexplicable manner. The Association points to Commissioner Jordan's statement "The officers, if involved, will say they are not involved" as evidence the decision was politically motivated. In addition, the Association relied on the statement made by Commissioner Jordan that he was going to conduct his own investigation. Such an action is contrary to established practice for dealing with these matters in the Bureau. Finally, the Association urges that the statement by Commissioner Jordan that he would announce disciplinary actions against W__ and G__ on March 25, 1981, the day before the scheduled disciplinary hearing, is evidence of political motivation.

The Association maintains that substantial procedural irregularities exist in the way in which the City reached the decision to discharge. First, the Association argues that under the City Charter only Commissioner Jordan has authority to discharge, yet the City referred to the decision of Jordan and Baker at the commencement of the hearing. Second, the complete lack of any investigation performed by Commissioner Jordan warrants overturning the discharge. Third, the failure of the City to convene either the Disciplinary Review Committee or the Disciplinary Hearing Board constitutes in the mind of the Association a substantial procedural irregularity. Thus, the Association reasons that the grievants were not accorded due process and the discharges should be set aside.

Moreover, the Association claims that the City failed to fairly and objectively handle the cases of Officers W__ and G__. The Association cites the failure of Commissioner Jordan to speak with the grievants as an indication that W__ and G__ were singled out for disciplinary action. Further, the Association maintains that Commissioner Jordan's statement that he was looking for a reason not to discharge the grievants should not be credited. According to the Association, one who was looking for a reason not to discharge them would have spoken with the grievants, their supervisors, and significantly would have studied the imposition of discipline imposed by the Bureau in the past. Consequently, the Association argues that Commissioner Jordan had his mind made up long before all the facts were known.

Finally, the Association alleges that the public response does not support the discharges of W__ and G__. According to the Association, the arbitral authority does not support the position of the City that public opinion is a proper component of just cause. The Association contends that at the hearing Commissioner Jordan never testified that he took the public opinion or trust into consideration in deciding to terminate the grievants. In addition, the Association argues that the City's public trust argument assumes the public was properly informed about the March 12 incident. The Association maintains the record establishes that the public was not fully and accurately informed about the incident. Hence, the Association concludes that just cause must be based on proven facts before the Arbitrator and "not on some posited public opinion which the City has alleged but not proven."

The Association believes that some sort of suspension is in order for Officers W__ and G__. The Association maintains that the grievants have "learned their lesson" and have already been punished beyond measure for the March 12 incident. The Association concludes that based on past discipline imposed by the Bureau the grievants should be returned to work with a two-week suspension.

V. Discussion

There is no dispute that Officers W— and G— did deposit four dead oppossums on a public sidewalk in front of the Burger Barn Restaurant on March 12, 1981. Nor is it denied by the Association that the grievants should not be punished for their conduct on March 12. The question before the Arbitrator is whether or not there was just cause to terminate the grievants. The question of the appropriateness of the penalty imposed by the City brought into consideration a wide array of factors. The hearing took eight days to complete and consumed some 1650 pages of transcript. The parties filed lengthy and comprehensive post-hearing briefs.

At the outset, it is necessary for the Arbitrator to discuss the question of whether or not the March 12 incident was a racially motivated act. The Burger Barn Restaurant is a black owned and operated business on Union Avenue in Northeast Portland. In order to accurately understand the situation, it must be realized that the term Burger Barn had a meaning to Portland police officers separate and distinct from the restaurant itself. One officer testified that the words Burger Barn referred to the geographic area of Union and Shaver. It includes the parking lot area between the Burger Barn Restaurant and Wimers Hardware. The public sidewalks and several buildings in the immediate vicinity are included in the geographic area referred to by police officers as the Burger Barn.

The Burger Barn geographic area as opposed to the restaurant represented to the police a symbol of a place where illegal transactions took place. Grievant G— testified "that's where most people congregate when they are dealing their dope, prostitution, pimping, fencing hot items." The evidence demonstrated that the geographical area known as the Burger Barn was a source of frustration to police officers because they were unable to stop the illegal activity that transpired in the area.

The grievants' stated reason for engaging in their conduct was to help solve a peer problem among officers on the shift. The grievants thought it would be funny to display the opossums to their fellow officers and leave them at the Burger Barn in an attempt to get the officers laughing. The reason they chose the Burger Barn geographic area was because it was a trouble spot known to all officers. The grievants felt it would have the greatest humorous effect in the area of lawless troublemakers.

The grievants denied that their act was racially motivated. The Internal Affairs Division report found no evidence of racial intent. Chief Baker was unable to attribute any racial motivation for the grievants' conduct. Commissioner Jordan testified as follows:

"Q. (By Mr. Mortland) Did you consider it to be an act of either racial harassment or harassment?

A. Harassment, yes, harassment. I did not think it was racial, I really didn't."

There is not a scintilla of evidence in the record to suggest that the grievants' conduct was racially motivated. The record in this case clearly and convincingly establishes that the act of leaving the dead opossums on the sidewalk was a way of getting back at what the officers viewed as "lawless troublemakers," white or black, who frequented the geographic area known as the Burger Barn. The evidence in the record leaves no doubt that the decision to leave the opossums at the Burger Barn was made on the spur-of-the-moment. The Arbitrator finds that G__'s and W__'s act was a mistaken and ill advised attempt at humor in order to get their fellow officers to laugh. No evidence exists in this record to even suggest the conduct was racially motivated.

This finding of no racial motivation is not to suggest that the grievants' conduct was justified and should go unpunished. The City maintains it had just cause to discharge the grievants. The critical issue in this case is the appropriateness of the penalty. According to the City, the Association is asking the Arbitrator to overturn a judgmental decision of Commissioner Jordan and Chief Baker. Therefore, the City concludes that the Arbitrator must find that the judgmental conclusion of Commissioner Jordan and Chief Baker was arbitrary, capricious or an abuse of discretion before he may set the discharge aside.

The basic consideration in this arbitration is the collective bargaining agreement which exists between the parties. The contract provides "disciplinary action shall be for just cause. . . ." The burden of proving just cause for the discharges is on the City. The

City cautioned the Arbitrator that he is not free to impose his "own brand of industrial justice" upon the parties. United Steelworkers v. Enterprise Corp., 363 U.S. 593, 4 L.Ed. 2d 1424, 34 LA 569 (1960). Continuing in that same case, Justice Douglas states:

"When an arbitrator is commissioned to interpret and apply the collective bargaining agreement, he is to bring his informed judgment to bear in order to reach a fair solution to the problem. This is especially true when it comes to formulating remedies. There the need is for flexibility in meeting a wide variety of situations. The draftsmen (of the contract) may never have thought what specific remedies should be awarded to meet a particular contingency."

The task of reviewing the decision of the City is not one taken lightly by this Arbitrator. However, there is no basis in the contract to require the Arbitrator to find that the decision of the City to terminate the grievants was arbitrary, capricious or an abuse of discretion in order to modify the punishment imposed.

The termination notices to the grievants gave the reason for termination as a violation of Section 310.10 of the Standard of Conduct. The notices specified "you obtained four (4) opossums and placed them on the sidewalk in front of the Burger Barn restaurant, 3962 NE Union, thereby bringing discredit upon the Bureau of Police." The major thrust of the City's case was that as police officers, the grievants are public trustees. The evidence is undisputed that Commissioner Jordan and Chief Baker gave great weight to the public concern expressed in the various media and to the letters and telephone calls addressed to City officials about the incident.

The City stated in its brief that "Public trust, public concern and credibility of the police in the public eye are the focal points of this case." In the City's view, the incident had an extremely adverse impact on the credibility of the Bureau. Thus, the City reasons that the elements of public trust must be injected into the just cause concept. Against this backdrop, the City argues that it cannot be "concluded that Commissioner Jordan and Chief Baker acted arbitrarily, capriciously or in bad faith in exercising their judgment to discharge the grievants."

The just cause test mandates that the punishment assessed be reasonable in light of all the circumstances. Zapata Industries, Inc., 76 LA 467 (1981), City of Detroit, 76 LA 213 (1981). The point is that one must look at the entire situation involving the opossum incident before coming to the conclusion that discharge is

justified. The evidence in some cases will dictate that a lesser
penalty is more appropriate. There is no disagreement between the
parties or in the mind of the Arbitrator that the conduct of Officers
W__ and G__ warranted discipline.

The misconduct is admitted. The City presented evidence sufficient to establish a prima facie case. The burden, therefore, shifts
to the Association to show mitigating circumstances which made
the discipline imposed in this case unreasonable and excessive.
Linear Inc., 48 LA 319 (1966), Elkouri and Elkouri, How Arbitration Works, 624 (3rd ed., 1973). The Association identified some
twelve reasons why the discharges must be viewed as inappropriate. The reasons are outlined in the position of the parties
section of this report and will not be repeated in their entirety.

It is a cardinal rule of labor-management relations that the
degree of discipline must be reasonably related to the seriousness
of the offense and the employee's work record. Grief Brothers
Cooperage Corp., 42 LA 558, and City of Boulder, Colorado, 69
LA 1173 (1977). There is no dispute that both W__ and G__ were
superior police officers. The Association submitted in its opinion
ample evidence to support its position that the grievants' work
records demand that they be reinstated. The City does not deny
that the grievants were good police officers but views the gravity of
their actions on March 12 as overriding their good work records.

The Arbitrator will not unnecessarily lengthen this discussion by
restating the entire work history of the grievants. The best
summary of the work of Officer G__ was written in October, 1980
by Deputy Chief Gary Haynes in recognition of Officer G__'s
selection of "Officer of the Month by the Portland Kiwanis Club."
The memorandum states as follows:

"Officer G__ has been with the Bureau six and one half years, five of
which has been at North Precinct, his present assignment."

"Officer G__ is married; his wife's name is Molly."

G__ has received numerous letters of appreciation and/or commendations from citizens and Bureau personel. Several are noteworthy enough to
quote in part: 'May I take this opportunity to express my deep appreciation
to your Police Department and its fine officers and commend them for the
most prompt and efficient manner in which they performed at the time of my
distress when I was assaulted and robbed in Alberta Park...The response
...was most gratifying and the concern and courtesy shown was most
commendable . . . The friendly gesture in calling my home later in the
evening to check on how I was doing was most appreciated.' (Stanley S.
Ross) 'I have noted that your Afternoon Relief Officers, in particular

Officers G__ and __, arrested two robbery suspects just after the incident occurred . . . Please relay my complements . . . on an outstanding contribution especially for their timely and tactically appropriate responses to a highly dangerous situation.' (James T. Brouilette, Deputy Chief, Patrol Branch) 'Also I want the Department to know that they have 2 uniform officers and I fingerprint man who can deal with the public (me, at least) like civilized human beings and not like Gestapo officials. Thank them for their prompt and courteous handling of my problem.' (Rosemary W. Pollard) 'The recently concluded range training program was the most successful and worthwhile field training I have witnessed in 25 years on the Police Bureau . . . the interest and enthusiasm of the instructor staff was clearly evident to all who attended. I particularly wish to thank you for your energetic participation in this effort . . . Your contribution is sincerely appreciated.' (Capt. J.E. Harvey, Director, Training Division)

"All of Officer G__'s performance evaluation reports have been in the 'competent,' 'competent plus,' or 'superior' category. The following are excerpts from a few of them: '. . . is aware of peoples needs and problems and is quick to offer workable solutions for these things . . . is constantly working to improve in the areas where he is lacking . . . is continually aware of abnormal incidents on the district and takes corrective action without hesitation . . . a very mature and cool headed officer who handles all problems with ease and confidence . . . displays calmness and confidence when dealing with the public . . . possesses a keen insight into human behavior . . . has an excellent attitude and applies himself energetically to his work."

"Officer G__ is far and above a good 'street cop.' He is, and has been, one of North Precinct's top officers. His work habits and dedication to duty are truly exemplary. He has been an instructor at our semi-annual range for two years and, is active in the military reserve."

From time to time the standard methods of police patrol must be changed to achieve success. The criminal becomes so complacent that even a slight deviation gives us an edge. Such was the case recently when Officer G__ and two other North Precinct Officers came up with the idea of a burglary surveillance team using bicycles. With much planning, ingenuity and hard work, the operation was brought to a successful conclusion with the arrest of two subjects who were responsible for 80 – 90% of the residential burglaries in a particular area. What made this a particularly gratifying mission was the fact that the idea was conceived and well executed by G__ and his two fellow officers."

"Continuing to perform in a low-key professional manner makes Officer G__ an asset to North Precinct and to the Bureau."

Grievant G__ has never, prior to this incident been the subject of any disciplinary action by the Bureau.

The official evaluations of Officer W__ rate him as a superior officer. He has received numerous reports of meritorious service. Many of the instances described in the Haynes memorandum also relate to operations in which grievant W__ participated with his partner G__. Grievant W__ received the highest entry level score on the written examination in the history of the Bureau and has been commended for his work as an instructor in the Bureau's firing range program. Grievant W__ has never, prior to this incident, been the subject of disciplinary action in his 5 years with the Bureau.

Closely related to the evaluation of an employee's work record, is the concept of progressive discipline. The City's "Manager and Supervisors Handbook for Progressive Discipline" states:

"Although discipline is normally thought of in a narrow, punitive sense, the primary objective of discipline is corrective action. If applied fairly and consistently, it becomes a positive means of bringing about or increasing individual employee and organizational order and efficiency.

The concept of progressive discipline recognizes that as violations recur without correction despite disciplinary action, the severity of the disciplinary measures taken must increase. It also provides that as the seriousness of the violation increases, so must the seriousness of the disciplinary action taken.

The pattern followed in the City of Portland is oral warning(s); written reprimands(s); and suspension(s) preceding the ultimate penalty of discharge. However, there are cases where the action is of such a serious nature that discharge is justifiable even on a first offense.

We, therefore, have a program in which the penalties for unacceptable employee behavior become *progressively* more severe in accordance with *progressive* seriousness of the infraction."

The City did not consider progressive discipline because the conduct in this case was deliberate, intentional, and carried out without any thought to its adverse consequences to the Bureau. The City resisted the application of progressive discipline because it "will not heal the wound which has occurred."

Arbitrators frequently require progressive discipline where employees have not been given a chance to correct their behavior prior to discharge. Shields and Terrall Conv. Hosp., 56 LA 884 (1971), White Motor Corp., 50 LA 541 (1968) and Marion Power Shovel Co., Inc., 69 LA 339 (1977). The basis of progressive discipline was stated by Arbitrator Stouffer as follows:

"The primary purpose of discipline is to rehabilitate an employee and discourage repetition of the offense committed by the disciplined employee and by other employees. Discharge, the most extreme industrial penalty, is generally imposed where the offense committed is an extremely serious one, or where there is little reason to believe that the involved employee can be rehabilitated and made into a satisfactory employee."

Hankins Container Company, Division of Flint Kote Company, 69-1 ARB 118351 at p.4205 (Stouffer, 1969).

The City cannot seriously contend that the grievants are beyond rehabilitation. The grievants who have outstanding work records, and who have, for the first time made a mistake in the course of their jobs are the type of employees who will benefit from progressive discipline. Likewise, the City will benefit from the future services of these two officers who Chief Baker concluded will be unlikely to commit such an act again.

The defense of disparate treatment raised by the Association requires the City to be consistent in the imposition of discipline. That is, "All employees who engaged in the same type of misconduct must be treated essentially the same unless a reasonable basis exists for variations in the assessment of punishment." Stauffer Chemical Company, CCH 69-1, Para. 8392 (1968). The City contends that because of the public trust issue this case cannot be compared with any other disciplinary cases. The City argued "The Arbitrator simply must recognize the substantial difference in this case from prior cases of misconduct on the basis of lack of notoriety of other cases."

The record in this case contains abundant evidence of the facts and circumstances under which the City chose to discipline officers in the past. It would serve no purpose for the Arbitrator to discuss in detail the discipline imposed on police officers in the past. A review of the disciplinary log indicates that in the last seven years, excluding the grievants in this case, five officers have been discharged. The record of those discharges would indicate three were for receiving stolen property, one for violation of gun laws and one for theft. The Bureau has suspended officers in the past who have maced a business establishment for personal reasons, committed serious driving infractions, assaults, and alcohol abuse.

It is true that not all of the past situations that resulted in disciplinary action are comparable. For instance, some of the actions were not committed while on duty. The Arbitrator also notes that the other eight officers at the scene on March 12 received no discipline whatsoever. The grievants were not charged with the violation of any criminal statutes as was the case in past disciplinary actions which resulted in suspensions. Nor were the grievants discharged by the City for any alleged criminal activity.

The Arbitrator was persuaded that the overriding reason the

City chose to discharge the grievants in this case was because of the voluminous media attention the opposum incident attracted. The City in seeking to distinguish the differences between the prior discipline meted to police officers noted time and time again that the act of misconduct received little or no publicity. The City argued that none of the previous cases of wrongful conduct by officers even came close to the adverse publicity generated by this case. Under the unique set of circumstances of this termination, the Arbitrator is compelled to conclude that the grievants were "singled out" for discipline because of the substantial amount of media attention given this incident.

The City made a strong argument that public trust and public concern are the focal points of this case. The testimony of Commissioner Jordan and Chief Baker was extensive regarding their goals and philosophies dealing with public trust, public accountability, and community relations that provided the framework in which the decision to terminate the grievants was made. The necessity to preserve the public trust in the Portland Police Bureau and in its officers cannot be denied. The difficulty with any general principle is applying it to a particular situation. The point is especially true in this case; indeed, dealing with such nebulous concepts as public confidence and trust underscores this difficulty.

While not diminishing the City's position on the public trust factor, the fact remains that the collective bargaining agreement is the basic consideration in this arbitration. The City introduced 552 letters it had received from citizens, 401 in support of the discharge, and 121 opposing the discharge of W__ and G__. The record is replete with copies of newspaper articles covering the opossum incident. The record also indicates that substantial radio and television coverage was given the incident. Commissioner Jordan and Chief Baker both testified they were aware of and gave great weight to the expressions of public concern.

In the face of all the media coverage, Commissioner Jordan did not personally speak with the grievants. However, he spoke twice with the owners of the Burger Barn Restaurant. He appeared on radio and television and spoke with others who were not directly involved with the Bureau about the incident. Further, neither Commissioner Jordan nor Chief Baker ever spoke with the three immediate supervisors of Officers Ward and Gallaway prior to the decision to discharge them.

Furthermore, the Bureau must accept some of the responsibility for the public reaction to the incident of March 12. The Bureau did little to dispel unsound information that was being reported. Commissioner Jordan told the Oregonian on March 13, 1981 that he needed witnesses because "the officers, if involved, will say they were not involved." Thus, the implication was given that the officers would lie.

The City concedes it gave great weight to the public reaction in deciding to terminate the grievants for the March 12 incident. The City's motive of self-protection is understandable in the context of this case. However, the record contains no definite measures of the public reaction. The letters and news articles are hearsay in its most extreme form. The Arbitrator remains unconvinced that the extent of publicity generated is an accurate measure of the harm inflicted on the Bureau. The Arbitrator must base his decision on facts in the record and not on unsupported allegations of damage to the Bureau.

Moreover, in the context of the amount of publicity generated in this case, the failure of Commissioner Jordan to speak directly with the grievants or their immediate supervisors constitutes a serious flaw in the investigation. Commissioner Jordan testified on why he didn't want to speak with the grievants.:

"At that time I, for a couple of reasons and one of the reasons is I didn't know whether it was proper, but that was really secondary. I think my primary reason was, and I had a lot of input at that point from a lot of unwanted sources, you know, trying to influence my decision. And I really wanted to just get away *and not have any more input,* you know, anyone else or anything else that could influence my decision.

"I really didn't wrestle with that. It was hard enough as it was to make the decision. And so I didn't want to complicate it. I wasn't sure what my legal grounds were if I talked to the officers; did this mean that I had to record everything I said, it would be brought up in a hearing again. Chief Baker, as we've talked about this many times, about how involved I get into these hearings. The more involved I get into the investigation, then the more accountable I am to keep a record and be able to recall all those things. And I just didn't want to do it. *I didn't want to get that involved, so I refused to talk to them.*"

(Emphasis supplied)

In addition, the Commissioner responded to questions from counsel for the Union as follows:

"Well, the thought, let me explain, the thought was that I — I didn't want any more — any additional outside pressure. I really didn't because it was difficult enough as it was. And talking to W__ and G__ would have made it even more difficult to render what I would consider an objective decision.

Yeah, that's how I would characterize it. That's — those were the reasons I considered at this time . . .

"Q. (By Mr. Aitchison) You don't believe that as the manager of the Bureau charged with discharging employees, a decision that you have said is the most significant or the most drastic decision that you can make regarding the employee that you have any obligation to speak with the employees?

"A. No, I don't, Mr. Aitchison. Can I explain?

"Q. Sure. Please do.

"A. One of the reasons I'm glad that I did not is based on some of the things that have been regurgitated here today and some of the things you caused your witness to say I think damaged any policymaker like myself, myself relationship trying to work with employees as well as the Union, in trying to deal with mitigating circumstances. *Because if you try to temper your discipline with justice and with mercy, it's going to be regurgitated later on in some hearing like this. And so it just — you know, you really don't want to get involved in things like that.*" (Emphasis supplied.)

It is a well established rule that management has the obligation to fully and fairly investigate an incident before imposing discipline. Grief Brothers Cooperage, Inc., 42 LA 555 (1964). The Arbitrator is not holding that the decisionmaker must interview the grievant in all cases prior to discharge. Southern Bell Telephone & Telegraph Co., 75 LA 409 (1980). However, in this case Commissioner Jordan and others were speaking to the public about the incident. Commissioner Jordan admitted he was getting input from outside sources trying to influence his decision. In addition, the case had generated an immense amount of notoriety about Officers W— and G— of which the Commissioner was aware. For these reasons, the Arbitrator must find in the context of this case that the failure of Commissioner Jordan to personally speak with the grievants constituted a violation of the basic notions of fair play and justice.

The record in this case clearly established that the grievants will be able to return to work as effective police officers. The work records of the grievants leaves no doubt that they have the ability and experience to perform as responsible police officers for the City of Portland. The testimony of their fellow officers was unanimous that in their opinion the grievants could return to work as effective police officers. The testimony of these officers was credited because of their knowledge of police work and the special skills they attributed to the grievants in their ability to perform police tasks.

The supervisors within the Bureau testified in regards to the ability of the grievants to return to work as effective officers. The commander of the East Precinct testified as follows:

"I'd have no problem taking either one of these officers back."

The commander of Central Precinct testified:

"I would welcome them at Central Precinct . . . that I thought they had fine reputations and the best information I had to . . . we'd like to have them at Central Precinct."

The grievants' commander at North Precinct testified that W__ and G__ were excellent police officers. He further stated that to his knowledge W__ and G__ had never violated a department rule or regulation prior to March 12, 1981. The captain in charge of the Bureau's Community Affairs Division stated that after a period adjustment, they could be effective policemen within the Bureau's juvenile division.

The claim by the City that the grievants could not function effectively in the black community was unsupported by the record. Sergeant Charles Moose, a black officer, probably expressed it best on the ability of the grievants to return to police service:

"Q. (By Mr. Aitchison) Two other questions for you, Sergeant. The first, there has been some testimony that — not some testimony. There has been some statements that perhaps Officers W__ and G__ cannot return to the street, return to North Precinct because of what happened on March 12, 1981 or effectively function as police officers. How do you feel about that?

"MR. MORTHLAND: Objection.

"THE ARBITRATOR: Overruled.

"A. (Pause) Well, it confuses me when, you know, when you make such a general statement there about the — effectively communicating with people. Because I think part of the problem would be that there would be certain people, you know, that would want to say that they couldn't communicate with them or get along with them. But I think most of the — the way I perceive a lot of police work is there are a lot of victims and when you've got a victim out there and he's got a chance there to help the victim or if you've got someone that's willing to give you some information as to what they saw, maybe a lead or some information about a certain crime, then I think that these people are part of the community, too, and they are going to talk to anybody that's a policeman or anybody that's there to try to help them.

"Now to people I would see that wouldn't talk to W__ and G__ is, you know, there might be some guy there in front of the Burger Barn with no identification at 3:00 o'clock in the morning. When they go up and ask him his name, well, this person, well, he's not going to cooperate with them. But I don't even know if he's going to realize it's W__ and G__.

"It's going to be a certain percentage of people that won't cooperate with any policemen. But I think that's a small percentage."

The Arbitrator finds that the City's claim that the grievants could not return to work as effective police officers unsupported by the evidence in the record.

The grievants' conduct was offensive and stupid. The seriousness of their conduct cannot be understated. In this case, we are faced with two grievants with outstanding work records which prior to March 12 were completely unblemished. Both of the grievants deeply regret the incident of March 12. Under the circumstances of this case, reason and justice do not require that the supreme penalty of discharge be imposed on two grievants who made their first mistake in a combined total of twelve years service to the City. The City's legitimate interest in discouraging this type of behavior and maintaining its credibility will be served by a lesser penalty which will put the other police officers on notice that conduct such as the grievants' will not be tolerated. For these reasons and others stated in the discussion, the Arbitrator finds the decision to discharge the grievants was excessive and thus does not meet the test of just and sufficient cause.

The City argued against reinstatement because the Charter of the City of Portland precludes a suspension of more than 30 days. The City maintains that since Commissioner Jordan didn't have the power to suspend the grievants for more than 30 days that power cannot be delegated to an arbitrator in a collective bargaining agreement. The City submits that the only legal option Commissioner Jordan had for discipline beyond 30 days was termination. Hence, the City concluded that when faced with these two alternatives, a 30 day suspension is far too lenient.

The record in this case does contain evidence that a suspension in excess of 30 days might be appropriate. The Arbitrator, being fully cognizant of the City's legal position on the alleged limitations on the Arbitrator's authority, declines to set a suspension in excess of 30 days. The question of whether the City's position is legally correct will have to be settled in another forum. A review of the previous discipline imposed by the Bureau warrants a finding that a 30 day suspension without pay is appropriate under the facts of this case.

Finally, the Arbitrator fully and completely considered all of the contentions raised by the parties. The numerous points were well stated and documented. However, the manner in which the Arbitrator chose to decide this case makes it unnecessary to unduly lengthen this opinion with a discussion of each and every point made by the parties.

■ AWARD

Having reviewed all the evidence submitted on this matter, the Arbitrator concludes that the grievants were discharged without just cause within the meaning of the collective bargaining agreement. The discharge is reduced to a thirty day suspension without pay. The City is directed to reinstate the grievants to their former position with back pay and with all benefits and seniority restored as provided in the agreement. From the grievants' back pay there shall be deducted the thirty day's suspension and any earnings or wages received by the grievants during the period of discharge. Jurisdiction is reserved in the event the parties are unable to agree upon the amount of back pay.

Index

THE BOOK MANUFACTURE

The New Public Personnel Administration, Third Edition, was typeset at Auto-Graphics, Inc., Monterey Park, California. Printing and binding was by Braun–Brumfield, Inc., Ann Arbor, Michigan. Cover design was by Willis Proudfoot, Mt. Prospect, Illinois. The typeface is Caledonia.